Shooter's Bible

GUIDE TO COMBAT HANDGUNS

ROBERT A. SADOWSKI

SKYHORSE PUBLISHING

Because there are those who trespass against us, this book is dedicated to the women and men in the military who protect our homeland wherever the fight may take them; to law enforcement personnel who protect our cities, towns, and hamlets; and to those concerned citizens who recognize the responsibility and have made a conscious decision to conceal carry to defend their homes, families, friends, and neighbors. And this is especially for those who have made the ultimate sacrifice in our defense. You are all remembered.

Skyhorse Publishing books may be purchased in bulk at special discounts for sales promotion, corporate gifts, fund-raising, or educational purposes. Special editions can also be created to specifications. For details, contact the Special Sales Department, Skyhorse Publishing, 307 West 36th Street, 11th Floor, New York, NY 10018 or info@skyhorsepublishing.com.

Skyhorse® and Skyhorse Publishing® are registered trademarks of Skyhorse Publishing, Inc.®, a Delaware corporation.

Visit our website at www.skyhorsepublishing.com.

The following Gould and Goodrich photos on pages 242-243 are courtesy of Paul Riddell of On Duty Gear: 804 Shoulder, 890 Inside Trousers, and 891 Belt Slide.

10 9 8 7 6 5 4 3 2 1

Library of Congress Cataloging-in-Publication Data is available on file.

This 2013 edition printed for Barnes & Noble, Inc.
ISBN 978-1-4351-4507-8

Printed in China

CONTENTS

ACKNOWLEDGMENTS

I would like to thank Slaton White for his recommendation. To my editor at Skyhorse Publishing, Jay Cassell, who started our first conversation with the words: "I was wondering if..." What's that Bogart line? "I think this is the start of a beautiful friendship."

This book could not have been written without the support and help of all the handgun, ammo, holster, and accessory brands. Of those, special thanks (in no particular order) to Colt, Gould & Goodrich, Ruger, Remington, Les Baer, Buffalo Bore, DeSantis, Kahr, CZ, Sig Sauer, Federal, Bianchi, Blackhawk, CorBon, Winchester, Glock, Heckler & Koch, Crimson Trace, Springfield Armory, Laser Max, Beretta, Smith & Wesson, LaserLyte, and Gem Tech. I am sure I have forgotten some brands that were extraordinarily helpful. Thanks also to Union Station and the John M. Browning Museum.

Mother nature needs to be given her due as the abnormal amount of snow last winter turned what could have been a bout of cabin fever into a white heat of productivity. Thigh-high snow can do that. To Bella, who kept me company while she lounged on her bed outside the office door, and to Cooper, who poked his nose from under the desk to remind me it was time for a walk or to play ball. And especially to Deborah, whose patience, understanding, and camera skills helped me through the process. I love you and our two GSP kids.

INTRODUCTION

The *Shooter's Bible* has been a comprehensive resource for shooting enthusiasts for almost ninety years. Competitive shooters, hunters, weekend plinkers, and those who keep a pistol in their nightstand for protection, to name just a few, all have come to trust the *Shooter's Bible* as a source of valuable information. This, the first edition of the *Shooter's Bible Guide to Combat Handguns*, contains the most up-to-date information on combat and defensive handguns, training and defensive ammunition, handgun ballistics, tactical and concealment holsters, accessories, and training facilities. Throughout these pages are many well-known products that have been called into harm's way and literally battle and field tested. Others products are new and not yet proven, but are fresh takes on designs that employ the use of new materials and leverage technology. The new product section offers the very latest in all categories.

To write a book on combat handguns, especially on the 100th year anniversary of Colt's Model O, or more commonly referred to as the 1911, is a privilege. The pistol is legendary. It was adopted in 1911—hence the name—and has been in service with our armed forces ever since. Officially the Beretta 92 replaced the 1911 in 1985, but "replaced" is probably not the correct word. Old ways die hard in the military, especially old ways that work well. Some special forces units still use the 1911, but the 1911 they carry today is by no means your great-grandfather's pistol. Today's 1911 sports lowered and flared eject ports, beavertail-grip safeties, ambidextrous and extend thumb safeties, magazine well funnels, forward slide serrations, big visible sights, polished feed ramps—and that's just the short list of features on a modern 1911.

You will find in the handgun section not only 1911 manufacturers (and there are a lot of them), but also the usual suspects—Glock, Beretta, CZ, Heckler & Koch, Sig, Smith & Wesson, Ruger, Walther—as well as other lesser known gun makers who offer viable options for defensive handguns. Some designs hark back to the late 19th century with double barrels and spur triggers, like derringers from Bond and American Derringer, and tiny rimfire revolvers such as those from North American Arms. These designs may be old, but the techniques and materials used in the manufacturing are thoroughly modern. I suspect Wild Bill Hickok or Doc Holliday would take a liking to these 21st-century derringers. Or perhaps they'd take a look at the latest trend in handguns, highly concealable pocket pistols. Not that pocket pistols are new—they have been around since the early 1900s, with Fabrique Nationale creating the Baby Browning back in 1905 and Walther's Model 1 debuting in 1908. Today's manufacturers have redefined semi-automatic pocket pistols. Relative newcomers to firearm manufacturing, such as Kahr and Kel-Tec, have picked up where FN and Walther left off, and currently build pocket pistols that offer a nice compromise between weight and firepower. SeeCamp, Ruger, Taurus, Rohrbaugh, Masterpiece Arms, and others have picked up on the popularity of these mouse guns and produce their own versions in a variety of calibers. The original Baby Browning manufactured by FN was chambered in .25 ACP, but today's pocket pistol calibers range from .380 to .45 ACP.

At the other end of the spectrum are pistols from PTR, Sig, and Bushmaster. These pistols are essentially combat rifles modified to pistol size by removing the stock and shortening the barrel. They are chambered in .308 and 5.56mm/.223 and are not subtle about their ability to bring firepower to a gun fight. Obviously nostalgia is endemic in firearm manufacturing. Old-timers like the Thompson pistol with 50-round drum magazine would make a G-man like Melvin Purvis grin. A replica of a 1943 Polish-made machine pistol design, PPS-43C, manufactured to comply with current gun laws by I.O. Inc., seems like a relic from the Cold War. The Mac 10 design couples ease of manufacture with firepower, and the compliant models from Masterpiece Arms are civilian versions of this classic weapon. And yes, there are new 1911s that are built the same way as they were in 1911 when they were shipped from the Colt factory. Some will even eject dented .45 cases just like originals. Para USA, Springfield Armory, and even Colt offer retro styling that your great-grandfather would recognize. Other designs, like the Sig P210, which was the Swiss Army's sidearm from 1949 to 1975, are renowned for their classic lines and exceptional accuracy. Since

1899, Smith & Wesson has produced some six million Military & Police or Model 10 revolvers, a testament to its enduring design.

As nostalgic or archaic as the revolver may be—Samuel Colt carved the prototype out of wood in 1832 on a sea voyage—it is a fighting weapon. At the battle of Bandera Pass in 1841, a few Texas Rangers held off a slew of Comanches with the very first revolver, the Colt Paterson. The firepower that these five-shot guns brought to the battle was decimating. From there revolvers evolved into six-shooters, and as metallic cartridges became more reliable and commonplace, revolvers adapted to the new cartridges. Revolvers progressed from single-action, gate-loaded six-shooters through to double-action break-tops until finally settling on the swing-out cylinder. There is something to be said of a design that can handle calibers from .17 HRM up through the .500 S&W. Brands like Smith & Wesson, Ruger, Charter Arms, and Taurus have recently redefined the wheelgun with the use of polymers and alloys and added new technology. Taurus offers a polymer frame, while Ruger and S&W use lightweight alloys. These brands have also mashed up or integrated the 18th-century design with the latest high-tech laser sights. The latest trend is gargantuan revolvers chambered to fire shotgun shells or cartridge rounds interchangeably. It is rumored that Yosemite Sam traded in his six-shooters for a pair of one of these .45 Long Colt/.410 gauge uber revolvers.

But back to the usual suspects, these are combat handguns that were designed for military and LE use. Some have been game changers, such as Glock, with its striker-fire action, polygonal rifling, and polymer frame. Glock was not the first manufacturer to use polymers in the manufacturing of pistols, but the company came to market at the right time, with the right product. Their market share speaks for itself, and some established gunmakers who reeled at the thought of polymer handguns now offer their own striker-fired, polymer-framed pistols. This is not to say traditional metal-frame pistols with single- and double-action triggers are being decommissioned and sent to surplus retailers. Beretta, Sig, and most 1911 manufacturers all employ metal frames and all have their own philosophy on how a pistol should operate. There is no one correct solution, but many options. What the newer and traditional pistols have in common are calibers. Rounds like the 9mm, .357 Sig, .40 S&W, 10mm, and .45 ACP are proven performers and are strictly business. Any one of these calibers is a good choice for a defensive caliber.

In the ammunition section are the different types of cartridges available for training and defense. Bullet design, like handgun design, has evolved and continues to push the envelope on technology. Frangible bullets, such as the NyTrilium Handgun Round from Extreme Shock or CorBon's Blue and Silver Glaser Safety Slugs, literally disintegrate on contact and protect bystanders. Other bullet designs, like hollow points, have become more dependable and expand at a range of velocities and in different target materials. Names such as Federal's Hydra-Shok, Speer's Gold Dot, and Remington's Golden Saber are the latest in hollow-point design. Some hollow points aren't so hollow any more, either. Hornady's Critical Defense ammo uses their FTX bullet, and CorBon's Pow'R Ball either fills the opening with a pliable material or a polymer ball, respectively. Federal's Guard Dog brand encases a soft polymer in a thin metal jacket designed to expand without over penetrating. Ammo is also going green, meaning it is lead free and nontoxic; important especially if your training takes place indoors where fumes may be an issue.

The ballistics section provides factory data on many training and defensive calibers and compares muzzle velocity and energy head-to-head. Military and LE agencies chose to use calibers like the 9mm, .357 Sig, .40 S&W, 10mm, and .45 ACP because the data and real-life case studies prove these calibers perform in gun fights. The trend in calibers like the .380 cannot be ignored and is included here, as are other calibers that are not so much less popular but used less, including the .32 ACP, .44 Special, and .45 GAP.

The holster section looks at a cross section of manufacturers. Some, like Bianchi, DeSantis, Galco, and Safariland, have been in the gun-leather business for decades. But gun leather has almost become a misnomer. Fobus and BladeTech are just two brands that construct holsters out of injection-molded polymer or thermal-molded Kydex, respectively, to produce holsters that in some instances outperform old-fashioned horse hide. Other manufacturers, such as Cross Breed Holsters, are newcomers and offer hybrid holsters that combine leather and Kydex. There are virtually dozens of types of holsters and carry methods, from horizontal shoulder holsters a la Miami Vice to belt, paddle, clip-on, small-of-the-back, inside waistband, ankle, and pocket. One trend with holsters is the ability to tuck in a shirt over the weapon, so a gun is virtually invisible to untrained and unsuspecting eyes. With practice, a weak hand full of shirt tail, and a strong hand draw, a weapon can come into play almost as quickly as a less concealed carry option.

Bad things don't usually happen at high noon, they occur in the shadows and at night. Some accessories available to handgun shooters are designed to enlighten an otherwise dark and potentially lethal situation. Flashlights from the likes of SureFire and StreamLight can place a beam of light with surgical precision on any situation, and with most handgun manufacturers building in Picatinny rails on their pistols frames, the merging of weapon and light source combine to serve a specific purpose. Shooters can also hang laser sights, like those from Viridian, off a weapon's accessory rails or integrate the laser into the weapon's mechanism. LaserMax swaps a stock guide rod for a guide rod that contains a laser beam sight. Crimson Trace offers a simple solution that replaces the weapon's stock grip or attaches to the trigger guard. Laser sight systems bring a new meaning to the term light show, and allow shooters to project a red or green laser dot to aim in situations where normal open sights cannot be used.

Finally the section on training is where a shooter can bring it all together and learn how to effectively use a weapon, holster, and ammunition. The best advice I ever received from a firearms instructor was to run away and avoid a potential gunfight. Clint Smith, from Thunder Ranch, continued to say that if you can't get away from the bad guys and are forced to fight, here's what you need to know to survive and live to tell about it. Military and LE personnel are constantly training, refining skills, and learning new skill sets. The conceal-carry individual has a responsibility to acquire the skills necessary to be safe and win a gunfight quickly. The list of individuals and facilities offering training is staggering. Local instructors can provide all the necessary instruction to obtain a conceal-carry permit, while others, like the late Jeff Cooper's Gunsite facility, up the training to a higher level and different mindset. An investment in a course at one of these facilities or any other reputable and qualified training facility is critical to efficient and effective gun handling.

We have the right to protect our family, home, friends, and neighbors, and there are those who will do us wrong and invade our homes, our work place, and our space. It is my intent that readers with combat handgun experience, like military and law enforcement personnel, as well as private citizens who choose to conceal carry, plus those who are new to firearms, will find the information in this book valuable. Choose your weapon carefully and train with it often.

Exigo a me non ut optimis par sim, sed ut malis melior—I require myself not to be equal to the best, but to be better than the bad. (Seneca)

Robert A. Sadowski
East Haddam, Connecticut
March 29, 2011

1. THE 1911 RENAISSANCE

A Smart Pistol Design Thrives 100 Years Later

Ideas do not usually come sequentially but snarled and knotted up together. The trick is untangling the useful threads from the not so useful. I don't know if John Browning ever sat back from his drawing board and said eureka after finishing the design for the model 1911; I think his mind and dreams were animated with sears and levers and bushings and springs and all the other pieces that turn an idea for a firearm into an actual prototype. I suspect Browning was on to the next idea, maybe the P35 and high capacity magazine and external extractors and pivoting triggers. For certain, the 1911 design was momentous and forever changed the way firearms were designed thereafter.

The 1911 is simply defined as a single-action, semi-automatic, magazine-fed handgun chambered for the .45 ACP cartridge. It has and is chambered for other calibers, but the DNA of the 1911 and .45 ACP cartridge are entwined. The 1911 mechanism is a short-recoil system. In a short-recoil pistol, the barrel and slide recoil a short distance before unlocking and separating. While the barrel stops, the slide continues rearward, compressing the recoil spring, extracting and ejecting an empty casing, scraping a cartridge out of the magazine and pushing it into the chamber, and finally travels forward so the slide and barrel lock back into battery. This short-recoil system has been the basic mechanism for most modern pistols.

This is the actual prototype #1 that Browning made and took back East to the military for demonstration. Photo courtesy Ogden Union Station Foundation. Photo credit Lee Witten.

Some ideas provide new ways to accomplish old things; some ideas are solutions to problems. The 1911 was a solution to both. The problem was the Spanish-American and Philippine-American Wars in the early 1900s. In the Philippines, U.S. troops were up against Moro guerrilla fighters who frequently chewed coca leaves during battle. To say the Moros were fierce in battle is an understatement. In 1902, the standard issue handgun was the Colt M1892 revolver in .38 Long Colt, which had a muzzle velocity of 770 fps with a 150-grain solid lead bullet. It lacked power to stop the juiced-up guerrillas. The Army's solution was to bring back the Colt M1873 single-action revolver in .45 Long Colt that launched a 225-grain lead round-nose, flat-point bullet at 800 fps. The old six-shooters performed well during the Indian campaigns and there was reason to believe they would be effective in the jungles of the Philippines, too. The U.S. military's devotion to .45 caliber handguns was set. The Thompson-LaGarde Tests (caliber tests conducted in 1904 at the Nelson Morris Company Union Stock Yards) concluded ". . . a bullet, which will have the shock effect and stopping effect at short ranges necessary for a military pistol or revolver, should have a caliber not less than .45." The test pitted the .30 Luger, .38 Long Colt, .38 ACP, 9mm, .455 Webley, .45 Long Colt, and .476 Eley. Results firmly cemented the military's prejudice toward .45 caliber handguns. Then President Theodore Roosevelt assigned General William Crozier, who was the Chief of Ordance, the task of finding a new sidearm for the military. The rest, as they say, is history. Gun designs were submitted for review in

A pristine example of a Model 1911. This is serial number 39 from the personal collection of Mr. Charles W. Clawson, author of the book *Colt .45 Service Pistols Models of 1911 and 1911A1*. Photo credit Jeff Bell.

A Colt M1911A1 reproduction (top) manufactured from 2001–2004 is true to the last U.S. government spec compared to a current Springfield Tactical Response Pistol (TRP), the civilian version of the FBI contract pistol and an excellent example of a modern 1911. Note the lowered and flared eject port of the TRP and the longer aluminum trigger. The M1911A1 had a parkerized finish that resisted corrosion better than bluing. The TRP sports a matte black proprietary Teflon coating called Armory Kote. Photo courtesy Swamp Yankee Media.

The smaller grip safety of the M1911A1 top did not provide against "hammer bite" as does the TRP's extended beavertail grip safety. The TRP's hammer provides more grip, and it has an ambidextrous extended safety lever. The TRP, like many modern 1911s, brings the rear sight as far back on the slide as possible. The notch of the rear sight is large and snag free compared to the WWII-era 1911 rear sight. The TRP sights are also Tritium 3-dot that glow in the dark. Photo courtesy Swamp Yankee Media.

During WWI, many soldiers shot the 1911 low, so an arched mainspring housing was added to the M1911A1 (right) to slightly rotate the pistol higher in a shooter's grip. Modern 1911s like the TRPs have a flat mainspring housing and 20 lpi (lines per inch) checkering on the front strap of the grip. The M1911A1 has plain plastic checkered grips. The TRP has gritty G10 composite grips. Photo courtesy Swamp Yankee Media.

The magazine well of the TRP (top) makes fast reloads easier compared to the mil-spec 1911A1. Caution should be exercised when slamming home a magazine with the old-school lanyard ring. Photo courtesy Swamp Yankee Media.

Tighter tolerances on the bushing and barrel allow the barrel to return to the same position shot after shot, thus increasing accuracy. The solid ejector rod is the norm with the TRP (left) and many other modern 1911s. A hex wrench is required to field strip the TRP.

1906 from major firearm manufacturers in both the United States and Europe. By the time field trials were conducted, three prototypes remained: Colt, Savage, and Deutsche Waffen und Munitionsfabriken (DWM). All pistols designed were chambered in the new .45 ACP, which had similar ballistics as the .45 Long Colt. The .45 ACP featured a 230-grain full metal jacket bullet at a speed 855 fps. When the dust settled, the Colt prototype—the John Browning design—was formally adopted by the U.S. Army on March 29, 1911. The year and pistol were to become synonymous. Officially the pistol was adopted by the Navy and Marines in 1913, and not long after adoption of the 1911 it had its baptism under fire in World War I. The trenches in France exposed a few bugs in the design. The U.S. Army wanted enhancements to the pistol. One bug in the design was the short spur of the grip safety. Soldiers with meaty hands found the 1911's hammer prone to "hammer bite"–where the hammer pinches the skin of the shooter's hand between the thumb and trigger finger. Today's beavertail grip safeties nearly eliminate "hammer bite." The 1911's flat mainspring housing also caused soldiers to shoot low; an arched main spring housing was the solution. A shorter trigger, cutouts in the frame behind the trigger, a bigger front sight, and plastic checkered grip panels rounded out the minor tweaks, and the 1911 was designated the M1911A1. It then became standard issue and was used in World War II, the Korean War, the Vietnam War, and sporadically among troops in both Gulf Wars. The U.S. government purchased about 2.7 million pistols in total. What makes the 1911 such an enduring design? It works. It works in sand, in jungles, in frigid temperatures, and in just about any other environmental hell imaginable.

Civilians could, at one time, purchase any 1911 they wanted as long as it was a Colt. Where Browning and the U.S. military left off with the 1911 and M1911A1, a cadre of machinists, designers, gunsmiths, tinkerers and clever businessmen picked up and turned the early 20th-century design into one of the most modified and blatantly copied pistols the world has known. Today's manufacturers have stretched, compacted, microsized, rechambered, and adorned the 1911 with user-friendly enhancements that were the bread-and-butter trade for many custom gunsmiths in the 1950s through the 1970s. Not only did the 1911 perform on the battle field, with a little hand fitting of parts, the 1911 is transformed into a proverbial tack driver. It is the predominant pistol in centerfire bullseye competitions. Action pistol shooters know the 1911 is the starting point for tricked-out race guns. It's the grip angle, the trigger, the balance, and the calibers that make the 1911 a near-perfect pistol.

2. FANTASTIC PLASTICS

Polymer-Framed Pistols: Lightweight, Added Safety, and Modular

Heckler & Koch (H&K) introduced the P9S pistol in 1969 with a polymer-covered steel frame, steel slide, and a polygonal rifled barrel. It was chambered in either 9mm or .45 ACP in a single-stack magazine, employed a conventional single-action/double-action trigger system, used a decocking lever, and looked like no other handgun on the market at the time. It included features that are very common today, like the decocker, polygonal rifling, and polymer frame. A licensed variant of the P9S is still being manufactured in Greece.

It is fair to say that H&K was ahead of its time and the P9S was cutting edge, but polymer-framed pistols would not have wide spread acceptance among military, LE, and the shooting public until 1982 when the Glock 17 debuted. The Austrian government purchased the Glock 17 in that year with Norway and Sweden following shortly thereafter. Today some forty-eight countries use a variant of the Glock. In the United States, Glock pistols have a sixty-five percent market share among LE agencies. Initial response to the Glock was much like the response H&K received years early: How durable and reliable can a plastic gun be? Glock pistols have endured torture tests. They have been soaked in salt water, stuck in sludge, buried in sand, frozen in ice, dropped from helicopters, run over by vehicles, and the list goes on. Glock pistols consistently operate under the most adverse conditions. There is no question about the reliability and long life of polymer pistols.

The Glock 17 pistol completely transformed the industry. It is eighty-six percent lighter than conventional metal-framed pistols, plus the polymer is tougher than steel and corrosion resistant. It has a magazine capacity of seventeen 9mm rounds, has a polygonal-rifled barrel that offers better ballistics than conventionally rifled barrels—though pure-lead bullets should not be fired in Glocks since the lead will quickly build up in the barrel. Even the finish is high-tech. The Tenifer finish is highly corrosion resistant, hard, and antireflective, something many manufacturers have copied. The really ingenious part of the Glock is the action. The Glock is striker fired, which means after a round is fired or the slide is racked to load a round in the chamber, the striker is in a partially cocked position. The trigger completes the cocking process and releases the striker to fire the round. What Glock did was build the safety into the trigger. When the trigger is pulled, the three safeties are disengaged—the firing pin safety is pushed upward to release the firing pin for firing, the trigger lever prevents the trigger from being inadvertently pulled, and the trigger bar is deflected at the moment the shot is triggered. There are no grip safeties, thumb safeties, decockers, or any other controls—other than a slide release.

Since the introduction of Glock pistols, other manufacturers offer polymer-framed pistols. Springfield Armory's XD and XD(M) polymer-framed pistols have an added grip safety and a trigger that rivals a crisp single-action pistol. Ruger, Walther, Heckler & Koch, Smith & Wesson, Sig, and Steyr all have polymer-frame models. The latest trend is modular grip inserts that allow shooters to change the grip size.

The H&K P9S was radical in 1969 and still looks edgy. Photo courtesy of Heckler & Koch.

Can you tell which trigger came from what manufacturer and what model?

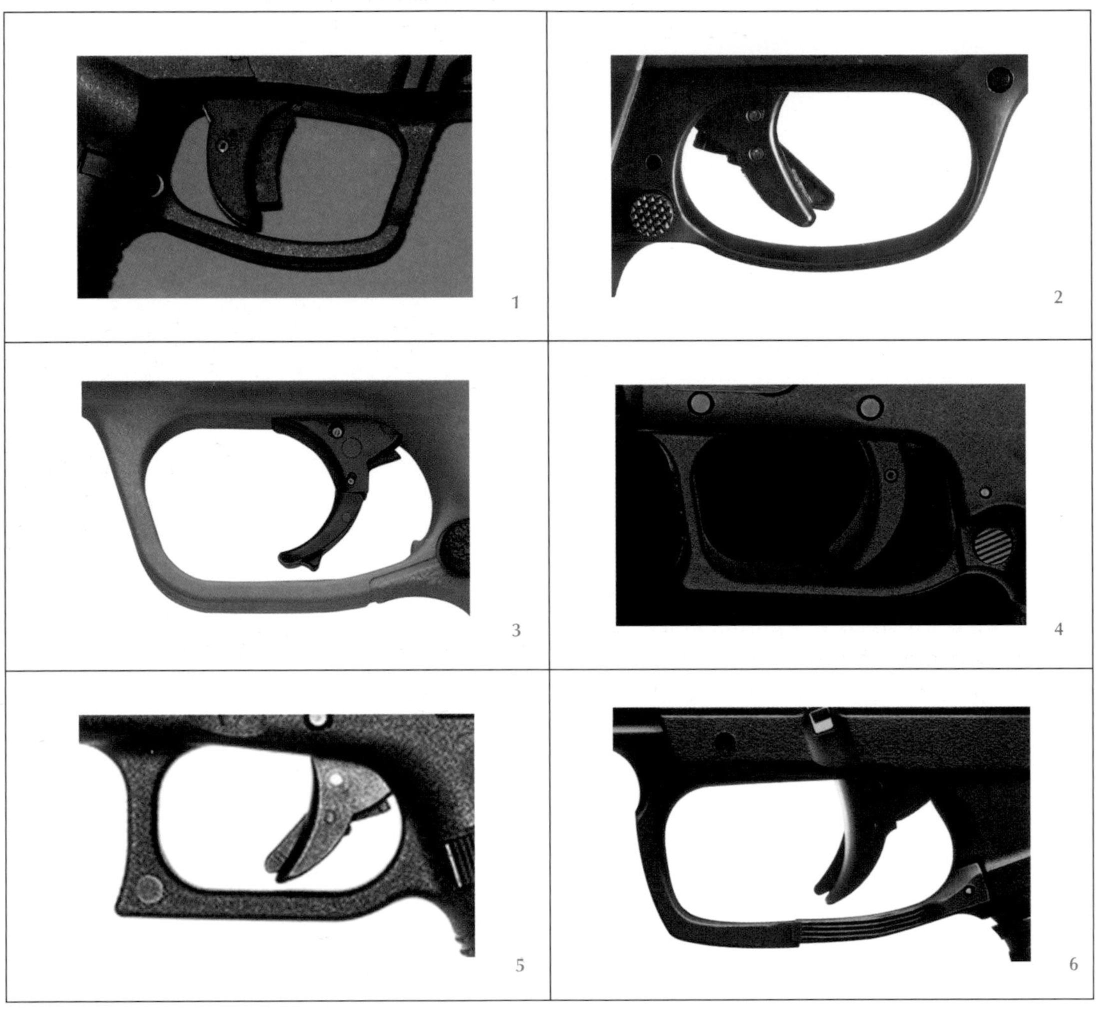

1: Steyr, Model M40-A1; 2: Ruger SR9B; 3: S&W, M&P; 4: Springfield, XDM; 5: G, G17; 6: Walther, PPS. Photos Courtesy of manufacturers.

3. WHEN THE BULLET HITS THE GEL

FBI Ballistics Test Protocol

Since the Thompson-LaGarde Tests in 1904, there has been a quest for the optimum way to test bullet type, velocity, and stopping effect. Back then, five unsuspecting cattle at the Nelson Morris Company Union stock yards were the unwitting participants in a test that eventually brought our military to the conclusion that a .45 caliber handgun provided the best shock and stopping effect. The test also used cadavers suspended in the air to measure the sway and movement of the bodies as they were hit with different calibers from varying distances. The wounds the calibers caused in the cattle and cadavers were examined in detail. Science does not always yield data in nice, easy, and clean methods.

Not until an incident with the FBI did the science of wound ballistics take a more humane approach. As in many cases, especially in these circumstances, humanity was born out of brutality. In 1986, the FBI was involved in a gunfight in Florida's Miami-Dade County. The gunfight involved ten participants—eight FBI agents, and two bank bankers. The event lasted less than five minutes and about 145 shots were exchanged. In the end, two FBI agents and the two bank robbers were killed. In the subsequent investigation, the FBI placed partial blame on the death of its agents on the lack of stopping power in the agents' service handguns. One suspect was hit six times, and the other twelve times, before they were killed. Soon after the shootout in Florida, the FBI developed a protocol for testing ammunition. The FBI protocol sets a standard for defensive ammunition.

Tests are conducted at a set distance with a block of ten percent ordinance-grade ballistic gel, which simulates human flesh. The protocol calls for ammunition to be tested in numerous test events through different material and into gel.

FBI Protocol – Minimum Bullet Requirements
• Minimum penetration into ballistic gelatin of 12 to 18 inches
• Expansion of bullet to at least 1.5 times original diameter
• 100% weight retention of expanded bullet

FBI Protocol – Test Events
1. Bare Gelatin @ 10 feet
2. Heavy Clothing @ 10 feet
3. Steel @ 10 feet
4. Wallboard @ 10 feet
5. Plywood @10 feet
6. Auto Glass @ 10 feet
7. Heavy Clothing @ 20 yards
8. Auto Glass @ 20 yards

.40 S&W Speer Gold Dot 165-grain bullet exiting two inches of ballistic gel. Photo credit Tom Burcinski.

Speer Gold Dot in wallboard

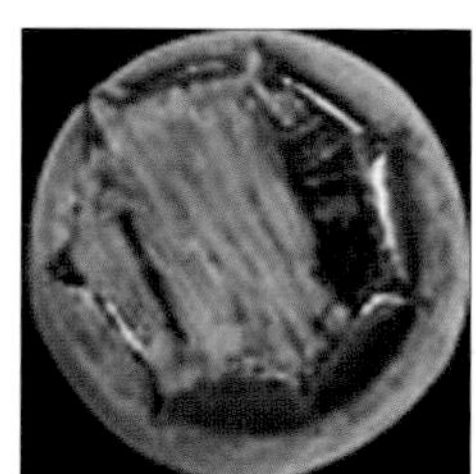

Speer Gold Dot in plywood

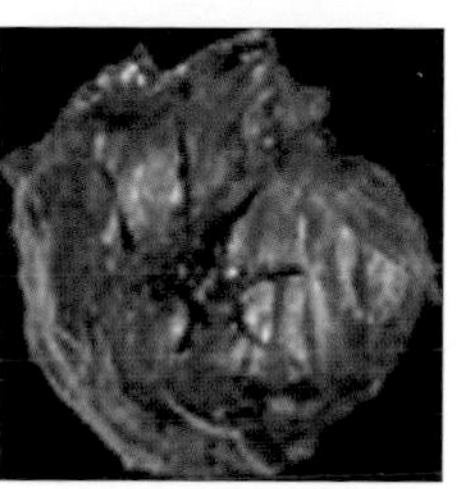

Speer Gold Dot in glass

Speer Gold Dot in heavy clothing

4. GET A GRIP

Proper Grip and Grasp Are Fundamental to Accurate Pistol Shooting

Bulls-eye target shooters pick up their pistols in their weak hands and place the pistols deep into the web of their shooting hands prior to getting in position. Action pistol shooters, who must draw their pistols from holsters, know they must grasp their pistols perfectly to get on target. What these two shooting disciplines can teach us is that grasp and grip are essential to shooting well.

The Grasp

Grasping a pistol from a holster should always be the same. The goal is to grasp the pistol so the web of your hand is as high as possible up the backstrap. The reason is that the closer the bore of the pistol to your hand, the easier it is to control recoil. Your index finger should comfortably access the trigger and should lie along the side of the pistol frame or the edge of the trigger guard. Only engage the trigger when you are ready to shoot.

The Grip

Your remaining fingers should grip the pistol as firmly as possible—a death grip, if you will. This hard, purposeful grip imprints in your muscle memory and tells your brain you are good to go. The death grip is also what you will have when you are in a high-stress situation, so it is beneficial to practice how you will perform. Your nonshooting, or weak, hand should clasp over the firing, or strong, hand with the thumb

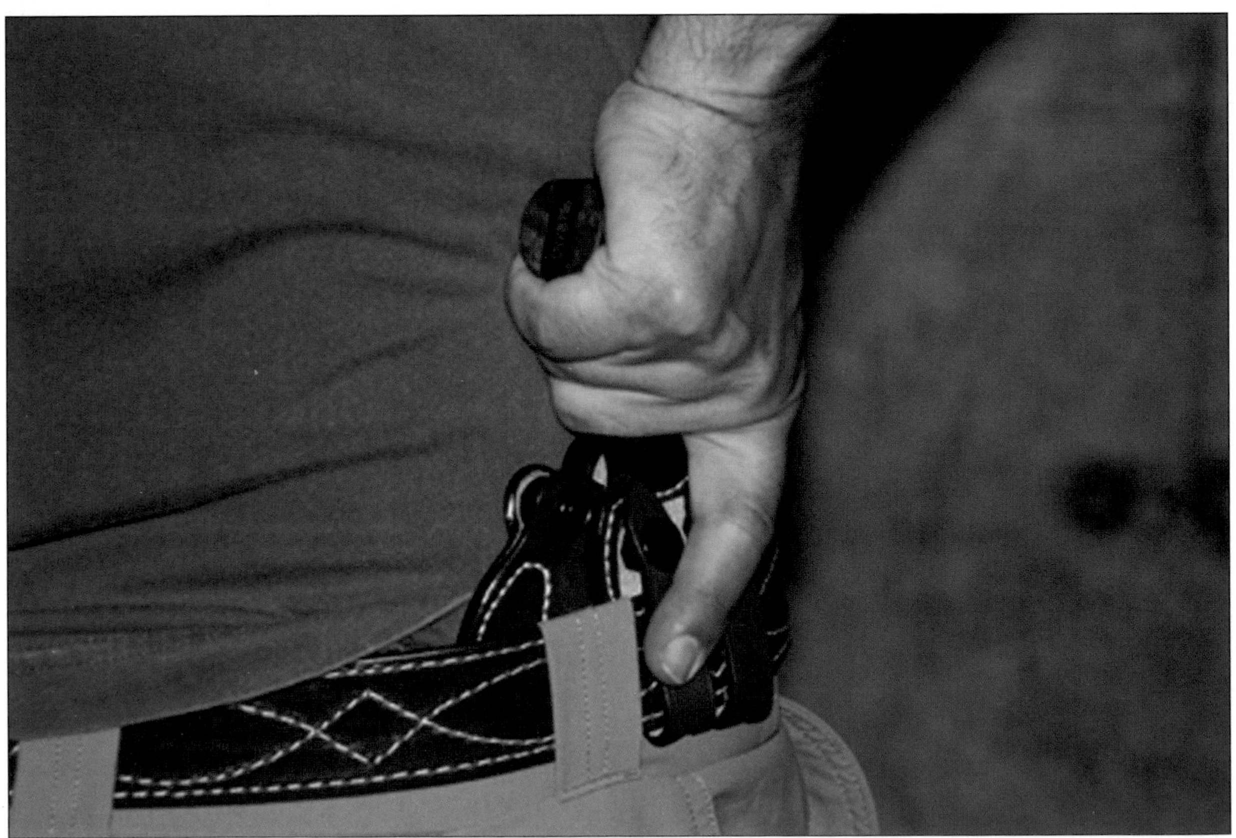

The three lower fingers have curled around the grip to extract the S&W Model 42 from the Desantis Cozy Partner holster. The grip is set even before the revolver exits the holster. Courtesy Swamp Yankee Media. Photo credit Deborah Moore–Sadowski.

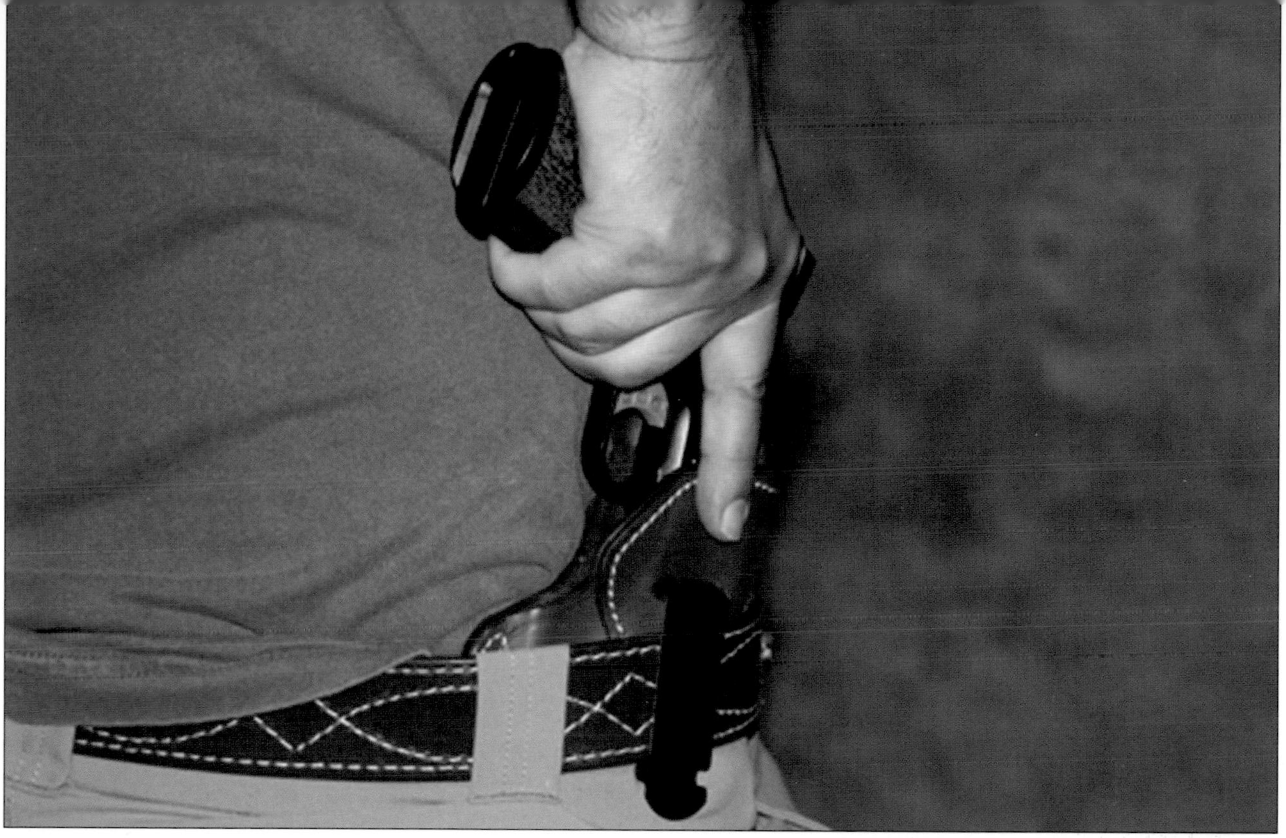

Note the high placement of the hand and the three lower fingers on the Springfield 1911 TRP. While partially extracted from the Blackhawk holster, the trigger finger lies straight against the 1911 until a target is ready to be engaged. Courtesy Swamp Yankee Media. Photo credit Deborah Moore–Sadowski.

A Glock G17 in a death grip. Courtesy Swamp Yankee Media. Photo credit Deborah Moore–Sadowski.

Opposite side of death grip.

A slight variation on thumb placement is to tuck the thumbs down.

For revolvers, one method is to lock the nonshooting hand thumb over the shooting hand thumb as shown with a S&W Model 42. Courtesy Swamp Yankee Media. Photo credit Deborah Moore–Sadowski.

Note how the pinky finger curls under the butt of the S&W Model 637. This method can be used with small, compact semi-automatic pistols, too. Courtesy Swamp Yankee Media. Photo credit Deborah Moore–Sadowski.

of your weak hand under the thumb of your strong hand. The index finger should tuck up under the trigger guard. Feel the grip panels on your palms and make sure you are in contact with as much surface area as possible. If your hands start to tremble, ease up on the death grip. As you practice you will find the right balance of grip strength, and you will have found your sweet spot. Finally, lock your wrists. This aids in recovering from recoil so you can get back on target faster.

Different types of weapons require a slight modification to grip and grasp. Here we illustrate the grasp and grip for a shooter with average-sized hands on a large pistol and small revolver.

5. BERETTA 92

A Quarter Century of Service

The Beretta 92 was officially adopted by the U.S. military in 1985, but the story of the Beretta doesn't start there. Beretta has been manufacturing firearms for nearly 500 years. They do know a thing or two about producing shotguns, rifles, and (as we know) pistols.

The 92 was designed in 1972 and was produced continuously from 1975 in many model versions and calibers. Its origins are from early 20th-century Berettas, where it received its characteristic open-slide design. It borrowed the alloy frame and locking block barrel from the WWII-era Walther P38. Where the U.S. military and Beretta crossed paths was in 1978, when the Joint Services Small Arms Program (JSSAP) began. The U.S. military decided the M1911A1 was getting long in the tooth and the aging platform needed to be replaced. While the military was deciding what sidearm to procure, law enforcement agencies were looking to replace their .38 Special and .357 Magnum revolvers. The Connecticut State Police adopted the 92 in 1980, and thereafter Florida, Indiana, Maryland, North Carolina, Pennsylvania, South Dakota, Utah, and Wyoming all equipped their troopers with 92s or variants like the 96. Some twenty-five U.S. state police agencies ended up acquiring the pistol. It was January 14, 1985, when the U.S. Army announced the Beretta 92 SB-F won the trials. In military parlance it is called the M9. Uncle Sam bought over 300,000 pistols in the first contract worth about $75 million. By 2009, another 450,000 pistols were ordered by the government along with spare parts making the $220 million deal the largest U.S. military pistol contract awarded since WWII.

Since the 92 was adopted, it has seen tours of duty in thirty-six countries from Panama, the Persian Gulf War, and Bosnia, to Somalia, Afghanistan, and Operation Iraqi Freedom.

The sight system on the M9 is dot-and-post style. Barrel length is 4.9 inches. Photo courtesy of Beretta.

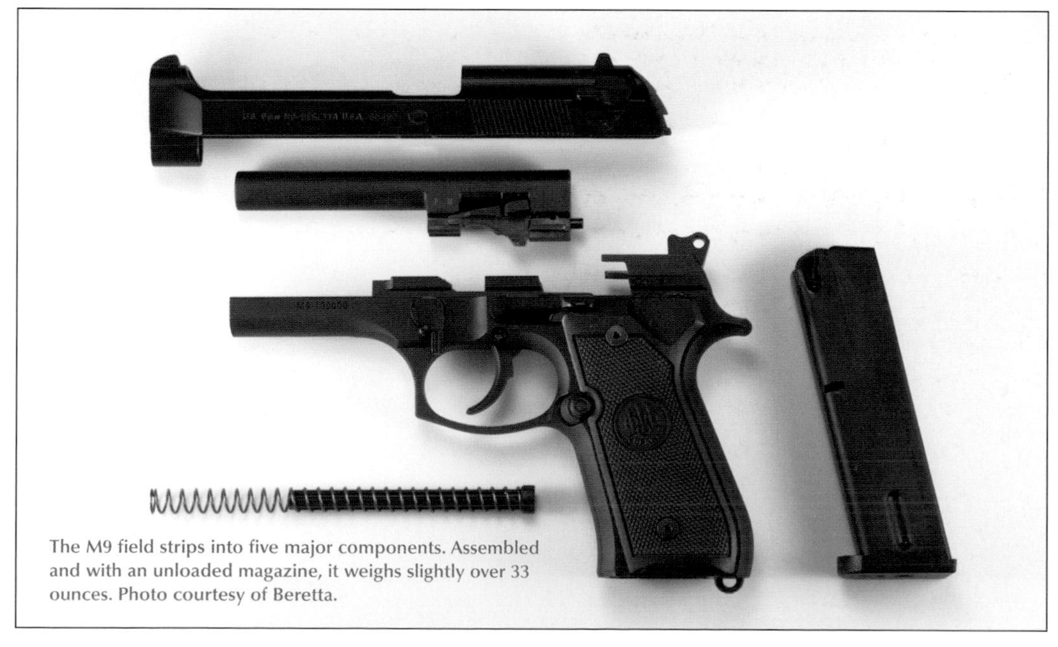

The M9 field strips into five major components. Assembled and with an unloaded magazine, it weighs slightly over 33 ounces. Photo courtesy of Beretta.

The M9, like all 92 variants, has an external hammer that can be thumbed back for single-action mode. It also operates in double action. Photo courtesy of Beretta.

The magazine capacity of the M9 is 15 rounds. The front and rear backstraps are grooved; the M9A1 is checkered. Note that the magazine release is reversible. Magazines drop clear when the magazine button is depressed. Photo courtesy of Beretta.

The M9A1 was upgraded with a Picatinny MIL-STD-1913 accessory rail to attach tactical lights and laser-aiming devices. The magazine well was aggressively beveled to assist fast reloads. Photo courtesy of Beretta.

The backstrap is checkered on the M9A1, as is the front-grip frame. Sights are upgraded to a 3-dot system. Overall length is 8.5 inches. Photo courtesy of Beretta.

6. WHEELGUN VIRTUES

Revolvers May Be Old-School and That's a Good Thing

The revolver as we know it, with its revolving cylinder that aligns a chamber with the barrel, has been around since the mid-19th century. The first commercially successful revolver, the Colt Paterson, held five rounds. Since then there have been six-shooters, seven-shooters, and revolvers that hold up to eight centerfire cartridges. Rimfire revolvers can hold even more. Not many handgun designs can tout the fact they can be chambered in nearly all handgun calibers. Nor can many designs flaunt barrel lengths like revolvers. Revolvers have at the short end snubbed nosed barrels that measure about one inch and at the long end Buntline barrels that are up to 16 inches. And as much as revolvers seem a relic from a different and older time, manufacturers have refined the design by using light weight alloys and polymer frames. Laser sights are a common feature on many small, five-shot revolvers. Here are just three reasons revolvers will still be around through this century.

Ease of Use

Unlike pistols, which have slide stops, decocking levers, thumb safeties, and magazine releases, a revolver is void of levers and buttons. A revolver has one thumb piece that is either pushed, pulled, or squeezed to open the cylinder for loading and unloading. Uncomplicated.

Misfire Reboot

If a round misfires in a pistol, you must go through a series of steps and procedures to fix the situation. If a round misfires in a revolver, just pull the trigger again. Simple.

Getting hammered: An S&W Model 42 has an enclosed hammer. Think snag free. S&W also manufactures J-frame .38 Specials and .357 Magnums with low-profile and shrouded hammers. Photo courtesy Swamp Yankee Media. photo credit Deborah Moore–Sadowski.

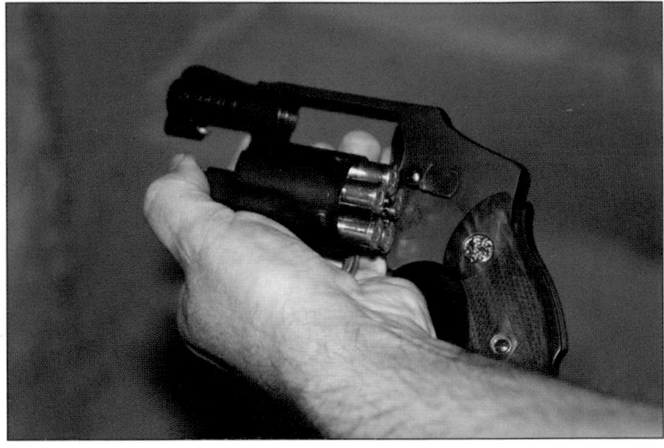

Getting Purged: Gravity can help speed the unloading process.

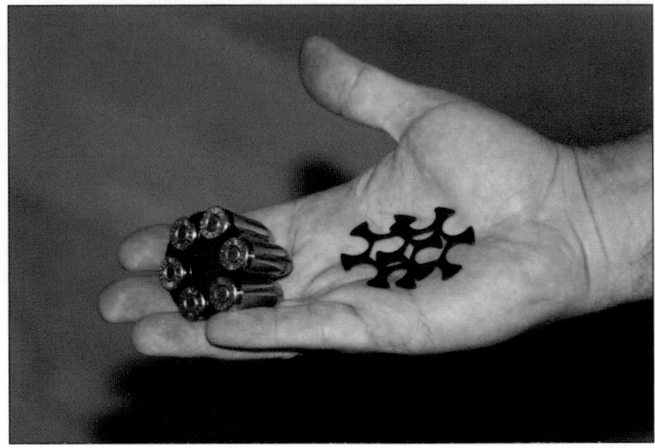

Getting Mooned: Full-moon clips loaded with .45 ACP cartridges and empty. Speedloaders, like half- and full-moon clips, do exactly that with revolvers—speed up the loading process.

Getting Fed: The full-moon clip falls fast and easy into the S&W's cylinder.

No Missing Parts

Drop a pistol magazine in the snow, in leaves, or in tall grass and your participation in a gunfight is immediately reduced to being a target. A revolver, though slower to reload, is self-contained and has no part that can be lost or misplaced. Easy.

7. NEW PRODUCTS

American Tactical Imports (ATI)

(www.americantactical.us)

ATI FX 45 GI I911

ATI FX 45 MILITARY 1911

FX 45 MILITARY 1911

Action: Autoloader, SA
Overall Length: 8.3 in.
Overall Height: 5.5 in.
Overall Width: 1.3 in.
Barrel: 5 in.
Grips: Checkered wood
Sights: Fixed blade front/dovetail rear, mil-spec style
Weight Unloaded: 37 oz.
Caliber: .45 ACP
Capacity: 8 + 1
Features: Colt 1911 design; thumb grip and firing pin block safeties; combat hammer; rear slide serrations; magazine bumper pad
Matte blue: $470

FX 45 GI 1911

Action: Autoloader, SA
Overall Length: 7.5 in.
Overall Height: 5.5 in.
Overall Width: 1.3 in.
Barrel: 4.3 in.
Grips: Checkered hardwood
Sights: Fixed blade front/dovetail rear, mil-spec style
Weight Unloaded: 32 oz.
Caliber: .45 ACP
Capacity: 8 + 1
Features: Colt 1911 design; extended thumb, beavertail grip, and firing pin block safeties; combat hammer; rear slide serrations; magazine bumper pad
Matte blue: $470

FX 45 TITAN 1911

Action: Autoloader, SA
Overall Length: 7.3 in.
Overall Height: 5 in.
Overall Width: 1.3 in.
Barrel: 3.2 in.
Grips: Checkered hardwood
Sights: Dovetail front/rear, Novak-style
Weight Unloaded: 32.5 oz.
Caliber: .45 ACP
Capacity: 5 + 1
Features: Colt 1911 design; extended thumb, beavertail grip, and firing pin block safeties; flared ejection port; extended slide stop; combat hammer; combat trigger; rear slide serrations; magazine bumper pad
Matte blue: $501
Stainless: $595

FX 45 THUNDERBOLT 1911

Action: Autoloader, SA
Overall Length: 8.4 in.
Overall Height: 5.5 in.
Overall Width: 1.3 in.
Barrel: 5 in.
Grips: Checkered hardwood
Sights: Dovetail front/adj. rear
Weight Unloaded: 37.3 oz.
Caliber: .45 ACP
Capacity: 8 + 1
Features: Colt 1911 design; ambidextrous extended thumb, beavertail grip, and firing pin block safeties; flared ejection port; extended slide stop; combat hammer; combat trigger; front and rear slide serrations; magazine bumper pad; Picatinny rail; textured front/rear strap
Matte blue: $790

ATI FX 45 THUNDERBOLT 1911

ATI FX 45 TITAN 1911 (BLUE)

ATI FX 45 TITAN 1911 (SS)

Beretta

(berettausa.com)

BERETTA NANO

Action: Autoloader; striker-fired
Overall Length: 5.6 in.
Overall Height: 4.2 in.
Overall Width: 0.9 in.
Barrel: 3.1 in.
Grips: Textured polymer
Sights: Dovetail front/rear, 3-dot
Weight Unloaded: 17.7 oz.
Caliber: 9mm
Magazine: 6 + 1
Features: Polymer frame; steel slide; reversible magazine release; removable sights; snag-free profile; stainless magazine; black nitride finish
MSRP: $475

BERETTA NANO

Bushmaster

(www.bushmaster.com)

BUSHMASTER PIT VIPER TYPE AP21

Action: Autoloader
Overall length: 23.0 in.
Barrel: 7.3 in.
Grips: Checkered black polymer grip
Sights: N/A
Weight Unloaded: 55 oz.
Caliber: 5.56mm/.223 Rem.
Capacity: 30 + 1
Features: AR-15 design; forged upper/lower receiver; thumb manual safety; manganese phosphate-finished bolt carrier; Picatinny rail; birdcage flash hider; matte black finish; Hogue OverMolded grip; chrome-lined barrel
MSRP: $874

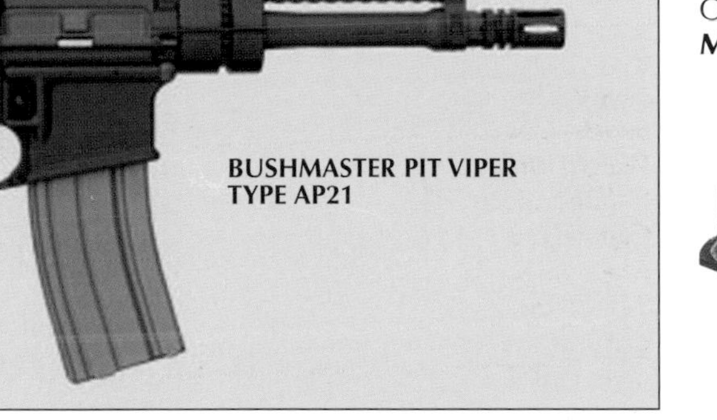

BUSHMASTER PIT VIPER TYPE AP21

COLT NEW AGENT DAO

Colt

(www.coltsmfg.com)

NEW AGENT SERIES

Action: Autoloader, DAO
Overall Length: 6.3 in.
Barrel: 3 in.
Grips: Double-diamond slim checkered walnut
Sights: None
Weight Unloaded: 24 oz.
Caliber: .45 ACP
Capacity: 7 + 1
Features: Rear slide serrations; aluminum frame; stainless steel slide and barrel
Matte blue: $992

1991 SERIES

Action: Autoloader, DAO
Overall Length: 8.5 in.
Overall Height: 5.4 in.
Overall Width: 1.3 in.
Barrel: 5 in.
Grips: Double-diamond checkered slim fit
Sights: Fixed-blade front/dovetail rear
Weight Unloaded: 32 oz.
Caliber: .45 ACP
Capacity: 7 + 1
Features: Aluminum alloy frame/steel slide; hammerless, beveled magazine well
MSRP: $1017

COLT 1991 SERIES DAO

Glock

(www.glock.com)

G26 GEN 4

Action: Autoloader, striker-fire
Overall Length: 6.3 in.
Overall Height: 4.2 in.
Overall Width: 1.2 in.
Barrel: 3.5 in.
Grips: Checkered polymer with finger grooves, modular
Sights: Fixed front/dovetail rear, dot/outline
Weight Unloaded: 19.8 oz.
Caliber: 9mm
Capacity: 10 + 1
Features: Rough Textured Frame (RTF) polymer frame; three back strap sizes; dual recoil spring; reversible magazine release; magazine bumper pad; textured front strap; external extractor; loaded-chamber indicator; serrated combat trigger guard; trigger, firing pin, and drop safeties; hexagonal rifling; matte black Tenifer finish
MSRP: $649

GLOCK G26 GEN 4

G27 GEN 4 and G35 GEN 4

Action: Autoloader, striker-fire
Overall Length: 6.3 in. (G27), 8.2 in. (G35)
Overall Height: 4.2 in. (G27), 5.4 in. (G35)
Overall Width: 1.2 in.
Barrel: 3.5 in. (G27), 5.3 in. (G35)
Grips: Textured polymer with finger grooves, modular
Sights: Fixed front/dovetail rear; dot/outline
Weight Unloaded: 19.8 oz. (G27), 24.5 oz. (G35)
Caliber: .40 S&W
Capacity: 9 + 1 (G27), 15 + 1 (G35)
Features: Rough Textured Frame (RTF) polymer frame; three back strap sizes; dual recoil spring; reversible magazine release; magazine bumper pad; textured front strap; external extractor; loaded-chamber indicator; serrated combat trigger guard; trigger, firing pin, and drop safeties; hexagonal rifling; matte black Tenifer finish
G27 Gen 4: $649
G35 Gen 4: $729

GLOCK G27 GEN 4

Kahr

(www.kahr.com)

CM9

Action: Autoloader, DAO
Overall Length: 5.3 in.
Overall Height: 4 in.
Width: .9 in.
Barrel: 3 in.
Grips: Textured polymer
Sights: Dovetail front/rear; white bar-dot
Weight Unloaded: 14 oz.
Caliber: 9mm
Capacity: 7 + 1
Features: Polymer frame; serrated front/rear back straps; passive striker block safety
Two-tone: $549

KAHR CM9

Kimber

(www.kimberamerica.com)

ROYAL II

Action: Autoloader, SA
Overall Length: 8.7 in.
Overall Height: 5.3 in.
Overall Width: 1.3 in.
Barrel: 5 in.
Grips: Solid smooth bone
Sights: Fixed dovetail front/rear
Weight Unloaded: 38 oz.
Caliber: .45 ACP
Capacity: 7 + 1
Features: Colt 1911 design; steel frame; grip-activated firing pin safety; loaded-chamber indicator port; extended thumb, beavertail grip safeties; lowered/flared ejection port; charcoal blue finish
MSRP: $1938

SOLO CARRY

Action: Autoloader, SA, striker-fired
Overall Length: 5.5 in.
Overall Height: 3.9 in.
Width: 1.2 in.
Barrel: 2.7 in.
Grips: Checkered synthetic
Sights: Fixed front/rear, 3-dot
Weight Unloaded: 17 oz., 17.2 oz. (stainless)
Caliber: 9mm
Capacity: 6 + 1
Features: Aluminum frame; ambidextrous thumb safety; slide stop; magazine release; external extractor
Two-tone: $725
Stainless: $725

KIMBER ROYAL II

KIMBER SOLO CARRY

KIMBER SUPER CARRY ULTRA HD

SUPER CARRY PRO HD

Action: Autoloader, SA
Overall Length: 6.8 in. (Super Carry Ultra HD), 7.7 in. (Super Carry Pro HD), 8.7 in. (Super Carry Custom HD)
Overall Height: 4.8 in. (Super Carry Ultra HD), 5.3 in. (Super Carry Pro HD, Super Carry Custom HD)
Overall Width: 1.3 in.
Barrel: 3 in. (Super Carry Ultra HD), 4 in. (Super Carry Pro HD), 5 in. (Super Carry Custom HD)
Grips: G-10 synthetic checkered
Sights: Fixed dovetail front/rear, 3-dot
Weight Unloaded: 32 oz. (Super Carry Ultra HD), 35 oz. (Super Carry Pro HD), 38 oz. (Super Carry Custom HD)
Caliber: .45 ACP
Capacity: 7 + 1 (Super Carry Ultra HD), 8+1 (Super Carry Pro HD, Super Carry Custom HD)
Features: Colt 1911 design; stainless steel frame; grip-activated firing pin safety; steel frame; loaded-chamber indicator port; extended thumb, beavertail grip safeties; lowered/flared ejection port; rounded and blended edges; fish-scale slide serrations

Super Carry Ultra HD: $1625
Super Carry Pro HD: $1625
Super Carry Custom HD: . . . $1625

KIMBER SUPER CARRY PRO HD

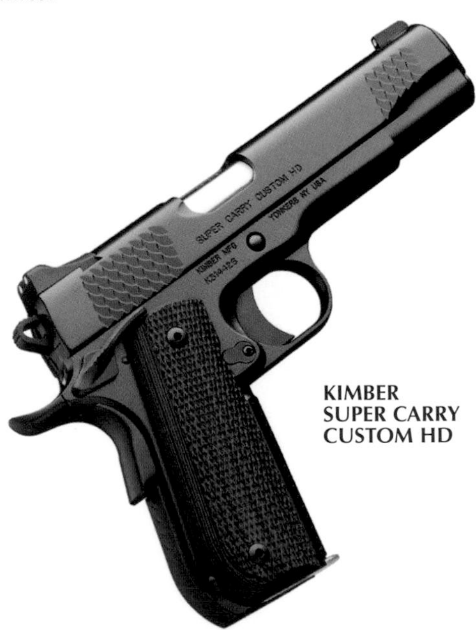

KIMBER SUPER CARRY CUSTOM HD

LES BAER 1911 BOSS .45

Les Baer

(www.lesbaer.com)

BAER 1911 BOSS .45

Action: Autoloader, SA
Overall Length: 8.5 in.
Overall Height: 5.5 in.
Overall Width: .8 in.
Barrel: 5 in.
Grips: Checkered cocobola
Sights: Dovetail fiber optic front/adj. rear
Weight Unloaded: 37 oz.
Caliber: .45 ACP
Capacity: 8 + 1
Features: Colt 1911 Series 70 design; steel frame; extended thumb, beavertail grip safeties; lowered/flared ejection port; checkered front/rear grip straps; blue slide/stainless frame finish
MSRP: $2109

Remington

(www.remington.com)

MODEL 1911 R1 ENHANCED

Action: Autoloader, SA
Overall Length: 8.5 in.
Overall Height: 5.5 in.
Width: 1.3 in.
Barrel: 5 in.
Grips: Checkered wood laminate
Sights: Dovetail fiber optic front/adj. rear
Weight Unloaded: 40 oz.
Caliber: .45 ACP
Capacity: 8 + 1
Features: Colt 1911 design; steel frame; thumb, grip safeties; lowered/flared ejection port; serrated front grip; satin black oxide finish
MSRP: $940

REMINGTON MODEL 1911 R1 ENHANCED

Rossi

(www.rossiusa.com)

RANCH HAND

Action: Lever action, SA
Overall Length: 24 in.
Barrel: 12 in.
Grips: Brazilian hardwood
Sights: Fixed, front/adj. rear
Weight Unloaded: 4.0 lbs.–14.4 oz.
Caliber: .38 Special/.357 Mag., .44 Mag., .45 LC
Capacity: 6
Features: Oversized lever loop; saddle ring with leather strap; matte blue or case hardened finishes
MSRP: . . . . $536–$614
(depending on caliber and finish)

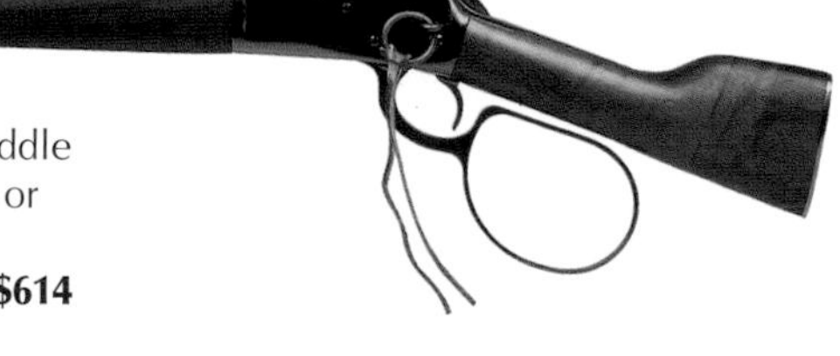

ROSSI RANCH HAND

SIG SAUER P210

SIG SAUER P290

Sig Sauer

(sigsauer.com)

P210

Action: Autoloader, SA
Overall Length: 8.5 in.
Overall Height: 5.6 in.
Width: 1.3 in.
Barrel: 4.7 in.
Grips: Checkered wood
Sights: Dovetail front/rear
Weight Unloaded: 37.4 oz.
Caliber: 9mm
Capacity: 8 + 1
Features: Reintroduction of classic Swiss Army pistol; steel frame/slide; manual thumb, drop safeties; thumb magazine release
MSRP: $2100

P290

Action: Autoloader, DAO
Overall Length: 5.5 in.
Overall Height: 3.9 in.
Width: 1.1 in.
Barrel: 2.9 in.
Grips: Textured polymer
Sights: Dovetail front/rear
Weight Unloaded: 20.5 oz.
Caliber: 9mm
Capacity: 6 + 1
Features: Polymer frame; steel slide; removable grip panels; automatic firing pin block, hammer intercept, and trigger bar disconnect safeties
Nitron (matte black)**: $758**

Smith & Wesson (S&W)

(www.smith-wesson.com)

GOVERNOR

Action: Revolver, SA/DA
Overall Length: 8.5 in.
Overall Height: 5.5 in.
Width: 1.8 in.
Barrel: 2.8 in.
Grips: Textured, finger-groove synthetic
Sights: Tritium front/fixed rear
Weight Unloaded: 29.6 oz.
Caliber: .45 Long Colt/.45 ACP/.410
Capacity: 6
Features: Scandium frame; 2.5-in. chamber
Matte black:. $679
Matte black (Crimson Trace laser sight grip)**: $899**

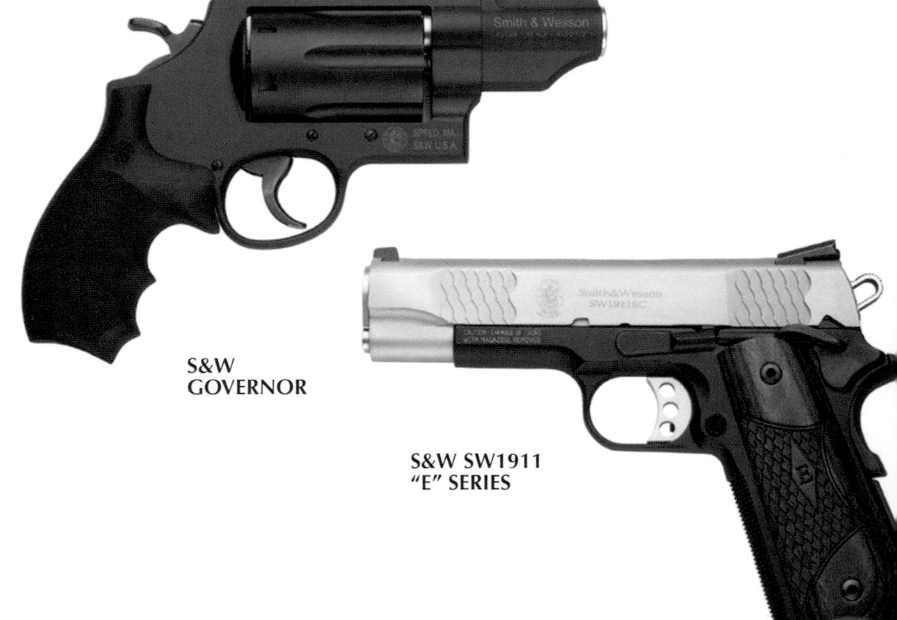
S&W GOVERNOR

S&W SW1911 "E" SERIES

SW1911 "E" SERIES

Action: Autoloader, SA
Overall Length: 8 in. (SW1911SC), 8.7 in.
Overall Height: 5.5 in.
Width: 1.5 in.
Barrel: 4.3 in. (SW1911SC), 5 in.
Grips: Checkered hardwood
Sights: Fixed front/dovetail rear, 3-dot
Weight Unloaded: 29.9 oz. (SW1911SC), 39 oz.
Caliber: .45 ACP
Capacity: 7 + 1 (SW1911SC), 8 + 1
Features: Colt 1911 design; steel frame; extended thumb, beavertail grip safeties; lower/flared ejection port; magazine bumper pad; oversized external extractor; chamfered/recessed muzzle; titanium firing pin
SW1911: $919
SW1911CT (stainless, Crimson Trace laser grip)**: $1089**
SW1911TA (stainless or blue, Picatinny rail, ambidextrous thumb safety, 40.5 oz.)**: $1319**
SW1911SC (scandium round butt frame, two-tone or blue, ambidextrous thumb safety)**: $1369**

Springfield Armory
(www.springfield-armory.com)

RANGE MASTER
Action: Autoloader, SA
Overall Length: 8.5 in.
Overall Height: 5.5 in.
Width: 1.5 in.
Barrel: 5 in.
Grips: Checkered hardwood
Sights: Fixed front/adj. rear
Weight Unloaded: 40 oz.
Caliber: .45 ACP
Capacity: 7 + 1
Features: Colt 1911 design; steel frame; thumb/beavertail grip safeties; lower/flared ejection port; parkerized finish
MSRP: $939

SPRINGFIELD ARMORY RANGE MASTER PACK

SPRINGFIELD ARMORY RANGE MASTER

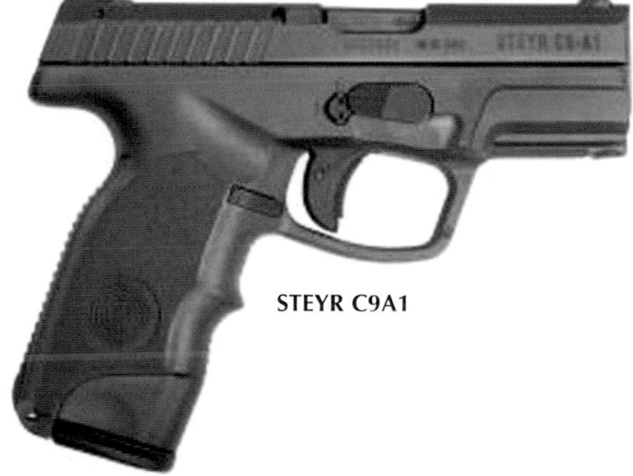

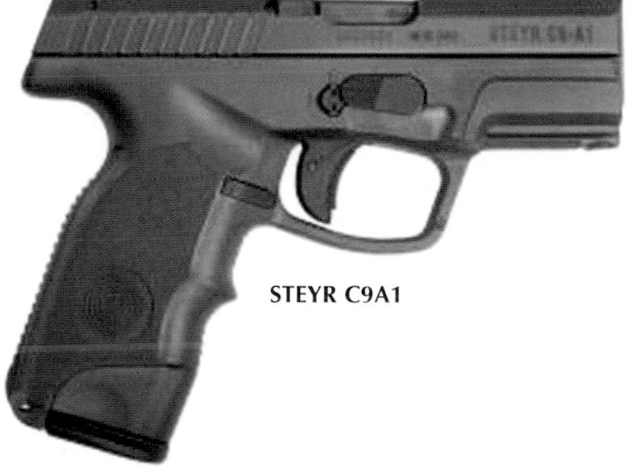

STEYR C9A1

STOEGER COUGAR COMPACT

Steyr Arms
(www.steyr-mannlicher.com)

C9 A1
Action: Autoloader, striker-fired
Overall Length: 6.7 in.
Overall Height: 5.1 in.
Overall Width: 1.2 in.
Barrel: 3.6 in.
Grips: Textured polymer
Sights: Fixed triangular/trapezoid
Weight Unloaded: 25.6 oz.
Caliber: 9mm
Capacity: 17 + 1
Features: Polymer frame; trigger, internal striker, internal gun-lock safeties; polygonal rifling; black matte Mannox finish; Picatinny rail
MSRP: $649

Stoeger Industries
(www.stoegerindustries.com)

STOEGER COUGAR COMPACT
Action: Autoloader, SA/DA
Overall Length: 7 in.
Overall Height: 4.8 in.
Overall Width: 1.4 in.
Barrel: 3.5 in.
Grips: Checkered polymer
Sights: Dovetail front and rear, white 3-dot
Weight Unloaded: 28.8 oz.
Caliber: 9mm
Capacity: 13 + 1
Features: Beretta rotating barrel design; aluminum alloy frame; steel slide and barrel; ambidextrous thumb, firing pin block, and decocking safeties; external hammer; loaded-chamber indicator; combat trigger guard; serrated front/back grip strap
Bruniton matte black: $449

STURM, RUGER & CO. SR1911

STURM, RUGER & CO. LC9

STURM, RUGER & CO. LCR XS

Sturm, Ruger & Co.

(www.ruger.com)

SR1911

Action: Autoloader, SA
Overall Length: 8.7 in.
Overall Height: 5.5 in.
Width: 1.5 in.
Barrel: 5 in.
Grips: Checkered hardwood
Sights: Dovetail front/rear, Novak 3-dot
Weight Unloaded: 39 oz.
Caliber: .45 ACP
Capacity: 8 + 1
Features: Colt 1911 Series 70 design; stainless frame; thumb/beavertail grip safeties; lower/flared ejection port; titanium firing pin; loaded-chamber inspection port; matte stainless finish
MSRP: $799

LC9

Action: Autoloader, DAO
Overall Length: 6 in.
Overall Height: 4.5 in.
Width: .9 in.
Barrel: 3.1 in.
Grips: Textured polymer
Sights: Fixed front/rear
Weight Unloaded: 17.1 oz.
Caliber: 9mm
Capacity: 7 + 1
Features: Glass-filled nylon frame; textured front/rear grip straps; black finish
MSRP: $443

LCR XS

Action: Revolver, DAO
Overall Length: 6.5 in.
Overall Height: 4.5 in.
Width: 1.3 in.
Barrel: 1.9 in.
Grips: Rubber; Hogue Tamer
Sights: Fixed front/rear, Tritium dot
Weight Unloaded: 13.5 oz.
Caliber: .38 Spl. +P
Capacity: 5
Features: Matte black aluminum frame; stainless fluted cylinder
MSRP: $525

Taurus

(www.taurususa.com)

TAURUS DT HYBRID

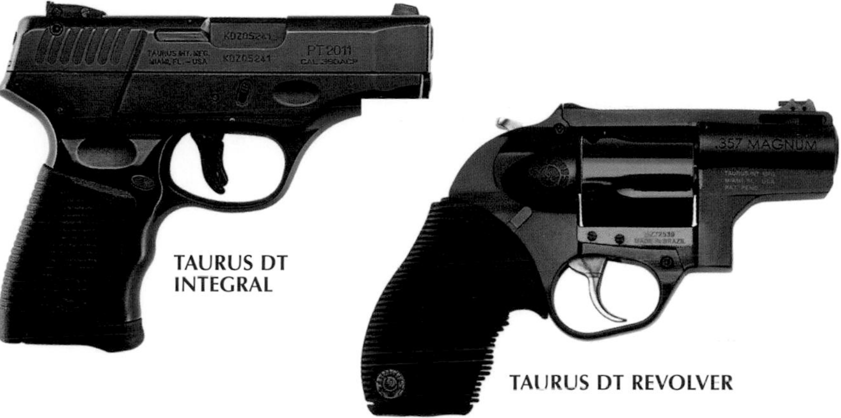

TAURUS DT INTEGRAL

TAURUS DT REVOLVER

DT HYBRID

Action: Autoloader, hybrid striker-fire
Overall Length: 6.3 in.
Barrel: 3.2 in.
Grips: Textured polymer
Sights: Fixed front/adj. rear
Weight Unloaded: 24 oz.
Caliber: 9mm, .40 S&W
Capacity: 13 + 1 (9mm), 11 + 1 (.40 S&W)
Features: Polymer frame; ambidextrous magazine release; thumb safety; external extractor; loaded-chamber indicator; blue and matte stainless finishes
MSRP: . . . . $545–$561
(depending on finish)

DT INTEGRAL

Action: Autoloader, hybrid striker-fire
Overall Length: 6.3 in.
Barrel: 3.2 in.
Grips: Textured polymer; modular
Sights: Fixed front/adj. rear
Weight Unloaded: 21 oz.
Caliber: .380, 9mm, .40 S&W
Capacity: 15 + 1 (.380), 15 + 1 (9mm), 11 + 1 (.40 S&W)
Features: Polymer frame; ambidextrous magazine release; thumb safety; external extractor; loaded-chamber indicator; blue and matte stainless finishes
MSRP: . . . . $545–$561
(depending on finish)

PROTECTOR 605 PLY and 85 PLY POLYMER

Action: Revolver, SA/DA
Overall Length: 5.1 in.
Barrel: 1.3 in.
Grips: Checkered brown polymer (.38 Spl.), ribbed rubber (.357 Mag.)
Sights: Fiber optic fixed front/fixed rear
Weight Unloaded: 16.5 oz.
Caliber: .38 Spl. +P, .357 Mag.
Capacity: 5
Features: Polymer frame; external low profile hammer; ambidextrous thumb rest; black and matte stainless finishes
MSRP: . . . . $445–$461
(depending on caliber and finish)

DT REVOLVER

Action: Revolver, SA/DA
Overall Length: 6.7 in.
Barrel: 2 in.
Grips: Ribbed rubber
Sights: Fiber optic fixed front/fixed rear
Weight Unloaded: 20.2 oz.
Caliber: .357 Mag.
Capacity: 5
Features: Polymer frame; external low profile hammer; ambidextrous thumb rest; black finish
MSRP: $445

709 G2 SLIM and 740 G2 SLIM

Action: Autoloader, hybrid striker-fire
Overall Length: 6.3 in.
Barrel: 3.2 in.
Grips: Textured polymer

NEW Products: Handguns

TAURUS 740 G2 SLIM

TAURUS 638 PRO COMPACT

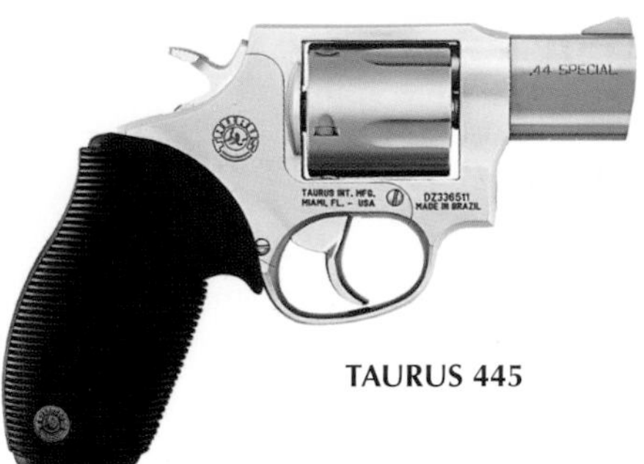

TAURUS 445

TAURUS 405

Sights: Fixed front/adj. rear
Weight Unloaded: 19 oz.
Caliber: 9mm (709 G2 Slim), .40 S&W (740 G2 Slim)
Capacity: 7 + 1 (9mm), 6 + 1 (.40 S&W)
Features: Polymer frame; ambidextrous magazine release; magazine base pad; loaded-chamber indicator; trigger/thumb safeties; black and matte stainless finishes
709 G2 Slim: . . . . $483–$498
(depending on finish)
740 G2 Slim: . . . . $483–$498
(depending on finish)

638 PRO COMPACT

Action: Autoloader, SA
Overall Length: 6.2 in.
Barrel: 3.2 in.
Grips: Textured polymer
Sights: Dovetail front/adj. rear
Weight Unloaded: 28 oz.
Caliber: .380
Capacity: 15 + 1
Features: Polymer frame; ambidextrous thumb safety; combat trigger guard; Picatinny rail; black and matte stainless finishes
MSRP: . . . . $483–$498
(depending on finish)

MODEL 405 and 445

Action: Revolver, SA/DA
Overall Length: 7 in.
Barrel: 2 in.
Grips: Ribbed rubber
Sights: Fixed front/rear
Weight Unloaded: 22 oz. (445), 29 oz. (405)
Caliber: .44 Spl. (445), .40 S&W (405)
Capacity: 5
Features: Lightweight steel frame; external hammer; black and matte stainless finishes
405: . . . . $452–$498
445: . . . . $483–$415
(depending on finish)

Walther

(www.smith-wesson.com)

WALTHER PPQ

Action: Autoloader, striker-fired
Overall Length: 7.1 in.
Overall Height: 5.3 in.
Width: 1.3 in.
Barrel: 4 in.
Grips: Textured polymer, modular
Sights: Adj. front/rear
Weight Unloaded: 24.5 oz.
Caliber: 9mm, .40 S&W
Capacity: 15 + 1 (9mm), 12 + 1 (.40 S&W)
Features: Quick Defense Trigger (QDT) with short reset; ambidextrous magazine release; manual safety; polymer frame; two grip insert sizes; Picatinny rail; loaded-chamber indicator; black finish
MSRP: $729

WALTHER PPQ

Federal

(www.federalpremium.com)

GUARD DOG

Guard Dog ammunition is designed for home defense. It offers terminal performance to stop threats while reducing overpenetration through walls. The bullet is constructed similar to a FMJ and filled with an expanding polymer designed to minimize overpenetration through interior walls.

Caliber	Bullet Weight in Grains	Bullet Type	Case Type	Primer Type	Cartridges Per Box	MSRP
9mm	105	Guard Dog	Brass	Boxer	20	$24.95
.40 S&W	135	Guard Dog	Brass	Boxer	20	$26.95
.45 ACP	165	Guard Dog	Brass	Boxer	20	$27.95

FEDERAL GUARD DOG

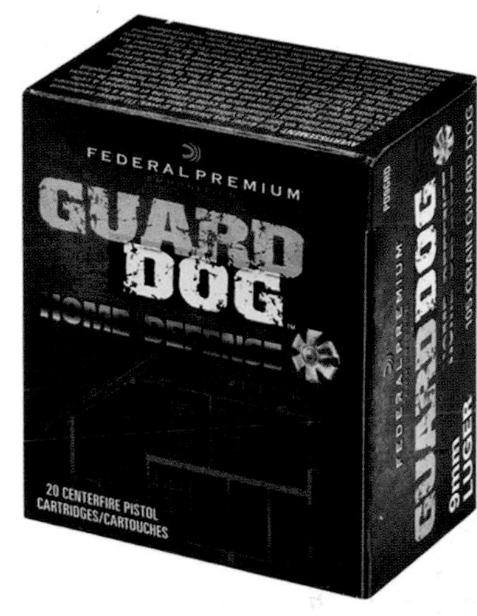

Winchester

(www.winchester.com)

SUPREME ELITE BONDED PDX1

Supreme Elite Bonded PDX1 ammo was chosen by the FBI as its primary service round and is engineered to maximize terminal ballistics, as defined by the demanding FBI test protocol. The bonding process welds lead and jacket together to control expansion and retain weight. The hollow point jacket is notched in six segments to help promote consistent expansion at a variety of impact velocities and ranges. It is new-manufacture loaded in nickel-plated, reloadable brass.

Caliber	Bullet Weight In Grains	Bullet Type	Case Type	Primer Type	Cartridges Per Box	MSRP
.357 Magnum	125	Bonded PDX1 JHP	Nickel-plated brass	Boxer	20	$17
.357 Sig	125	Bonded PDX1 JHP	Nickel-plated brass	Boxer	20	$19

Gauge	Length	Shot Size	Case Type	Cartridges Per Box	MSRP
.410	3 in.	16 plated BB pellets and 4 Defense Disc projectiles	Plastic hull	10	$12

GUARD DOG BULLETS ARE LIKE FMJ BULLETS BUT ARE FILLED WITH A POLYMER CORE THAT MINIMIZES OVER PENETRATION WHILE PROVIDING EXPANSION. THIS IS A TOP VIEW OF AN EXPANDED 105-GR. 9MM.

WINCHESTER BONDED PDX1

NEW PRODUCTS

LASER SIGHTS

Crimson Trace

(www.crimsontrace.com)

LASER GUARD

Compatible Firearms: Diamondback, H&K, Ruger, Sig, Springfield, Taurus
Activation: Ambidextrous button under trigger guard, one-hand operation
Master Switch: No
Beam Color/Intensity/Mode: Red/5mw, 633nm, class IIIa/constant
Sight Adjustments: Windage and elevation
Battery Size/Life: One 1/3N 3V lithium or two 357 silver oxide/4 hr.
Features: Polymer construction; matte black finish; water resistant
MSRP: $209

PRO-CUSTOM LASER GRIP

Compatible Firearms: 1911
Activation: Ambidextrous button under trigger guard, one-hand operation/constant
Master Switch: Yes
Beam Color/Intensity/Mode: Red/5mw, 633nm, class IIIa/constant
Sight Adjustments: Windage and elevation
Battery Size/Life: Two #2032 lithium/4 hr.
Features: Water resistant; walnut finish with double-diamond checkered wood
MSRP: $359

LASER GRIP

Compatible Firearms: Kimber (Solo Carry)
Activation: Ambidextrous button under trigger guard, one-hand operation/constant
Master Switch: Yes
Beam Color/Intensity/Mode: Red/5mw, 633nm, class IIIa/constant
Sight Adjustments: Windage and elevation
Battery Size/Life: Two #2032 lithium/4 hr.
Features: Water resistant; checkered rosewood finish
MSRP: $209

CRIMSON TRACE LG-401 PRO-CUSTOM

CRIMSON TRACE LG-407 LASER GUARD

LASERLYTE RL-SR REAR SIGHT

LaserLyte

(www.laserlyte.com)

REAR SIGHT LASER

Compatible Firearms: 1911, Kahr, Kel-Tec, Ruger, Taurus, Smith & Wesson
Activation: Button behind rear sight
Master Switch: No
Beam Color/Intensity/Mode: Red/5mw, 650nm, class IIIa/constant and pulsating
Sight Adjustments: Windage and elevation
Battery Size/Life: Four #377/5 hr.
Features: Waterproof
MSRP: $199

SIDE MOUNT LASER

Compatible Firearms: Taurus, Smith & Wesson
Activation: Ambidextrous button under trigger guard, one-hand operation
Master Switch: No
Beam Color/Intensity/Mode: Red/5mw, 650nm, class IIIa/constant and pulsating
Sight Adjustments: Windage and elevation
Battery Size/Life: Four #377/5 hr.
Features: Designed for revolvers; waterproof
MSRP: $150

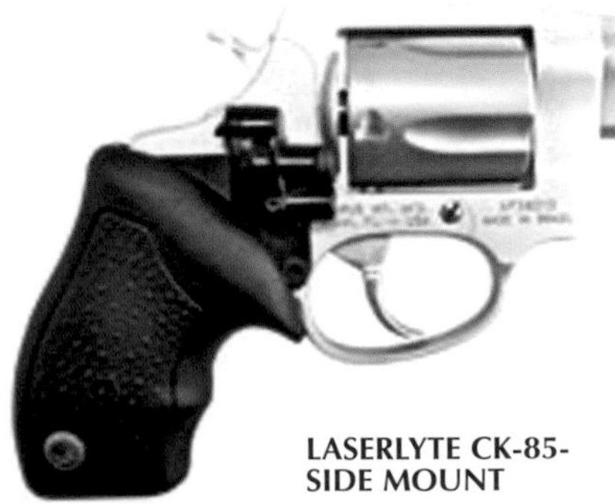

LASERLYTE CK-85-SIDE MOUNT

LaserMax
(www.lasermax.com)

GENESIS
Compatible Firearms: Most pistols with an accessory rail
Activation: Ambidextrous button on unit
Master Switch: No
Beam Color/Intensity/Mode: Green/5mw, 532nm/constant
Sight Adjustments: Windage and elevation
Battery Size/Life: Rechargeable lithium/2.5 hr.
Features: Water resistant; rechargeable battery
MSRP: $259

LASERMAX GENESIS

UNI-MAX MICRO
Compatible Firearms: Most pistols with an accessory rail
Activation: Ambidextrous button on unit
Master Switch: No
Beam Color/Intensity/Mode: Red/5mw, 650nm/constant
Sight Adjustments: Windage and elevation
Battery Size/Life: One 1/3N 3V lithium/5 hr.
Features: Water resistant; compact design
MSRP: $129

LASERMAX UNI-MAX MICRO

UNI-IR
Compatible Firearms: Most pistols with an accessory rail
Activation: Ambidextrous button on unit
Master Switch: No
Beam Color/Mode: Infrared/constant
Sight Adjustments: Windage and elevation
Battery Size/Life: Two 357 silver oxide/3.5 hr.
Features: Compact design; beam is only visible with night vision devices
MSRP: $189

Viridian
(www.viridiangreenlaser.com)

X5L
Compatible Firearms: Most pistols with an accessory rail
Activation: Ambidextrous button
Master Switch: No
Beam Color/Intensity/Mode: Green/5mw, 532nm/constant or multiple pulsating
Sight Adjustments: Windage and elevation
Battery Size/Life: One #CR123/6 hr. (constant), 10 hr. (pulsating), 60 min. (laser and light)
Features: Zytel polymer construction; compact design; integrated tactical light 154 lumen continuous, 187 strobe
MSRP: . . not available at press time

VIRIDIAN X5L

TACTICAL LIGHTS

LEAPERS UTG 16MM IRB LED FLASH-LIGHT WITH INTEGRAL WEAVER MOUNT

Leapers
(www.leapers.com)

UTG 16MM IRB LED
Activation: Ambidextrous toggle switch
Compatible Firearms: Designed for most pistols with an accessory rail
Beam Output/Modes: 90 Lumens/ constant
Overall Length: 3.4 in.
Weight With Batteries: 3.1 oz.
Battery Size/Life: Two CR123A/120 min.
Bulb Type: LED
Features: Aluminum construction
MSRP: $35

NEW Products: Accessories

UTG COMBAT 23MM IRB LED

Activation: Ambidextrous toggle switch
Compatible Firearms: Designed for most pistols with an accessory rail
Beam Output/Modes: 150 Lumens/constant
Overall Length: 3.4 in.
Weight With Batteries: 4.9 oz.
Battery Size/Life: Two CR123A/120 min.
Bulb Type: LED
Features: Aluminum construction
MSRP: $53

LEAPERS UTG COMBAT 23MM IRB LED WITH BUILT-IN WEAVER MOUNT

NEW Products: Holsters

Galco
(www.usgalco.com)

V-HAWK

Use/Type: Concealment/belt
Retention: None
Material/Finish: Leather/plain black
Carry: Strong side
Compatible Firearms: Full-size pistols and revolvers
Features: Reinforced opening; low profile; fits belts up to 1.3 in.; polymer c-hooks and metal clips; allows shirt to be tucked
MSRP: $112

GALCO V-HAWK

GALCO TACSLIDE

TACSLIDE

Use/Type: Concealment/belt, inside waistband
Retention: None
Material/Finish: Kydex and leather/black
Carry: Strong side
Compatible Firearms: Compact and full-size pistols, small-and medium-frame revolvers
Features: Open muzzle; neutral cant; fits belts up to 1.8 in.
MSRP: $40

Training Facilities

CorBon Training Center
(www.corbon.com)

Location: Sturgis, SD

Training Offered: handgun, rifle, and CCW courses available

COURSE: LEVEL I PISTOL

Duration: 3 days
Prerequisite: None, entry level
Estimated Round Count: TBD
Tuition: $375
Details: Heavy repetition course emphasizing proficiency with a pistol; basic marksmanship fundamentals and safety; concentrates on personal defense

COURSE: LEVEL II PISTOL

Duration: 3 days
Prerequisite: Level I Pistol
Estimated Round Count: TBD
Tuition: $375
Details: Heavy repetition course; combat skills; high stress course drills; carry and deploy pistols from carry mode; operation and conflict resolution

COURSE: CONCEAL CARRY WEAPON (CCW)

Duration: 1 day
Prerequisite: None, entry level
Estimated Round Count: TBD
Tuition: $125
Details: Carrying and using a weapon; carry options; drills utilizing a carry method

8. Handguns

Image Courtesy of Sig Sauer.

LEGEND

ACP – AUTOMATIC COLT PISTOL
SA – SINGLE ACTION
DA – DOUBLE ACTION
DAO – DOUBLE ACTION ONLY
FED. – FEDERAL
LC – LONG COLT
LR – LONG RIFLE
MAG. – MAGNUM
MSRP – MANUFACTURER'S SUGGESTED RETAIL PRICE
NAA – NORTH AMERICAN ARMS
REM. – REMINGTON
SAO – SINGLE ACTION ONLY
SPL. – SPECIAL
S&W – SMITH AND WESSON
TB – THREADED BARREL
WIN. – WINCHESTER

Accu-Tek

(www.accu-tekfirearms.com)

ACCU-TEK AT-380 II

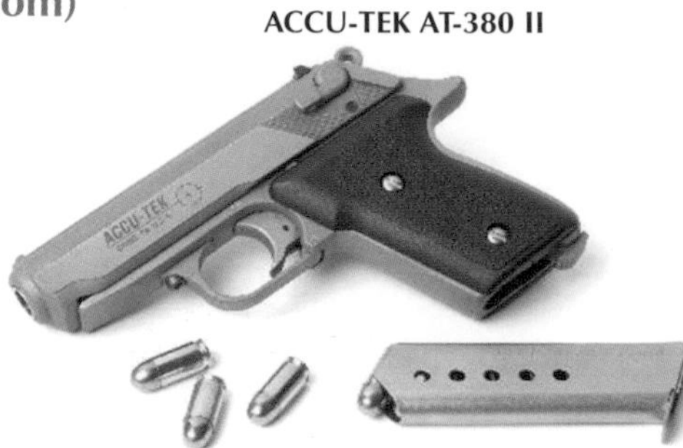

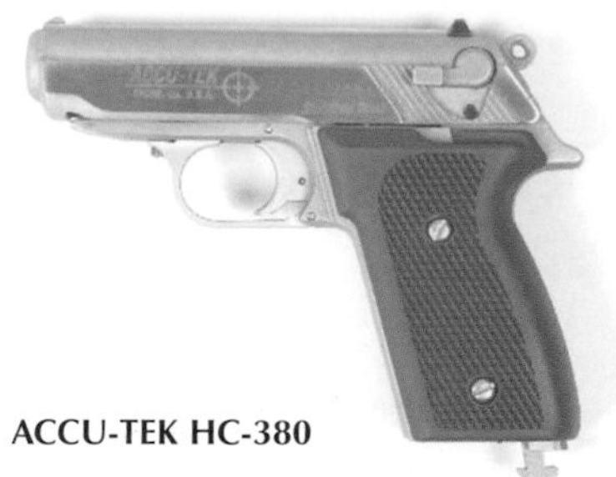

ACCU-TEK HC-380

AT-380 II

Action: Autoloader, SA
Overall Length: 5.6 in.
Overall Height: 4.2 in.
Overall Width: 8 in.
Barrel: 2.8 in.
Grips: Composite
Sights: Fixed front/adj. rear
Weight Unloaded: 23.5 oz.
Caliber: .380
Capacity: 6 + 1
Features: Stainless frame; exposed hammer; slide-mounted safety; satin stainless finish
MSRP: $275

HC-380

Action: Autoloader, SA
Overall Length: 6 in.
Overall Height: 4.9 in.
Overall Width: 8 in.
Barrel: 2.8 in.
Grips: Checkered composite
Sights: Fixed front/adj. rear
Weight Unloaded: 26 oz.
Caliber: .380
Capacity: 13 + 1
Features: Stainless frame; exposed hammer; slide-mounted safety; satin stainless
MSRP: $314

American Classic

(www.americanclassic1911.com)

AMERICAN CLASSIC
CLASSIC (BLUE)

AMERICAN CLASSIC
CLASSIC II (CHROME)

HANDGUNS

CLASSIC

Action: Autoloader, SA
Overall Length: 8.3 in.
Overall Height: 5.5 in.
Overall Width: 1.3 in.
Barrel: 5 in.
Grips: Checkered wood
Sights: Fixed blade front/dovetail rear, mil-spec style
Weight Unloaded: 37 oz.
Caliber: .45 ACP
Capacity: 8 + 1
Features: Colt 1911 design; thumb, grip, and firing pin block safeties; lowered ejection port; mil-spec slide serrations; magazine bumper pad
Matte blue: $500
Hard chrome: $550

CLASSIC II

Action: Autoloader, SA
Overall Length: 8.4 in.
Overall Height: 5.5 in.
Overall Width: 1.3 in.
Barrel: 5 in.
Grips: Double-diamond checkered hardwood
Sights: Dovetail front/rear, Novak-style
Weight Unloaded: 37.3 oz.
Caliber: .45 ACP
Capacity: 8 + 1
Features: Colt 1911 design; extended thumb, beavertail grip, and firing pin block safeties; flared ejection port; extended slide stop; combat hammer; combat trigger; front and rear slide serrations; magazine bumper pad
Deep blue: $550
Hard chrome: $600

American Classic

(www.americanclassic1911.com)

AMERICAN CLASSIC COMMANDER

AMERICAN CLASSIC TROPHY

AMERICAN CLASSIC AMIGO (CHROME)

COMMANDER

Action: Autoloader, SA
Overall Length: 7.5 in.
Overall Height: 5.5 in.
Overall Width: 1.3 in.
Barrel: 4.3 in.
Grips: Double-diamond checkered hardwood
Sights: Dovetail front/rear, Novak-style
Weight Unloaded: 32 oz.
Caliber: .45 ACP
Capacity: 8 + 1
Features: Colt 1911 design; extended thumb, beavertail grip, and firing pin block safeties; flared ejection port; extended slide stop; combat hammer; combat trigger; rear slide serrations; magazine bumper pad
Deep blue: $480
Hard chrome: $540

TROPHY

Action: Autoloader, SA
Overall Length: 8.4 in.
Overall Height: 5.5 in.
Overall Width: 1.3 in.
Barrel: 5 in.
Grips: Double-diamond checkered hardwood
Sights: Dovetail fiber optic front/rear, Novak-style
Weight Unloaded: 37.3 oz.
Caliber: .45 ACP
Capacity: 8 + 1
Features: Colt 1911 design; extended thumb, beavertail grip, and firing pin block safeties; flared ejection port; standard slide stop; combat hammer; combat trigger; front and rear slide serrations; magazine bumper pad; checkered mainspring housing; beveled magazine well; reverse plug recoil system with full-length guide rod
Hard chrome: $680

AMIGO

Action: Autoloader, SA
Overall Length: 7.3 in.
Overall Height: 5 in.
Overall Width: 1.3 in.
Barrel: 3.5 in.
Grips: Checkered hardwood
Sights: Dovetail front/rear, Novak-style
Weight Unloaded: 32.5 oz.
Caliber: .45 ACP
Capacity: 7 + 1
Features: Colt 1911 design; extended thumb, beavertail grip, and firing pin block safeties; flared ejection port; extended slide stop; combat hammer; combat trigger; rear slide serrations; magazine bumper pad
Deep blue: $560
Hard chrome: $640

HANDGUNS

American Derringer

(www.amderringer.com)

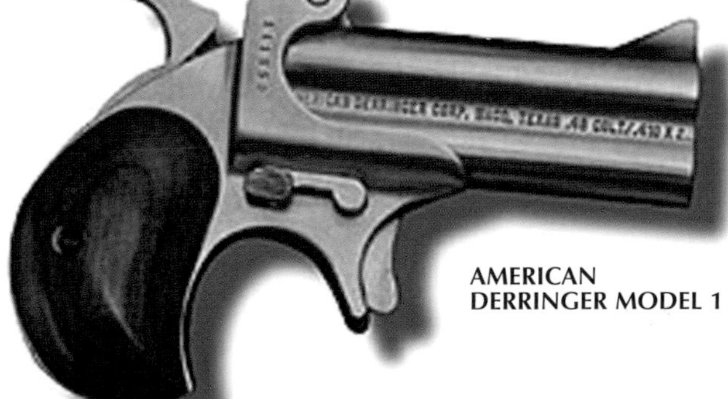

AMERICAN DERRINGER MODEL 1

MODEL 1

Action: Hinged breech, SA
Overall Length: 4.82 in.
Overall Height: 5 in.
Overall Width: 1.3 in.
Barrel: 3 in.
Grips: Rosewood or stag
Sights: Fixed front/rear
Weight Unloaded: 15 oz.
Caliber: .22 LR, .22 Mag., .223 Rem., .30 M1 Carbine, .30-30 Win., .32 Mag./.32 S&W Long, .32-20, .357 Mag., .357 Maximum, .38 Spl., .38 Super, .380, 9mm, .40 S&W, 10mm, .41 Mag., .44 Mag., .44 Spl., .44-40, .45 ACP, .45 LC, .45 Win. Mag., .45 LC/.410, .45-70
Capacity: 2
Features: Remington Model 95 design; exposed hammer; automatic barrel selection; manually operated hammer-block type safety; satin stainless finish
MSRP: . . . . $400–$600 (depending on caliber)

American Derringer

(www.amderringer.com)

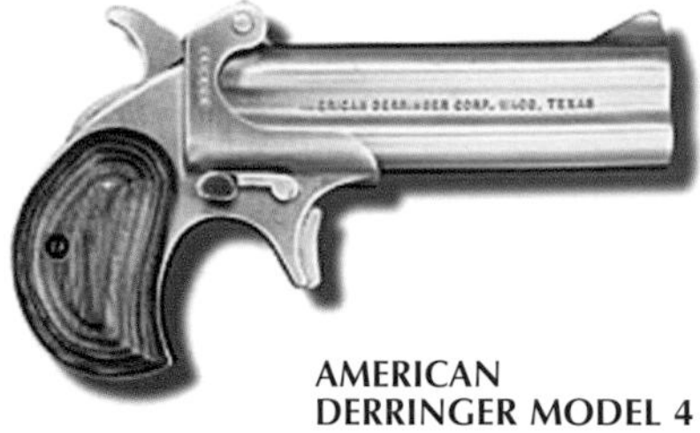

AMERICAN DERRINGER MODEL 4

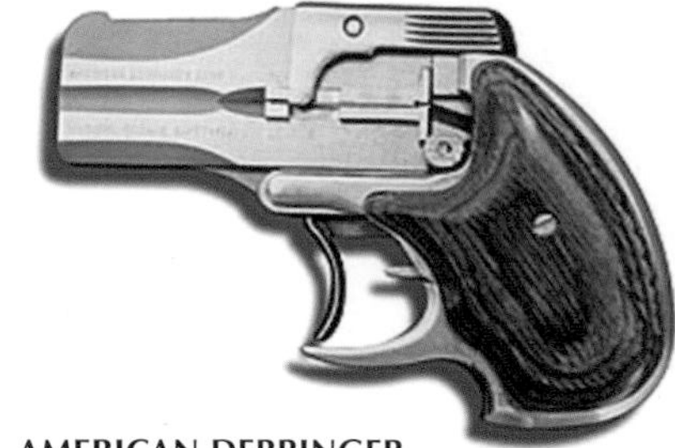
AMERICAN DERRINGER DA 38

MODEL 4

Action: Hinged breech, SA
Overall Length: 6 in.
Overall Height: 5 in.
Overall Width: 1.3 in.
Barrel: 3 in.
Grips: Rosewood or stag
Sights: Fixed front/rear
Weight Unloaded: 16.5 oz.
Caliber: .357 Mag., .357 Maximum, .44 Mag., .45 ACP, .45 LC, .45 LC/.410, .45-70
Capacity: 2
Features: Remington Model 95 design; exposed hammer; automatic barrel selection; manually operated hammer-block-type safety; satin or high polish stainless finish
Model 4: . . . . $500–$600
(depending on caliber)
Model M-4 Alaskan Survival (.45-70-top barrel and .45 LC-bottom barrel, .45-70-top barrel and .45 LC/.410-lower barrel)**: $528**

MODEL 7 LIGHTWEIGHT and ULTRALIGHTWEIGHT

Action: Hinged breech, SA
Overall Length: 4.82 in.
Overall Height: 5 in.
Overall Width: 1.3 in.
Barrel: 3 in.
Grips: Blackwood
Sights: Fixed front/rear
Weight Unloaded: 7.5 oz.
Caliber: 22LR and .22 Mag., .32 Mag./.32 S&W Long, .38 Spl., .380, .44 Spl.
Capacity: 2
Features: Remington Model 95 design; aluminum frame and barrel; exposed hammer; automatic barrel selection; manually operated hammer-block type safety; grey matte finish
MSRP: . . . . $450–$600
(depending on caliber)

DA 38

Action: Hinged breech, DAO
Overall Length: 4.84 in.
Overall Height: 3.3 in.
Overall Width: 1.2 in.
Barrel: 3.3 in.
Grips: Rosewood, walnut, or other hardwood
Sights: Fixed front/rear
Weight Unloaded: 14.5 oz.
Caliber: .38 Spl., .40 S&W
Capacity: 2
Features: Aluminum frame; stainless barrels; manually operated hammer-block-type safety; satin stainless finish
MSRP: . . . . $350–$530
(depending on caliber)

DS22 DERRINGER STANDARD

Action: Hinged breech, DAO
Overall Length: 5 in.
Overall Height: 3 in.
Overall Width: 1.3 in.
Barrel: 3 in.
Grips: Rosewood, walnut, or other hardwood
Sights: Fixed front/rear
Weight Unloaded: 11 oz.
Caliber: .22 Mag.
Capacity: 2
Features: Manually operated hammer-block-type safety; blued finish
MSRP: $500

LM4 SIMMERLING

Action: Static, fully-locked breech, DAO
Overall Length: 5.2 in.
Overall Height: 3.7 in.
Barrel: 3.5 in.
Grips: Checkered plastic
Sights: Fixed front/rear
Weight Unloaded: 24 oz.
Caliber: .45 ACP
Capacity: 4 + 1
Features: Manually operated slide; available in limited quantities; blued finish
MSRP: $2750

LM5

Action: Autoloader, SA
Overall Length: 3 in.
Overall Height: 4 in.
Barrel: 2 in.
Grips: Smooth wood
Sights: Fixed front/rear
Weight Unloaded: 15 oz.
Caliber: .25 ACP, .32 Win. Mag.
Capacity: 4 + 1 (.25 ACP), 3 + 1 (.32 Win. Mag.)
Features: Frame-mounted safety; available in limited quantities; blued finish
MSRP: . . . . $460–$600
(depending on caliber)

AMERICAN DERRINGER LM4 SIMMERLING

AMERICAN DERRINGER LM5

American Tactical Imports (ATI)

(www.americantactical.us)

ATI C45

C45

Action: Autoloader, SA/DA
Overall Length: 8.2 in.
Overall Height: 5.6 in.
Overall Width: 1.4 in.
Barrel: 4.7 in.
Grips: Textured polymer
Sights: Fixed front/dovetail rear
Weight Unloaded: 32.2 oz.
Caliber: .45 ACP
Capacity: 9 + 1
Features: Exposed hammer; ambidextrous thumb safety; external extractor; Picatinny rail
Matte black:. $400
Black and chrome:. $430
Chrome: $440

ATI CS9

CS9 and CS40

Action: Autoloader, SA/DA
Overall Length: 7.6 in.
Overall Height: 5.6 in.
Overall Width: 1.4 in.
Barrel: 4 in.
Grips: Textured polymer
Sights: Fixed front/dovetail rear
Weight Unloaded: 32.2 oz.
Caliber: 9mm (CS9), .40 S&W (CS40)
Capacity: 20 + 1 (9mm), 12 + 1 (.40 S&W)
Features: Exposed hammer; ambidextrous thumb safety; external extractor; Picatinny rail
CS9 matte black: $400
CS9 black and chrome: $420
CS9 chrome: $446
CS40 matte black: $423
CS40 black and chrome: $420
CS40 chrome: $446

FS9 and FS40

Action: Autoloader, SA/DA
Overall Length: 8.7 in.
Overall Height: 5.6 in.
Overall Width: 1.4 in.
Barrel: 5.1 in.
Grips: Textured polymer
Sights: Fixed front/dovetail rear
Weight Unloaded: 32.2 oz.
Caliber: 9mm (FS9), .40 S&W (FS40)
Capacity: 20 + 1 (9mm), 12 + 1 (.40 S&W)
Features: Exposed hammer; ambidextrous thumb safety; external extractor; Picatinny rail
FS9 matte black: $400
FS9 black and chrome: $420
FS9 chrome:. $446
FS40 matte black:. $423
FS40 black and chrome:. $420
FS40 chrome:. $446

HP9

Action: Autoloader, SA/DA
Overall Length: 8.4 in.
Overall Height: 5.5 in.
Overall Width: 1.4 in.
Barrel: 5 in.
Grips: Textured polymer
Sights: Fixed front/dovetail rear
Weight Unloaded: 32.2 oz.
Caliber: 9mm
Capacity: 20 + 1
Features: Exposed hammer; ambidextrous thumb safety; external extractor; Picatinny rail
Matte black:. $400
Black and chrome:. $430
Chrome: $440

ATI FS9

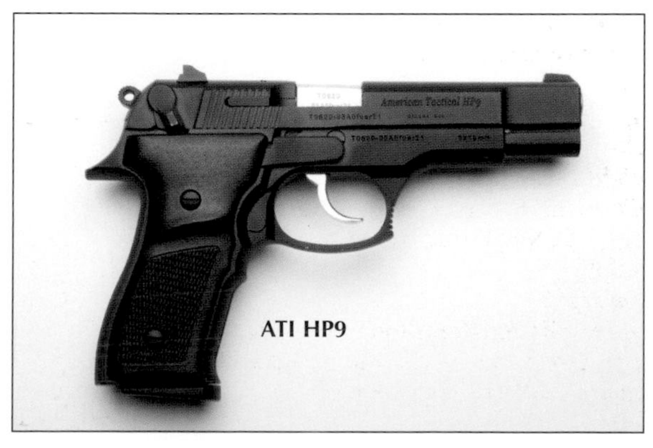
ATI HP9

ArmaLite

(www.armalite.com)

ARMALITE 24K-13C

ARMALITE 24-15C

ARMALITE 24-15

ARMALITE 24K-13

HANDGUNS

24-10 and 24-10C

Action: Autoloader, SA/DA
Overall Length: 7.5 in.
Overall Height: 5.1 in.
Barrel: 3.9 in.
Grips: Checkered rubber
Sights: Fixed front/rear, 3-dot luminous (24-10), dovetail front/adj. rear, 3-dot luminous (24-10)
Weight Unloaded: 34.9 oz.
Caliber: 9mm
Capacity: 10 + 1
Features: CZ-75 design; forged steel frame, slide and barrel; thumb, firing pin block, and half-cock safeties; serrated front/rear grip straps (24-10); checkered front/rear grip straps (24-10C); manganese phosphate, heat-cured epoxy black finish

24-10: $550
24-10C: $631

24K-10 and 24K-10C

Action: Autoloader, SA/DA
Overall Length: 7.5 in.
Overall Height: 5.1 in.
Barrel: 3.9 in.
Grips: Checkered rubber
Sights: Fixed front/rear, 3-dot luminous (24K-10), dovetail front/adj. rear, 3-dot luminous (24K-10C)
Weight Unloaded: 33.4 oz.
Caliber: 9mm
Capacity: 10 + 1
Features: CZ-75 design; forged steel frame, slide and barrel; thumb, firing pin block, and half-cock safeties; serrated front/rear grip straps (24-10); checkered front/rear grip straps (24-10C); manganese phosphate, heat-cured epoxy black finish

24K-10: $550
24K-10C: $631

24K-13 and 24K-13C

Action: Autoloader, SA/DA
Overall Length: 7.5 in.
Overall Height: 5.1 in.
Barrel: 3.9 in.
Grips: Checkered rubber
Sights: Fixed front/rear, 3-dot luminous (24K-13), dovetail front/adj. rear, 3-dot luminous (24K-13C)
Weight Unloaded: 33.4 oz.
Caliber: 9mm
Capacity: 13 + 1
Features: CZ-75 design; forged steel frame, slide and barrel; thumb, firing pin block, and half-cock safeties; serrated front/rear grip straps (24K-13); checkered front/rear grip straps (24K-13C); manganese phosphate, heat-cured epoxy black finish

24K-13: $550
24K-13C: $631

ArmaLite

(www.armalite.com)

24-15 and 24-15C

Action: Autoloader, SA/DA
Overall Length: 8.3 in.
Overall Height: 5.6 in.
Barrel: 4.8 in.
Grips: Checkered rubber
Sights: Fixed front/rear, 3-dot luminous (24-15), dove-tail front/adj. rear, 3-dot luminous (24-15C)
Weight Unloaded: 34.9 oz.
Caliber: 9mm
Capacity: 15 + 1
Features: CZ-75 design; forged steel frame, slide and barrel; thumb, firing pin block, and half-cock safeties; serrated front/rear grip straps (24-15); checkered front/rear grip straps (24-15C); manganese phosphate, heat-cured epoxy black finish
24-15: $550
24-15C: $631

Auto-Ordnance

(www.auto-ordnance.com)

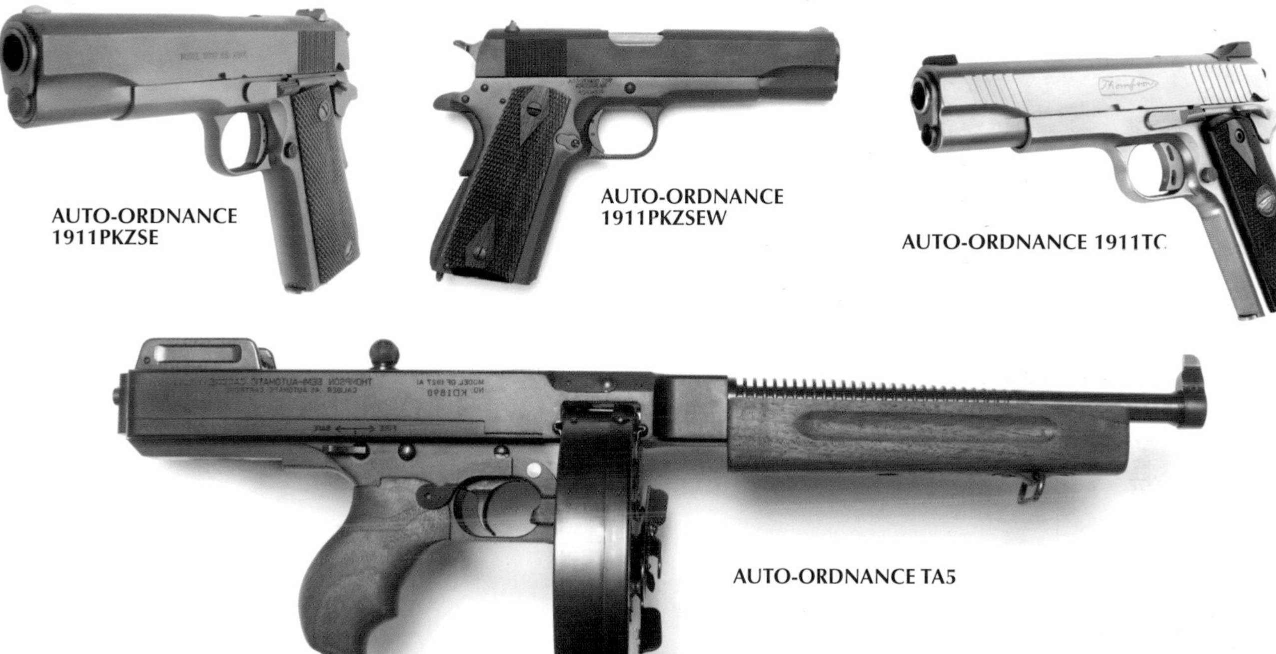

AUTO-ORDNANCE 1911PKZSE

AUTO-ORDNANCE 1911PKZSEW

AUTO-ORDNANCE 1911TC

AUTO-ORDNANCE TA5

1911PKZSE and 1911PKZSEW

Action: Autoloader, SA
Overall Length: 8.5 in.
Overall Height: 5.5 in.
Overall Width: 1.3 in.
Barrel: 5 in.
Grips: Checkered plastic (1911PKZSE), checkered wood (1911PKZSEW)
Sights: Fixed blade front/dovetail rear
Weight Unloaded: 39 oz.
Caliber: .45 ACP
Capacity: 7 + 1
Features: Colt 1911 design, Series 80 configuration; thumb, grip, and firing pin block safeties; parkerized finish
1911PKZSE: $627
1911PKZSEW: $662

TA5

Action: Autoloader, SA
Overall Length: 23.3 in.
Barrel: 10.5 in.
Grips: Walnut
Sights: Fixed blade front/adj. rear
Weight Unloaded: 94.5 oz.
Caliber: .45 ACP
Capacity: 50
Features: Aluminum receiver; horizontal foregrip; top cocking; drum magazine; manual safety; blued finish
MSRP: $1377

1911TC

Action: Autoloader, SA
Overall Length: 8.5 in.
Overall Height: 5.5 in.
Overall Width: 1.3 in.
Barrel: 5 in.
Grips: Checkered laminate
Sights: Fixed front/dovetail rear
Weight Unloaded: 39 oz.
Caliber: .45 ACP
Capacity: 7 + 1
Features: Stainless steel frame/slide; thumb, grip, and firing pin block safeties
MSRP: $813

Beretta

(www.berettausa.com)

BERETTA
21 BOBCAT

BERETTA
3032 TOMCAT

BERETTA 84FS
CHEETAH

21 BOBCAT

Action: Autoloader, SA/DA
Overall Length: 4.8 in.
Overall Height: 3.7 in.
Overall Width: 1.1 in.
Barrel: 2.4 in.
Grips: Checkered plastic
Sights: Fixed front/rear
Weight Unloaded: 12 oz.
Caliber: .22 LR, .25 ACP
Magazine: 7 + 1 (.22 LR), 8 + 1 (.25 ACP)
Features: Aluminum alloy frame; steel slide and barrel; stainless barrel (Inox), thumb, and inertia firing pin block safeties; tip-up barrel
Matte black (.22 LR or .25 ACP): **$335**
Inox matte stainless (.22 LR): **. . $420**

3032 TOMCAT

Action: Autoloader, SA/DA
Overall Length: 4.9 in.
Overall Height: 3.7 in.
Overall Width: 1.1 in.
Barrel: 2.4 in.
Grips: Checkered plastic
Sights: Fixed front/dovetail rear
Weight Unloaded: 14.5 oz.
Caliber: .32 ACP
Capacity: 7 + 1
Features: Aluminum alloy frame; steel slide and barrel; stainless barrel (Inox), thumb, and inertia-firing pin block safeties; tip-up barrel
Matte black: $435
Inox matte stainless: $555

84FS CHEETAH

Action: Autoloader, SA/DA
Overall Length: 6.8 in.
Overall Height: 4.8 in.
Overall Width: 1.4 in.
Barrel: 3.8 in.
Grips: Checkered plastic (matte black), checkered walnut (nickel)
Sights: Fixed front/dovetail rear, 2-dot
Weight Unloaded: 23.3 oz.
Caliber: .380
Capacity: 13 + 1
Features: Aluminum alloy frame; steel slide and barrel; ambidextrous thumb, inertia-firing pin block safeties; loaded-chamber indicator; reversible magazine release; combat-style trigger guard
Matte black: $770
Nickel: $830

85FS CHEETAH

Action: Autoloader, SA/DA
Overall Length: 6.8 in.
Overall Height: 4.8 in.
Overall Width: 1.2 in.
Barrel: 3.8 in.
Grips: Checkered plastic (matte black), checkered walnut (nickel)
Sights: Fixed front/dovetail rear, 2-dot
Weight Unloaded: 21.9 oz.
Caliber: .380
Capacity: 8 + 1
Features: Aluminum alloy frame; steel slide and barrel; ambidextrous thumb, inertia-firing pin block safeties; loaded-chamber indicator; reversible magazine release; combat-style trigger guard
Matte black: $770
Nickel: $830

PX4 STORM COMPACT TYPE F

Action: Autoloader, SA/DA
Overall Length: 6.8 in.
Overall Height: 5 in.
Overall Width: 1.4 in.
Barrel: 3.2 in.
Grips: Polymer, modular
Sights: Dovetail front/rear, 3-dot
Weight Unloaded: 27.3 oz.
Caliber: 9mm, .40 S&W
Capacity: 15 + 1 (9mm), 12 + 1 (.40 S&W)
Features: Rotating barrel design; polymer frame; steel slide and barrel; three grip insert sizes; ambidextrous thumb, firing pin block, and half-cock safeties; ambidextrous slide stop lever; reversible magazine release; Picatinny rail; external hammer; compatible with full-size PX4 magazines
Matte black:. $550

(www.berettausa.com)

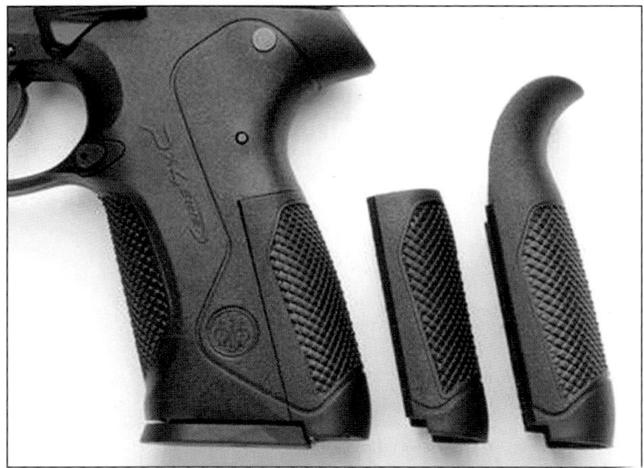

BERETTA PX4 STORM MODULAR GRIP SYSTEM.

BERETTA 92 FS

PX4 STORM SUB-COMPACT TYPE F

Action: Autoloader, SA/DA
Overall Length: 6.2 in.
Overall Height: 4.8 in.
Overall Width: 1.4 in.
Barrel: 3 in.
Grips: Polymer, modular
Sights: Dovetail front/rear, 3-dot
Weight Unloaded: 26.1 oz.
Caliber: 9mm, .40 S&W
Capacity: 13 + 1 (9mm), 10 + 1 (.40 S&W)
Features: Polymer frame; steel slide and barrel; three grip insert sizes; ambidextrous thumb, firing pin block, and half-cock safeties; ambidextrous slide stop lever; reversible magazine release; Picatinny rail; external hammer; compatible with full-size and compact PX4 magazines
Matte black: $550

PX4 STORM TYPE F and TYPE C

Action: Autoloader, SA/DA (Type F), DAO (Type C)
Overall Length: 7.6 in., 8.2 in. (.45 ACP)
Overall Height: 5.5 in.
Overall Width: 1.4 in.
Barrel: 4 in.
Grips: Polymer, modular
Sights: Dovetail front/rear, 3-dot
Weight Unloaded: 27.7 oz., 28.2 oz. (.45 ACP)
Caliber: 9mm, .40 S&W (Type F and C), .45 ACP (Type F)
Capacity: 17 + 1 (9mm), 14 + 1 (.40 S&W), 9 + 1 (.45 ACP)
Features: Rotating barrel design; polymer frame; steel slide and barrel; three grip insert sizes; ambidextrous thumb with decocker (Type F); firing pin block and half-cock safeties; ambidextrous slide stop lever; reversible magazine release; Picatinny rail; external hammer (Type F); matte black finish
Type F (9mm and .40 S&W): **. . . $550**
Type F (.45 ACP): **. $550**
Type C (9mm and .40 S&W): **. . $650**

PX4 STORM SPECIAL DUTY

Action: Autoloader, SA/DA
Overall Length: 8.2 in.
Overall Height: 5.7-in.
Overall Width: 1.4 in.
Barrel: 4.6 in.
Grips: Polymer, modular
Sights: Dovetail front/rear, 3-dot
Weight Unloaded: 28.6 oz.
Caliber: .45 ACP
Capacity: 9 + 1
Features: Rotating barrel design; developed to meet SOCOM specifications for Joint Combat Pistol (JCP); extended barrel suitable for threading; polymer frame; steel slide and barrel; three grip insert sizes; ambidextrous thumb with decocker, firing pin block, and half-cock safeties; ambidextrous slide stop lever; reversible magazine release; Picatinny rail; external hammer; matte black slide and earth tone frame finishes; lanyard loop
MSRP: $1035

92 FS and M9

Action: Autoloader, SA/DA
Overall Length: 8.5 in.
Overall Height: 5.4 in.
Overall Width: 1.5 in.
Barrel: 4.9 in.
Grips: Checkered plastic
Sights: Fixed front/dovetail rear, 3-dot
Weight Unloaded: 33.3 oz.
Caliber: 9mm
Capacity: 15 + 1
Features: Civilian version of U.S. military model (M9); open slide; aluminum alloy frame; steel slide and barrel; ambidextrous thumb with decocker, firing pin block, and half-cock safeties; reversible magazine release; external hammer; loaded-chamber indicator; checkered front/back grip frame; lanyard loop; drop-free magazine; beveled magazine well; sand-resistant PVC coated magazine; Picatinny rail
92 FS/M9 Bruniton matte black: $650
92 FS Inox: $795

BERETTA PX4 STORM

Beretta

(www.berettausa.com)

BERETTA PX4 STORM SUBCOMPACT

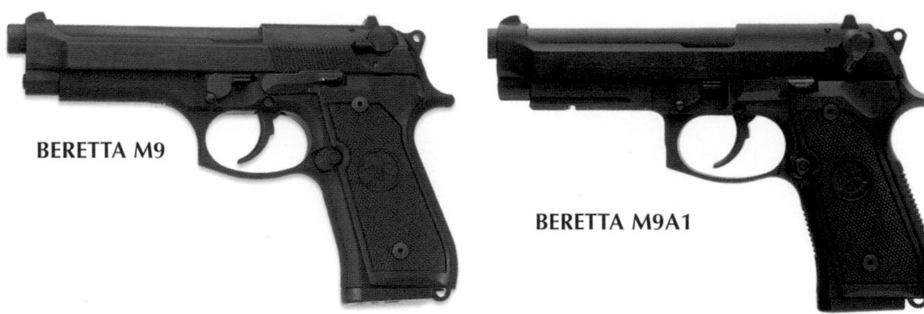

BERETTA M9

BERETTA M9A1

M9A1

Action: Autoloader, SA/DA
Overall Length: 8.5 in.
Overall Height: 5.4 in.
Overall Width: 1.5 in.
Barrel: 4.9 in.
Grips: Checkered plastic
Sights: Fixed front/dovetail rear, 3-dot
Weight Unloaded: 33.3 oz.
Caliber: 9mm
Capacity: 15 + 1
Features: U.S. Marine Corp. spec M9; open slide; aluminum alloy frame; steel slide and barrel; ambidextrous thumb with decocker, firing pin block, and half-cock safeties; reversible magazine release; external hammer; loaded-chamber indicator; checkered front/back grip frame; lanyard loop; drop-free magazine; Picatinny accessory rail; Bruniton matte black finish
MSRP: $750

92A1 and 96A1

Action: Autoloader, SA/DA
Overall Length: 8.5 in.
Overall Height: 5.5 in.
Overall Width: 1.5 in.
Barrel: 4.9 in.
Grips: Checkered plastic
Sights: Fixed, removable front/dovetail rear, 3-dot
Weight Unloaded: 34.4 oz.
Caliber: 9mm (92A1), .40 S&W (96A1)
Capacity: 17 + 1 (9mm), 12 + 1 (.40 S&W)
Features: Open slide; aluminum alloy frame; round trigger guard; steel slide and barrel; ambidextrous thumb with decocker, firing pin block and half-cock safeties; reversible magazine release; external hammer; loaded-chamber indicator; serrated front/back grip frame; lanyard loop; drop-free magazine; Picatinny accessory rail; internal recoil buffer (96A1); captive recoil spring assembly; Bruniton matte black finish
MSRP: $690

BERETTA 90-TWO

90-TWO TYPE F

Action: Autoloader, SA/DA
Overall Length: 8.5 in.
Overall Height: 5.5 in.
Overall Width: 1.5 in.
Barrel: 4.9 in.
Grips: Checkered plastic, modular
Sights: Fixed, removable front/dovetail rear, 3-dot
Weight Unloaded: 32.5 oz.
Caliber: 9mm (92A1), .40 S&W (96A1)
Capacity: 17 + 1 (9mm), 12 + 1 (.40 S&W)
Features: Open slide; skeletonized aluminum alloy frame; round trigger guard; steel slide and barrel; arched or straight grip inserts; ambidextrous thumb with decocker, firing pin block, and half-cock safeties; reversible magazine release; external hammer; loaded-chamber indicator; lanyard loop; drop-free magazine; Picatinny accessory rail with removable cover; internal recoil buffer (.40 S&W); captive recoil spring assembly; Bruniton matte black finish
MSRP: $700

BERETTA PX4 STORM SPECIAL DUTY

BERETTA PX4 STORM COMPACT

Bersa
(www.bersa.com)

BERSA FIRESTORM .38

BERSA FIRESTORM .380

THUNDER 380
Action: Autoloader, SA/DA
Overall Length: 6.6 in.
Overall Height: 4.9 in.
Overall Width: 1.3 in.
Barrel: 3.5 in.
Grips: Checkered polymer
Sights: Fixed front/dovetail rear, 3-dot
Weight Unloaded: 20 oz.
Caliber: .380
Capacity: 7 + 1
Features: Alloy frame; combat trigger guard; steel slide and barrel; integral locking system, manual thumb, firing pin safeties; external hammer; duotone, satin nickel, and matte black finishes; extended finger rest on magazine
MSRP: $260

THUNDER 380 CONCEAL CARRY
Action: Autoloader, DAO
Overall Length: 6 in.
Overall Height: 4.5 in.
Overall Width: 1 in.
Barrel: 3.2 in.
Grips: Checkered polymer
Sights: Fixed front/dovetail rear, 3-dot
Weight Unloaded: 20.6 oz.
Caliber: .380
Capacity: 15 + 1
Features: Alloy frame; combat trigger guard; steel slide and barrel; integral locking system, manual thumb, firing pin safeties; matte black finish; extra low profile sights
MSRP: $270

THUNDER 380 PLUS
Action: Autoloader, SA/DA
Overall Length: 6.6 in.
Overall Height: 4.9 in.
Overall Width: 1.4 in.
Barrel: 3.5 in.
Grips: Checkered polymer
Sights: Fixed front/dovetail rear
Weight Unloaded: 16.4 oz.
Caliber: .380
Capacity: 15 + 1
Features: Alloy frame; combat trigger guard; steel slide and barrel; integral locking system, manual thumb, firing pin safeties; external hammer; satin nickel, matte black finishes; extended finger rest on magazine
MSRP: $330

BERSA THUNDER 380

BERSA THUNDER 380 CONCEAL CARRY

Bersa

(www.bersa.com)

BERSA THUNDER 9

FIRESTORM .380

Action: Autoloader, SA/DA
Overall Length: 6.6 in.
Overall Height: 4.9 in.
Overall Width: 1.3 in.
Barrel: 3.5 in.
Grips: Rubber wrap around
Sights: Fixed front/dovetail rear
Weight Unloaded: 20 oz.
Caliber: .380
Capacity: 7 + 1
Features: Alloy frame; round trigger guard; steel slide and barrel; integral locking system; manual thumb, firing pin safeties; external hammer; duotone, matte black finishes; extended finger rest on magazine
MSRP: $310

FIRESTORM .38 REVOLVER

Action: DAO
Overall Length: 6.5 in.
Barrel: 2 in.
Grips: Black checkered wood
Sights: Fixed front/rear
Weight Unloaded: 24 oz.
Caliber: .38 Spl. +P
Capacity: 7 + 1

BERSA THUNDER 9 ULTRA COMPACT

BERSA 45 ULTRA COMPACT

Features: Steel frame; bobbed hammer
Satin nickel finish: $300

THUNDER 9, 40, and 45 ULTRA COMPACT

Action: Autoloader, SA/DA
Overall Length: 6.5 in., 6.8 in. (.45 ACP)
Overall Height: 4.8 in., 5.1 in. (.45 ACP)
Overall Width: 1.5 in.
Barrel: 3.3 in., 3.6 in. (.45 ACP)
Grips: Checkered black polymer
Sights: Fixed interchangeable front/ interchangeable dovetail rear, 3-dot
Weight Unloaded: 23 oz.
Caliber: 9mm, .40 S&W, .45 ACP
Capacity: 13 + 1 (9mm), 10 + 1 (.40 S&W), 7 + 1 (.45 ACP)
Features: Alloy frame; combat trigger guard; steel slide and barrel; integral locking system, manual thumb, firing and pin safeties; external hammer; duotone, matte black finishes; extended finger rest on magazine; Picatinny rail; polygonal rifling; loaded-chamber indicator; ambidextrous safety, slide release and magazine release
MSRP: . . . . $400–$450
(depending on caliber)

Bersa

(www.bersa.com)

BERSA THUNDER
.40 HIGH CAPACITY

THUNDER 9 and 40 HIGH CAPACITY PRO

Action: Autoloader, SA/DA
Overall Length: 7.6 in.
Overall Height: 5.5 in.
Overall Width: 1.5 in.
Barrel: 4.3 in.
Grips: Checkered black polymer
Sights: Fixed interchangeable front/ interchangeable dovetail rear, 3-dot
Weight Unloaded: 30.7 oz.
Caliber: 9mm, .40 S&W
Capacity: 17 + 1 (9mm), 13 + 1 (.40 S&W)
Features: Alloy frame; combat trigger guard; steel slide and barrel; integral locking system; manual thumb, firing pin safeties; external hammer; duotone, matte black finishes; extended finger rest on magazine; Picatinny rail; polygonal rifling and loaded-chamber indicator; ambidextrous safety, slide release and magazine release; reversible extended magazine release; link-free locked breech design
MSRP: . . . . $350–$400
(depending on caliber)

Bond Arms

(www.bondarms.com)

RANGER

Action: Hinged breech, SA
Overall Length: 6.3 in.
Overall Height: 3.6 in.
Overall Width: 1.4 in.
Barrel: 4.3 in.
Grips: Black ash
Sights: Fixed front/rear
Weight Unloaded: 23.5 oz.
Caliber: .45 LC/.410 3-inch chambers
Capacity: 2
Features: Remington Model 95 design; stainless steel frame/barrels; spur trigger; exposed hammer; automatic extractor; cross bolt, rebounding hammer safeties; interchangeable barrels; satin polish finish; retracting firing pins
MSRP: $649

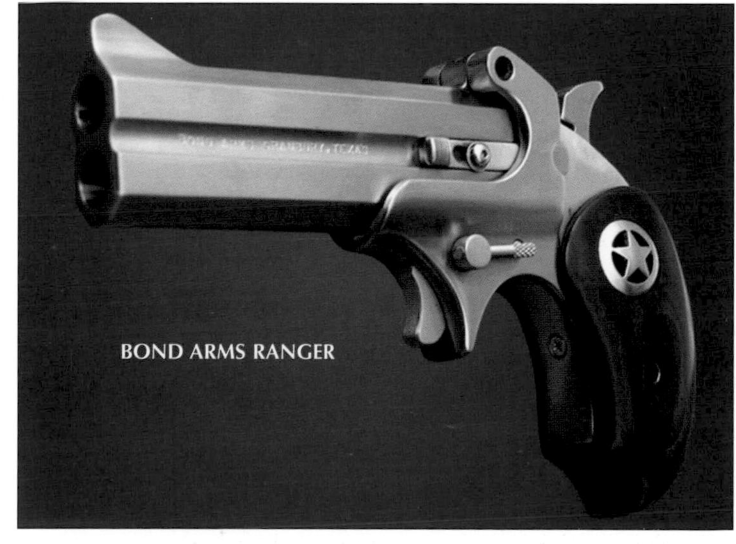

BOND ARMS RANGER

HANDGUNS

Bond Arms

(www.bondarms.com)

BOND ARMS SNAKE SLAYER

SNAKE SLAYER and SNAKE SLAYER IV

Action: Hinged breech, SA
Overall Length: 6.3 in.
Overall Height: 3.6 in.
Overall Width: 1.4 in.
Barrel: 3.5 in. (Snake Slayer), 4.3 in. (Snake Slayer IV)
Grips: Rosewood
Sights: Fixed front/rear
Weight Unloaded: 22 oz. (Snake Slayer), 23.5 oz. (Snake Slayer IV)
Caliber: .45 LC/.410 3-inch chambers
Capacity: 2
Features: Remington Model 95 design; stainless steel frame/barrels; spur trigger; exposed hammer; automatic extractor; cross bolt, rebounding hammer safeties; interchangeable barrels; satin polish finish; trigger guard; retracting firing pins
Snake Slayer: $469
Snake Slayer IV: $499

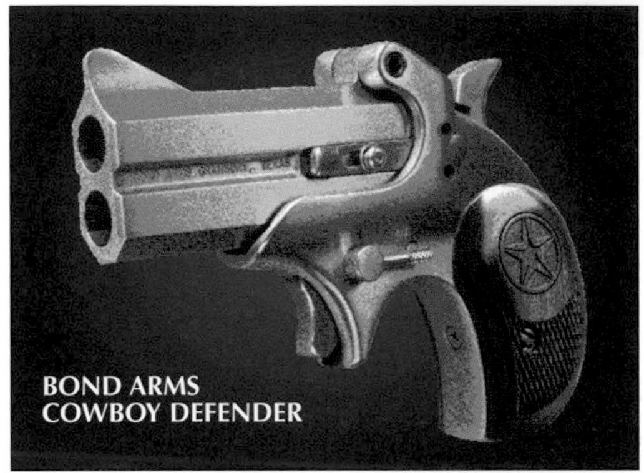
BOND ARMS COWBOY DEFENDER

COWBOY DEFENDER and TEXAS DEFENDER

Action: Hinged breech, SA
Overall Length: 5 in.
Overall Height: 5 in.
Overall Width: 1.4 in.
Barrel: 3 in.
Grips: Rosewood or laminated ash
Sights: Fixed front/rear
Weight Unloaded: 19 oz.
Caliber: .22 LR, .32 H&R Mag., 38 Spl., .357 Mag., .357 Maximum, 9mm, .40 S&W, 10mm, .44 Spl., .44-40, .45 ACP, .45 GAP, .45 LC, .45 LC/.410
Capacity: 2
Features: Remington Model 95 design; stainless steel frame/barrels; spur trigger; exposed hammer; automatic extractor (except for 9mm, .40 S&W, 10mm, .45 ACP); cross bolt, rebounding hammer safeties; interchangeable barrels; satin polish finish; retracting firing pins
Cowboy Defender: $429
Texas Defender (trigger guard): **..$399**

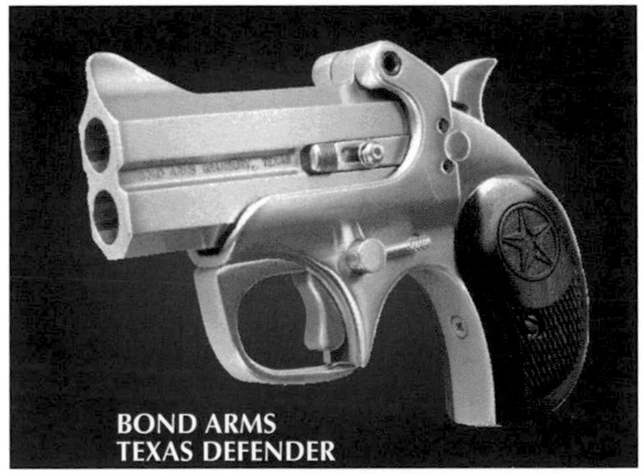
BOND ARMS TEXAS DEFENDER

CENTURY 2000

Action: Hinged breech, SA
Overall Length: 5.5 in.
Overall Height: 3.6 in.
Overall Width: 1.4 in.
Barrel: 3.5 in.
Grips: Rosewood or laminated ash
Sights: Fixed front/rear
Weight Unloaded: 21 oz.
Caliber: .45 LC/.410
Capacity: 2
Features: Remington Model 95 design; stainless steel frame/barrels; spur trigger; exposed hammer; automatic extractor; cross bolt, rebounding hammer safeties; interchangeable barrels; retracting firing pins
Satin stainless: $420

BOND ARMS CENTURY 2000

Browning

(www.browning.com)

BROWNING HI-POWER MARK III

HI-POWER STANDARD

Action: Autoloader, SA
Overall Length: 7.8 in.
Overall Height: 5 in.
Overall Width: 1.4 in.
Barrel: 4.6 in.
Grips: Checkered walnut
Sights: Fixed front/adj. rear, fixed front/rear
Weight Unloaded: 32 oz. (9mm), 32.2 oz. (.40 S&W)
Caliber: 9mm, .40 S&W
Capacity: 13 + 1 (9mm), 10 + 1 (.40 S&W)
Features: Steel frame; slide and barrel; ambidextrous manual thumb, half-cock, magazine disconnect, and firing pin block safeties; external hammer; external extractor; blued finish
Adjusted sights: $1100
Fixed sights: $1030

HI-POWER MARK III

Action: Autoloader, SA
Overall Length: 7.8 in.
Overall Height: 5 in.
Overall Width: 1.4 in.
Barrel: 4.6 in.
Grips: Checkered molded composite
Sights: Dovetail front/rear
Weight Unloaded: 32 oz. (9mm), 32.3 oz. (.40 S&W)
Caliber: 9mm, .40 S&W
Capacity: 13 + 1 (9mm), 10 + 1 (.40 S&W)
Features: Steel frame; slide and barrel; ambidextrous manual thumb, half-cock, magazine disconnect, and firing pin block safeties; external hammer; external extractor; black epoxy finish
MSRP: $999

BROWNING HI-POWER STANDARD

The Hi-Power was the last pistol design by John Browning. The French military was in need of a new service pistol—the *Grande Puissance*, which translates to "high power." It was to be compact, have a minimum 10-round magazine capacity, magazine disconnect and thumb safeties, external hammer, as well as be easy to disassemble and reassemble. Browning died before the pistol was finished and the design was finalized by FN designer, Dieudonné Saive, in 1935. The French government ultimately went with a pistol design by a former French military officer.

HANDGUNS

Bushmaster

(www.bushmaster.com)

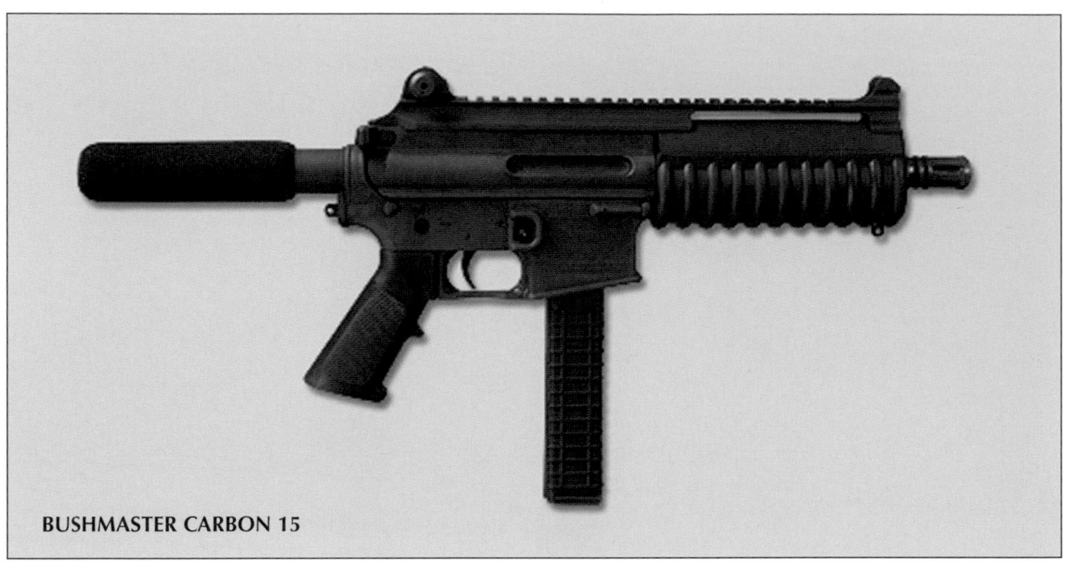

BUSHMASTER CARBON 15

CARBON 15

Action: Autoloader
Overall Length: 22.8 in.
Barrel: 7.3 in.
Grips: Checkered polymer grip, grooved foregrip
Sights: Adj. A2 front post/dual aperture rear
Weight Unloaded: 76 oz.
Caliber: 9mm
Capacity: 30 + 1
Features: AR-15 design; carbon fiber composite receiver, fore-end; thumb manual safety; manganese phosphate-finished bolt carrier; Picatinny rail; birdcage flash hider; sling swivel studs; matte black finish
MSRP: $1055

CARBON 15 TYPE 97

Action: Autoloader
Overall Length: 20 in.
Barrel: 7.3 in.
Grips: Rubber, finger groove grip
Sights: Fixed front post/adj. ghost ring rear
Weight Unloaded: 50 oz.
Caliber: 5.56mm/.223 Rem.
Capacity: 30 + 1
Features: AR-15 design; carbon fiber composite receiver; fluted match-grade stainless steel barrel; Hogue OverMolded grip; thumb manual safety; birdcage flash hider; matte black finish
MSRP: $1020

HANDGUNS

BUSHMASTER CARBON 15 TYPE 97

Bushmaster

(www.bushmaster.com)

BUSHMASTER CARBON 15 TYPE 97S

CARBON 15 TYPE 97S

Action: Autoloader
Overall Length: 20 in.
Barrel: 7.3 in.
Grips: Rubber, finger groove grip, grooved fore end
Sights: Adj. A2 front post/dual aperture rear
Weight Unloaded: 62 oz.
Caliber: 5.56mm/.223 Rem.
Capacity: 30 + 1
Features: AR-15 design; carbon fiber composite receiver, fore-end; thumb manual safety; Picatinny rail; birdcage flash hider; sling swivel studs; matte black finish; Hogue OverMolded grip; chrome bolt carrier
MSRP: $1130

CARBON 15 TYPE 21S

Action: Autoloader
Overall Length: 20 in.
Barrel: 7.3 in.
Grips: Checkered black polymer grip, grooved fore-end
Sights: Adj. A2 front post/dual aperture rear
Weight Unloaded: 62 oz.
Caliber: 5.56mm/.223 Rem.
Capacity: 30 + 1
Features: AR-15 design; carbon fiber composite receiver, fore-end; thumb manual safety; manganese phosphate-finished bolt carrier; Picatinny rail; birdcage flash hider; sling swivel studs; matte black finish; Hogue OverMolded grip
MSRP: $1080

HANDGUNS

BUSHMASTER CARBON 15 TYPE 21S

Charter Arms

(www.charterfirearms.com)

CHARTER ARMS UNDERCOVER ON DUTY WITH CRIMSON TRACE LASER GRIP

.38 UNDERCOVER and DAO

Action: Revolver, SA/DA (Undercover), DAO (DAO)
Overall Length: 6.4 in.
Overall Height: 4.8 in.
Overall Width: 1.3 in.
Barrel: 2 in.
Grips: Checkered black rubber
Sights: Fixed front ramp/rear groove
Weight Unloaded: 16 oz.
Caliber: .38 Spl. +P
Capacity: 5
Features: Hammer block safety; external hammer; 3-point cylinder lock-up; protected ejector rod
Blue: $393
Custom finishes available *(OD, tiger/black, grey/stainless)*: $429–$454
Stainless: $407
Stainless *(Crimson Trace laser sight grip)*: $701
DAO *(blue)*: $401
DAO *(stainless)*: $415
DAO *(stainless, Crimson Trace laser sight grip)*: $701
DAO *(grey/stainless)*: $429

.38 POLICE UNDERCOVER

Action: Revolver, SA/DA
Overall Length: 6.4 in.
Overall Height: 4.9 in.
Overall Width: 1.5 in.
Barrel: 2 in.
Grips: Checkered black rubber
Sights: Fixed front ramp/rear groove
Weight Unloaded: 20 oz.
Caliber: .38 Spl. +P
Capacity: 6
Features: Hammer block safety; 3-point cylinder lock-up; protected ejector rod; uses .44 Special Bulldog frame; stainless finish
MSRP: $448

CHARTER ARMS .38 UNDERCOVER DAO

.38 UNDERCOVER ON DUTY

Action: Revolver, SA/DA
Overall Length: 6.4 in.
Overall Height: 4.9 in.
Overall Width: 1.5 in.
Barrel: 2 in.
Grips: Checkered black rubber
Sights: Fixed front ramp/rear groove
Weight Unloaded: 12 oz.
Caliber: .38 Spl. +P
Capacity: 5
Features: Hammer block safety; 3-point cylinder lock-up; protected ejector rod; aluminum frame; hammer shroud; stainless finish
Stainless: $457
Stainless *(Crimson Trace laser sight grip)*: $736

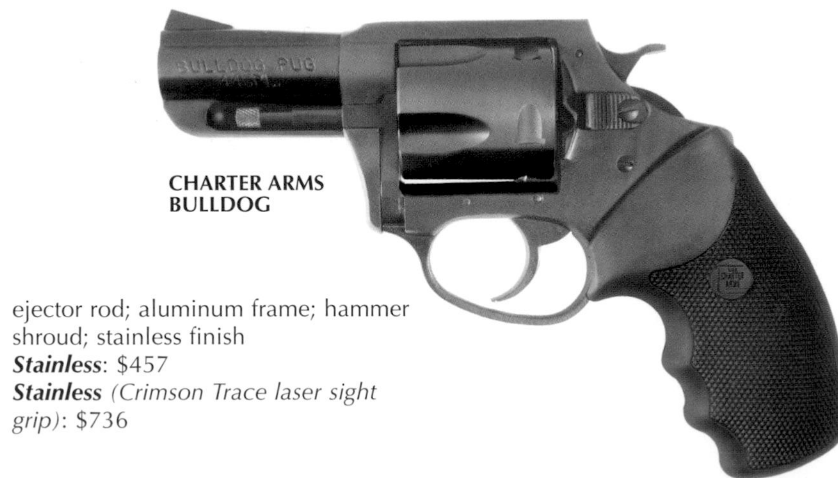

CHARTER ARMS BULLDOG

.38 UNDERCOVER OFF DUTY

Action: Revolver, DAO
Overall Length: 6.4 in.
Overall Height: 4.9 in.
Overall Width: 1.5 in.
Barrel: 2 in.
Grips: Small-checkered black rubber
Sights: Fixed front ramp/rear groove
Weight Unloaded: 12 oz.
Caliber: .38 Spl. +P
Capacity: 5
Features: Hammer block safety; 3-point cylinder lock-up; protected ejector rod; aluminum frame; enclosed hammer
Stainless: $458
Stainless *(Crimson Trace laser sight grip)*: $736
Pink lady *(pink/stainless finish)*: $482

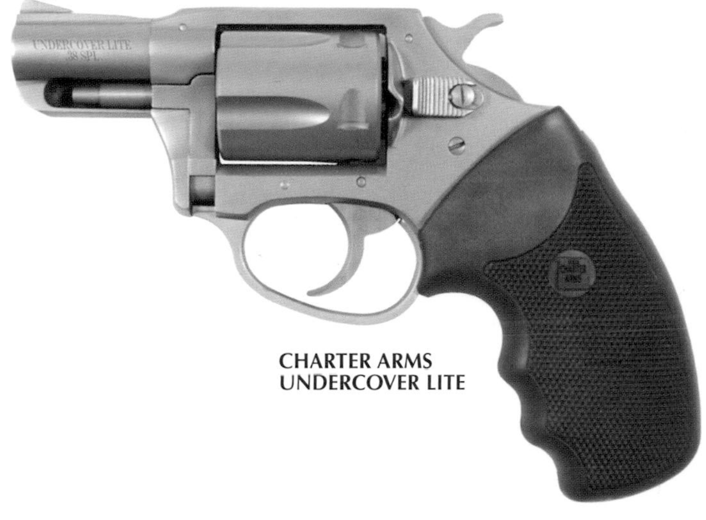

CHARTER ARMS UNDERCOVER LITE

.32 UNDERCOVERETTE

Action: Revolver, SA/DA
Overall Length: 6.4 in.
Overall Height: 4.9 in.
Overall Width: 1.5 in.
Barrel: 2 in.
Grips: Checkered black rubber
Sights: Fixed front ramp/rear groove
Weight Unloaded: 12 oz.
Caliber: .32 H&R
Capacity: 5
Features: Hammer block safety; 3-point cylinder lock-up; protected ejector rod; aluminum frame; external hammer
Stainless: $422
Stainless *(Crimson Trace laser sight grip)*: $715
Pink lady *(pink/stainless, Crimson Trace laser sight grip)*: $764
Custom finished *(pink/stainless, lavender/stainless, black/gold-tone)*: $477

CHARTER ARMS UNDERCOVER LITE (RED/STAINLESS)

.357 MAG PUG DOA

Action: Revolver, DAO
Overall Length: 7 in.
Overall Height: 4.9 in.
Overall Width: 1.5 in.
Barrel: 2.2 in.
Grips: Checkered black rubber
Sights: Fixed front/rear groove
Weight Unloaded: 23 oz.
Caliber: .357 Mag.
Capacity: 5
Features: Hammer block safety; 3-point cylinder lock-up; protected ejector rod; stainless steel frame
MSRP: $450

Charter Arms

(www.charterfirearms.com)

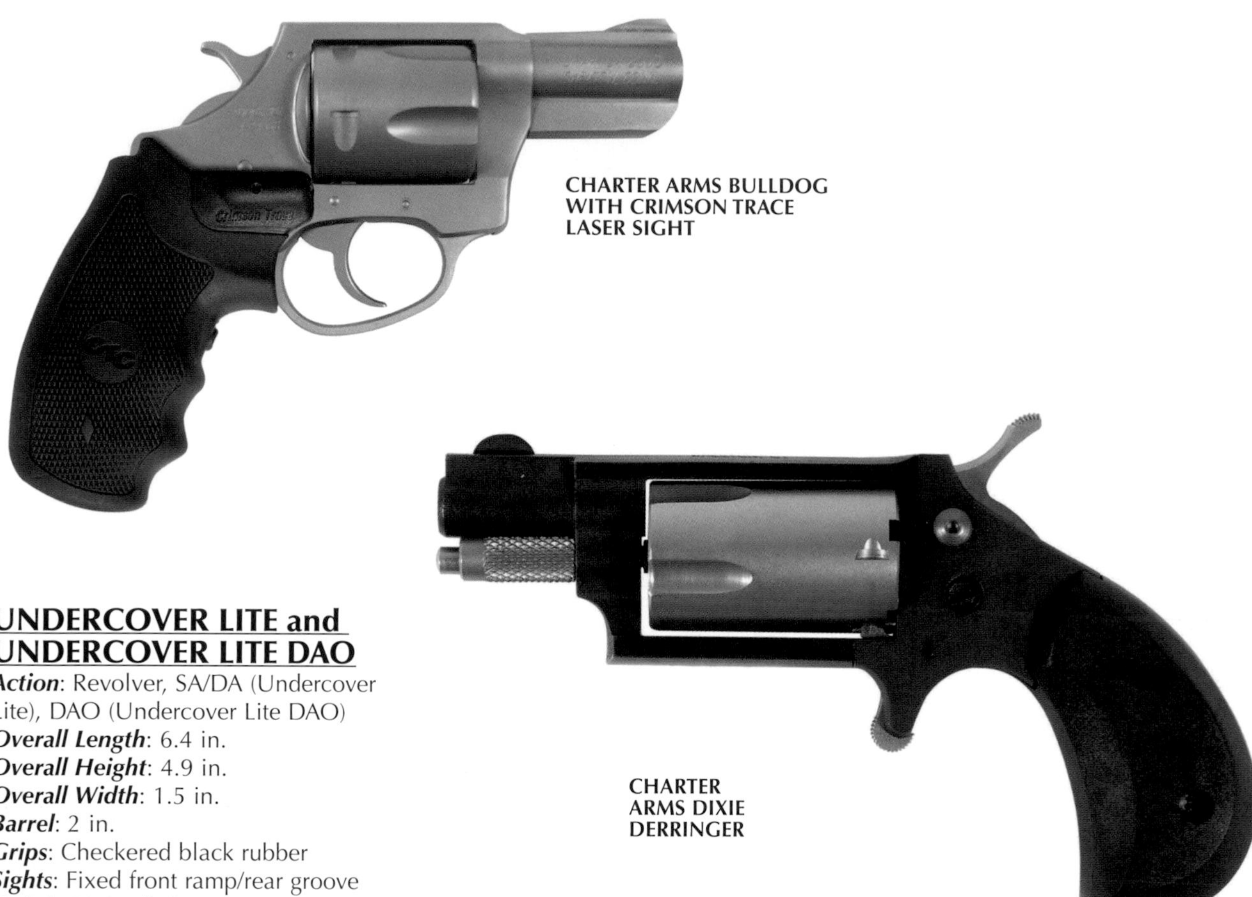

CHARTER ARMS BULLDOG WITH CRIMSON TRACE LASER SIGHT

CHARTER ARMS DIXIE DERRINGER

UNDERCOVER LITE and UNDERCOVER LITE DAO

Action: Revolver, SA/DA (Undercover Lite), DAO (Undercover Lite DAO)
Overall Length: 6.4 in.
Overall Height: 4.9 in.
Overall Width: 1.5 in.
Barrel: 2 in.
Grips: Checkered black rubber
Sights: Fixed front ramp/rear groove
Weight Unloaded: 12 oz.
Caliber: .38 Spl. +P
Capacity: 5
Features: Hammer block safety; 3-point cylinder lock-up; protected ejector rod; aluminum frame; external hammer
Aluminum: $450
Custom finishes available *(red/stainless, red/black, pink/stainless, green/black, turquoise/stainless, turquoise/black, black/stainless, bronze/black camo, bronze/black, black/gold-tone, lavender/stainless)*: $469–$493
DOA custom finishes available *(black, pink/stainless)*: $477
Southpaw *(aluminum; right side swing-out cylinder)*: $476
Southpaw Pink Lady *(pink/stainless; right side swing-out cylinder)*: $513

BULLDOG and BULLDOG DAO

Action: Revolver, SA/DA (Bulldog), DAO (Bulldog DAO)
Overall Length: 7.4 in.
Overall Height: 4.9 in.
Overall Width: 1.5 in.
Barrel: 2.5 in.
Grips: Checkered black rubber
Sights: Fixed front ramp/rear groove
Weight Unloaded: 21 oz.
Caliber: .44 Spl.
Capacity: 5
Features: Hammer block safety; 3-point cylinder lock-up; protected ejector rod; stainless steel frame; external hammer
Custom finishes available *(black, tiger and black)*: $461–$519
Stainless: $474
Stainless *(Crimson Trace laser sight grip)*: $768
DOA blue: $465
DOA stainless: $480

DIXIE DERRINGER

Action: Revolver, SA
Overall Length: 3.6 in.
Overall Height: 2.4 in.
Overall Width: .8 in.
Barrel: 1.2 in.
Grips: Smooth polymer

Charter Arms

(www.charterfirearms.com)

CHARTER ARMS
BULLDOG DOA

CHARTER ARMS
UNDERCOVER
SOUTHPAW

Sights: Fixed front ramp/rear groove
Weight Unloaded: 6 oz.
Caliber: .22 LR; .22 Mag.
Capacity: 5
Features: Spur trigger; exposed hammer
Black and stainless *(.22 Mag.)*: $249
Stainless *(.22 Mag.)*: $245
Stainless *(.22 LR)*: $238
Stainless *(.22 LR/.22 Mag. combo)*: $297

Chiappa Firearms

(www.chiappafirearms.com)

CHIAPPA FIREARMS RHINO

RHINO

Action: Revolver, SA/DA
Overall Length: 6.5 in. (2 in. barrel)
Overall Width: 1.4 in.
Barrel: 2 in., 4 in., 5 in., 6 in.
Grips: Wood or neoprene
Sights: Fixed front/rear or fixed front/adj. rear
Weight Unloaded: 25.3 oz. (2 in. barrel)
Caliber: .357 Mag.
Capacity: 6
Features: Alloy frame; flat-sided cylinder; external hammer; barrel aligns with bottom chamber of cylinder; blue and stainless finishes
2 in. barrel: $795

Cobra Firearms

(www.cobrafirearms.net)

STANDARD DERRINGER

Action: Hinged breech, SA
Overall Length: 4 in.
Barrel: 2.4 in.
Grips: Rosewood or pearl
Sights: Fixed open
Weight Unloaded: 9.5 oz.
Caliber: .22 LR, .22 Mag., .25 ACP, .32 ACP
Capacity: 2
Features: Remington Model 95 design; alloy frame; spur trigger; exposed hammer; automatic barrel selection; manually operated hammer-block type, half-cock safeties; custom finishes available (ruby red, majestic pink, king cobra copper, royal blue, imperial purple, black chrome)
Standard finishes *(chrome, black powder coat, satin nickel)*: $150

BIG BORE DERRINGER

Action: Hinged breech, SA
Overall Length: 4.7 in.
Barrel: 2.8 in.
Grips: Rosewood, pink, white, or black
Sights: Fixed open
Weight Unloaded: 14 oz.
Caliber: .22 Mag., .32 H&R Mag., .38 Spl., .380
Capacity: 2
Features: Remington Model 95 design; alloy frame; spur trigger; exposed hammer; automatic barrel selection; manually operated hammer-block type, half-cock safeties; custom finishes available (ruby red, majestic pink, king cobra copper, royal blue, imperial purple, black chrome)
Standard finishes *(chrome, black powder coat, satin nickel)*: $200

LONG BORE DERRINGER

Action: Hinged breech, SA
Overall Length: 5.4 in.
Barrel: 3.5 in.
Grips: Rosewood, pink, white, or black
Sights: Fixed open
Weight Unloaded: 16 oz.
Caliber: .22 Mag., .38 Spl.
Capacity: 2
Features: Remington Model 95 design; alloy frame; spur trigger; exposed hammer; automatic barrel selection; manually operated hammer-block type, half-cock safeties; custom finishes available (ruby red, majestic pink, king cobra copper, royal blue, imperial purple, black chrome)
Standard finishes *(chrome, black powder coat, satin nickel)*: $250

TITAN DERRINGER

Action: Hinged breech, SA
Overall Length: 5.5 in.
Barrel: 3.5 in.
Grips: Rosewood
Sights: Fixed open
Weight Unloaded: 16.4 oz.
Caliber: .45 LC/.410, 9mm
Capacity: 2
Features: Remington Model 95 design; stainless steel frame; rebounding hammer; removable trigger guard; spur trigger; exposed hammer; automatic barrel selection; manually operated hammer-block type, half-cock safeties
Standard finishes *(brushed stainless, black stainless, satin stainless)*: $300

CA SERIES

Action: Autoloader, SA
Overall Length: 5.4 in.
Overall Height: 4 in.
Barrel: 2.8 in.
Grips: Black, white
Sights: Fixed open
Weight Unloaded: 22 oz.
Caliber: .32 ACP, .380
Capacity: 6 + 1 (.32 ACP), 5 + 1 (.380)
Features: Alloy frame; frame-mounted safety; butt-mounted magazine release; custom finishes available (ruby red, majestic pink, king cobra copper, royal blue, imperial purple, black chrome)
Standard finishes *(chrome, black powder coat, satin nickel)*: $200

FREEDOM SERIES

Action: Autoloader, SA
Overall Length: 6.4 in.
Overall Height: 5 in.
Barrel: 3.5 in.
Grips: Black, white
Sights: Fixed open
Weight Unloaded: 33.6 oz.
Caliber: .32 ACP, .380
Capacity: 8 + 1 (.32 ACP), 7 + 1 (.380)
Features: Alloy frame; frame-mounted safety; butt-mounted magazine release; magazine finger rest; custom finishes available (ruby red, majestic pink, king cobra copper, royal blue, imperial purple, black chrome)
Standard finishes *(chrome, black powder coat, satin nickel)*: $150

PATRIOT .45

Action: Autoloader, DAO
Overall Length: 6.4 in.
Overall Height: 4.8 in.
Barrel: 3.3 in.
Grips: Black checkered polymer
Sights: Fixed front; dovetail rear
Weight Unloaded: 18.6 oz.
Caliber: .45 ACP
Capacity: 6 + 1
Features: Black polymer frame; stainless steel slide; combat trigger guard
Standard finishes *(brushed stainless, polished stainless, black melonite)*: $370

PATRIOT 9 and 380

Action: Autoloader, DAO
Overall Length: 6 in.
Overall Height: 4.8 in.
Barrel: 3.3 in.
Grips: Black checkered polymer
Sights: Fixed
Weight Unloaded: 17.5 oz.
Caliber: 9mm, .380
Capacity: 10 + 1
Features: Black polymer frame; stainless steel slide; loaded-chamber indicator
Standard finishes *(brushed stainless, polished stainless, black melonite)*: $300

SHADOW REVOLVER

Action: Revolver, DAO
Overall Length: 6.4 in.
Overall Height: 4.2 in.
Overall Width: 1.3 in.
Barrel: 1.9 in.
Grips: Black rubber, rosewood
Sights: Fixed
Weight Unloaded: 17.5 oz.
Caliber: .38 Spl. +P
Capacity: 5
Features: S&W J-frame design; aluminum frame; stainless steel cylinder; internal hammer; custom finishes available (anodized titanium, red, pink, gold, blue, black)
Standard finishes *(brushed stainless, polished stainless, black melonite)*: $425

Colt

(www.coltsmfg.com)

COLT
1991 SERIES

SERIES 70

Action: Autoloader, SA
Overall Length: 8.5 in.
Overall Height: 5.4 in.
Overall Width: 1.3 in.
Barrel: 5 in.
Grips: Double-diamond checkered rosewood
Sights: Fixed blade front/dovetail rear
Weight Unloaded: 36.8 oz.
Caliber: .45 ACP
Capacity: 7 + 1
Features: Mil-spec thumb and grip safeties; rear mil-spec slide serrations; short trigger
Blue: $974
Stainless steel: $1007

COLT DELTA ELITE

COLT
SERIES 70

1991 SERIES

Action: Autoloader, SA
Overall Length: 7.6 in. (Combat Commander), 8.5 in. (Government)
Overall Height: 5.4 in.
Overall Width: 1.3 in.
Barrel: 4.3 in. (Combat Commander), 5 in. (Government)
Grips: Double diamond checkered rosewood or checkered rubber composite
Sights: Fixed blade front/dovetail rear, 3-dot
Weight Unloaded: 32 oz. (Combat Commander); 35.2 oz. (Government)
Caliber: .45 ACP
Capacity: 7 + 1
Features: Mil-spec thumb and beavertail grip safeties; rear mil-spec slide serrations; aluminum trigger; spur hammer
Government *(blue, wood grip)*: $883
Government *(stainless steel, rubber grip)*: $942
Combat Commander *(blue, wood grip)*: $883
Combat Commander *(stainless steel, rubber grip)*: $942

COLT DELTA ELITE

Action: Autoloader, SA
Overall Length: 8.5 in.
Overall Height: 5.4 in.
Overall Width: 1.3 in.
Barrel: 5 in.
Grips: Wrap around pebbled rubber
Sights: Fixed blade front/dovetail rear, 3-dot
Weight Unloaded: 35.2 oz.
Caliber: 10mm
Capacity: 8 + 1
Features: Series 80; stainless frame/slide; extended thumb and beavertail grip safeties; rear mil-spec slide serrations; aluminum trigger; combat hammer
MSRP: $983

Colt

(www.coltsmfg.com)

COLT SPECIAL COMBAT GOVERNMENT (STAINLESS)

COLT SPECIAL COMBAT GOVERNMENT

SPECIAL COMBAT GOVERNMENT

Action: Autoloader, SA
Overall Length: 8.5 in.
Overall Height: 5.5 in.
Overall Width: 1.4 in.
Barrel: 5 in.
Grips: Double-diamond checkered
Sights: Dovetail Heinie blade front/ adj. Bomar rear, 3-dot
Weight Unloaded: 39.2 oz.
Caliber: .45 ACP
Capacity: 8 + 1
Features: Series 80; firing pin, extended ambidextrous thumb and beavertail grip safeties; rear slide serrations; aluminum 3-hole trigger; enhanced hammer; checkered front/ rear grip; flared ejection port; extended magazine well; magazines bumper
Blue: $1899
Two-tone: $1899
Hard chrome: $1899

XSE SERIES

Action: Autoloader, SA
Overall Length: 7.6 in. (Combat Commander), 8.5 in. (Government)
Overall Height: 5.5 in.
Overall Width: 7.6 in. (Combat Commander), 1.5 in.
Barrel: 1.4 in. (LightWeight Commander), 5 in. (Government)
Grips: Double-diamond checkered rosewood
Sights: Fixed blade front/Novak rear, 3-dot
Weight Unloaded: 26.4 oz. (LightWeight Commander), 32.6 oz. (Combat Commander), 36 oz. (Government)
Caliber: .45 ACP
Capacity: 8 + 1
Features: Series 80; firing pin, extended ambidextrous thumb and beavertail grip safeties; front/rear slide serrations; aluminum 3-hole trigger; enhanced hammer
Government *(blue or brushed stainless)*: $1001
Government Rail Gun *(stainless, Picatinny rail)*: $1087
Government Rail Gun *(matte black, Picatinny rail)*: $1188
Government Combat Elite *(duo-tone)*: $1087
Combat Commander *(brushed stainless)*: $1001
Combat Commander LightWeight *(aluminum frame)*: $1001

COLT XSE SERIES

COLT 1991 SERIES (BRIGHT STAINLESS)

HANDGUNS

Colt

(www.coltsmfg.com)

COLT XSE SERIES COMMANDER

COLT DEFENDER SERIES

COLT 1991 SERIES COMMANDER

DEFENDER SERIES

Action: Autoloader, SA
Overall Length: 6.8 in.
Overall Height: 4.9 in.
Overall Width: 1.3 in.
Barrel: 3 in.
Grips: Double-diamond checkered rosewood or wraparound rubber
Sights: Fixed blade front/dovetail rear, 3-dot
Weight Unloaded: 24.8 oz. (9mm), 24 oz. (.45 ACP)
Caliber: 9mm, .45 ACP
Capacity: 8 + 1 (9mm), 7 + 1 (.45 ACP)
Features: Series 80; firing pin, standard thumb and beavertail grip safeties; rear slide serrations; black aluminum 3-hole trigger; enhanced hammer; beveled magazine well; aluminum frame; stainless steel slide and barrel; matte aluminum finish
MSRP: $995

COLT NEW AGENT SERIES

NEW AGENT SERIES

Action: Autoloader, SA
Overall Length: 6.8 in.
Overall Height: 4.6 in.
Overall Width: 1.1 in.
Barrel: 3 in.
Grips: Double-diamond checkered rosewood or wraparound rubber
Sights: None
Weight Unloaded: 22.4 oz.
Caliber: 9mm, .45 ACP
Capacity: 8 + 1 (9mm), 7 + 1 (.45 ACP)
Features: Series 80; firing pin, standard thumb and beavertail grip safeties; rear slide serrations; black aluminum 3-hole trigger; enhanced hammer; beveled magazine well; aluminum frame; stainless steel slide and barrel; matte aluminum finish
MSRP: $995

CZ

(www.cz-usa.com)

CZ P06

Action: Autoloader, SA/DA
Overall Length: 7.2 in.
Overall Height: 5.3 in.
Overall Width: 1.4 in.
Grip Overall Width: 1.3 in.
Barrel: 3.9 in.
Grips: Checkered rubber
Sights: Fixed front/dovetail rear, Tritium 3-dot
Weight Unloaded: 16.8 oz.
Caliber: .40 S&W
Capacity: 10 + 1
Features: Alloy frame; combat trigger guard; decocking lever, safety stop on hammer, and firing pin safeties; external hammer; black polycoat finish; lanyard loop; magazine bumper pad
MSRP: $648

CZ 75 COMPACT

Action: Autoloader, SA/DA
Overall Length: 7.2 in.
Overall Height: 5 in.
Overall Width: 1.4 in.
Barrel: 3.8 in.
Grips: Checkered rubber
Sights: Fixed front/dovetail rear, Tritium 3-dot
Weight Unloaded: 16.7 oz.
Caliber: 9mm
Capacity: 14 + 1
Features: Alloy frame; combat trigger guard; manual thumb, safety stop on hammer, and firing pin safeties; external hammer; magazine bumper pad; Picatinny rail

CZ P06

Black polycoat: $518
Duo-tone: $559
Satin nickel: $559

CZ 75 D PCR COMPACT

CZ 75 COMPACT

CZ 75 D PCR COMPACT

Action: Autoloader, SA/DA
Overall Length: 7.2 in.
Overall Height: 5 in.
Overall Width: 1.4 in.
Barrel: 3.8 in.
Grips: Checkered plastic
Sights: Fixed front/dovetail rear, Tritium 3-dot
Weight Unloaded: 32 oz.
Caliber: 9mm
Capacity: 14 + 1
Features: Steel frame; combat trigger guard; decocking lever, manual thumb, safety stop on hammer, and firing pin safeties; external hammer; magazine bumper pad; lanyard loop; black polycoat finish
MSRP: $518

CZ 75 P01

CZ 75 P01

Action: Autoloader, SA/DA
Overall Length: 7.2 in.
Overall Height: 5 in.
Overall Width: 1.4 in.
Barrel: 3.8 in.
Grips: Checkered rubber
Sights: Fixed front/dovetail rear, Tritium 3-dot
Weight Unloaded: 16.8 oz.
Caliber: 9mm
Capacity: 14 + 1
Features: Polymer frame; combat trigger guard; decocking lever, safety stop on hammer, and firing pin safeties; external hammer; magazine bumper pad; lanyard loop; Black polycoat finish
MSRP: $598

CZ

(www.cz-usa.com)

CZ 75 P07 DUTY

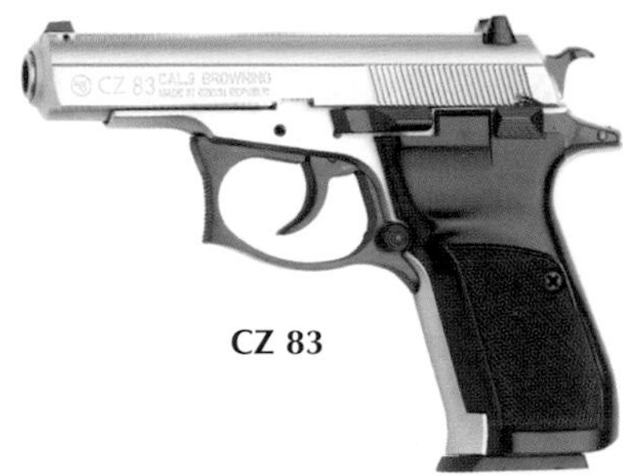

CZ 83

CZ 75 P07 DUTY

Action: Autoloader, SA/DA
Overall Length: 7.3 in.
Overall Height: 5.1 in.
Overall Width: 1.5 in.
Barrel: 3.8 in.
Grips: Textured polymer
Sights: Fixed front/dovetail rear, Tritium 3-dot
Weight Unloaded: 16.7 oz.
Caliber: 9mm, .40 S&W
Capacity: 16 + 1 (9mm), 12 + 1 (.40 S&W)
Features: Alloy frame; combat trigger guard; decocking lever or manual safety, safety stop on hammer, and firing pin safeties; external hammer; magazine bumper pad; lanyard loop; black matte finish
9mm: $467
.40 S&W: $487

CZ 83

Action: Autoloader, SA/DA
Overall Length: 6.8 in.
Overall Height: 5 in.
Overall Width: 1.4 in.
Barrel: 3.8 in.
Grips: Checkered plastic
Sights: Fixed front/dovetail rear, Tritium 3-dot
Weight Unloaded: 16.8 oz.
Caliber: .32 ACP; .380
Capacity: 15 + 1 (.32 ACP), 12 + 1 (.380)
Features: Steel frame; combat trigger guard; ambidextrous manual sear, rebounding hammer safeties; external hammer; magazine bumper pad
Glossy blue: $444
Satin nickel (.380): $479

CZ 2075 RAMI

Action: Autoloader, SA/DA
Overall Length: 6.5 in.
Overall Height: 4.7 in.
Overall Width: 1.3 in.
Barrel: 3 in.
Grips: Checkered rubber
Sights: Fixed front/dovetail rear, Tritium 3-dot
Weight Unloaded: 16.6 oz.
Caliber: 9mm, .40 S&W
Capacity: 10 + 1 (9mm), 7 + 1 (.40 S&W)
Features: Alloy frame; rounded trigger guard; manual thumb, safety stop on hammer, and firing pin safeties; external hammer; magazine bumper pad; black polycoat finish
9mm: $585
.40 S&W: $604

CZ 2075 RAMI P

CZ 2075 RAMI P

Action: Autoloader, SA/DA
Overall Length: 6.5 in.
Overall Height: 4.7 in.
Overall Width: 1.3 in.
Barrel: 3 in.
Grips: Textured polymer
Sights: Fixed front/dovetail rear, Tritium 3-dot
Weight Unloaded: 16.5 oz.
Caliber: 9mm, .40 S&W
Capacity: 10 + 1 (9mm), 7 + 1 (.40 S&W)
Features: Polymer frame; rounded trigger guard; manual thumb, safety stop on hammer, and firing pin safeties; external hammer; magazine bumper pad; black polycoat finish
9mm: $491
.40 S&W: $517

CZ 2075 RAMI BD

Action: Autoloader, SA/DA
Overall Length: 6.5 in.
Overall Height: 4.7 in.
Overall Width: 1.3 in.
Barrel: 3 in.
Grips: Checkered rubber
Sights: Fixed front/dovetail rear, Tritium 3-dot
Weight Unloaded: 16.6 oz.
Caliber: 9mm
Capacity: 10 + 1
Features: Alloy frame; rounded trigger guard; decocking lever, safety stop on hammer, and firing pin safeties; external hammer; magazine bumper pad; black polycoat finish
MSRP: $620

2075 RAMI BD

CZ

(www.cz-usa.com)

CZ 75B (SATIN NICKEL)

CZ 75B

Action: Autoloader, SA/DA
Overall Length: 8.1 in.
Overall Height: 5.4 in.
Overall Width: 1.4 in.
Barrel: 4.7 in.
Grips: Checkered plastic
Sights: Fixed front/dovetail rear, Tritium 3-dot
Weight Unloaded: 32.2 oz.
Caliber: 9mm, .40 S&W
Capacity: 16 + 1 (9mm), 10 + 1 (.40 S&W)
Features: Steel frame; combat trigger guard; manual thumb, safety stop on hammer, and firing pin safeties; external hammer; magazine bumper pad
Black polycoat: $499 (9mm), $546 (.40 S&W)
Duo-tone: $559 (9mm), $615 (.40 S&W)
Satin nickel: $559 (9mm), $615 (.40 S&W)
Matte stainless: $699
High polish stainless: $699

CZ 75BD

CZ 75B SA

CZ 75BD

Action: Autoloader, SA/DA
Overall Length: 8.1 in.
Overall Height: 5.4 in.
Overall Width: 1.4 in.
Barrel: 4.7 in.
Grips: Checkered plastic
Sights: Fixed front/dovetail rear, Tritium 3-dot
Weight Unloaded: 32.2 oz.
Caliber: 9mm
Capacity: 16 + 1
Features: Steel frame; combat trigger guard; decocking lever, safety stop on hammer, and firing pin safeties; external hammer; magazine bumper pad; black polycoat finish
MSRP: $518

CZ 75B SA

Action: Autoloader, SA
Overall Length: 8.1 in.
Overall Height: 5.4 in.
Overall Width: 1.4 in.
Barrel: 4.7 in.
Grips: Checkered plastic
Sights: Fixed front/dovetail rear, Tritium 3-dot
Weight Unloaded: 32.2 oz.
Caliber: 9mm, .40 S&W
Capacity: 16 + 1 (9mm), 10 + 1 (.40 S&W)
Features: Steel frame; combat trigger guard; ambidextrous manual thumb, safety stop on hammer, and firing pin safeties; external hammer; drop-free magazine; magazine bumper pad; black polycoat finish
9mm: $546
.40 S&W: $585

CZ 75B

CZ 85 B

CZ 85 B

Action: Autoloader, SA/DA
Overall Length: 8.1 in.
Overall Height: 5.4 in.
Overall Width: 1.4 in.
Barrel: 4.7 in.
Grips: Checkered plastic
Sights: Dovetail front/dovetail rear, Tritium 3-dot
Weight Unloaded: 32.1 oz.
Caliber: 9mm
Capacity: 16 + 1
Features: Steel frame; combat trigger guard; ambidextrous manual thumb, safety stop on hammer, and firing pin safeties; ambidextrous slide release; drop-free magazine; external hammer; magazine bumper pad; black polycoat finish
MSRP: $572

CZ 85 COMBAT

CZ 85 COMBAT

Action: Autoloader, SA/DA
Overall Length: 8.1 in.
Overall Height: 5.4 in.
Overall Width: 1.4 in.
Barrel: 4.7 in.
Grips: Checkered plastic
Sights: Dovetail front/adj. rear, Tritium 3-dot
Weight Unloaded: 32.1 oz.
Caliber: 9mm
Capacity: 16 + 1
Features: Steel frame; combat trigger guard; ambidextrous manual thumb, safety stop on hammer, and firing pin safeties; ambidextrous slide release; drop-free magazine; external hammer; magazine bumper pad
Black polycoat: $604
Satin nickel: $630
Two-tone: $630

CZ 75 SP-01

CZ 75 SP-01

Action: Autoloader, SA/DA
Overall Length: 8.2 in.
Overall Height: 5.8 in.
Overall Width: 1.5 in.
Barrel: 4.7 in.
Grips: Checkered rubber
Sights: Dovetail front/rear, Tritium 3-dot
Weight Unloaded: 32.4 oz.
Caliber: 9mm
Capacity: 18 + 1
Features: Steel frame; combat trigger guard; manual thumb, safety stop on hammer, and firing pin safeties; Picatinny rail; full dust cover; external hammer; magazine bumper pad; extended beavertail; black polycoat finish
MSRP $648

CZ 75 SP-01 TACTICAL

CZ 75 SP-01 TACTICAL

Action: Autoloader, SA/DA
Overall Length: 8.2 in.
Overall Height: 5.8 in.
Overall Width: 1.5 in.
Barrel: 4.7 in.
Grips: Checkered rubber
Sights: Dovetail front/rear, Tritium 3-dot
Weight Unloaded: 32.4 oz.
Caliber: 9mm, .40 S&W
Capacity: 18 + 1 (9mm), 12 + 1 (.40 S&W)
Features: Steel frame; combat trigger guard; ambidextrous decocker, safety stop on hammer, and firing pin safeties; Picatinny rail; full dust cover; external hammer; magazine bumper pad; extended beavertail; black polycoat finish
9mm: $648
.40 S&W: $724

CZ

(www.cz-usa.com)

CZ 75 SP-01 PHANTOM

Action: Autoloader, SA/DA
Overall Length: 8.2 in.
Overall Height: 5.8 in.
Overall Width: 1.5 in.
Barrel: 4.7 in.
Grips: Checkered rubber
Sights: Dovetail front/rear, Tritium 3-dot
Weight Unloaded: 16.8 oz.
Caliber: 9mm
Capacity: 18 + 1
Features: Polymer frame; combat trigger guard; decocking lever, safety stop on hammer, and firing pin safeties; Picatinny rail; full dust cover; external hammer; magazine bumper pad; extended beavertail; black polycoat finish
MSRP: $648

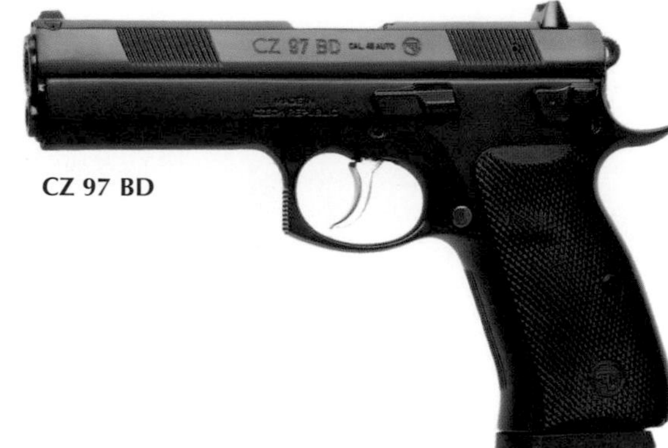

CZ 97 BD

CZ 75 SP-01 PHANTOM

CZ 97 B

Action: Autoloader, SA/DA
Overall Length: 8.3 in.
Overall Height: 5.9 in.
Overall Width: 1.4 in.
Barrel: 4.8 in.
Grips: Checkered wood
Sights: Dovetail front/rear, Tritium 3-dot
Weight Unloaded: 32.5 oz.
Caliber: .45 ACP
Capacity: 10 + 1
Features: Steel frame; combat trigger guard; manual thumb, safety stop on hammer, and firing pin safeties; loaded-chamber indicator; full dust cover; external hammer; magazine bumper pad; extended beavertail; screw in barrel bushing
Black polycoat: $644
Glossy blue: $700

CZ 97 B

CZ 97 BD

Action: Autoloader, SA/DA
Overall Length: 8.3 in.
Overall Height: 5.9 in.
Overall Width: 1.4 in.
Barrel: 4.8 in.
Grips: Checkered rubber
Sights: Dovetail front/rear, Tritium 3-dot
Weight Unloaded: 32.5 oz.
Caliber: .45 ACP
Capacity: 10 + 1
Features: Steel frame; combat trigger guard; decoking lever, safety stop on hammer, and firing pin safeties; loaded-chamber indicator; full dust cover; external hammer; magazine bumper pad; extended beavertail; screw in barrel bushing; black polycoat finish
MSRP: $778

HANDGUNS

Dan Wesson

(www.cz-usa.com)

DAN WESSON V-BOB

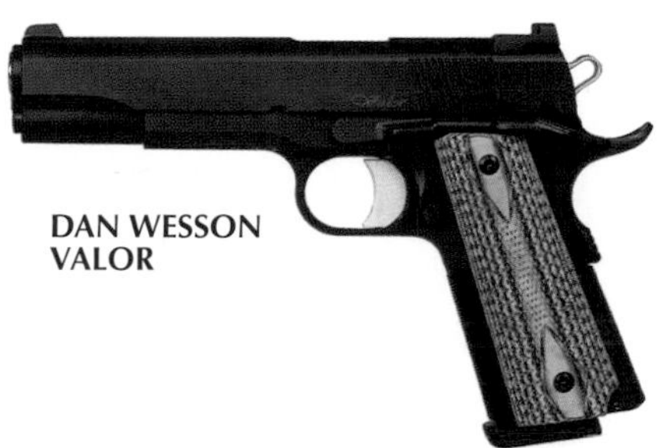
DAN WESSON VALOR

DAN WESSON VALOR (STAINLESS)

VALOR

Action: Autoloader, SA
Overall Length: 8.8 in.
Overall Height: 5.5 in.
Overall Width: 1.5 in.
Barrel: 5 in.
Grips: Checkered composite
Sights: Dovetail front/rear, Heine Straight Eight night sight
Weight Unloaded: 32.8 oz.
Caliber: .45 ACP
Capacity: 8 + 1
Features: Colt 1911 design; thumb and beavertail grip safeties; rear slide serrations; checkered front strap and mainspring housing
Black: $1977
Stainless: $1594

RZ-45 HERITAGE

Action: Autoloader, SA
Overall Length: 8.8 in.
Overall Height: 5.5 in.
Overall Width: 1.5 in.
Barrel: 5 in.
Grips: Checkered double-diamond cocobolo
Sights: Fixed blade front/dovetail rear, night sight
Weight Unloaded: 32.4 oz.
Caliber: .45 ACP
Capacity: 8 + 1
Features: Colt 1911 design; thumb and beavertail grip safeties; rear slide serrations; serrated slide top; stainless finish
MSRP: $1275

CCO BOBTAIL

Action: Autoloader, SA
Overall Length: 8 in.
Overall Height: 5 in.
Overall Width: 1.5 in.
Barrel: 4.3 in.
Grips: Textured wood
Sights: Novak style fixed blade front/dovetail rear, night sight
Weight Unloaded: 16.6 oz.
Caliber: .45 ACP
Capacity: 7 + 1
Features: Colt 1911 design; aluminum frame; thumb and beavertail grip safeties; rear slide serrations; chain-link serrations on slide top, front strap, mainspring housing; black ceramic coat finish
MSRP: $1530

V-BOB

Action: Autoloader, SA
Overall Length: 8 in.
Overall Height: 5.5 in.
Overall Width: 1.5 in.
Barrel: 4.3 in.
Grips: Slim line G10 laminate
Sights: Dovetail front/rear, Heine Straight Eight night sight
Weight Unloaded: 32.2 oz.
Caliber: .45 ACP
Capacity: 7 + 1
Features: Colt 1911 design; steel frame; thumb and beavertail grip safeties; rear slide serrations; checkered front and backstrap
Black: $2040
Matte stainless: $1658

HANDGUNS

Doublestar Corp.

(www.star15.com)

DOUBLESTAR COMBAT PISTOL

COMBAT PISTOL

Action: Autoloader, SA
Overall Length: 8.75 in.
Overall Height: 5.5 in.
Overall Width: 1.3 in.
Barrel: 5 in.
Grips: Checkered polymer
Sights: Novak white dot front/Novak LoMount 2-dot dovetail adj. rear
Weight Unloaded: 39 oz.
Caliber: .45 ACP
Capacity: 8 + 1
Features: Colt 1911 design; thumb, beavertail memory groove grip, and firing pin block safeties; matte black finish; funneled magazine well; checkered front grip; Picatinny rail
MSRP: $1350

Ed Brown

(www.edbrown.com)

ED BROWN CLASSIC CUSTOM

ED BROWN EXECUTIVE ELITE

ED BROWN EXECUTIVE CARRY

ED BROWN KOBRA

CLASSIC CUSTOM

Action: Autoloader, SA
Overall Length: 8.8 in.
Overall Height: 5.5 in.
Overall Width: 1.3 in.
Barrel: 5 in.
Grips: Double-diamond checkered wood
Sights: Dovetail front/adj. rear
Weight Unloaded: 39 oz.
Caliber: .45 ACP
Capacity: 8 + 1
Features: Colt 1911 design; Series 70 configuration; extended thumb, beavertail safeties; checkered front/rear grip strap; oversized magazine release; slide top grooved; two-piece rod guide; stainless, dual tone, blue finishes
MSRP: $3155

EXECUTIVE ELITE

Action: Autoloader, SA
Overall Length: 8.8 in.
Overall Height: 5.5 in.
Overall Width: 1.3 in.
Barrel: 5 in.
Grips: Double-diamond checkered wood
Sights: Dovetail front/rear, 3-dot night sights
Weight Unloaded: 38 oz.
Caliber: .45 ACP
Capacity: 8 + 1
Features: Colt 1911 design; Series 70 configuration; extended thumb, beavertail safeties; checkered front/rear grip strap; magazine bumper pad; matte stainless, matte dual tone, matte blue finishes
MSRP: $2395

EXECUTIVE CARRY

Action: Autoloader, SA
Overall Length: 8 in.
Overall Height: 5.5 in.
Overall Width: 1.3 in.
Barrel: 4.25 in.
Grips: Double-diamond checkered wood
Sights: Dovetail front/rear, 3-dot night sights
Weight Unloaded: 35 oz.
Caliber: .45 ACP
Capacity: 8 + 1
Features: Colt 1911 design; Series 70 configuration; bobtail steel frame; extended thumb, beavertail safeties; checkered front/rear grip strap; matte stainless, matte dual tone, matte blue finishes
MSRP: $2645

KOBRA

Action: Autoloader, SA
Overall Length: 8.8 in.
Overall Height: 5.5 in.
Overall Width: 1.3 in.
Barrel: 5 in.
Grips: Double-diamond checkered wood
Sights: Dovetail front/rear, 3-dot night sights
Weight Unloaded: 38 oz.
Caliber: .45 ACP
Capacity: 8 + 1
Features: Colt 1911 design; Series 70 configuration; extended thumb, beavertail safeties; snakeskin texture on front/rear grip straps; magazine bumper pad; matte stainless, matte dual tone, matte blue finishes
MSRP: $2195

ED BROWN KOBRA CARRY

KOBRA CARRY

Action: Autoloader, SA
Overall Length: 8 in.
Overall Height: 5.5 in.
Overall Width: 1.3 in.
Barrel: 4.25 in.
Grips: Double-diamond checkered wood
Sights: Dovetail front/rear, 3-dot night sights
Weight Unloaded: 35 oz.
Caliber: .45 ACP
Capacity: 8 + 1
Features: Colt 1911 design; Series 70 configuration; bobtail steel frame; extended thumb, beavertail safeties; snakeskin texture on front/rear grip straps; matte stainless, matte dual tone, matte blue finishes
MSRP: $2445

Ed Brown

(www.edbrown.com)

ED BROWN KOBRA CARRY LW

ED BROWN SPECIAL FORCES

ED BROWN SPECIAL FORCES CARRY

ED BROWN SPECIAL FORCES LIGHT RAIL

KOBRA CARRY LW

Action: Autoloader, SA
Overall Length: 8 in.
Overall Height: 5.5 in.
Overall Width: 1.3 in.
Barrel: 4.25 in.
Grips: Double-diamond checkered wood
Sights: Dovetail front/rear, U-notch; 3-dot night sights
Weight Unloaded: 27 oz.
Caliber: .45 ACP
Capacity: 8 + 1
Features: Colt 1911 design; Series 70 configuration; bobtail aluminum frame; extended thumb, beavertail safeties; snakeskin texture on front/rear grip straps; matte stainless, matte dual tone, matte blue finishes
MSRP: $2920

SPECIAL FORCES

Action: Autoloader, SA
Overall Length: 8.8 in.
Overall Height: 5.5 in.
Overall Width: 1.3 in.
Barrel: 5 in.
Grips: Double-diamond checkered wood
Sights: Dovetail front/rear, 3-dot night sights
Weight Unloaded: 38 oz.
Caliber: .45 ACP
Capacity: 8 + 1
Features: Colt 1911 design; Series 70 configuration; extended thumb, beavertail safeties; chainlink texture on front/rear grip straps; magazine bumper pad; matte stainless, matte dual tone, matte blue finishes
MSRP: $2195

SPECIAL FORCES CARRY

Action: Autoloader, SA
Overall Length: 8 in.
Overall Height: 5.5 in.
Overall Width: 1.3 in.
Barrel: 4.25 in.
Grips: Double-diamond checkered wood
Sights: Dovetail front/rear, U-notch; 3-dot night sights
Weight Unloaded: 35 oz.
Caliber: .45 ACP
Capacity: 8 + 1
Features: Colt 1911 design; Series 70 configuration; bobtail steel frame; extended thumb, beavertail safeties; chainlink texture on front/rear grip straps; matte stainless, matte dual tone, matte blue finishes
MSRP: $2445

SPECIAL FORCES LIGHT RAIL

Action: Autoloader, SA
Overall Length: 8.8 in.
Overall Height: 5.5 in.
Overall Width: 1.3 in.
Barrel: 5 in.
Grips: Double-diamond checkered wood
Sights: Dovetail front/rear, 3-dot night sights
Weight Unloaded: 38 oz.
Caliber: .45 ACP
Capacity: 8 + 1
Features: Colt 1911 design; Series 70 configuration; extended thumb, beavertail safeties; chainlink texture on front/rear grip straps; magazine bumper pad; Picatinny rail; matte stainless, matte dual tone, matte blue finishes
MSRP: $2295

European American Armory(EAA)

(www.eaacorp.com)

WITNESS

Action: Autoloader, SA/DA
Overall Length: 8.1 in.
Overall Height: 5.5 in.
Overall Width: 1.4 in.
Barrel: 4.5 in.
Grips: Pebbled rubber
Sights: Fixed front/dovetail rear, 3-dot
Weight Unloaded: 33 oz.
Caliber: 9mm, .40 S&W, 10mm, .45 ACP
Capacity: 17 + 1 (9mm), 15 + 1 (.40 S&W, 10mm), 10 + 1 (.45 ACP)
Features: CZ 75 design; steel frame; thumb safety; Picatinny rail; external hammer; magazine bumper pad; extended beavertail
Blue: $400
Matte silver Wonder finish: $450

European American Armory(EAA)

(www.eaacorp.com)

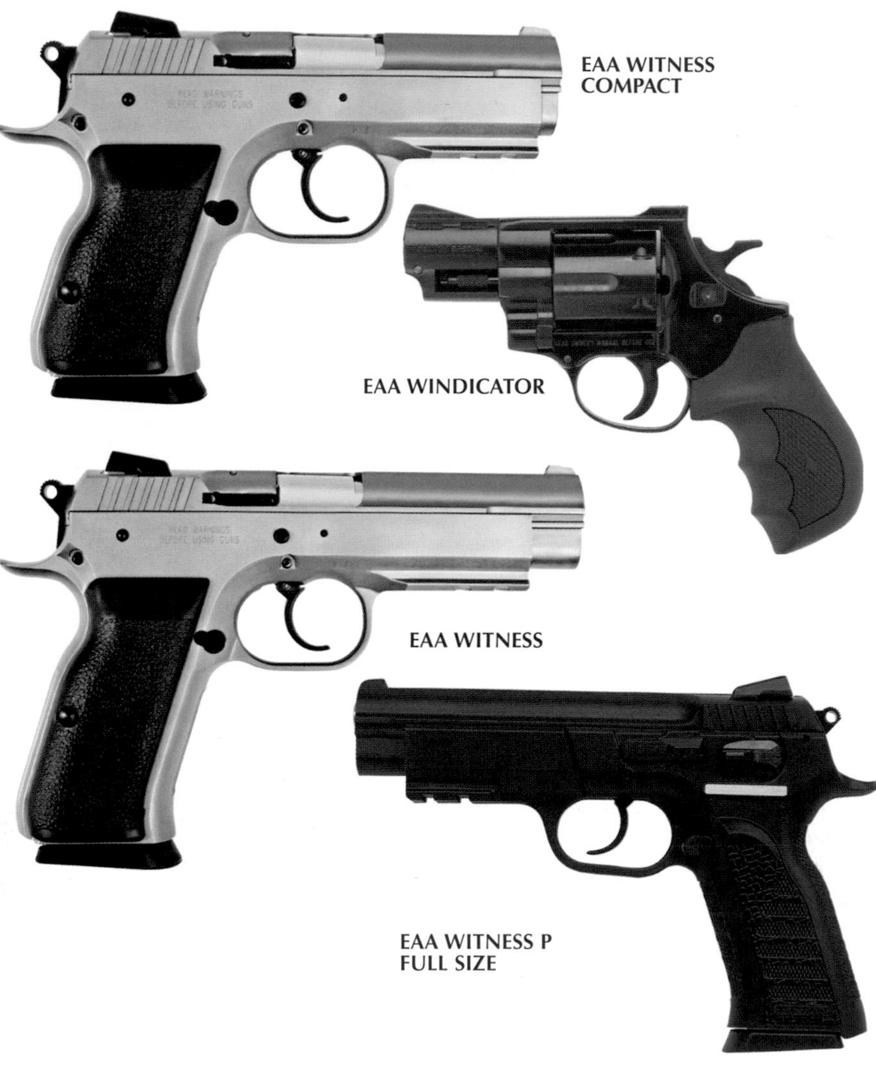

EAA WITNESS COMPACT

EAA WINDICATOR

EAA WITNESS

EAA WITNESS P FULL SIZE

WITNESS COMPACT

Action: Autoloader, SA/DA
Overall Length: 7.3 in.
Overall Height: 4.5 in.
Overall Width: 1.4 in.
Barrel: 3.6 in.
Grips: Pebbled rubber
Sights: Fixed front/dovetail rear, 3-dot
Weight Unloaded: 30 oz.
Caliber: 9mm, .40 S&W, 10mm, .45 ACP
Capacity: 14 + 1 (9mm), 12 + 1 (.40 S&W, 10mm), 8 + 1 (.45 ACP)
Features: CZ 75 design; steel frame; thumb safety; Picatinny rail; external hammer; magazine bumper pad; extended beavertail
Blue: $400
Matte silver Wonder finish: $542

WITNESS P FULL SIZE

Action: Autoloader, SA/DA
Overall Length: 8.1 in.
Overall Height: 5.5 in.
Overall Width: 1.4 in.
Barrel: 4.5 in.
Grips: Pebbled polymer
Sights: Fixed front/dovetail rear, 3-dot
Weight Unloaded: 30 oz.
Caliber: 9mm, .40 S&W, 10mm, .45 ACP
Capacity: 17 + 1 (9mm), 15 + 1 (.40 S&W, 10mm), 10 + 1 (.45 ACP)
Features: CZ 75 design; polymer frame; thumb safety; Picatinny rail; external hammer; magazine bumper pad; extended beavertail; pebbled front and back grip straps; matte black finish
MSRP: $511

WITNESS P CARRY

Action: Autoloader, SA/DA
Overall Length: 7.5 in.
Overall Height: 5.5 in.
Overall Width: 1.4 in.
Barrel: 3.6 in.
Grips: Pebbled polymer
Sights: Fixed front/dovetail rear, 3-dot
Weight Unloaded: 27 oz.
Caliber: 9mm, .40 S&W, 10mm, .45 ACP
Capacity: 17 + 1 (9mm), 15 + 1 (.40 S&W, 10mm), 10 + 1 (.45 ACP)
Features: CZ 75 design; polymer frame; thumb safety; Picatinny rail; external hammer; magazine bumper pad; extended beavertail; matte black finish
MSRP: $635

WINDICATOR

Action: Revolver, SA/DA
Overall Length: 7 in. (2-in. barrel), 8.5 in. (4-in. barrel)
Overall Height: 5.5 in.
Overall Width: 1.5 in.
Barrel: 2in., 4in.
Grips: Textured black rubber
Sights: Fixed front ramp/rear
Weight Unloaded: 25 oz. (2-in. barrel), 36 oz. (4-in. barrel)
Caliber: .38 Spl. (alloy frame), .357 Mag. (steel frame)
Capacity: 6
Features: Hammer block safety; external hammer; protected ejector rod
MSRP: . . . . $309–$380
(depending on finish and barrel length)

EAA WITNESS P CARRY

HANDGUNS

European American Armory(EAA)

(www.eaacorp.com)

EAA WITNESS P COMPACT

EAA WITNESS ELITE SERIES MATCH

WITNESS P COMPACT

Action: Autoloader, SA/DA
Overall Length: 7.3 in.
Overall Height: 4.5 in.
Overall Width: 1.4 in.
Barrel: 3.6 in.
Grips: Pebbled polymer
Sights: Fixed front/dovetail rear, 3-dot
Weight Unloaded: 26 oz. (9mm, .40 S&W), 27 oz. (10mm, .45 ACP)
Caliber: 9mm, .40 S&W, 10mm, .45 ACP
Capacity: 14 + 1 (9mm), 12 + 1 (.40 S&W, 10mm), 8 + 1 (.45 ACP)
Features: CZ 75 design; polymer frame; thumb safety; Picatinny rail; external hammer; magazine bumper pad; extended beavertail; matte black finish
MSRP: $511

WITNESS ELITE SERIES MATCH

Action: Autoloader, SA
Overall Length: 8.8 in.
Overall Height: 5 in.
Overall Width: 1.4 in.
Barrel: 4.8 in.
Grips: Pebbled rubber
Sights: Fixed front/dovetail rear, 3-dot
Weight Unloaded: 33 oz.
Caliber: 9mm, .40 S&W, 10mm, .45 ACP
Capacity: 17 + 1 (9mm), 15 + 1 (.40 S&W, 10mm), 10 + 1 (.45 ACP)
Features: CZ 75 design; steel frame; thumb safety; Picatinny rail; external hammer; extended magazine release; magazine bumper pad; extended beavertail; trigger over travel stop; two-tone finish
MSRP: $570

WITNESS ELITE SERIES STOCK 1 and STOCK 2

Action: Autoloader, single/DA
Overall Length: 8 in.
Overall Height: 5 in.
Overall Width: 1.4 in.
Barrel: 4.5 in.
Grips: Checkered wood
Sights: Fixed front/dovetail rear, 3-dot
Weight Unloaded: 33 oz.
Caliber: 9mm, .40 S&W, 10mm, .45 ACP
Capacity: 17 + 1 (9mm), 15 + 1 (.40 S&W, 10mm), 10 + 1 (.45 ACP)
Features: CZ 75 design; steel frame; extended thumb safety; Picatinny rail; external hammer; extended magazine release; magazine bumper pad; extended beavertail; checkered front/backstrap; matte silver Wonder finish
Stock 1: $976
Stock 2 *(beveled magazine well, combat trigger guard, extended beavertail)*: $1085

EAA WITNESS ELITE SERIES STOCK 1

EAA WITNESS ELITE SERIES STOCK 2

HANDGUNS

Glock

(www.glock.com)

GLOCK G17 GEN 4

GLOCK G27 GEN 4

G22, G23, and G27

Action: Autoloader, striker-fired
Overall Length: 7.3 in. (G22), 6.9 in. (G23), 6.3 in. (G27)
Overall Height: 5.4 in. (G22), 5 in. (G23), 4.2 in. (G27)
Overall Width: 1.2 in.
Barrel: 4.5 in. (G22), 4 in. (G23), 3.5 in. (G27)
Grips: Textured polymer with finger grooves
Sights: Fixed front/dovetail rear, dot/outline
Weight Unloaded: 22.9 oz. (G22), 21.6 oz. (G23), 19.8 oz. (G27)
Caliber: .40 S&W
Capacity: 15 + 1 (G22), 13 + 1 (G23), 9 + 1 (G27)
Features: Polymer frame; Picatinny rail (except for G27); magazine bumper pad; textured front/back grip straps; external extractor; loaded-chamber indicator; serrated combat trigger guard; trigger, firing pin, and drop safeties; hexagonal rifling; matte black Tenifer finish
G22: $599
G23: $599
G27: $599
G22C *(compensated barrel/slide)*: $621
G23C *(compensated barrel/slide)*: $621

G20 and G29

Action: Autoloader, striker-fired
Overall Length: 7.6 in. (G20), 6.8 in. (G29)
Overall Height: 5.5 in. (G20), 4.5 in. (G29)
Overall Width: 1.3 in.
Barrel: 4.6 in. (G20), 3.8 in. (G29)
Grips: Textured polymer with finger grooves
Sights: Fixed front/dovetail rear, dot/outline
Weight Unloaded: 27.7 oz. (G20), 24.7 oz. (G29)
Caliber: 10mm
Capacity: 15 + 1 (G20), 10 + 1 (G29)
Features: Polymer frame; Picatinny rail; magazine bumper pad; textured front/back grip straps; external extractor; loaded-chamber indicator; serrated combat trigger guard; trigger, firing pin, and drop safeties; hexagonal rifling; matte black Tenifer finish
G20: $637
G29: $637
G20C *(compensated barrel/slide)*: $676

G21, G30, and G36

Action: Autoloader, striker-fired
Overall Length: 7.6 in. (G21), 6.8 in. (G30, G36)
Overall Height: 5.5 in. (G21), 4.8 in. (G30, G36)
Overall Width: 1.3 in. (G21, G30), 1.1 in. (G36)
Barrel: 4.6 in. (G21), 3.8 in. (G30, G36)
Grips: Textured polymer with finger grooves
Sights: Fixed front/dovetail rear, dot/outline
Weight Unloaded: 26.3 oz. (G21), 24 oz. (G30), 20.1 oz. (G36)
Caliber: .45 ACP
Capacity: 13 + 1 (G21), 10 + 1 (G30), 6 + 1 (G36)
Features: Polymer frame; Picatinny rail (except for G36); magazine bumper pad; textured front/back grip straps; external extractor; loaded-chamber indicator; serrated combat trigger guard; trigger, firing pin, and drop safeties; hexagonal rifling; matte black Tenifer finish
G21: $637
G30: $637
G36: $637
G21C *(compensated barrel/slide)*: $676

GLOCK G31 GEN 4

G31, G32, and G33

Action: Autoloader, striker-fired
Overall Length: 7.3 in. (G31), 6.9 in. (G32), 6.3 in. (G33)
Overall Height: 5.4 in. (G31), 5 in. (G32), 4.2 in. (G33)
Overall Width: 1.2 in.
Barrel: 4.5 in. (G31), 4 in. (G32), 3.5 in. (G33)
Grips: Textured polymer with finger grooves
Sights: Fixed front/dovetail rear, dot/outline
Weight Unloaded: 23.3 oz. (G31), 21.5 oz. (G32), 19.8 oz. (G33)
Caliber: .357 SIG
Capacity: 15 + 1 (G31), 13 + 1 (G32), 9 + 1 (G33)
Features: Polymer frame; Picatinny rail (except for G33); magazine bumper pad; textured front/back grip straps; external extractor; loaded-chamber indicator; serrated combat trigger guard; trigger, firing pin, and drop safeties; hexagonal rifling; matte black Tenifer finish
G31: $599
G32: $599
G33: $599
G31C *(compensated barrel/slide)*: $621
G32C *(compensated barrel/slide)*: $621

Glock

(www.glock.com)

GLOCK G35 GEN 4

G34 and G35

Action: Autoloader, striker-fired
Overall Length: 8.2 in.
Overall Height: 5.4 in.
Overall Width: 1.2 in.
Barrel: 5.3 in.
Grips: Textured polymer with finger grooves
Sights: Fixed front/dovetail rear, dot/outline
Weight Unloaded: 22.9 oz. (G34) 24.5 oz. (G35)
Caliber: 9mm (G34), .40 S&W (G35)
Capacity: 17 + 1 (G34), 15 + 1 (G35)
Features: Polymer frame; Picatinny rail; magazine bumper pad; textured front/back grip straps; external extractor; loaded-chamber indicator; serrated combat trigger guard; trigger, firing pin, and drop safeties; hexagonal rifling; matte black Tenifer finish
G34: $679
G35: $679

G37, G38 and G39

Action: Autoloader, striker-fired
Overall Length: 6.3 in. (G39), 6.9 in. (G38), 7.3 in. (G37)
Overall Height: 4.7 in. (G39), 5 in. (G38), 5.5 in. (G37)
Overall Width: 1.2 in.
Barrel: 3.5 in. (G39), 4.5 in. (G37, G36)
Grips: Textured polymer with finger grooves
Sights: Fixed front/dovetail rear, dot/outline
Weight Unloaded: 19.3 oz. (G39), 24.2 oz. (G38), 30 oz. (G37)
Caliber: .45 GAP
Capacity: 6 + 1 (G39), 8 + 1 (G38), 10 + 1 (G37)
Features: Polymer frame; Picatinny rail (except for G39); magazine bumper pad; textured front/back grip straps; external extractor; loaded chamber indicator; serrated combat trigger guard; trigger, firing pin, drop safeties; hexagonal rifling; matte black Tenifer finish
G39: $637
G38: $637
G37: $637

G17 GEN 4 and G22 GEN 4

Action: Autoloader, striker-fired
Overall Length: 7.3 in.
Overall Height: 5.4 in.
Overall Width: 1.2 in.
Barrel: 4.5 in.
Grips: Checkered with finger grooves; modular backstrap
Sights: Fixed front/dovetail rear, dot/outline
Weight Unloaded: 22 oz. (G17 Gen 4), 22.9 oz. (G22 Gen 4)
Caliber: 9mm (G17 Gen 4), .40 S&W (G22 Gen 4)
Capacity: 17 + 1 (G17 Gen 4), 15 + 1 (G22 Gen 4)
Features: RTF (rough textured frame) polymer frame; three backstrap sizes; dual recoil spring; reversible magazine release; Picatinny rail; magazine bumper pad; textured front strap; external extractor; loaded-chamber indicator; serrated combat trigger guard; trigger, firing pin, and drop safeties; hexagonal rifling; matte black Tenifer finish
G17 Gen 4: $649
G22 Gen 4: $649

Heckler & Koch (H&K)

(www.hk-usa.com)

H&K P30

P30 and P30L

Action: Autoloader, SA/DA
Overall Length: 7 in. (P30), 7.6 in. (P30L)
Overall Height: 5.4 in. (P30), 5.4 in. (P30L)
Overall Width: 1.4 in. (P30), 1.4 in. (P30L)
Barrel: 3.9 in. (P30), 4.5 in. (P30L)
Grips: Textured polymer, modular
Sights: Dovetail front/rear, luminous 3-dot
Weight Unloaded: 16.6 oz. (P30), 16.7 in. (P30L)
Caliber: 9mm, .40 S&W
Capacity: 15 + 1 (9mm), 13 + 1 (.40 S&W, P30)
Features: Polymer frame; three backstrap and grip panel sizes; ambidextrous slide and magazines releases; Picatinny rail; magazine

Heckler & Koch (H&K)

(www.hk-usa.com)

GERMAN OFFICER TRAINING WITH H&K P30

bumper pad; textured front strap; external extractor; loaded-chamber indicator; combat trigger guard; front/rear slide serrations; external hammer; polygonal rifling; matte black finish; numerous trigger variants
P30: $1005
P30L: $1059

HK45 and HK45 COMPACT

Action: Autoloader, SA/DA
Overall Length: 7.5 in. (HK45), 7.2 in. (HK45 Compact)
Overall Height: 5.8 in. (HK45), 5.1 in. (HK45 Compact)
Overall Width: 1.4 in. (HK45), 1.1 in. (HK45 Compact)
Barrel: 4.5 in. (HK45), 3.9 in. (HK45 Compact)
Grips: Textured polymer, modular
Sights: Dovetail front/rear, luminous 3-dot
Weight Unloaded: 16.9 oz. (HK45), 16.8 in. (HK45 Compact)
Caliber: .45 ACP
Capacity: 10 + 1 (HK45), 8 + 1 (HK45 Compact)
Features: Developed for the U.S. Joint Combat Pistol Program; polymer frame; similar grip angle as 1911; full dust cover; O-ring barrel; two backstrap options; ambidextrous decocking lever, slide and magazine releases; Picatinny rail; magazine bumper pad; textured front strap; external extractor; loaded-chamber indicator; serrated combat trigger guard; front/rear slide serrations; external hammer; polygonal rifling; matte black finish; numerous trigger variants
HK45, HK45 Compact: $1147
HK45 *(DAO model)*, ***HK45 Compact*** *(DAO model)*: $1237

H&K P30 ENDURANCE TEST-PISTOL

HANDGUNS

SWAT TRAINING WITH H&K HK45

H&K HK45

H&K HK45 COMPACT

Heckler & Koch (H&K)

(www.hk-usa.com)

USMC OPERATOR WITH H&K HK45

P2000

Action: Autoloader, SA/DA
Overall Length: 6.8 in.
Overall Height: 5 in.
Overall Width: 1.3 in.
Barrel: 3.7 in.
Grips: Textured polymer, modular
Sights: Dovetail front/rear, luminous 3-dot
Weight Unloaded: 16.6 oz.
Caliber: 9mm, .40 S&W, .357 SIG
Capacity: 13 + 1 (9mm), 12 + 1 (.40 S&W), 12 + 1 (.357 SIG)
Features: Polymer frame; four backstrap sizes; ambidextrous slide and magazines releases; Picatinny rail; magazine bumper pad; textured front strap; external extractor; loaded-chamber indicator; combat trigger guard; external hammer; polygonal rifling; matte black finish; numerous trigger variants; limited availability for .357 SIG model
MSRP: $941

P2000 SK

Action: Autoloader, SA/DA
Overall Length: 6.4 in.
Overall Height: 4.6 in.
Overall Width: 1.3 in.
Barrel: 3.3 in.
Grips: Textured polymer, modular
Sights: Dovetail front/rear, luminous 3-dot
Weight Unloaded: 16.5 oz.
Caliber: 9mm, .40 S&W, .357 SIG
Capacity: 10 + 1 (9mm), 9 + 1 (.40 S&W), 9 + 1 (.357 SIG)
Features: Polymer frame; four backstrap sizes; ambidextrous slide and magazines releases; Picatinny rail; magazine bumper pad; textured front strap; external extractor; loaded-chamber indicator; combat trigger guard; external hammer; polygonal rifling; matte black finish; numerous trigger variants; limited availability for .357 SIG model
MSRP: $983

H&K USP 9MM

USP

Action: Autoloader, SA/DA
Overall Length: 7.6 in. (9mm, .40 S&W), 7.9 in. (.45 ACP)
Overall Height: 5.4 in. (9mm, .40 S&W), 5.6 in. (.45 ACP)
Overall Width: 1.3 in.
Barrel: 4.3 in. (9mm, .40 S&W), 4.4 in. (.45 ACP)
Grips: Textured polymer
Sights: Dovetail front/rear, luminous 3-dot
Weight Unloaded: 16.7 oz. (9mm), 16.8 oz. (.40 S&W), 32 oz. (.45 ACP)
Caliber: 9mm, .40 S&W, .45 ACP
Capacity: 15 + 1 (9mm), 13 + 1 (.40 S&W), 12 + 1 (.45 ACP)
Features: Polymer frame; decocking lever; ambidextrous magazine release; Picatinny rail; magazine bumper pad; checkered front strap; external extractor; loaded-chamber indicator; serrated oversized combat trigger guard; external hammer; polygonal rifling; matte black finish; numerous trigger variants
9mm, .40 S&W: $902
9mm, .40 S&W, DOA model: . . $952
.45 ACP: $983
.45 ACP, DOA model: $1033

H&K P2000

H&K P2000 SK

USP COMPACT

Action: Autoloader, SA/DA
Overall Length: 6.8 in. (9mm, .40 S&W), 7.1 in. (.45 ACP)
Overall Height: 5 in. (9mm, .40 S&W), 5.1 in. (.45 ACP)
Overall Width: 1.1 in.
Barrel: 3.6 in. (9mm, .40 S&W), 3.8 in. (.45 ACP)
Grips: Textured polymer
Sights: Dovetail front/rear, luminous 3-dot
Weight Unloaded: 16.6 oz. (9mm), 16.7 oz. (.40 S&W), 16.8 oz. (.45 ACP)
Caliber: 9mm, .40 S&W, .45 ACP
Capacity: 13 + 1 (9mm), 12 + 1 (.40 S&W), 8 + 1 (.45 ACP)

Heckler & Koch

(www.hk-usa.com)

Features: Polymer frame; decocking lever; ambidextrous magazine release; Picatinny rail; magazine bumper pad; checkered front strap; external extractor; loaded-chamber indicator; serrated oversized combat trigger guard; external hammer; polygonal rifling; matte black finish; numerous trigger variants

9mm, .40 S&W: $941
9mm, .40 S&W, DOA model: . . $991
.45 ACP: $1086
.45 ACP, DOA model: $1086

H&K US TACTICAL .45ACP

H&K USP COMPACT 9MM

H&K MARK 23

H&K USP TACTICAL COMPACT

USP TACTICAL

Action: Autoloader, SA/DA
Overall Length: 8.4 in. (9mm), 8.3 in. (.40 S&W), 8.6 in. (.45 ACP)
Overall Height: 5.6 in. (9mm, .40 S&W), 5.9 in. (.45 ACP)
Overall Width: 1.3 in.
Barrel: 4.8 in. (9mm), 4.9 in. (.40 S&W), 5.1 in. (.45 ACP)
Grips: Textured polymer
Sights: Dovetail front/adj. rear, luminous 3-dot
Weight Unloaded: 16.6 oz. (9mm), 16.7 oz. (.40 S&W), 16.8 oz. (.45 ACP)
Caliber: 9mm, .40 S&W, .45 ACP
Capacity: 15 + 1 (9mm), 13 + 1 (.40 S&W), 12 + 1 (.45 ACP)
Features: Polymer frame; threaded barrel with rubber O-ring; adj. trigger stop; extended slide release; decocking lever; ambidextrous magazine release; Picatinny rail; magazine bumper pad; checkered front strap; external extractor; loaded-chamber indicator; serrated oversized combat trigger guard; external hammer; polygonal rifling; matte black finish; numerous trigger variants

9mm: $1112,
.40 S&W: $1262,
.45 ACP: $1301

USP TACTICAL COMPACT

Action: Autoloader, DAO
Overall Length: 7.7 in.
Overall Height: 5.6 in.
Overall Width: 1.3 in.
Barrel: 4.5 in.
Grips: Textured polymer
Sights: Dovetail front/adj. rear, luminous 3-dot
Weight Unloaded: 16.7 oz.
Caliber: .45 ACP
Capacity: 8 + 1
Features: Developed for U.S. special operations; polymer frame; threaded barrel with rubber O-ring; adj. trigger stop; extended slide release; decocking lever; ambidextrous magazine release; Picatinny rail; magazine bumper pad; checkered front strap; external extractor; loaded-chamber indicator; serrated oversized combat trigger guard; external hammer; polygonal rifling; matte black finish; numerous trigger variants

MSRP: $1238

MARK 23

Action: Autoloader, SA/DA
Overall Length: 9.7 in.
Overall Height: 5.9 in.
Overall Width: 1.5 in.
Barrel: 5.9 in.
Grips: Textured polymer
Sights: Dovetail front/adj. rear, luminous 3-dot
Weight Unloaded: 32.6 oz.
Caliber: .45 ACP
Capacity: 12 + 1
Features: Developed for U.S. special operations; polymer frame; threaded barrel with rubber O-ring; adj. match grade trigger; extended slide release; decocking lever; ambidextrous safety and magazine release; Picatinny rail; magazine bumper pad; checkered front strap; external extractor; loaded-chamber indicator; serrated oversized combat trigger guard; external hammer; polygonal rifling; matte black finish

MSRP: $2310

Hi-Point Firearms

(www.hi-pointfirearms.com)

HI-POINT CF-380

CF-380

Action: Autoloader, striker-fired
Overall Length: 6.8 in.
Overall Height: 5.3 in.
Overall Width: 1.4 in.
Barrel: 3.5 in.
Grips: Textured polymer
Sights: Fixed front/adj. rear, 3-dot
Weight Unloaded: 29 oz.
Caliber: .380
Capacity: 8 + 1
Features: Polymer frame; thumb and magazine disconnect safeties; matte black finish
MSRP: $140

C-9

Action: Autoloader, striker-fired
Overall Length: 6.8 in.
Overall Height: 5.2 in.
Overall Width: 1.5 in.
Barrel: 3.5 in.
Grips: Textured polymer
Sights: Fixed front/adj. rear, 3-dot
Weight Unloaded: 29 oz.
Caliber: 9mm
Capacity: 8 + 1
Features: Polymer frame; thumb and magazine disconnect safeties; matte black finish
MSRP: $165

HI-POINT C-9

HI-POINT 45ACP

HANDGUNS

HI-POINT 40 SW-B

40 SW-B

Action: Autoloader, striker-fired
Overall Length: 7.8 in.
Barrel: 4.5 in.
Grips: Textured polymer
Sights: Fixed front/adj. rear, 3-dot
Weight Unloaded: 35 oz.
Caliber: .40 S&W
Capacity: 10 + 1
Features: Polymer frame; thumb and magazine disconnect safeties; Picatinny rail; matte black finish
MSRP: $165

45ACP

Action: Autoloader, striker-fired
Overall Length: 7.8 in.
Barrel: 4.5 in.
Grips: Textured polymer
Sights: Fixed front/adj. rear, 3-dot
Weight Unloaded: 35 oz.
Caliber: .45 ACP
Capacity: 9 + 1
Features: Polymer frame; thumb and magazine disconnect safeties; Picatinny rail; matte black finish
MSRP: $200

High Standard

(www.highstandard.com)

HIGH STANDARD UNITED STATES MODEL 1911A1

HIGH STANDARD COMPACT ELITE

HIGH STANDARD BACKUP

UNITED STATES MODEL 1911A1 and UNITED STATES MODEL 1911 CUSTOM

Action: Autoloader, SA
Overall Length: 8.8 in.
Overall Height: 5.5 in.
Overall Width: 1.3 in.
Barrel: 5 in.
Grips: Deluxe cocobolo
Sights: Fixed dovetail front/rear, Novak style; fixed dovetail front/Adj. rear (custom)
Weight Unloaded: 40 oz.
Caliber: .45 ACP
Capacity: 7 + 1
Features: Colt 1911 design; steel frame; thumb, beavertail grip safeties; lowered/flared ejection port; long trigger with overtravel stop; flat serrated mainspring housing; beveled magazine well
MSRP: **$645**
MSRP (custom): **$995**

COMPACT ELITE

Action: Autoloader, SA
Overall Length: 6.8 in.
Overall Height: 4.3 in.
Overall Width: 1.3 in.
Barrel: 3.6 in.
Grips: Deluxe cocobolo
Sights: Fixed dovetail front/rear, Novak style; fixed dovetail front/Adj. rear (custom)
Weight Unloaded: 25 oz.
Caliber: .45 ACP
Capacity: 7 + 1
Features: Colt 1911 design; steel frame; thumb, beavertail grip safeties; lowered/flared ejection port; long trigger with overtravel stop; flat serrated mainspring housing; beveled magazine well
MSRP: **$645**

G-MAN MODEL

Action: Autoloader, SA
Overall Length: 8.8 in.
Overall Height: 5.5 in.
Overall Width: 1.3 in.
Barrel: 5 in.
Grips: Deluxe cocobolo
Sights: Fixed dovetail front/rear, Novak style
Weight Unloaded: 39 oz.
Caliber: .45 ACP
Capacity: 7 + 1
Features: Colt 1911 design; steel frame; thumb, grip safeties; lowered/flared ejection port; long trigger with overtravel stop; flat serrated mainspring housing; beveled magazine well; black Teflon finish
MSRP: **$1395**

BACKUP

Action: Autoloader, DAO
Overall Length: 5 in. (.380), 5.8 in. (9mm, .40 S&W, 400 CorBon, .45 ACP)
Overall Height: 4.1 in.
Overall Width: 1 in.
Barrel: 2.5 in. (.380), 3 in. (9mm, .40 S&W, 400 CorBon, .45 ACP)
Grips: Checkered fiberglass
Sights: Fixed groove
Weight Unloaded: 18 oz. (.380), 23 oz. (9mm, .45 ACP), 25 oz. (.40 S&W, 400 CorBon)
Caliber: .380; 9mm, .40 S&W, 400 CorBon; .45 ACP
Capacity: 5 + 1 (.40 S&W, .45 ACP)
Features: Butt magazine release; ported barrel/slide (400 CorBon), matte stainless finish
MSRP (.380, 9mm, .40 S&W,.45 ACP): **$525**
MSRP (400 Cor-Bon): **$625**

I.O. Inc.

(www.ioinc.us)

HELLCAT

Action: Autoloader, DAO
Overall Length: 5.16 in.
Overall Height: 3.60 in.
Overall Width: .82 in.
Barrel: 2.75 in.
Grips: Checkered polymer
Sights: Fixed front/rear
Weight Unloaded: 9.4 oz.
Caliber: 380
Capacity: 6 round magazine
Features: Steel slide; polymer frame
Blued: $350

I.O. INC. HELLCAT

I.O. Inc.

(www.ioinc.us)

I.O. INC. PPS-43C

I.O. INC. HELLPUP

PPS-43C

Action: Autoloader
Overall Length: 24.2 in.
Barrel: 9.8 in.
Grips: Polymer
Sights: Fixed front/rear
Weight Unloaded: 129 oz.
Caliber: 7.62x25mm
Capacity: 35-round magazine
Features: Stamped steel receiver; matte black finish; muzzle brake
MSRP: $400

HELLPUP

Action: Autoloader
Grips: Polymer
Sights: Fixed front/rear
Caliber: 7.63x39mm
Capacity: 30 round magazine
Features: AK47-style action; steel receiver; matte black finish
MSRP: $450

Kahr Arms

(www.kahr.com)

P380

Action: Autoloader, striker-fired
Overall Length: 4.9 in.
Overall Height: 3.9 in.
Overall Width: .8 in.
Barrel: 2.5 in.
Grips: Textured polymer
Sights: Dovetail front/rear, white bar-dot
Weight Unloaded: 10 oz.
Caliber: .380
Capacity: 6 + 1
Features: Polymer frame; serrated front/backstraps; loaded-chamber indicator (LCI model)
LCI: $733
LCI *(Tritium sights)*: $846
Two-tone: $649
Two-tone *(Tritium sights)*: $758
Matte black: $690
Matte black *(Tritium sights)*: $790
Black Rose *(engraved slide)*: $949

P9

Action: Autoloader, striker-fired
Overall Length: 5.8 in.
Overall Height: 4.5 in.
Overall Width: .9 in.
Barrel: 3.6 in.
Grips: Textured polymer
Sights: Dovetail front/rear, white bar-dot
Weight Unloaded: 15 oz.
Caliber: 9mm
Capacity: 7 + 1
Features: Polymer frame; serrated front/backstraps; passive striker block safety; polygonal rifling; magazine bumper pad
Two-tone: $739
Two-tone *(Tritium sights)*: $846
Matte black: $786
Matte black *(Tritium sights)*: $903

KAHR ARMS P380

TP9

Action: Autoloader, striker-fired
Overall Length: 6.5 in.
Overall Height: 5.1 in.
Overall Width: .9 in.
Barrel: 4 in.
Grips: Textured polymer
Sights: Dovetail front/rear, white bar-dot
Weight Unloaded: 18.3 oz.

Kahr Arms

(www.kahr.com)

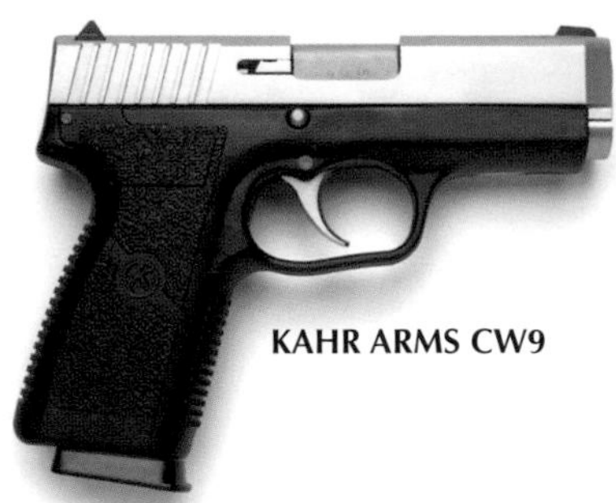
KAHR ARMS CW9

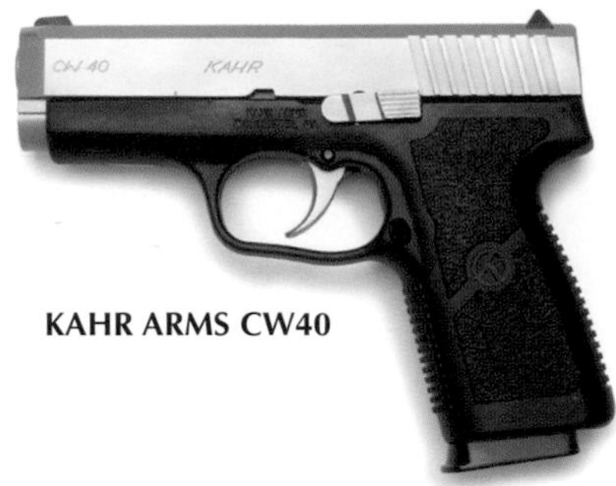
KAHR ARMS CW40

KAHR ARMS PM9 BLACK ROSE

Caliber: 9mm
Capacity: 8 + 1
Features: Polymer frame; serrated front/backstraps; passive striker block safety; polygonal rifling; magazine bumper pad
Two-tone: $697
Two-tone *(Novak Tritium sights)*: $838

CW9

Action: Autoloader, striker-fired
Overall Length: 5.9 in.
Overall Height: 4.5 in.
Overall Width: .9 in.
Barrel: 3.6 in.
Grips: Textured polymer
Sights: Dovetail front/rear, white bar-dot
Weight Unloaded: 15.8 oz.
Caliber: 9mm
Capacity: 7 + 1
Features: Polymer frame; serrated front/backstraps; passive striker block safety; magazine bumper pad
Two-tone: $549

PM9

Action: Autoloader, striker-fired
Overall Length: 5.3 in.
Overall Height: 4 in.
Overall Width: .9 in.
Barrel: 3 in.
Grips: Textured polymer
Sights: Dovetail front/rear, white bar-dot
Weight Unloaded: 14 oz.
Caliber: 9mm
Capacity: 6 + 1
Features: Polymer frame; serrated front/backstraps; passive striker block safety; polygonal rifling
Two-tone: $786
Two-tone *(Tritium sights)*: $908
Matte black: $837
Matte black *(Tritium sights)*: $958
Two-tone *(Crimson Trace laser sight grip)*: $991
Black Rose *(engraved slide)*: $1049
External safety and LCI: $924
External safety and LCI *(Tritium sights)*: $1049

T9

Action: Autoloader, striker-fired
Overall Length: 6.5 in.
Overall Height: 5 in.
Overall Width: .9 in.
Barrel: 4 in.
Grips: Checkered wood
Sights: Dovetail front/rear, white bar-dot
Weight Unloaded: 18.3 oz.
Caliber: 9mm
Capacity: 8 + 1
Features: Steel frame; passive striker block safety; polygonal rifling; magazine bumper pad; matte stainless finish
MSRP: $831
Novak Tritium sights: $968

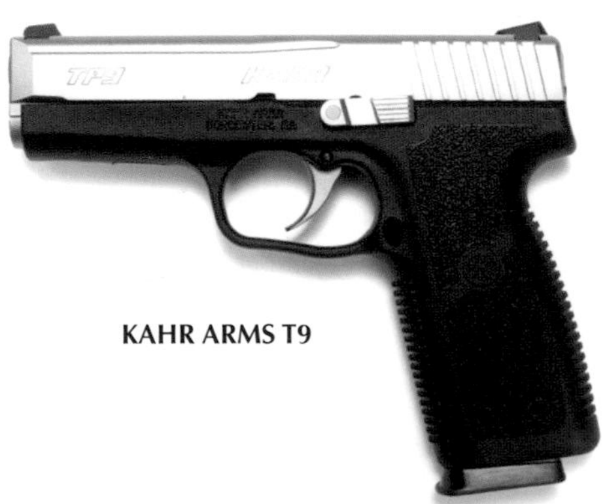
KAHR ARMS T9

KAHR ARMS PM9

Kahr Arms

(www.kahr.com)

KAHR ARMS K9

K9

Action: Autoloader, striker-fired
Overall Length: 6 in.
Overall Height: 4.5 in.
Overall Width: .9 in.
Barrel: 3.5 in.
Grips: Wraparound textured rubber
Sights: Dovetail front/rear, white bar-dot
Weight Unloaded: 18.3 oz.
Caliber: 9mm
Capacity: 7 + 1
Features: Steel frame; passive striker block safety; polygonal rifling; magazine bumper pad
Matte stainless: $855
Matte stainless *(Tritium sights)*: $985
Matte black: $891
Matte black *(Tritium sights)*: $1021
Elite *(polished stainless)*: $932
Elite *(polished stainless, Tritium sights)*: $1054

MK9

Action: Autoloader, striker-fired
Overall Length: 5.3 in.
Overall Height: 4 in.
Overall Width: .9 in.
Barrel: 3 in.
Grips: Wraparound textured nylon
Sights: Dovetail front/rear, white bar-dot
Weight Unloaded: 22.1 oz.
Caliber: 9mm
Capacity: 6 + 1
Features: Steel frame; passive striker block safety; polygonal rifling
Matte stainless: $855
Matte stainless *(Tritium sights)*: $958
Elite *(polished stainless)*: $932
Elite *(polished stainless, Tritium sights)*: $958

TP40

Action: Autoloader, striker-fired
Overall Length: 6.5 in.
Overall Height: 5.1 in.
Overall Width: .94 in.
Barrel: 4 in.
Grips: Textured polymer
Sights: Dovetail front/rear, white bar-dot
Weight Unloaded: 20.1 oz.
Caliber: .40 S&W
Capacity: 8 + 1
Features: Polymer frame; serrated front/backstraps; passive striker block safety; polygonal rifling; magazine bumper pad
Two-tone: $697
Two-tone *(Novak Tritium sights)*: $838

KAHR ARMS MK9

KAHR ARMS TP40

Kahr Arms

(www.kahr.com)

KAHR ARMS T40

KAHR ARMS PM40 WITH CRIMSON TRACE LASER

P40

Action: Autoloader, striker-fired
Overall Length: 6.1 in.
Overall Height: 4.6 in.
Overall Width: .94 in.
Barrel: 3.6 in.
Grips: Textured polymer
Sights: Dovetail front/rear, white bar-dot
Weight Unloaded: 16.8 oz.
Caliber: .40 S&W
Capacity: 6 + 1
Features: Polymer frame; serrated front/backstraps; passive striker block safety; polygonal rifling; magazine bumper pad
Two-tone: $739
Two-tone *(Tritium sights)*: $857
Matte black: $786
Matte black *(Tritium sights)*: $903

CW40

Action: Autoloader, striker-fired
Overall Length: 6.4 in.
Overall Height: 4.6 in.
Overall Width: .9 in.
Barrel: 3.6 in.
Grips: Textured polymer
Sights: Fixed front/dovetail rear, white bar-dot
Weight Unloaded: 16.8 oz.
Caliber: .40 S&W
Capacity: 6 + 1
Features: Polymer frame; serrated front/backstraps; passive striker block safety; magazine bumper pad
Two-tone: $549

PM40

Action: Autoloader, striker-fired
Overall Length: 5.4 in.
Overall Height: 4 in.
Overall Width: .9 in.
Barrel: 3 in.
Grips: Textured polymer
Sights: Dovetail front/rear, white bar-dot
Weight Unloaded: 15.8 oz.
Caliber: .40 S&W
Capacity: 5 + 1
Features: Polymer frame; serrated front/backstraps; passive striker block safety; polygonal rifling
Two-tone: $786
Two-tone *(Tritium sights)*: $908
Two-tone *(Crimson Trace laser sight grip)*: $991
Matte black: $837
Matte black *(Tritium sights)*: $939
Black Rose *(engraved slide)*: $1049
External safety and LCI: $924

KAHR ARMS P40

HANDGUNS

Kahr Arms

(www.kahr.com)

KAHR ARMS MK40

KAHR ARMS K40

K40

Action: Autoloader, striker-fired
Overall Length: 6.1 in.
Overall Height: 4.6 in.
Overall Width: .9 in.
Barrel: 3.5 in.
Grips: Wraparound textured rubber
Sights: Dovetail front/rear, white bar-dot
Weight Unloaded: 24.1 oz.
Caliber: .40 S&W
Capacity: 6 + 1
Features: Steel frame; passive striker block safety; polygonal rifling; magazine bumper pad
Matte stainless: $855
Matte stainless *(Tritium sights)*: $985
Matte black: $891
Matte black *(Tritium sights)*: $1021
Elite *(polished stainless)*: $932
Elite *(polished stainless, Tritium sights)*: $1054

T40

Action: Autoloader, striker-fired
Overall Length: 6.6 in.
Overall Height: 5 in.
Overall Width: .9 in.
Barrel: 4 in.
Grips: Checkered wood
Sights: Dovetail front/rear, white bar-dot
Weight Unloaded: 24.1 oz.
Caliber: .40 S&W
Capacity: 7 + 1
Features: Steel frame; passive striker block safety; polygonal rifling; magazine bumper pad; matte stainless finish
MSRP: $831
Novak Tritium sights: $968

MK40

Action: Autoloader, striker-fired
Overall Length: 5.4 in.
Overall Height: 4 in.
Overall Width: .9 in.
Barrel: 3 in.
Grips: Wraparound textured nylon
Sights: Dovetail front/rear, white bar-dot
Weight Unloaded: 23.1 oz.
Caliber: .40 S&W
Capacity: 5 + 1
Features: Steel frame; passive striker block safety; polygonal rifling
Matte stainless: $855
Matte stainless *(Tritium sights)*: $958
Elite *(polished stainless)*: $932
Elite *(polished stainless, Tritium sights)*: $958

KP45

Action: Autoloader, striker-fired
Overall Length: 6.1 in.
Overall Height: 4.8 in.
Overall Width: 1 in.
Barrel: 3.1 in.
Grips: Textured polymer
Sights: Dovetail front/rear, white bar-dot
Weight Unloaded: 20.5 oz.
Caliber: .45 ACP
Capacity: 6 + 1
Features: Polymer frame; serrated front/backstraps; passive striker block safety; magazine bumper pad
Two-tone: $805
Matte black: $855
Two-tone *(Tritium sights)*: $921
Matte black *(Tritium sights)*: $973

KAHR ARMS KP45

Kahr Arms

(www.kahr.com)

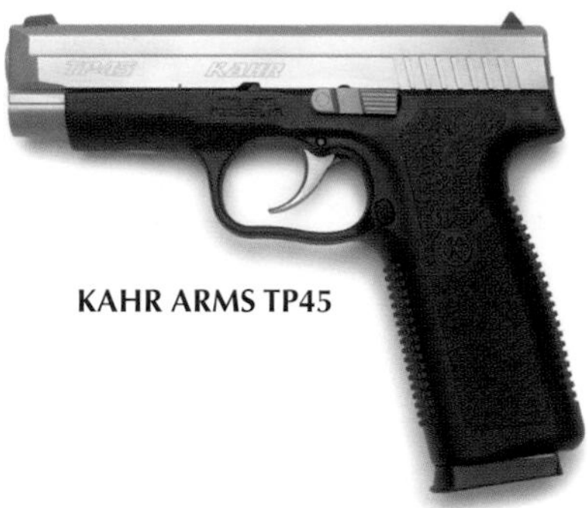

KAHR ARMS TP45

KAHR ARMS CW45

KAHR ARMS PM45

TP45

Action: Autoloader, striker-fired
Overall Length: 6.6 in.
Overall Height: 5.2 in.
Overall Width: 1 in.
Barrel: 4 in.
Grips: Textured polymer
Sights: Dovetail front/rear, white bar-dot
Weight Unloaded: 22.1 oz.
Caliber: .45 ACP
Capacity: 7 + 1
Features: Polymer frame; serrated front/backstraps; passive striker block safety; magazine bumper pad
Two-tone: $697
Two-tone *(Tritium sights)*: $839

CW45

Action: Autoloader, striker-fired
Overall Length: 6.3 in.
Overall Height: 4.8 in.
Overall Width: 1 in.
Barrel: 3.6 in.
Grips: Textured polymer
Sights: Dovetail front/rear, white bar-dot
Weight Unloaded: 21.7 oz.
Caliber: .45 ACP
Capacity: 6 + 1
Features: Polymer frame; serrated front/backstraps; passive striker block safety; magazine bumper pad
Two-tone: $606

PM45

Action: Autoloader, striker-fired
Overall Length: 5.8 in.
Overall Height: 4.5 in.
Overall Width: 1 in.
Barrel: 3.1 in.
Grips: Textured polymer
Sights: Dovetail front/rear, white bar-dot
Weight Unloaded: 19.3 oz.
Caliber: .45 ACP
Capacity: 5 + 1
Features: Polymer frame; serrated front/backstraps; passive striker block safety; magazine bumper
Two-tone: $805
Two-tone *(Tritium sights)*: $974
Matte black: $903
Matte black *(Tritium sights)*: $1022

Kel-Tec

(www.keltecweapons.com)

PF-9

Action: Autoloader, striker-fired
Overall Length: 5.9 in.
Overall Height: 4.3 in.
Overall Width: .9 in.
Barrel: 3.1 in.
Grips: Textured polymer
Sights: Fixed front/adj. rear, 3-dot
Weight Unloaded: 27.7 oz.
Caliber: 9mm
Capacity: 7 + 1
Features: Polymer frame; hammer block safety; Picatinny rail; magazine base pad with finger rest
Blue: $333
Parkerized: $377
Hard chrome: $390

PF-11

Action: Autoloader, striker-fired
Overall Length: 5.6 in.
Overall Height: 4.3 in.
Overall Width: 1 in.
Barrel: 3.1 in.
Grips: Textured polymer
Sights: Fixed front/adj. rear, 3-dot
Weight Unloaded: 14 oz.
Caliber: 9mm
Capacity: 10 + 1
Features: Polymer frame; hammer block safety; compatible with S&W model 59 series magazines
Blue: $333
Parkerized: $377
Hard chrome: $390

KEL-TEC PF-9

KEL-TEC PF-11

Kel-Tec

(www.keltecweapons.com)

KEL-TEC PF-32

KEL-TEC PLR-16

KEL-TEC PF-3AT

PF-32

Action: Autoloader, striker-fired
Overall Length: 5.1 in.
Overall Height: 3.5 in.
Overall Width: 1 in.
Barrel: 2.7 in.
Grips: Textured polymer
Sights: Fixed front/rear
Weight Unloaded: 6.6 oz.
Caliber: .32 ACP
Capacity: 7 + 1
Features: Polymer frame; hammer block safety
Blue: $318
Parkerized: $361
Hard chrome: $377

PF-3AT

Action: Autoloader, striker-fired
Overall Length: 5.2 in.
Overall Height: 3.5 in.
Overall Width: .8 in.
Barrel: 2.7 in.
Grips: Textured polymer
Sights: Fixed front/rear
Weight Unloaded: 8.3 oz.
Caliber: .380
Capacity: 6 + 1
Features: Polymer frame; hammer block safety
Blue: $318
Parkerized: $361
Hard chrome: $377

PLR-16

Action: Autoloader, SA
Overall Length: 18.5 in.
Barrel: 9.2 in.
Grips: Textured polymer
Sights: Fixed front/adj. rear
Weight Unloaded: 48.3 oz.
Caliber: .223 Rem.
Capacity: 10
Features: AR-15 design; gas piston action; polymer frame; threaded muzzle; Picatinny rail; compatible with AR-15 magazines; matte black
MSRP: $665

Kimber

(www.kimberamerica.com)

KIMBER CUSTOM II

CUSTOM II

Action: Autoloader, SA
Overall Length: 8.7 in.
Overall Height: 5.3 in.
Overall Width: 1.3 in.
Barrel: 5 in.
Grips: Black synthetic checkered double diamond
Sights: Fixed front/dovetail rear
Weight Unloaded: 38 oz.
Caliber: .45 ACP
Capacity: 7 + 1
Features: Colt 1911 design; steel frame; grip-activated firing pin safety; steel frame; loaded-chamber indicator port; extended thumb, beavertail grip safeties; lowered/flared ejection port
Matte black: $828
Matte black with 3-dot night sights: $956
Royal II *(polished blue)*: $1013
Stainless II: $964
Stainless II *(3-dot night sights)*: $1092
Desert Warrior *(Picatinny rail, lanyard loop, ambidextrous safety, magazine base pad, dark earth finish)*: $1458
Desert Warrior *(Picatinny rail, lanyard loop, ambidextrous safety, magazine base pad, matte black)*: $1441
Stainless TLE II *(front grip strap checkering, Tritium 3-dot night sight)*: $1177
Custom TLE II *(front grip strap checkering, Tritium 3-dot night sight, matte black)*: $1044
Custom TLE/RL II *(Picatinny rail, front grip strap checkering, Tritium 3-dot night sight, matte black)*: $1139
Stainless TLE II *(Picatinny rail, front grip strap checkering, Tritium 3-dot night sight)*: $1272
Custom Crimson Carry II *(Crimson Trace laser sight grip rosewood grip, blue slide/stainless frame)*: $1156

Kimber

(www.kimberamerica.com)

KIMBER PRO CARRY II

KIMBER ULTRA CDP II

KIMBER ULTRA TLE II

KIMBER STAINLESS ULTRA CARRY II

PRO CARRY II

Action: Autoloader, SA
Overall Length: 7.7 in.
Overall Height: 4.8 in. (Compact Stainless II), 5.3 in.
Overall Width: 1.3 in.
Barrel: 4 in.
Grips: Gray synthetic checkered double diamond
Sights: Dovetail front/rear, 3-dot
Weight Unloaded: 28 oz. (9mm), 35 oz. (.45 ACP)
Caliber: 9mm, .45 ACP
Capacity: 9 + 1 (9mm), 7 + 1(.45 ACP)
Features: Colt 1911 design; aluminum frame; grip-activated firing pin safety; steel frame; loaded-chamber indicator port; extended thumb, beavertail grip safeties; lowered/flared ejection port
Matte black *(.45 ACP)*: $888
Matte black *(9mm)*: $929
Matte black *(.45 ACP, 3-dot night sights)*: $997
Stainless II *(.45 ACP)*: $979
Stainless II *(9mm)*: $1020
Stainless II *(.45 ACP, 3-dot night sights)*: $1088
Stainless Pro TLE II *(front grip strap checkering, Tritium3-dot night sight)*: $1210
Stainless Pro TLE II LG *(Crimson Trace laser sight grip, front grip strap checkering, Tritium 3-dot night sight)*: $1462
Compact Stainless II: $1009
Pro Carry HD II *(stainless frame)*: $1008
Pro TLE/RL II *(steel frame, Picatinny rail, front grip strap checkering, Tritium 3-dot night sight, matte black)*: $1197
Pro Stainless TLE/RL II *(stainless frame, Picatinny rail, front grip strap checkering, Tritium 3-dot night sight)*: $1322
Pro Crimson Carry II *(Crimson Trace laser sight grip rosewood grip, blue slide/stainless frame)*: $1156

ULTRA CARRY II

Action: Autoloader, SA
Overall Length: 6.8 in.
Overall Height: 4.3 in.
Overall Width: 1.3 in.
Barrel: 3 in.
Grips: Gray synthetic checkered double diamond
Sights: Dovetail front/rear, 3-dot
Weight Unloaded: 25 oz.
Caliber: 9mm, .45 ACP
Capacity: 8 + 1 (9mm), 7 + 1 (.45 ACP)
Features: Colt 1911 design; steel frame; grip-activated firing pin safety; loaded-chamber indicator port; extended thumb, beavertail grip safeties; lowered/flared ejection port; rounded and blended edges; beveled magazine well
Matte black: $888
Matte black *(Tritium 3-dot night sight)*: $996
Stainless II *(.45 ACP)*: $980
Stainless II *(9mm)*: $1021
Ultra TLE II *(aluminum frame, front grip strap checkering, Tritium 3-dot night sight)*: $1102
Ultra TLE II LG *(Crimson Trace laser sight grip, front grip strap checkering, Tritium3-dot night sight)*: $1346
Stainless Ultra TLE II: *(aluminum frame, front grip strap checkering, Tritium 3-dot night sight)*: $1210
Stainless Ultra TLE II LG *(Crimson Trace laser sight grip, front grip strap checkering, Tritium3-dot night sight)*: $1462
Ultra Crimson Carry II *(Crimson Trace laser sight grip rosewood grip, blue slide/stainless frame)*: $1156

Kimber

(www.kimberamerica.com)

TACTICAL II

Action: Autoloader, SA
Overall Length: 6.8 in. (Ultra), 7.7 in. (Pro), 8.7 in. (Custom)
Overall Height: 5 in.
Overall Width: 1.3 in.
Barrel: 3 in. (Ultra), 4 in. (Pro), 5 in. (Custom)
Grips: Laminated checkered double diamond
Sights: Dovetail front/rear, Tritium 3-dot
Weight Unloaded: 25 oz. (Ultra), 28 oz. (Pro), 31 oz. (Custom)
Caliber: 9mm (Pro), .45 ACP
Capacity: 9 + 1 (9mm), 7 + 1 (.45 ACP)
Features: Colt 1911 design; aluminum frame; grip-activated firing pin safety; loaded-chamber indicator port; ambidextrous extended thumb, beavertail grip safeties; lowered/flared ejection port; magazine bumper pad; checkered under trigger guard/front strap; magazine well; matte gray finish
Ultra: $1250
Pro *(.45 ACP)*: $1250
Pro *(9mm)*: $1291
Custom: $1250
Custom HD *(steel frame)*: $1333
Tactical Entry *(steel frame, Picatinny rail)*: $1428

KIMBER TACTICAL CUSTOM HD II

KIMBER TACTICAL ENTRY II

KIMBER TACTICAL ULTRA II

KIMBER TACTICAL CUSTOM II

ECLIPSE II

Action: Autoloader, SA
Overall Length: 6.8 in. (Ultra), 7.7 in. (Pro), 8.7 in. (Custom)
Overall Height: 4.8 in. (Ultra), 5.3
Overall Width: 1.3 in.
Barrel: 3 in. (Ultra), 4 in. (Pro), 5 in. (Custom)
Grips: Laminated checkered double diamond
Sights: Dovetail front/rear, Tritium 3-dot
Weight Unloaded: 31 oz. (Ultra), 35 oz. (Pro), 31 oz. (Custom)
Caliber: .45 ACP
Capacity: 7 + 1 (Ultra), 8 + 1
Features: Colt 1911 design; stainless steel frame; grip-activated firing pin safety; loaded-chamber indicator port; extended thumb, beavertail grip safeties; lowered/flared ejection port; checkered front strap; brushed polish finish on flats
Ultra II: $1236
Pro: $1236
Custom *(front/rear slide serrations)*: $1250

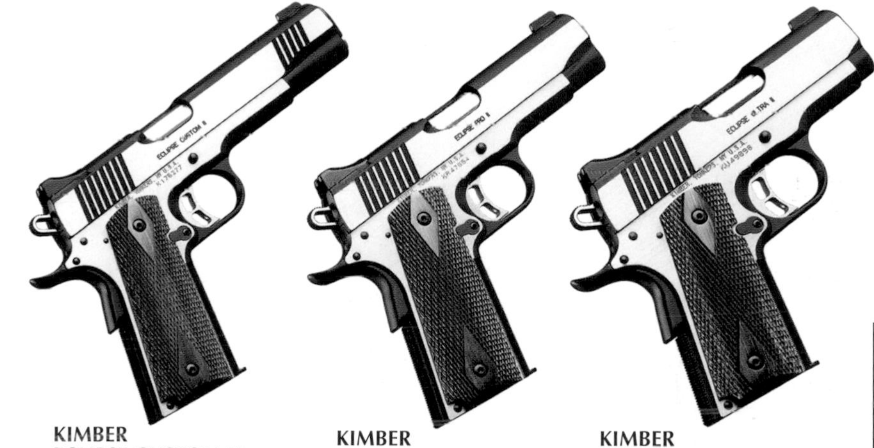

KIMBER ECLIPSE CUSTOM II

KIMBER ECLIPSE PRO II

KIMBER ECLIPSE ULTRA II

COVERT II

Action: Autoloader, SA
Overall Length: 6.8 in. (Ultra), 7.7 in. (Pro), 8.7 in. (Custom)
Overall Height: 4.8 in. (Ultra), 5.3
Overall Width: 1.3 in.
Barrel: 3 in. (Ultra), 4 in. (Pro), 5 in. (Custom)
Grips: Crimson Trace laser sight grip digital camo
Sights: Dovetail front/rear, Tritium 3-dot
Weight Unloaded: 25 oz. (Ultra), 35 oz. (Pro), 31 oz. (Custom)
Caliber: .45 ACP
Capacity: 7 + 1 (Ultra), 8 + 1
Features: Colt 1911 design; aluminum frame; grip-activated firing pin safety; loaded-chamber indicator port; extended thumb, beavertail grip safeties; lowered/flared ejection port; checkered front strap; front/rear slides serrations (Custom), beveled magazine well; magazine bumper pad; lanyard loop; rounded/blended edges; matte black slide/dark earth frame finish
MSRP: $1603

KIMBER CUSTOM COVERT II

HANDGUNS

Kimber

(www.kimberamerica.com)

KIMBER CUSTOM AEGIS II

KIMBER COMPACT CDP II

KIMBER SUPER CARRY CUSTOM

KIMBER STAINLESS ULTRA RAPTOR II

AEGIS II

Action: Autoloader, SA
Overall Length: 6.8 in. (Ultra), 7.7 in. (Pro), 8.7 in. (Custom)
Overall Height: 4.8 in. (Ultra), 5.3
Overall Width: 1.2 in.
Barrel: 3 in. (Ultra), 4 in. (Pro), 5 in. (Custom)
Grips: Thin, fluted rosewood
Sights: Dovetail front/rear, Tritium 3-dot
Weight Unloaded: 25 oz. (Ultra), 28 oz. (Pro), 31 oz. (Custom)
Caliber: 9mm
Capacity: 8 + 1 (Ultra), 9 + 1
Features: Colt 1911 design; aluminum frame; grip-activated firing pin safety; loaded-chamber indicator port; bobbed thumb, beavertail grip safeties; lowered/flared ejection port; checkered front strap; front/rear slides serrations (Custom), rounded/blended edges; blue slide/stainless frame finish
MSRP: $1277

CDP II

Action: Autoloader, SA
Overall Length: 6.8 in. (Ultra), 7.7 in. (Compact, Pro), 8.7 in. (Custom)
Overall Height: 4.8 in. (Ultra), 5.3 in.
Overall Width: 1.3 in.
Barrel: 3 in. (Ultra), 4 in. (Compact, Pro), 5 in. (Custom)
Grips: Double-diamond checkered rosewood
Sights: Dovetail front/rear, Tritium 3-dot
Weight Unloaded: 25 oz. (Ultra), 27 oz. (Compact), 28 oz. (Pro), 31 oz. (Custom)
Caliber: .45 ACP
Capacity: 7 + 1
Features: Colt 1911 design; aluminum frame; grip-activated firing pin safety; loaded-chamber indicator port; extended ambidextrous thumb, beavertail grip safeties; lowered/flared ejection port; checkered under trigger guard/front strap front/rear slides serrations (Custom), beveled magazine well; rounded/blended edges; stainless slide/matte black frame finish
MSRP: $1318
Ultra CDP LG *(Crimson Trace rosewood double-diamond laser sight grip)*: $1603

RAPTOR II

Action: Autoloader, SA
Overall Length: 6.8 in. (Ultra), 7.7 in. (Pro), 8.7 in. (Raptor, Grand Raptor)
Overall Height: 4.8 in. (Ultra), 5.3
Overall Width: 1.3 in.
Barrel: 3 in. (Ultra), 4 in. (Pro), 5 in. (Raptor, Grand Raptor)
Grips: Scale pattern zebra wood
Sights: Dovetail front/rear, Tritium3-dot
Weight Unloaded: 25 oz. (Ultra), 35 oz. (Pro), 38 oz. (Raptor, Grand Raptor)
Caliber: .45 ACP
Capacity: 7 + 1 (Ultra; Pro), 8 + 1 (Raptor, Grand Raptor)

KIMBER STAINLESS PRO TLE II (LG)

KIMBER STAINLESS PRO TLE RL II

KIMBER WARRIOR

KIMBER GOLD COMBAT II

HANDGUNS

Kimber

(www.kimberamerica.com)

Features: Colt 1911 design; steel frame; grip-activated firing pin safety; loaded-chamber indicator port; extended thumb, beavertail grip safeties; lowered/flared ejection port; scaled front/rear strap, slide serrations, slide top
Ultra, Pro *(matte black)*: $1248
Ultra, Pro *(stainless)*: $1359
Raptor *(matte black)*: $1379
Raptor *(stainless)*: $1509
Grand Raptor *(matte black slide/ stainless frame)*: $1587

SUPER CARRY

Action: Autoloader, SA
Overall Length: 6.8 in. (Ultra), 7.7 in. (Pro), 8.7 in. (Custom)
Overall Height: 4.8 in. (Ultra), 5.3
Overall Width: 1.3 in.
Barrel: 3 in. (Ultra), 4 in. (Pro), 5 in. (Custom)
Grips: Checkered micarta/laminate wood
Sights: Dovetail front/rear, Tritium3-dot
Weight Unloaded: 25 oz. (Ultra), 28 oz. (Pro), 38 oz. (Custom)
Caliber: .45 ACP
Capacity: 7 + 1 (Ultra), 8 + 1
Features: Colt 1911 design; aluminum frame; grip-activated firing pin safety; loaded-chamber indicator port; extended thumb, beavertail grip safeties; rounded mainspring housing (Pro, Custom), lowered/flared ejection port; serrations front/rear strap; front/ rear/top slide serrations; matte black slide/stainless frame finish
MSRP: $1530

HANDGUNS

Les Baer

(www.lesbaer.com)

LES BAER 1911 PREMIER II

LES BAER H.C. 40

BAER 1911 PREMIER II

Action: Autoloader, SA
Overall Length: 8.5 in.
Overall Height: 5.5 in.
Overall Width: 1.3 in.
Barrel: 5 in.
Grips: Checkered cocobola
Sights: Dovetail front/adj. rear
Weight Unloaded: 37 oz.
Caliber: .45 ACP
Capacity: 8 + 1
Features: Colt 1911 Series 70 design; steel frame; extended ambidextrous thumb, beavertail grip safeties; lowered/flared ejection port; checkered front/rear grip straps; beveled magazine well; front/ rear slide serrations; blue finish
MSRP: $1790

BAER H.C. 40

Action: Autoloader, SA
Overall Length: 8 in.
Overall Height: 5.5 in.
Overall Width: 1.4 in.
Barrel: 5 in.
Grips: Checkered cocobola
Sights: Dovetail front/adj. rear
Weight Unloaded: 39 oz.
Caliber: .40 S&W
Capacity: 18 + 1
Features: Colt 1911 Series 70 design; steel frame; extended ambidextrous thumb, beavertail grip safeties; lowered/flared ejection port; checkered front/rear grip straps; beveled magazine well; front/rear slide serrations; combat trigger guard; blue finish
MSRP: $2960

BAER 1911 PREMIER II SUPER-TAC

Action: Autoloader, SA
Overall Length: 8.5 in.
Overall Height: 5.5 in.
Overall Width: 1.3 in.
Barrel: 5 in.
Grips: Checkered cocobola
Sights: Dovetail front/adj. rear
Weight Unloaded: 37 oz.
Caliber: .45 ACP
Capacity: 8 + 1
Features: Colt 1911 Series 70 design; steel frame; extended ambidextrous thumb, beavertail grip safeties; lowered/flared ejection port; checkered front/rear grip straps; beveled magazine well; front/rear slide serrations; blue finish
MSRP: $2280

BAER 1911 PROWLER III

Action: Autoloader, SA
Overall Length: 8.5 in.
Overall Height: 5.5 in.
Overall Width: 1.3 in.
Barrel: 5 in.
Grips: Checkered cocobola
Sights: Dovetail front/adj. rear
Weight Unloaded: 37 oz.
Caliber: .45 ACP
Capacity: 8 + 1
Features: Colt 1911 Series 70 design; steel frame; extended ambidextrous thumb, beavertail grip safeties; lowered/flared ejection port; checkered front/rear grip straps; beveled magazine well; front/rear slide serrations; tapered cone stub weight; blue finish
MSRP: $2580

LES BAER PREMIER II SUPER-TAC

LES BAER 1911 PROWLER III

LES BAER 1911 CUSTOM CARRY

BAER 1911 CUSTOM CARRY

Action: Autoloader, SA
Overall Length: 8.5 in.
Overall Height: 5.5 in.
Overall Width: 1.3 in.
Barrel: 5 in.
Grips: Checkered cocobola
Sights: Dovetail front/rear, night sights
Weight Unloaded: 37 oz.
Caliber: .45 ACP
Capacity: 8 + 1
Features: Colt 1911 Series 70 design; steel frame; extended ambidextrous thumb, beavertail grip safeties; lowered/flared ejection port; checkered front/rear grip straps; beveled magazine well; front/rear slide serrations; rounded/blended edges; blue finish
MSRP: $1830

BAER 1911 ULTIMATE RECON

Action: Autoloader, SA
Overall Length: 8.5 in.
Overall Height: 5.5 in.
Overall Width: 1.3 in.
Barrel: 5 in.
Grips: Checkered cocobola
Sights: Dovetail front/rear, Tritium 3-dot
Weight Unloaded: 37 oz.
Caliber: .45 ACP
Capacity: 8 + 1
Features: Colt 1911 Series 70 design; steel frame; extended ambidextrous thumb, beavertail grip safeties; lowered/flared ejection port; checkered front/rear grip straps; beveled magazine well; front/rear slide serrations; rounded/blended edges; Picatinny rail; Streamlight TLR-1 flash light
Bead blast blue: $2290
Bead blast chrome: $2590

LES BAER 1911 ULTIMATE RECON

LES BAER 1911 ULTIMATE TACTICAL CARRY

BAER 1911 ULTIMATE TACTICAL CARRY

Action: Autoloader, SA
Overall Length: 8.5 in.
Overall Height: 5.5 in.
Overall Width: 1.3 in.
Barrel: 5 in.
Grips: Checkered cocobola
Sights: Dovetail front/rear, Tritium 3-dot
Weight Unloaded: 37 oz.
Caliber: .45 ACP
Capacity: 8 + 1
Features: Colt 1911 Series 70 design; steel frame; extended ambidextrous thumb, beavertail grip safeties; lowered/flared ejection port; checkered front/rear grip straps; beveled magazine well; front/rear slide serrations; rounded/blended edges; blue finish
MSRP: $1890

BAER 1911 SWIFT RESPONSE PISTOL (SRP)

Action: Autoloader, SA
Overall Length: 8.5 in.
Overall Height: 5.5 in.
Overall Width: 1.3 in.
Barrel: 5 in.
Grips: Checkered cocobola
Sights: Dovetail front/rear, Tritium 3-dot
Weight Unloaded: 37 oz.
Caliber: .45 ACP
Capacity: 8 + 1
Features: Colt 1911 Series 70 design; steel frame; extended ambidextrous thumb, beavertail grip safeties; lowered/flared ejection port; checkered front/rear grip straps; beveled magazine well; front/rear slide serrations; rounded/blended edges; blue finish
MSRP: $2490

LES BAER 1911 SRP

Les Baer

(www.lesbaer.com)

LES BAER 1911 STINGER

LES BAER 1911 CONCEPT 1

LES BAER 1911 MONOLITH COMMANCHE

BAER 1911 MONOLITH

Action: Autoloader, SA
Overall Length: 7.5 in. (Commanche), 8.5 in.
Overall Height: 5.5 in. (Commanche), 5.5 in.
Overall Width: 1.3 in.
Barrel: 4.5 in. (Commanche), 5 in.
Grips: Checkered cocobola
Sights: Dovetail front/adj. rear, dovetail front/rear Tritium sight (Commanche, Commanche Heavy)
Weight Unloaded: 34 oz. (Commanche), 37 oz.
Caliber: .45 ACP
Capacity: 8 + 1
Features: Colt 1911 Series 70 design; steel frame; extended ambidextrous thumb, beavertail grip safeties; lowered/flared ejection port; checkered front/rear grip straps; beveled magazine well; front/rear slide serrations; rounded/blended edges; full dustcover; blue finish
MSRP: $2190
Heavy Weight Unloaded *(added weight)*: $1870
Tactical Illuminator *(mounted Streamlight TLR-1 flash light)*: $2290
Commanche *(dovetail front/rear Tritium sight)*: $1870
Commanche Heavy *(dovetail front/rear Tritium sight, added weight)*: $1870

BAER 1911 STINGER

Action: Autoloader, SA
Overall Length: 7.5 in.
Overall Height: 5 in.
Overall Width: 1.3 in.
Barrel: 4.5 in.
Grips: Checkered cocobola
Sights: Dovetail front/rear, Tritium 3-dot
Weight Unloaded: 34 oz.
Caliber: .45 ACP
Capacity: 7 + 1
Features: Colt 1911 Series 70 design; steel frame; extended ambidextrous thumb, beavertail grip safeties; lowered/flared ejection port; checkered front/rear grip straps; beveled magazine well; front/rear slide serrations; rounded/blended edges; blue finish
Blue: $1890
Stainless: $1995

BAER 1911 CONCEPT I

Action: Autoloader, SA
Overall Length: 8.5 in.
Overall Height: 5.5 in.
Overall Width: 1.3 in.
Barrel: 5 in.
Grips: Checkered cocobola
Sights: Dovetail front/adj. rear
Weight Unloaded: 37 oz.
Caliber: .45 ACP
Capacity: 8 + 1
Features: Colt 1911 Series 70 design; steel frame; extended ambidextrous thumb, beavertail grip safeties; lowered/flared ejection port; checkered front/rear grip straps; beveled magazine well; front/rear slide serrations; blue finish
MSRP: $1690
Concept II *(Tritium sights)*: $1690
Concept III *(dovetail front/adj. rear sights, two-tone finish)*: $1840
Concept IV *(Tritium sights, two-tone finish)*: $1840
Concept V *(dovetail front/adj. rear sights, stainless)*: $1870
Concept VI *(Tritium sights, stainless)*: $1890
Concept VI I *(Commanche frame, Tritium sights, blue)*: $1830
Concept VI I (Commanche frame, Tritium sights, stainless): $1830

BAER/EMERSON CQC

Action: Autoloader, SA
Overall Length: 8.5 in.
Overall Height: 5.5 in.
Overall Width: 1.3 in.
Barrel: 5 in.
Grips: Checkered laminate
Sights: Dovetail front/rear, Tritium sights
Weight Unloaded: 37 oz.
Caliber: .45 ACP
Capacity: 8 + 1
Features: Colt 1911 Series 70 design; steel frame; extended ambidextrous thumb, beavertail grip safeties; lowered/flared ejection port; checkered front/rear strap; beveled magazine well; front/rear slide serrations; blue finish; Emerson folding knife
MSRP: $3123

LES BAER 1911 MONOLITH

LES BAER/EMERSON CQC

Magnum Research

(www.magnumresearch.com)

MAGNUM RESEARCH BABY DESERT EAGLE II

MAGNUM RESEARCH 1911 C

MAGNUM RESEARCH DESERT EAGLE MARK VII

MAGNUM RESEARCH 1911 G

BABY DESERT EAGLE II

Action: Autoloader, DA/SA
Overall Length: 8.3 in.
Overall Height: 5.8 in.
Overall Width: 1.3 in.
Barrel: 4.5 in.
Grips: Textured polymer
Sights: Dovetail front/rear
Weight Unloaded: 38.6 oz. (9mm), 37.9 oz. (.40 S&W)
Caliber: 9mm, .40 S&W
Capacity: 15 +1 (9mm), 13+ 1 (.40 S&W)
Features: Steel frame; polygonal rifling; slide and decocker safeties; Picatinny rail; black finish
MSRP: $630

DESERT EAGLE MARK VII

Action: Autoloader, SA
Overall Length: 10.5 in.
Overall Height: 6.1 in.
Overall Width: 1.3 in.
Barrel: 6 in.
Grips: Textured polymer
Sights: Dovetail front/rear
Weight Unloaded: 62.9 oz. (.357 Mag.), 67 oz. (.44 Mag.)
Caliber: .357 Mag., .44 Mag.
Capacity: 9 + 1 (.357 Mag.), 8 + 1 (.44 Mag.)
Features: Steel frame; polygonal rifling; slide safety; black finish
MSRP: $2910

1911 C and 1911 G

Action: Autoloader, SA
Overall Length: 7.9 in. (1911 "C"), 8.6 in. (1911 "G")
Overall Height: 5.3 in.
Overall Width: 1.3 in.
Barrel: 4.3 in. (1911 "C"), 5 in. (1911 "G")
Grips: Wood
Sights: Dovetail front/rear, Novak style
Weight Unloaded: 33.9 oz. (1911 "C"), 36.2 oz. (1911 "G")
Caliber: .45 ACP
Capacity: 7 + 1
Features: Colt 1911 design; steel frame; extended thumb, beavertail grip safeties; lowered/flared ejection port; beveled magazine well; magazine base pad; black oxide finish
MSRP: $799

MR EAGLE "FAST ACTION"

Action: Autoloader, striker-fired
Overall Length: 7.1 in. (9mm), 7.2 in. (.40 S&W)
Overall Height: 5.3 in.
Overall Width: 1.3 in.
Barrel: 4 in. (9mm), 4.2 in. (.40 S&W)
Grips: Textured polymer
Sights: Fixed front/dovetail rear.
Weight Unloaded: 24.8 oz. (9mm), 26.4 oz. (.40 S&W)
Caliber: 9mm, .40 S&W
Capacity: 15 +1 (9mm), 12 + 1 (.40 S&W)
Features: Walther P99 design; polymer frame; ambidextrous magazine release; cocking indicator; decocker safety; Picatinny rail; black finish
MSRP: $699.00

MICRO DESERT EAGLE

Action: Autoloader, DOA
Overall Length: 4.5 in.
Overall Height: 3.2 in.
Overall Width: .9 in.
Barrel: 2.2 in.
Grips: Textured polymer
Sights: Fixed front/rear
Weight Unloaded: 14 oz.
Caliber: .380
Capacity: 6 +1
Features: Polymer frame; magazine base pad; external extractor
Nickel: $535.00
Two-tone: $535.00
Blue: $500.00

MAGNUM RESEARCH MICRO DESERT EAGLE

MAGNUM RESEARCH MR EAGLE "FAST ACTION"

Masterpiece Arms

(www.masterpiecearms.com)

PROTECTOR

Action: Autoloader, DAO
Overall Length: 4.4 in.
Overall Height: 3.2 in.
Overall Width: .9 in.
Barrel: 2.3 in.
Grips: Textured polymer
Sights: None
Weight Unloaded: 10.9 oz. (.32 ACP), 11.3 oz. (.380)
Caliber: .32 ACP, .380
Capacity: 6 + 1 (.32 ACP), 5 + 1 (.380)
Features: Steel frame
Matte black: $323
Matte black frame/stainless slide: $346

MASTERPIECE ARMS DEFENDER MPA10T

MASTERPIECE ARMS PROTECTOR MPA 32

DEFENDER

Action: Autoloader, SA
Barrel: 6 in.
Grips: Steel and polymer
Sights: Fixed front/rear
Caliber: 9mm, .45 ACP
Capacity: 35 + 1 (9mm), 30 + 1 (.45 ACP)
Features: MAC design; steel frame; treaded barrel; matte black finish; Picatinny optic mount (side cocking)
Top cocking: $489
Side cocking: $570

MASTERPIECE ARMS DEFENDER MPA30T

DEFENDER MINI

Action: Autoloader, SA
Barrel: 3.3 in.
Grips: Steel and polymer
Sights: Fixed front/rear
Caliber: 9mm, .45 ACP
Capacity: 35 + 1 (9mm), 30 + 1 (.45 ACP)
Features: MAC design; steel frame; treaded barrel; matte black finish; Picatinny optic mount (side cocking)
Top cocking: $489
Top cocking *(camo)*: $538
Side cocking: $570

TACTICAL MINI

Action: Autoloader, SA
Barrel: 3.3 in.
Grips: Steel and polymer
Sights: Fixed front/rear
Caliber: 9mm
Capacity: 35 + 1
Features: MAC design; steel frame; treaded barrel; side cocking; matte black finish; Picatinny optic mount; safety barrel extension; multireticle holosight; 40 lumens flashlight; accessory rail
MSRP: $688

TACTICAL

Action: Autoloader, SA
Barrel: 6 in.
Grips: Steel and polymer
Sights: Fixed front/rear
Caliber: 9mm, .45 ACP
Capacity: 35 + 1 (9mm), 30 + 1 (.45 ACP)
Features: MAC design; steel frame; treaded barrel; side cocking; matte black finish; Picatinny optic mount; safety barrel extension; multi reticle holosight; 40 lumens flashlight; accessory rail
MSRP: $688

MASTERPIECE ARMS DEFENDER MPA30SST

MASTERPIECE ARMS MINI MPA930T

MASTERPIECE ARMS PROTECTOR MPA 380

HANDGUNS

Nighthawk Tactical

(www.nighthawktactical.com)

GLOBAL RESPONSE PISTOL (GRP)

Action: Autoloader, SA
Overall Length: 8.5 in.
Overall Height: 5.8 in.
Overall Width: 1.4 in.
Barrel: 5 in.
Grips: Textured micarta
Sights: Heinie or Novak night sights
Weight Unloaded: 36.7 oz.
Caliber: .45 ACP
Capacity: 7 + 1
Features: Colt 1911 design; steel frame; extended thumb, beavertail grip safeties; lowered/flared ejection port; lanyard loop; magazine base pad; front/rear slide serrations; checkered front grip strap; various Perma Kote finishes
MSRP: $2695

GRP RECON

Action: Autoloader, SA
Overall Length: 8.5 in.
Overall Height: 5.6 in.
Overall Width: 1.4 in.
Barrel: 5 in.
Grips: Textured micarta
Sights: Heinie or Novak night sights
Weight Unloaded: 36.7 oz.
Caliber: .45 ACP
Capacity: 7 + 1
Features: Colt 1911 design; steel frame with Picatinny rail; extended thumb, beavertail grip safeties; lowered/flared ejection port; lanyard loop; magazine base pad; front/rear slide serrations; checkered front grip strap; various Perma Kote finishes
MSRP: $2795

ENFORCER

Action: Autoloader, SA
Overall Length: 8.5 in.
Overall Height: 5.6 in.
Overall Width: 1.4 in.
Barrel: 5 in.
Grips: Textured composite
Sights: Heinie or Novak night sights
Weight Unloaded: 36.7 oz.
Caliber: .45 ACP
Capacity: 7 + 1
Features: Colt 1911 design; steel frame; extended thumb, beavertail grip safeties; lowered/flared ejection port; magazine base pad; front/rear slide serrations; checkered front/back grip strap; extended magazine release; various Perma Kote finishes
MSRP: $2995

T3

Action: Autoloader, SA
Overall Length: 7.6 in.
Overall Height: 5.6 in.
Overall Width: 1.4 in.
Barrel: 4.3 in.
Grips: Textured polymer
Sights: Heinie or Novak night sights
Weight Unloaded: 32.8 oz.
Caliber: .45 ACP
Capacity: 7 + 1
Features: Colt 1911 design; steel frame with Picatinny rail; extended thumb, beavertail grip safeties; lowered/flared ejection port; magazine base pad; checkered front/back grip strap; extended magazine release; notched magazine well; slide top serrated
Various Perma Kote finishes: $2799
Stainless: $2999
Compensated: $3295

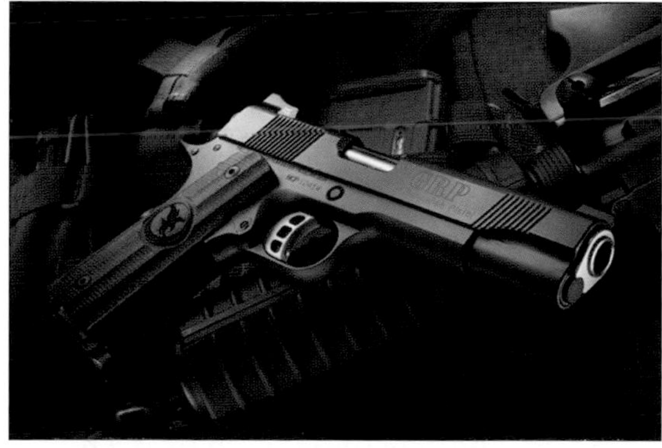

NIGHTHAWK GRP

NIGHTHAWK GRP RECON

NIGHTHAWK TACTICAL ENFORCER

NIGHTHAWK T3

Olympic Arms

(www.olyarms.com)

OLYMPIC ARMS JOURNEYMAN

OLYMPIC ARMS WESTERNER

OLYMPIC ARMS STREET DEUCE

OLYMPIC ARMS CONSTABLE

JOURNEYMAN

Action: Autoloader, SA
Overall Length: 7.8 in.
Overall Height: 5.5 in.
Overall Width: 1.3 in.
Barrel: 4 in.
Grips: Checkered double-diamond walnut
Sights: Dovetail front/adj. rear
Weight Unloaded: 35 oz.
Caliber: .45 ACP
Capacity: 7 + 1
Features: Colt 1911 design; steel frame; extended thumb, beavertail grip safeties; lowered/flared ejection port; two-tone finish
MSRP: $1299

STREET DEUCE

Action: Autoloader, SA
Overall Length: 8.8 in.
Overall Height: 5.5 in.
Overall Width: 1.3 in.
Barrel: 5.2 in.
Grips: Checkered double-diamond walnut
Sights: Dovetail front/adj. rear
Weight Unloaded: 38 oz.
Caliber: .45 ACP
Capacity: 7 + 1
Features: Colt 1911 design; steel frame; extended thumb, beavertail grip safeties; lowered/flared ejection port; two-tone finish
MSRP: $1294

WESTERNER

Action: Autoloader, SA
Overall Length: 8.8 in.
Overall Height: 5.5 in.
Overall Width: 1.3 in.
Barrel: 5 in.
Grips: Smooth ivory polymer
Sights: Dovetail front/adj. rear
Weight Unloaded: 39 oz.
Caliber: .45 ACP
Capacity: 7 + 1
Features: Colt 1911 design; steel frame; extended thumb, beavertail grip safeties; lowered/flared ejection port; case hardened finish
MSRP: $1039

CONSTABLE

Action: Autoloader, SA
Overall Length: 7.8 in.
Overall Height: 5.5 in.
Overall Width: 1.3 in.
Barrel: 4 in.
Grips: Smooth ivory polymer
Sights: Dovetail front/adj. rear
Weight Unloaded: 35 oz.
Caliber: .45 ACP
Capacity: 7 + 1
Features: Colt 1911 design; steel frame; extended thumb, beavertail grip safeties; lowered/flared ejection port; case hardened finish
MSRP: $1164

Para USA

(www.paraord.com)

PARA WARTHOG

PARA P14-45

PARA PXT LDA PDA

PARA PXT LDA CARRY SAFE

WARTHOG

Action: Autoloader, SA
Overall Length: 6.8 in.
Overall Height: 4.8 in. (Slim Hawg), 4.5 in., 5 in. (Hawg 7)
Overall Width: 1.3 in.
Barrel: 3 in.
Grips: Checkered polymer
Sights: Dovetail front/rear, 3-dot
Weight Unloaded: 24 oz., 31 oz. (Warthog stainless), 32 oz. (Hawg 7)
Caliber: .45 ACP
Capacity: 6 + 1 (.45 ACP, Slim Hawg), 7 + 1 (.45 ACP, Hawg 7), 10 + 1 (.45 ACP)
Features: Colt 1911 design; alloy or stainless frame; thumb, beavertail grip safeties; lowered/flared ejection port; magazine bumper pad; Griptor grasping grooves (Hawg 7); matte black or stainless finishes
Slim Hawg: $999
Warthog: $999
Warthog stainless: $1099
Hawg 7: $919

P14-45

Action: Autoloader, SA
Overall Length: 8.5 in.
Overall Height: 5.8 in.
Overall Width: 1.4 in.
Barrel: 5 in.
Grips: Checkered polymer
Sights: Dovetail front/rear, 3-dot
Weight Unloaded: 40 oz.
Caliber: .45 ACP
Capacity: 14 + 1
Features: Colt 1911 design; alloy frame; thumb, beavertail grip safeties; lowered/flared ejection port; magazine bumper pad
Matte black: $919
Stainless: $1159

PXT

Action: Autoloader, SA
Overall Length: 8.5 in.
Overall Height: 5.8 in.
Overall Width: 1.4 in.
Barrel: 5.5 in.
Grips: Checkered wood or polymer
Sights: Dovetail front/rear, 3-dot
Weight Unloaded: 39 oz., 40 oz. (14-45 Limited, 16-40 Limited)
Caliber: 9mm, .40 S&W, .45 ACP
Capacity: 8 + 1 (.45 ACP, 1911 Limited), 18 + 1 (9mm), 16 + 1 (.40 S&W), 10 + 1 (.45 ACP)
Features: Colt 1911 design; alloy frame; thumb, beavertail grip safeties; lowered/flared ejection port; magazine bumper pad
1911 Limited: $1289
14-45 Limited: $1289
16-40 Limited: $1289
18-9 Limited: $1289

PXT LIGHT DOUBLE ACTION (LDA) CARRY SAFE

Action: Autoloader, DAO
Overall Length: 6.5 in., 7.1 in. (Companion), 7.8 in. (Companion II)
Overall Height: 4.8 in., 5 in. (Companion), 5.1 in. (Companion II)
Overall Width: 1.4 in.
Barrel: 3 in.
Grips: Checkered wood or polymer
Sights: Dovetail front/rear, 3-dot
Weight Unloaded: 23 oz. (9mm, PDA), 24 oz. (Carry 9, PDA .45 ACP), 24 oz. (9mm), 30 oz. (Carry), 32 oz. (Companion), 35 oz. (Companion II)
Caliber: 9mm, .45 ACP
Capacity: 8 + 1 (9mm), 6 + 1 (.45 ACP, Carry, PDA), 7 + 1 (Companion), 8 + 1 (Companion II)

PARA PXT LDA COMPANION II

PARA PXT TACTICAL LTC

PARA PXT TACTICAL 14-45

Para USA

(www.paraord.com)

Features: Colt 1911 design; LDA (Light Double Action) trigger; spurless hammer; stainless frame; thumb, beavertail grip safeties; lowered/flared ejection port; magazine bumper pad; Griptor grooved front grip strap; matte black or matte stainless finishes
Carry: $1169
PDA *(.45 ACP)*: $1299
Carry 9: $999
PDA *(9mm)*: $1249
Companion: $999
Companion II: $899

PARA GI EXPERT WILD BUNCH

PXT TACTICAL

Action: Autoloader, SA
Overall Length: 7.8 in. (LTC Tactical), 8.5 in. (14-45 Tactical)
Overall Height: 4.3 in. (LTC Tactical), 5 in. (14-45 Tactical)
Overall Width: 1.4 in.
Barrel: 4.3 in. (LTC Tactical), 5 in. (14-45 Tactical)
Grips: Textured wood
Sights: Dovetail front/adj. rear
Weight Unloaded: 36 oz. (LTC Tactical), 42 oz. (14-45 Tactical)
Caliber: .45 ACP
Capacity: 8 + 1 (LTC Tactical), 14 + 1 (14-45 Tactical)
Features: Colt 1911 design; alloy frame; ambidextrous extend thumb, beavertail grip safeties; lowered/flared ejection port; magazine bumper pad; checkered front/rear grip strap; Picatinny rail; matte black finish
LTC Tactical: $1599
14-45 Tactical: $1599

PARA GI EXPERT

GI EXPERT

Action: Autoloader, SA
Overall Length: 7.8 in. (GI LTC), 8.5 in. (GI Expert, 1911 Wild Bunch)
Overall Height: 5.8 in.
Overall Width: 1.4 in.
Barrel: 4.3 in. (GI LTC), 5 in. (GI Expert, 1911 Wild Bunch)
Grips: Double diamond checkered cocobolo (GI LTC, 1911 Wild Bunch), checkered polymer (GI Expert)
Sights: Dovetail front/rear, 3-dot
Weight Unloaded: 28 oz. (GI LTC), 39 oz. (GI Expert, 1911 Wild Bunch)
Caliber: .45 ACP
Capacity: 8 + 1
Features: Colt 1911 design; steel frame; alloy frame (GI LTC); thumb, grip safeties; lowered/flared ejection port; magazine bumper pad; black or stainless finishes
GI EXPERT LTC: $849
GI Expert: $659
GI Expert *(stainless)*: $749
Wild Bunch: $789

PARA GI EXPERT LTC

PXT 1911

Action: Autoloader, SA
Overall Length: 7.8 in. (LTC), 8.5 in. (SSP)
Overall Height: 5.8 in.
Overall Width: 1.4 in.
Barrel: 4.3 in. (LTC), 5 in. (SSP)
Grips: Checkered cocobolo
Sights: Dovetail fiber optic front/rear, 3-dot
Weight Unloaded: 35 oz. (LTC), 39 oz. (SSP)
Caliber: .45 ACP
Capacity: 8 + 1
Features: Colt 1911 design; steel frame; thumb, grip safeties; lowered/flared ejection port; magazine bumper pad
LTC: $999
SSP: $999

PARA WARTHOG SLIM HAWG

PARA WARTHOG HAWG 7

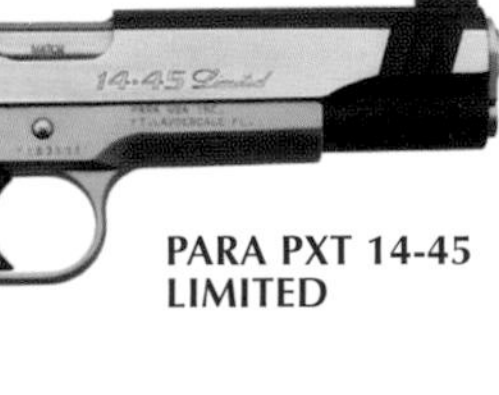

PARA PXT 14-45 LIMITED

Precision Small Arms

(www.precisionsmallarms.com)

PSA-25

Action: Autoloader, striker-fired
Overall Length: 4.1 in.
Overall Height: 2.9 in.
Overall Width: .9 in.
Barrel: 2.1 in.
Grips: Checkered polymer
Sights: Fixed front/rear
Weight Unloaded: 9.7 oz.
Caliber: .25 ACP
Capacity: 6 + 1
Features: "Baby Browning" design; steel frame; magazine butt release; loaded-chamber indicator; magazine disconnect, thumb safeties; numerous deluxe finishes
Blue: $525
Matte nickel: $555
Bright nickel: $555
Stainless: $590
FeatherWeight (aluminum frame): $1000

PTR-91

(www.ptr91.com)

PTR-32 PDW

PTR-91 PDW

PTR-32 PERSONAL DEFENSE WEAPON (PDW)

Action: Autoloader, SA
Overall Length: 23.5 in.
Barrel: 8.1 in.
Grips: Polymer, steel handguard
Sights: Fixed front/adj. rear
Weight Unloaded: 7 lbs.-8 oz.
Caliber: 7.62x39mm
Capacity: 30 + 1
Features: H&K G3 design; steel receiver; thumb manual safety; flash hider; aluminum hand guard; machined butt cap; matte black finish
MSRP: $999

PTR-91 PERSONAL DEFENSE WEAPON (PDW)

Action: Autoloader, SA
Overall Length: 23.5 in.
Barrel: 8.1 in.
Grips: Polymer, steel handguard
Sights: Fixed front/adj. rear
Weight Unloaded: 7 lbs.-8 oz.
Caliber: .308
Capacity: 20 + 1
Features: H&K G3 design; steel receiver; thumb manual safety; flash hider; aluminum hand guard; machined butt cap; matte black finish
MSRP: $999

Remington

(www.remington.com)

REMINGTON MODEL 1911 R1

MODEL 1911 R1

Action: Autoloader, SA
Overall Length: 8.5 in.
Overall Height: 5.5 in.
Overall Width: 1.3 in.
Barrel: 5 in.
Grips: Checkered double-diamond walnut
Sights: Dovetail front/rear, 3-dot
Weight Unloaded: 38.5 oz.
Caliber: .45 ACP
Capacity: 7 + 1
Features: Colt 1911 design; steel frame; thumb, grip safeties; lowered/ flared ejection port, blue finish
MSRP: $692

Rohrbaugh Firearms

(www.rohrbaughfirearms.com)

ROHRBAUGH R9 and R9S

Action: Autoloader, DAO
Overall Length: 5.2 in.
Overall Height: 3.7 in.
Overall Width: .95 in.
Barrel: 2.9 in.
Grips: Polymer
Sights: None (R9), fixed front and rear (R9s)
Weight Unloaded: 13.5 oz.
Caliber: 9mm
Capacity: 6 + 1
Features: Stainless steel slide; aluminum alloy frame; butt-style magazine release; loaded-chamber indicator; two-tone, matte black Titan Kote C12, matte grey NP3 finishes (R9s), black (R9)
MSRP: $1195

ROHRBAUGH 380S

ROHRBAUGH R9

Rohrbaugh Firearms

(www.rohrbaughfirearms.com)

ROHRBAUGH 380

ROHRBAUGH 380 and 380S

Action: Autoloader, DA
Overall Length: 5.2 in.
Overall Height: 3.7 in.
Overall Width: .95 in.
Barrel: 2.9 in.
Grips: Polymer
Sights: None (380), fixed front and rear (380s)
Weight Unloaded: 13.5 oz.
Caliber: 380
Capacity: 6 + 1
Features: Stainless steel slide; aluminum alloy frame; butt-style magazine release; loaded-chamber indicator; two-tone or matte black Titan Kote C12 finishes
MSRP: $1195

Rossi

(www.rossiusa.com)

MODEL R97104

Action: Revolver, SA/DA
Barrel: 4 in.
Grips: Checkered black rubber with finger grooves
Sights: Fixed, front ramp, adj. rear
Weight Unloaded: 32 oz.
Caliber: .357 Mag.
Capacity: 6
Features: Underlug barrel; blue finish
MSRP: $452

MODEL R85104

Action: Revolver, SA/DA
Barrel: 4 in.
Grips: Checkered black rubber with finger grooves
Sights: Fixed, front ramp, adj. rear
Weight Unloaded: 32 oz.
Caliber: .38 Spl. +P
Capacity: 6
Features: Underlug barrel; vent rib; blue finish
MSRP: $389

ROSSI MODEL R35202 (BRIGHT STAINLESS)

MODEL R46202 and R46102

Action: Revolver, SA/DA
Overall Length: 6.7 in.
Overall Height: 4.8 in.
Overall Width: 1.5 in.
Barrel: 2 in.
Grips: Textured black rubber with finger grooves

HANDGUNS

Rossi

(www.rossiusa.com)

Sights: Fixed, front ramp/groove rear
Weight Unloaded: 26 oz.
Caliber: .357 Mag.
Capacity: 6
Features: Forged frame
R46202 *(bright stainless)*: $452
R46102 *(blue)*: $389

ROSSI MODEL R35102 (BLUE)

MODEL R35202 and R35102

Action: Revolver, SA/DA
Barrel: 2 in.
Grips: Textured black rubber with finger grooves
Sights: Fixed, front ramp/groove rear
Weight Unloaded: 24 oz.
Caliber: .38 Spl. +P
Capacity: 5
Features: Forged frame
R35202 *(bright stainless)*: $452
R35102 *(blue)*: $389

Seecamp

(www.seecamp.com)

SEECAMP LWS .380

LWS .32 and LWS .380

Action: Autoloader, DAO
Overall Length: 4.3 in.
Overall Height: 3.3 in.
Overall Width: .9 in.
Barrel: 2.1 in.
Grips: Checkered polymer
Sights: None
Weight Unloaded: 13.3 oz. (.32 ACP), 13.7 oz. (.380)
Caliber: .32 ACP; .380
Capacity: 6 + 1
Features: Stainless frame; recommend ammo for LWS .32 is Win. Silvertips, Win. 71 gr. FMJ, Hornady 60 gr. SJH/XTP, Speer Gold Dot, or Federal Hydra Shoks
LWS .32: $446
LWS .32 California Edition *(thumb safety)*: $525
LWS .380: $795

SEECAMP LWS .32

Sig Sauer

(www.sigsauer.com)

SIG SAUER P238
TWO-TONE
BLACKWOOD GRIPS

P238

Action: Autoloader, SA
Overall Length: 5.5 in.
Overall Height: 3.9 in.
Overall Width: 1.1 in.
Barrel: 2.7 in.
Grips: Fluted polymer
Sights: Dovetail front/rear, night sights
Weight Unloaded: 15.2 oz.
Caliber: .380
Capacity: 6 + 1
Features: Alloy beavertail frame; thumb safety
Two-tone *(matte black frame/stainless slide)*: $643
Two-tone Blackwood Grips *(matte black frame/stainless slide, checkered blackwood grips)*: $699
Nitron *(matte black)*: $629
Nitron Rosewood Grips *(matte black, checkered rosewood grips)*: $699
Rainbow Titanium Finish *(Rainbow Titanium slide/controls)*: $699
Equinox *(two-tone slide, matte black frame, checkered wood grips)*: $699
HD *(matte stainless finish, checkered laminate grips)*: $719
Tactical Laser *(matte black frame/stainless slide, checkered aluminum grips, integrated laser sight grip)*: $749

SIG SAUER
P250 TACTICAL

SAS *(matte black frame/stainless slide, rounded/blended edges, checkered wood grips)*: $735

P250

Action: Autoloader, DAO
Overall Length: 8 in.
Overall Height: 5.5 in.
Overall Width: 1.4 in.
Barrel: 4.7 in.

SIG SAUER P250
DIGITAL CAMO

Grips: Textured polymer, modular
Sights: Dovetail front/rear, night sights
Weight Unloaded: 29.4 oz.
Caliber: 9mm, .357 SIG, .40 S&W, .45 ACP
Capacity: 17 + 1(9mm), 14 + 1(.357 SIG, .40 S&W), 10 + 1(.45 ACP)
Features: Polymer frame; interchangeable calibers; full dust cover; Picatinny rail; serrated combat trigger guard; textured front/rear grip straps

SIG SAUER
P250

Nitron matte black finish: $640
Nitron matte black finish *(.45 ACP)*: $712
Two-tone *(matte black frame/stainless slide, 9mm, .40 S&W)*: $655

P250 COMPACT

Action: Autoloader, DAO
Overall Length: 7.2 in.
Overall Height: 5.1 in.
Overall Width: 1.3 in.
Barrel: 3.9 in.
Grips: Textured polymer, modular
Sights: Dovetail front/rear, night sights
Weight Unloaded: 25.1 oz. (9mm), 26.9 oz. (.45 ACP)
Caliber: 9mm, .357 SIG, .40 S&W, .45 ACP
Capacity: 15 + 1(9mm), 13 + 1(.357 SIG, .40 S&W), 9 + 1(.45 ACP)
Features: Polymer frame; interchangeable calibers; full dust cover; Picatinny rail; serrated combat trigger guard; textured front/rear grip straps
Nitron matte black: $640
Nitron matte black *(.45 ACP)*: $712
Two-tone *(matte black frame/stainless slide, 9mm, .40 S&W)*: $655

SIG SAUER P250
COMPACT

P250 SUBCOMPACT

Action: Autoloader, DAO
Overall Length: 6.7 in.
Overall Height: 4.7 in.
Overall Width: 1.1 in.
Barrel: 3.6 in.
Grips: Textured polymer
Sights: Dovetail front/rear, night sights
Weight Unloaded: 24.9 oz.
Caliber: 9mm, .357 SIG, .40 S&W, .45 ACP
Capacity: 12 + 1(9mm), 10 + 1(.357 SIG, .40 S&W), 6 + 1(.45 ACP)
Features: Polymer frame; interchangeable calibers; full dust cover; textured front/rear grip straps
Nitron matte black: $640
Nitron matte black *(.45 ACP)*: $712
Two-tone *(matte black frame/stainless slide, 9mm, .40 S&W)*: $655

Sig Sauer

(www.sigsauer.com)

SIG SAUER P556

SIG SAUER 220 COMBAT TB

SIG SAUER P220 CARRY

SIG SAUER P220 CARRY GEN2 45

SIG SAUER P220 TWO-TONE SAO

P556

Action: Autoloader, SA
Overall Length: 20.5 in.
Barrel: 10 in.
Grips: Grooved polymer grip/ handguard
Sights: Mini red dot, flip up adj. front/ adj. rear
Weight Unloaded: 6.3 lbs.
Caliber: 5.56 x 45mm NATO/.223 Rem.
Capacity: 30 + 1
Features: AR-15 design; full-length gas piston; A2 style muzzle devise; threaded muzzle; matte black finish
MSRP: $1876
SWAT *(aluminum Picatinny quad-rail handguard, 6.7 lbs)*: $2023

P220

Action: Autoloader, SA/DA
Overall Length: 7.7 in.
Overall Height: 5.5 in.
Overall Width: 1.5 in.
Barrel: 4.4 in.
Grips: Textured polymer
Sights: Dovetail front/rear, 3-dot
Weight Unloaded: 30.4 oz.
Caliber: .45 ACP
Capacity: 8 + 1
Features: Alloy frame; Picatinny rail; serrated combat trigger guard, front/rear grip straps; thumb and decocking safeties; magazine bumper pad
Nitron matte black: $976
Nitron matte black *(night sights)*: $1050
SAO *(Nitron matte black, SAO, night sights, ambidextrous thumb safety)*: $1050
Two-tone *(matte black frame/ stainless slide)*: $1110
SAO two-tone *(matte black frame/ stainless slide, SAO, night sights, ambidextrous thumb safety)*: $1050
DAK (DAO): $853
Equinox *(two-tone slide/matte black frame, checkered wood grips)*: $1200
Elite *(Nitron matte black, beavertail frame, textured rosewood grips, night sights)*: $1200
Elite stainless *(matte stainless, beavertail frame, textured rosewood grips, night sights)*: $1350
Platinum Elite *(matte black frame/ stainless slide, beavertail frame, checkered aluminum grips, night sights)*: $1405
Elite Dark *(Nitron matte black, beavertail frame, checkered aluminum grips, night sights, short reset trigger, checkered front/rear grip strap)*: $1306
Elite Dark TB *(Nitron matte black, beavertail frame, checkered aluminum grips, night sights, short reset trigger, checkered front/back grip strap, 5 in. threaded barrel)*: $1200
Combat *(flat dark earth frame/matte black slide, night sights, checkered front/back grip strap)*: $1200
Combat TB *(flat dark earth frame/ matte black slide, night sights, checkered front/back grip strap, 5 in. threaded barrel)*: $1350

P220 CARRY

Action: Autoloader, single/DA
Overall Length: 7.1 in.
Overall Height: 5.5 in.
Overall Width: 1.5 in.
Barrel: 3.9 in.

SIG SAUER P250 SUBCOMPACT

Sig Sauer

(www.sigsauer.com)

SIG SAUER P220R COMPACT

SIG SAUER P226 ELITE STAINLESS

SIG SAUER 226 DAK

Grips: Textured polymer
Sights: Dovetail front/rear, 3-dot
Weight Unloaded: 30.4 oz.
Caliber: .45 ACP
Capacity: 8 + 1
Features: Alloy frame; Picatinny rail; serrated combat trigger guard, front/rear grip straps; thumb and decocking safeties; magazine bumper pad
Nitron matte black finish: $976
Nitron matte black finish *(night sights)*: $1050
Carry SAO *(nitron matte black finish, SA only, night sights, ambidextrous thumb safety)*: $1029
Carry two-tone *(matte black frame/stainless slide)*: $1110
Carry two-tone SAO *(matte black frame/stainless slide, SA only, night sights, ambidextrous thumb safety)*: $1086
Carry DAK *(DAO, bobbed hammer)*: $1070
Carry two-tone DAK *(matte black frame/stainless slide, DAO, bobbed hammer)*: $907
Carry two-tone DAK *(matte black frame/stainless slide, DAO, bobbed hammer, night sights)*: $973
Carry Equinox *(two-tone slide, matte black frame, checkered wood grips)*: $1200
Carry Elite *(Nitron matte black finish, beavertail frame, textured rosewood grips, night sights)*: $1200
Carry Elite stainless *(matte stainless finish, beavertail frame, textured rosewood grips, night sights)*: $1350
Carry Elite SAO *(SA only, Nitron matte black finish, beavertail frame, textured rosewood grips, night sights)*: $1107
Carry SAS Gen 2 *(rounded/beveled edges, night sights, textured polymer grips, Nitron matte black finish)*: $1049
Carry SAS Gen 2 two-tone *(rounded/beveled edges, night sights, textured polymer grips, matte black frame/stainless slide)*: $1126
Elite Dark *(Nitron matte black finish, beavertail frame, checkered aluminum grips, night sights, short reset trigger, checkered front/rear grip strap)*: $1200

P220R COMPACT

Action: Autoloader, SA/DA
Overall Length: 7.1 in.
Overall Height: 5 in.
Overall Width: 1.5 in.
Barrel: 3.9 in.
Grips: Textured polymer
Sights: Dovetail front/rear, night sight
Weight Unloaded: 29.6 oz.
Caliber: .45 ACP
Capacity: 6 + 1
Features: Alloy frame; Picatinny rail; serrated combat trigger guard, front/rear grip straps; thumb and decocking safeties; magazine bumper pad
Nitron matte black: $1050
Compact SAS Gen 2 *(rounded/beveled edges, Nitron matte black)*: $1095
Carry SAS Gen 2 two-tone *(rounded/beveled edges, matte black frame/stainless slide)*: $1125

HANDGUNS

SIG SAUER P226 NAVY

SIG SAUER P226 SCT

SIG SAUER P226 COMBAT

Sig Sauer

(www.sigsauer.com)

P226 X-FIVE TACTICAL

Action: Autoloader, SA/DA
Overall Length: 8.8 in.
Overall Height: 5.7 in.
Overall Width: 1.6 in.
Barrel: 5 in.
Grips: Textured polymer
Sights: Dovetail front/rear, night sights
Weight Unloaded: 35.5 oz.
Caliber: 9mm
Capacity: 15 + 1
Features: Alloy beavertail frame; decocking lever safety; Picatinny rail; serrated combat trigger guard; textured front/rear grip straps; Nitron matte black finish
MSRP: $1800

SIG SAUER P226 X-FIVE TACTICAL

P226 X-FIVE ALLROUND

Action: Autoloader, SA/DA
Overall Length: 8.8 in.

SIG SAUER P229 ELITE DARK

Overall Height: 5.6 in.
Overall Width: 1.6 in.
Barrel: 5 in.
Grips: Textured polymer
Sights: Dovetail front/rear, night sights
Weight Unloaded: 45 oz.
Caliber: 9mm, .40 S&W
Capacity: 17 + 1 (9mm), 12 + 1 (.40 S&W)
Features: Stainless beavertail frame; decocking lever safety; Picatinny rail; serrated combat trigger guard; textured front/rear grip straps
MSRP: $1800

P226

Action: Autoloader, SA/DA
Overall Length: 7.7 in.
Overall Height: 5.5 in.
Overall Width: 1.5 in.
Barrel: 4.4 in.
Grips: Textured polymer
Sights: Dovetail front/rear, 3-dot

SIG SAUER P226 X-5 ALLROUND

Weight Unloaded: 34 oz.
Caliber: 9mm, .357 SIG, .40 S&W
Capacity: 15 + 1(9mm), 12 + 1(.357 SIG, .40 S&W)
Features: Alloy frame; Picatinny rail; serrated combat trigger guard; textured front/rear grip straps; decocking lever safety
Nitron matte black: $976
Nitron matte black *(night sights)*: $1050

SIG SAUER P229 TWO-TONE

SIG SAUER P229 EQUINOX

Two-tone *(matte black frame/stainless slide, 9mm, .40 S&W)*: $1110
DAK *(DAO, bobbed hammer)*: $900
Equinox *(two-tone slide/matte black frame, checkered wood grips, .40 S&W)*: $1200
Elite Dark *(Nitron matte black, beavertail frame, textured rosewood grips, night sights, 9mm, .40 S&W)*: $1200
Elite stainless *(matte stainless, beavertail frame, textured rosewood grips, night sights, 9mm, .40 S&W)*: $1350
Navy *(U.S. Navy Seal version, Nitron matte black)*: $1020
SCT *(extra capacity magazine, Nitron matte black)*: $1156
Platinum Elite *(matte black frame/stainless slide, beavertail frame, checkered aluminum grips, night*

SIG SAUER P229 SCT

sights, 9mm, .40 S&W): $1276
Elite Dark *(Nitron matte black, beavertail frame, checkered aluminum grips, night sights, short reset trigger, checkered front/rear grip strap)*: $1200
Elite Dark TB *(Nitron matte black, beavertail frame, checkered aluminum grips, night sights, short reset trigger, checkered front/back grip strap, 4.9 in. threaded barrel, 9mm)*: $1306
Combat *(flat dark earth frame/matte black slide, night sights, checkered front/back grip strap, 9mm)*: $1199
Combat TB *(flat dark earth frame/matte black slide, night sights, checkered front/back grip strap, 5 in. threaded barrel, 9mm)*: $1349

HANDGUNS

Sig Sauer

(www.sigsauer.com)

SIG SAUER P229 SAS GEN-2

SIG SAUER P2022

SIG SAUER P239 SAS GEN 2

SIG SAUER P239 TACTICAL

SIG SAUER 239 DAK

SIG SAUER 229 DAK

E2 *(contoured screwless grips, Nitron matte black, night sights, 9mm)*: $1149
Enhanced Elite *(contoured screwless grips, Nitron matte black, night sights, 9mm, .40 S&W)*: $1200
Tactical Operations *(extended magazine capacity, magazine well grips)*: $1300

P229

Action: Autoloader, SA/DA
Overall Length: 7.1 in.
Overall Height: 5.4 in.
Overall Width: 1.5 in.
Barrel: 3.9 in.
Grips: Textured polymer
Sights: Dovetail front/rear, 3-dot
Weight Unloaded: 32 oz.
Caliber: 9mm, .357 SIG, .40 S&W
Capacity: 13 + 1(9mm), 12 + 1(.357 SIG, .40 S&W)
Features: Alloy frame; Picatinny rail; serrated combat trigger guard; textured front/rear grip straps; decocking lever safety
Nitron matte black: $976
Nitron matte black *(night sights)*: $1050
Two-tone *(matte black frame/stainless slide, 9mm, .40 S&W)*: $1110
DAK *(DAO, bobbed hammer)*: $853
DAK *(DAO, bobbed hammer, night sights)*: $920
Equinox *(two-tone slide/ matte black frame, checkered wood grips, .40 S&W)*: $1200
Elite *(Nitron matte black, beavertail frame, textured rosewood grips, night sights, 9mm, .40 S&W)*: $1200
Elite stainless *(matte stainless, beavertail frame, textured rosewood grips, night sights, 9mm, .40 S&W)*: $1350
SCT *(extra capacity magazine, Nitron matte black)*: $1156

SIG SAUER P266 PLATINUM ELITE

Platinum Elite *(matte black frame/stainless slide, beavertail frame, checkered aluminum grips, night sights, 9mm, .40 S&W)*: $1276
Elite Dark *(Nitron matte black, beavertail frame, checkered aluminum grips, night sights, short reset trigger, checkered front/rear grip strap)*: $1200
Elite Dark TB *(Nitron matte black, beavertail frame, checkered aluminum grips, night sights, short reset trigger, checkered front/back grip strap, 4.4 in. threaded barrel, 9mm)*: $1306
E2 *(contoured screwless grips, Nitron matte black, night sights, 9mm)*: $1149
SAS Gen 2 *(rounded/beveled edges, night sights, Nitron matte black)*: $1096
SAS Gen 2 two-tone *(rounded/ beveled edges, night sights, matte black frame/stainless slide)*: $1126

SP2022

Action: Autoloader, SA/DA
Overall Length: 7.4 in.
Overall Height: 5.7 in.
Overall Width: 1.4 in.
Barrel: 3.9 in.
Grips: Textured polymer
Sights: Dovetail front/rear, night sights
Weight Unloaded: 29 oz.
Caliber: 9mm, .357 SIG, .40 S&W
Capacity: 15 + 1(9mm), 12 + 1(.357 SIG, .40 S&W)
Features: Polymer frame; Picatinny rail; serrated combat trigger guard; textured front/rear grip straps; Nitron matte black finish; decocking lever safety
MSRP: $720

Sig Sauer

(www.sigsauer.com)

SIG SAUER 1911 STX

SIG SAUER 1911 XO BLACK

SIG SAUER 1911 TACTICAL OPERTATIONS

SIG SAUER P232 STAINLESS

P239

Action: Autoloader, SA/DA
Overall Length: 6.6 in.
Overall Height: 5.1 in.
Overall Width: 1.2 in.
Barrel: 3.6 in.
Grips: Textured polymer
Sights: Dovetail front/rear, 3-dot
Weight Unloaded: 29.5 oz.
Caliber: 9mm, .357 SIG, .40 S&W
Capacity: 8 + 1(9mm), 7 + 1(.357 SIG, .40 S&W)
Features: Alloy frame; texture front/rear grip straps; decocking lever safety
Nitron matte black: $840
Nitron matte black *(night sights)*: $916
DAK *(DAO, bobbed hammer)*: $823
Tactical *(Nitron matte black, night sights, short reset trigger, 4 in. threaded barrel, 9mm, checkered front/rear grip straps)*: $976
SAS Gen 2 *(rounded/beveled edges, night sights, Nitron matte black)*: $1006
SAS Gen 2 two-tone *(rounded/beveled edges, night sights, matte black frame/stainless slide)*: $1050

P232

Action: Autoloader, SA/DA
Overall Length: 6.6 in.
Overall Height: 4.7 in.
Overall Width: 1.2 in.
Barrel: 3.6 in.
Grips: Textured polymer
Sights: Dovetail front/rear, night sights
Weight Unloaded: 17.6 oz.
Caliber: .380
Capacity: 7 + 1
Features: Alloy frame; decocking lever safety
Nitron matte black: $720
Two-tone *(matte black frame/stainless slide)*: $826
Stainless *(stainless frame/stainless slide, Hogue rubber grips)*: $900

1911

Action: Autoloader, SA
Overall Length: 8.7 in.
Overall Height: 5.5 in.
Overall Width: 1.4 in.
Barrel: 5 in.
Grips: Checkered wood
Sights: Fixed dovetail front/rear, Novak style
Weight Unloaded: 41.6 oz.
Caliber: .45 ACP
Capacity: 8 + 1
Features: Colt 1911 design; steel frame; extended thumb, beavertail grip safeties; lowered/flared ejection port; beveled magazine well; magazine base pad; external extractor; textured front/rear grip straps
Stainless: $1170
Nitron Rail *(Nitron matte black, Picatinny rail)*: $1200
XO black *(Nitron matte black, textured grips)*: $1006
STX *(stainless frame/matte black slide, burled maple grips)*: $1456
Platinum Elite *(matte black frame/stainless slide, aluminum grips)*: $1276
Tactical Operations *(Nitron matte black, Picatinny rail, ambidextrous safety, magazine well, textured grips)*: $1290

1911 CARRY

Action: Autoloader, SA
Overall Length: 7.7 in.
Overall Height: 5.5 in.
Overall Width: 1.4 in.
Barrel: 4.2 in.
Grips: Checkered rosewood
Sights: Fixed dovetail front/rear, Novak style
Weight Unloaded: 38.8 oz.
Caliber: .45 ACP
Capacity: 8 + 1
Features: Colt 1911 design; steel frame; extended thumb, beavertail grip safeties; lowered/flared ejection port; beveled magazine well; magazine base pad; external extractor; texture front/rear grip straps
Stainless: $1170
Nitron matte black: $1200

Sig Sauer

(www.sigsauer.com)

SIG SAUER 1911 COMPACT RCS

SIG SAUER 1911 CARRY STAINLESS

1911 COMPACT

Action: Autoloader, SA
Overall Length: 7.7 in.
Overall Height: 4.8 in.
Overall Width: 1.4 in.
Barrel: 4.2 in.
Grips: Checkered diamond@wood
Sights: Fixed dovetail front/rear, Novak style
Weight Unloaded: 30.3 oz.
Caliber: .45 ACP
Capacity: 7 + 1
Features: Colt 1911 design; steel frame; extended thumb, beavertail grip safeties; lowered/flared ejection port; beveled magazine well; external extractor; texture front/rear grip straps
Stainless: $1025
RCS Nitron *(Nitron matte black, rosewood grips)*: $1306
RCS two-Tone *(matte black frame/stainless slide, aluminum grips)*: $1363

SIG SAUER 1911 COMPACT RCS TWO-TONE

CERTIFIED PRE-OWNED

Models: P220, P225, P226, P228, P229, P230, P232, P239, SP2009, SP2340
Features: Trade in by law enforcement agencies; factory certified

Smith & Wesson (S&W)

(www.smith-wesson.com)

S&W SIGMA

S&W SD9

SIGMA

Action: Autoloader, striker-fired
Overall Length: 7.3 in.
Overall Height: 5.6 in.
Overall Width: 1.2 in.
Barrel: 4 in.
Grips: Textured polymer
Sights: Fixed front/dovetail rear, 3-dot
Weight Unloaded: 22.7 oz.
Caliber: 9mm, .40 S&W
Capacity: 16 + 1 (9mm), 14 + 1 (.40 S&W)
Features: Polymer frame; external extractor; textured front/rear grip straps; two-tone black Melonite finish
MSRP: $349

SD9 and SD40

Action: Autoloader, striker-fired
Overall Length: 7.2 in.
Overall Height: 5.3 in.
Overall Width: 1.3 in.
Barrel: 4 in.
Grips: Textured polymer
Sights: Dovetail front/rear, Tritium 3-dot
Weight Unloaded: 22.7 oz.
Caliber: 9mm, .40 S&W
Capacity: 16 + 1 (9mm), 14 + 1 (.40 S&W)
Features: Polymer frame; external extractor; textured front/rear grip straps; Picatinny rail; black Melonite finish
MSRP: $459

Smith & Wesson (S&W)

(www.smith-wesson.com)

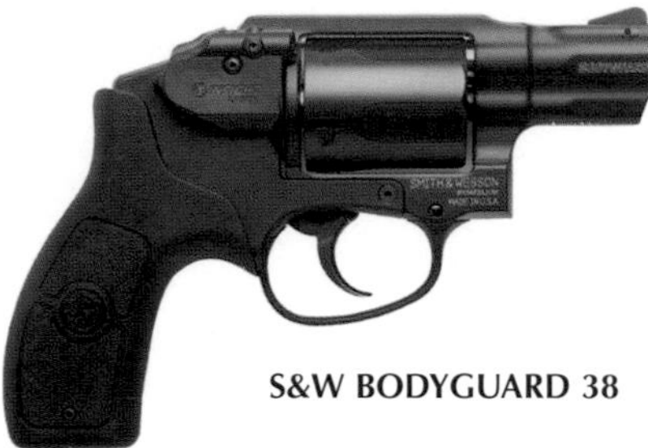

S&W BODYGUARD 38

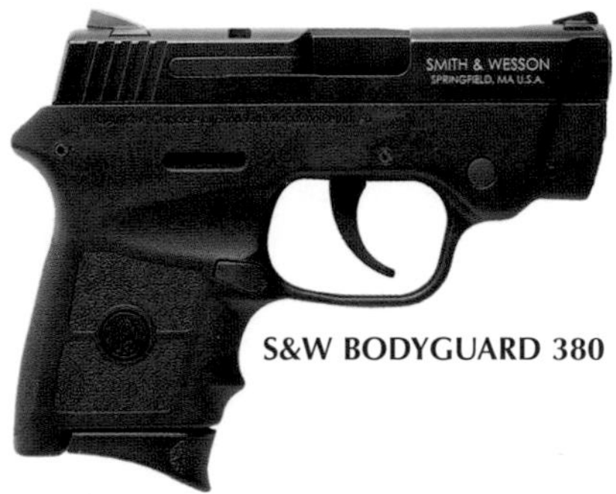

S&W BODYGUARD 380

BODYGUARD 380

Action: Autoloader, DAO
Overall Length: 7.3 in.
Overall Height: 3.9 in.
Overall Width: .9 in.
Barrel: 2.8 in.
Grips: Textured, finger groove polymer
Sights: Dovetail front/rear, Insight laser
Weight Unloaded: 11.9 oz.
Caliber: .380
Capacity: 6 + 1
Features: Polymer frame; ambidextrous laser controls; external extractor; extended finger tab magazine; black Melonite finish
MSRP: $399

M&P45

Action: Autoloader, striker-fired
Overall Length: 7.6 in. (Compact), 8.5 in.
Overall Height: 4.8 in. (Compact), 5.5 in.
Overall Width: 1.2 in.
Barrel: 4 in. (Compact), 4 in., 4.5 in.
Grips: Textured polymer; modular
Sights: Dovetail front/rear, 3-dot
Weight Unloaded: 26.2 oz. (Compact), 29.6 oz.
Caliber: .45 ACP
Capacity: 8 + 1 (Compact), 10 + 1
Features: Polymer frame; 3 interchangeable grip sizes; ambidextrous thumb safety, slide release; external extractor; Picatinny rail; available in various frame/barrel configurations
Black Melonite: $619
Black Melonite *(full-size frame/4 in. barrel)*: $619
Earth frame/black Melonite: $619
Earth frame/black Melonite *(full-size frame/4 in. barrel)*: $619
Compact earth frame/black Melonite: $619
Compact black Melonite: $619
Compact black Melonite *(no thumb safety)*: $599
Black Melonite *(no thumb safety)*: $599
Black Melonite *(no thumb safety, full-size frame/4 in. barrel)*: $599
Black Melonite *(no thumb safety, extra threaded barrel)*: $719
Black Melonite *(no thumb safety, Crimson Trace laser grips)*: $829

S&W M&P45

S&W MODEL 10 CLASSIC

S&W M&P9

M&P9

Action: Autoloader, striker-fired
Overall Length: 6.7 in. (Compact), 8.5 in.
Overall Height: 4.3 in. (Compact), 5.5 in.
Overall Width: 1.2 in.
Barrel: 3.5 in. (Compact), 5 in.
Grips: Textured polymer; modular
Sights: Dovetail front/rear, Novak 3-dot
Weight Unloaded: 21.7 oz. (Compact), 25.2 oz.
Caliber: 9mm
Capacity: 12 + 1 (Compact), 17 + 1
Features: Polymer frame; three interchangeable grip sizes; ambidextrous thumb safety, slide release; external extractor; Picatinny rail; available in various frame/barrel configurations
Black Melonite *(no thumb safety)*: $758
Black Melonite *(full-size frame/4 in. barrel)*: $569
Black Melonite *(no thumb safety, fiber optic front sight)*: $669
Vicking Tactics *(flat dark earth finish, no thumb safety, full-size frame/4 in. barrel), VTCA Warrior sights)*: $779
Compact black Melonite: $569
Compact black Melonite *(no thumb safety)*: $719
Compact black Melonite *(Crimson Trace laser sight grip)*: $809
Black Melonite *(no thumb safety)*: $669
Black Melonite *(no thumb safety, full-size frame/4 in. barrel)*: $569
Black Melonite *(no thumb safety, extra threaded barrel)*: $719
Black Melonite *(no thumb safety, Crimson Trace laser sight grip)*: $809

Smith & Wesson (S&W)

(www.smith-wesson.com)

S&W M&P357 COMPACT

M&P40 and M&P357

Action: Autoloader, striker-fired
Overall Length: 6.7 in. (Compact), 7.6 in.
Overall Height: 4.3 in. (Compact), 5.5 in.
Overall Width: 1.2 in.
Barrel: 3.5 in. (Compact), 4.3 in.
Grips: Textured polymer, modular
Sights: Dovetail front/rear, 3-dot
Weight Unloaded: 21.9 oz. (Compact), 24.3 oz.
Caliber: .40 S&W, .357 SIG
Capacity: 10 + 1 (Compact), 15 + 1
Features: Polymer frame; three interchangeable grip sizes; ambidextrous thumb safety, slide release; external extractor; Picatinny rail; available in various frame/barrel configurations
Black Melonite *(no thumb safety)*: $669
Black Melonite *(.40 S&W, fiber optic front sight, 5 in. barrel, no thumb safety)*: $669
Black Melonite: $569
Vicking Tactics *(.40 S&W, flat dark earth finish, no thumb safety, full-size frame/4 in. barrel), VTCA Warrior **sights**)*: $779
Compact black Melonite: $569
Compact black Melonite *(no thumb safety)*: $569
Compact black Melonite *(no thumb safety, Crimson Trace laser sight grip)*: $809
Black Melonite *(.40 S&W, no thumb safety, Crimson Trace laser sight grip)*: $809

SW1911

Action: Autoloader, SA
Overall Length: 6.5 in. (Sub Compact), 8.7 in.
Overall Height: 5 in. (Sub Compact), 5.5 in.
Overall Width: 1.5 in.
Barrel: 3 in. (Sub Compact), 4.3 in. (Commander configuration), 5 in.
Grips: Checkered hardwood
Sights: Fixed front/dovetail rear, 3-dot
Weight Unloaded: 26.5 oz. (Sub Compact), 30 oz. (Commander configuration), 39 oz.
Caliber: .45 ACP
Capacity: 7 + 1 (Sub Compact), 8 + 1
Features: Colt 1911 design; steel frame; extended thumb, beaver tail grip safeties; lower/flared ejection port; magazine bumper pad; external extractor; loaded-chamber indicator
Compact ES *(extended slide, 7 + 1, two-tone)*: $1139
TFP *(titanium firing pin, black Melonite, synthetic checkered grips)*: $1099
Tactical Rail *(stainless, Picatinny rail)*: $1225
Stainless *(adj. rear sight)*: $1229
Stainless *(synthetic checkered grips)*: $1019
Gunsite Edition *(scandium frame)*: $1229
Stainless *(OD green Crimson Trace laser sight grip)*: $1454
Black Melonite: $1039
Black Melonite *(Picatinny rail)*: $1149
Two-tone: $1379
Commander configuration *(OD green Crimson Trace laser sight grip, 4.3 in. barrel)*: $1349
Commander configuration *(black Melonite finish)*: $1109
Sub Compact *(black Melonite; textured synthetic grips)*: $1109

S&W MODEL SW1911 COMPACT ES

S&W SW1911 SUB COMPACT

S&W SW1911 TFP

S&W SW1911PD COMMANDER CONFIGURATION

S&W SW1911PD GUNSITE EDITION

S&W SW1911TA

Smith & Wesson (S&W)

(www.smith-wesson.com)

S&W MODEL 62

S&W MODEL 64

S&W MODEL 327

M&P360

Action: Revolver, SA/DA
Overall Length: 6.3 in. (1.9 in. barrel), 7.8 in. (3 in. barrel)
Overall Height: 4.2 in.
Overall Width: 1.3 in.
Barrel: 1.9 in., 3 in.
Grips: Textured rubber
Sights: Fixed front/rear, Tritium
Weight Unloaded: 13.3 oz. (1.9 in. barrel), 14.7 oz. (3 in. barrel)
Caliber: .38 Spl. +P/.357 Mag.
Capacity: 5
Features: Scandium J-frame; external hammer; matte black finish
M&P360: $869
M&P360 *(3 in. barrel)*: $980

M&P 38

Action: Revolver, SA/DA
Overall Length: 10.5 in.
Barrel: 5 in.
Grips: Textured rubber
Sights: Fixed interchangeable front/ adj. rear
Weight Unloaded: 36.3 oz.
Caliber: .38 Spl. +P/.357 Mag.
Capacity: 8
Features: Scandium N-frame; external hammer; Picatinny rail; matte black finish
MSRP: $1289

M&P340

Action: Revolver, DAO
Overall Length: 6.3 in.
Overall Height: 4.2 in.
Overall Width: 1.3 in.
Barrel: 1.9 in.
Grips: Textured rubber
Sights: Fixed front/rear, Tritium
Weight Unloaded: 13.3 oz.
Caliber: .38 Spl. +P/.357 Mag.
Capacity: 5
Features: Centennial design; scandium J-frame; internal hammer; matte black finish
M&P340: $869
M&P340 CT *(Crimson Trace laser sight grip)*: $1129

BODYGUARD 38

Action: Revolver, DAO
Overall Length: 6.6 in.
Overall Height: 4.2 in.
Overall Width: 1.3 in.
Barrel: 1.9 in.
Grips: Textured synthetic
Sights: Fixed front/rear, Insight laser
Weight Unloaded: 13.3 oz.
Caliber: .38 Spl. +P
Capacity: 5
Features: Aluminum/polymer/steel J-frame; internal hammer; matte black finish
MSRP: $509

HANDGUNS

S&W MODEL 340PD

S&W MODEL 360

S&W MODEL 627

(www.smith-wesson.com)

S&W MODEL 442

S&W MODEL 625

S&W MODEL 625JM

MODEL 10 CLASSIC

Action: Revolver, SA/DA
Overall Length: 8.9 in.
Overall Height: 5.5 in.
Overall Width: 1.4 in.
Barrel: 4 in.
Grips: Checkered wood
Sights: Fixed ramp front/groove rear
Weight Unloaded: 36 oz.
Caliber: .38 Spl. +P
Capacity: 6
Features: Steel K-frame; external hammer; blue finish
MSRP: $719

MODEL 15 CLASSIC

Action: Revolver, SA/DA
Overall Length: 9.3 in.
Barrel: 4 in.
Grips: Checkered wood
Sights: Fixed ramp front/adj. rear
Weight Unloaded: 37.6 oz.
Caliber: .38 Spl. +P
Capacity: 6
Features: Steel K-frame; external hammer; blue finish
MSRP: $719

MODEL 58 CLASSIC

Action: Revolver, SA/DA
Overall Length: 9.3 in.
Barrel: 4 in.
Grips: Checkered wood
Sights: Fixed ramp front/groove rear
Weight Unloaded: 40.8 oz.
Caliber: .41 Mag.
Capacity: 6
Features: Steel L-frame; external hammer
Bright blue: $969
Nickel: $1146

MODEL 57 CLASSIC

Action: Revolver, SA/DA
Overall Length: 9.5 in.
Barrel: 4 in.
Grips: Checkered walnut square butt
Sights: Fixed red ramp front/adj. rear
Weight Unloaded: 41 oz.
Caliber: .41 Mag.
Capacity: 6
Features: Steel L-frame; external hammer
Bright blue: $1098
Nickel: $1153

MODEL 36 CLASSIC

Action: Revolver, SA/DA
Overall Length: 6.9 in.
Overall Height: 4.4 in.
Overall Width: 1.3 in.
Barrel: 1.9 in.
Grips: Checkered walnut
Sights: Fixed ramp front/groove rear
Weight Unloaded: 19.5 oz.
Caliber: .38 Spl. +P
Capacity: 5
Features: Steel J-frame; small external hammer
Blue: $729
Nickel: $749

S&W MODEL 637 CT

S&W MODEL 638

S&W MODEL 36 CLASSIC

Smith & Wesson (S&W)

(www.smith-wesson.com)

S&W MODEL 27 CLASSIC

S&W M&P9 COMPACT

S&W MODEL 22 CLASSIC

MODEL 42 CLASSIC

Action: Revolver, DAO
Overall Length: 6.5 in.
Overall Width: 1.3 in.
Barrel: 1.9 in.
Grips: Checkered walnut
Sights: Fixed ramp front/groove rear
Weight Unloaded: 14.4 oz. (aluminum frame), 19.5 oz. (steel frame)
Caliber: .38 Spl. +P
Capacity: 5
Features: J-frame; internal hammer; grip safety
Blue: $877
Nickel: $909
Matte black *(aluminum J-frame)*: $861

MODEL 22 CLASSIC

Action: Revolver, SA/DA
Overall Length: 9.3 in.
Barrel: 4 in.
Grips: Checkered Altamont
Sights: Fixed half moon front/groove rear
Weight Unloaded: 36.8 oz.
Caliber: .45 ACP.
Capacity: 6
Features: Steel N-frame; external hammer
Blue: $1090
Model of 1917 *(5.5 in. barrel, lanyard loop, 37.2 oz., blue finish)*: $999

MODEL 27 CLASSIC

Action: Revolver, SA/DA
Overall Length: 9.5 in.
Barrel: 4 in.
Grips: Checkered walnut
Sights: Fixed ramp front/adj. rear
Weight Unloaded: 37 oz.
Caliber: .38 Spl +P/.357 Mag.
Capacity: 6
Features: Steel L-frame; external hammer
Bright blue: $989
Nickel: $1193

MODEL 442

Action: Revolver, DAO
Overall Length: 6.3 in.
Overall Width: 1.3 in.
Barrel: 1.9 in.
Grips: Textured synthetic
Sights: Fixed ramp front/groove rear
Weight Unloaded: 15 oz.
Caliber: .38 Spl. +P
Capacity: 5
Features: Centennial design; aluminum J-frame; internal hammer; matte black finish
Model 442: $449
Model 442 Pro Series *(cylinder cut for moon clips)*: $469

MODEL 340PD

Action: Revolver, DAO
Overall Length: 6.3 in.
Overall Width: 1.3 in.
Barrel: 1.9 in.
Grips: Textured synthetic
Sights: Fixed fiber optic front/groove rear
Weight Unloaded: 11.4 oz.
Caliber: .38 Spl. +P/.357 Mag.
Capacity: 5
Features: Centennial design; scandium J-frame; internal hammer; matte black finish
Model 340PD: $1019
Model 340PD *(fixed red ramp front/groove rear sights)*: $1019

MODEL 360PD

Action: Revolver, SA/DA
Overall Length: 6.3 in.
Overall Height: 4.4 in.
Overall Width: 1.3 in.
Barrel: 1.9 in.
Grips: Textured synthetic
Sights: Fixed fiber optic front/groove rear
Weight Unloaded: 11.4 oz.
Caliber: .38 Spl. +P/.357 Mag.
Capacity: 5
Features: Scandium J-frame; small external hammer; matte black finish
Model 360PD: $1019
Model 360PD *(fixed red ramp front/groove rear sights)*: $988

MODEL 638

Action: Revolver, SA/DA
Overall Length: 6.3 in. (1.9 in. barrel), 7 in. (2.5 in. barrel)
Overall Height: 4.5 in.
Overall Width: 1.3 in.
Barrel: 1.9 in., 2.5 in.
Grips: Textured synthetic
Sights: Fixed ramp front/groove rear
Weight Unloaded: 15.1 oz. (1.9 in. barrel), 16 oz. (2.5 in. barrel)
Caliber: .38 Spl. +P
Capacity: 5
Features: Aluminum J-frame; shrouded hammer; matte silver finish
Model 638: $449
Model 638 CT *(Crimson Trace laser sight grip)*: $669
Model 638 *(2.5 in. barrel)*: $640
Model 638 CT *(Crimson Trace laser sight grip, 2.5 in. barrel)*: $924

S&W MODEL 42 CLASSIC

Smith & Wesson (S&W)

(www.smith-wesson.com)

MODEL 637

Action: Revolver, SA/DA
Overall Length: 6.3 in. (1.9 in. barrel), 7 in. (2.5 in. barrel)
Overall Width: 1.3 in.
Barrel: 1.9 in., 2.5 in.
Grips: Textured synthetic
Sights: Fixed ramp front/groove rear
Weight Unloaded: 15 oz. (1.9 in. barrel), 16 oz. (2.5 in. barrel)
Caliber: .38 Spl. +P
Capacity: 5
Features: Aluminum J-frame; small exposed hammer; matte silver finish
Model 637: $449
Model 637 CT *(Crimson Trace laser sight grip)*: $669
Model 637 *(2.5 in. barrel)*: $640
Model 637 CT *(Crimson Trace laser sight grip, 2.5 in. barrel)*: $924
Model 637 Pro Series *(2.1 in. ported barrel, dovetail front/groove rear sights)*: $758

MODEL 642

Action: Revolver, SA/DA
Overall Length: 6.3 in. (1.9 in. barrel), 7 in. (2.5 in. barrel)
Overall Width: 1.3 in.
Barrel: 1.9 in., 2.5 in.
Grips: Textured synthetic
Sights: Fixed ramp front/groove rear
Weight Unloaded: 15 oz. (1.9 in. barrel), 16 oz. (2.5 in. barrel)
Caliber: .38 Spl. +P
Capacity: 5
Features: Centennial design; aluminum J-frame; internal hammer; matte silver finish
Model 642: $449
Model 642 Pro Series *(cylinder cut for moon clips)*: $469
Model 642 CT *(Crimson Trace laser sight grip)*: $669
Model 642 LS *(smooth wood grips)*: $479
Model 642 *(2.5 in. barrel)*: $640
Model 642 *(2.5 in. barrel, Crimson Trace laser sight grip)*: $924

MODEL 438

Action: Revolver, SA/DA
Overall Length: 6.3 in.
Overall Height: 4.2 in.
Overall Width: 1.3 in.
Barrel: 1.9 in.
Grips: Textured synthetic
Sights: Fixed ramp front/groove rear
Weight Unloaded: 15.1 oz.
Caliber: .38 Spl. +P
Capacity: 5
Features: Aluminum J-frame; shrouded hammer; matte black finish
MSRP: $449

MODEL 60

Action: Revolver, SA/DA
Overall Length: 6.6 in. (2.1 in. barrel), 7.5 in. (3 in. barrel)
Overall Width: 1.3 in.
Barrel: 2.1 in., 3 in.
Grips: Textured synthetic
Sights: Fixed ramp front/groove rear
Weight Unloaded: 22.6 oz. (2.1 in. barrel), 24.5 oz. (3 in. barrel)
Caliber: .38 Spl. +P/.357 Mag.
Capacity: 5
Features: Stainless J-frame; small exposed hammer; satin stainless finish
Model 60: $729
Model 60 LS *(smooth wood grips)*: $759
Model 60 *(3 in. barrel, fixed ramp front/adj. rear sights)*: $759
Model 60 Pro Series *(3 in. barrel, fixed ramp front/adj. rear sights, checkered wood grips)*: $779

MODEL 640

Action: Revolver, DAO
Overall Length: 6.6 in.
Overall Width: 1.3 in.
Barrel: 2.1 in.
Grips: Textured synthetic
Sights: Fixed ramp front/groove rear
Weight Unloaded: 23 oz.
Caliber: .38 Spl. +P/.357 Mag.
Capacity: 5
Features: Centennial design; stainless J-frame; internal hammer; satin stainless finish
Model 640: $729
Model 640 *(dovetail front/rear night sights, cylinder cut for moon clips)*: $809
Model 640 Pro Series *(cylinder cut for moon clips)*: $845

MODEL 649

Action: Revolver, DAO
Overall Length: 6.6 in.
Overall Width: 1.3 in.
Barrel: 2.1 in.
Grips: Textured synthetic

S&W MODEL 57 CLASSIC

S&W MODEL 60

S&W MODEL 632 PRO SERIES

Sights: Fixed ramp front/groove rear
Weight Unloaded: 23 oz.
Caliber: .38 Spl. +P/.357 Mag.
Capacity: 5
Features: Stainless J-frame; shrouded hammer; satin stainless finish
MSRP: $729

MODEL 632

Action: Revolver, SA/DA
Overall Length: 7.5 in.
Overall Width: 1.3 in.
Barrel: 3 in., ported
Grips: Textured synthetic
Sights: Fixed ramp front/adj. rear
Weight Unloaded: 24.5 oz.
Caliber: .327 Fed.
Capacity: 6
Features: Steel J-frame; small exposed hammer; matte black finish
Model 632 Pro Series: $809

Smith & Wesson (S&W)

(www.smith-wesson.com)

S&W MODEL 686 PLUS

MODEL 686

Action: Revolver, SA/DA
Overall Length: 7.5 in. (2.5 in. barrel), 9.6 in (4 in. barrel)
Overall Height: 6.3 in.
Overall Width: 1.6 in.
Barrel: 2.5 in., 4 in.
Grips: Textured finger groove synthetic
Sights: Fixed red ramp front/adj. rear
Weight Unloaded: 34.7 oz. (2.5 in. barrel), 39.7 oz. (4 in. barrel)
Caliber: .38 Spl. +P/.357 Mag.
Capacity: 6
Features: Stainless L-frame; exposed hammer; satin stainless finish
Model 686: $829
Model 686 *(2.5 in. barrel)*: $829
Model 686 SSR Pro Series *(custom barrel, chamfered chambers, textured wood grips)*: $969
Model 686 Plus *(2.5 in. barrel, 7 round cylinder, 34.1 oz.)*: $849
Model 686 Plus *(3 in. barrel, 7 round cylinder, 36.8 oz.)*: $849
Model 686 Plus *(4 in. barrel, 7 round cylinder, 38.9 oz.)*: $849

MODEL 64 and 67

Action: Revolver, SA/DA
Overall Length: 8.9 in.
Barrel: 4 in.
Grips: Textured finger groove synthetic
Sights: Fixed front/groove rear
Weight Unloaded: 35.5 oz.
Caliber: .38 Spl. +P
Capacity: 6
Features: Stainless K-frame; exposed hammer; satin stainless finish
Model 64: $689
Model 67 *(fixed ramp front/adj. rear sights)*: $749

MODEL 627

Action: Revolver, SA/DA
Overall Length: 9.8 in.
Overall Height: 6.1 in.
Overall Width: 1.7 in.
Barrel: 4 in.
Grips: Textured finger groove synthetic
Sights: Fixed red ramp front/adj. rear
Weight Unloaded: 41.2 oz.
Caliber: .38 Spl. +P/.357 Mag.
Capacity: 8
Features: Stainless N-frame; exposed hammer; satin stainless finish
Model 627 Pro Series: $969
Model 627 V-Comp *(5 in. barrel, smooth finger groove wood grips)*: $1249
Model 627 V-Comp *(5 in. barrel, removal barrel compensator)*: $1509
Model 627 Performance Center *(2.6 in. barrel, unfluted cylinder, checkered finger groove wood grips)*: $1049

MODEL 625

Action: Revolver, SA/DA
Overall Length: 9.8 in.
Overall Height: 5.5 in.
Overall Width: 1.7 in.
Barrel: 4 in.
Grips: Smooth wood
Sights: Fixed gold bead ramp front/adj. rear
Weight Unloaded: 40.3 oz.
Caliber: .45 ACP
Capacity: 6
Features: Stainless N-frame; exposed hammer; satin stainless finish
Model 625 JM *(Jerry Mikluk model full under lug barrel)*: $979
Model 625 Performance Center *(Hogue combat laminate grips)*: $1049

MODEL 327

Action: Revolver, SA/DA
Overall Length: 7 in.
Barrel: 2 in.
Grips: Smooth finger groove wood
Sights: Fixed red ramp front/adj. rear
Weight Unloaded: 21.4 oz.
Caliber: .38 Spl. +P/.357 Mag.
Capacity: 8
Features: Scandium N-frame; exposed hammer; cylinder cut for moon clips; matte black frame/gray cylinder finish
Model 327 Performance Center: $1269
Model 327 Night Guard *(2.5 in. barrel, Tritium sights, synthetic grips, matte black finish)*: $1049
Model 327 TRR8 *(5 in. barrel, interchangeable front/adj. rear sights, textured synthetic finger groove grips, detachable Picatinny rail, matte black finish)*: $1289

MODEL 657

Action: Revolver, SA/DA
Overall Length: 7.6 in.
Barrel: 2.6 in.
Grips: Checkered finger groove wood
Sights: Dovetail ramp front/adj. rear
Weight Unloaded: 39.6 oz.
Caliber: .41 Mag.
Capacity: 6
Features: Stainless N-frame; exposed hammer; unfluted cylinder; matte stainless finish
MSRP: $1049

S&W MODEL 327 TRR8

S&W MODEL 325 NIGHT GUARD

S&W MODEL 64

S&W MODEL 58 CLASSIC

Smith & Wesson (S&W)

(www.smith-wesson.com)

S&W MODEL 629

MODEL 629

Action: Revolver, SA/DA
Overall Length: 7.6 in.
Overall Height: 6 in.
Overall Width: 1.7 in.
Barrel: 2.6 in.
Grips: Checkered finger groove wood
Sights: Dovetail ramp front/adj. rear
Weight Unloaded: 39.6 oz.
Caliber: .44 Spl./.44 Mag.
Capacity: 6
Features: Stainless N-frame; exposed hammer; unfluted cylinder; matte stainless finish
MSRP: $1049

MODEL 329PD

Action: Revolver, SA/DA
Overall Length: 9.5 in.
Overall Height: 5.6 in.
Overall Width: 1.7 in.
Barrel: 4 in.
Grips: Finger groove wood and rubber
Sights: Fixed HI-VIZ red dot front/adj. rear
Weight Unloaded: 25.1 oz.
Caliber: .44 Spl./.44 Mag.
Capacity: 6
Features: Scandium N-frame/titanium alloy cylinder; large exposed hammer; matte black finish
MSRP: $1159

MODEL 629 PERFORMANCE CENTER

Action: Revolver, SA/DA
Overall Length: 7.6 in.
Overall Height: 5.6 in.
Overall Width: 1.7 in.
Barrel: 2.6 in.
Grips: Finger groove wood
Sights: Dovetail red ramp front/adj. white outline rear
Weight Unloaded: 39.6 oz.
Caliber: .44 Spl./.44 Mag.
Capacity: 6
Features: Stainless N-frame/stainless unfluted cylinder; large exposed hammer
MSRP: $1049

MODEL 310 NIGHT GUARD

Action: Revolver, SA/DA
Overall Length: 7.6 in.
Overall Width: 1.7 in.
Barrel: 2.8 in.
Grips: Checkered synthetic
Sights: Fixed Tritium front/Cylinder & Slide notched rear
Weight Unloaded: 28 oz.
Caliber: .40 S&W/10mm
Capacity: 6
Features: Scandium N-frame; large exposed hammer; matte black finish
MSRP: $1185

MODEL 325

Action: Revolver, SA/DA
Overall Length: 7.6 in.
Overall Height: 5.6 in.
Overall Width: 1.7 in.
Barrel: 2.8 in.
Grips: Checkered synthetic
Sights: Fixed Tritium front/Cylinder & Slide notched rear
Weight Unloaded: 28 oz.
Caliber: .45 ACP
Capacity: 6
Features: Scandium N-frame; large exposed hammer; matte black finish
Model 325 Night Guard: $1049
Model 325 Thunder Ranch *(4 in. barrel, interchangeable front/adj. rear sights, textured synthetic finger groove grips)*: $1289

MODEL 329 NIGHT GUARD

Action: Revolver, SA/DA
Overall Length: 7.6 in.
Overall Height: 5.6 in.
Overall Width: 1.7 in.
Barrel: 2.5 in.
Grips: Checkered synthetic
Sights: Fixed Tritium front/Cylinder & Slide notched rear
Weight Unloaded: 29.3 oz.
Caliber: .44 Spl./.44 Mag.
Capacity: 6
Features: Scandium N-frame; large exposed hammer; matte black finish
MSRP: $1049

MODEL 357 NIGHT GUARD

Action: Revolver, SA/DA
Overall Length: 7.6 in.
Overall Height: 5.6 in.
Overall Width: 1.7 in.
Barrel: 2.5 in.
Grips: Checkered synthetic
Sights: Fixed Tritium front/Cylinder & Slide notched rear
Weight Unloaded: 29.7 oz.
Caliber: .41Mag.
Capacity: 6
Features: Scandium N-frame; large exposed hammer; matte black finish
MSRP: $1185

MODEL 386 NIGHT GUARD

Action: Revolver, SA/DA
Overall Length: 7.6 in.
Overall Height: 5.6 in.
Overall Width: 1.7 in.
Barrel: 2.5 in.
Grips: Checkered synthetic
Sights: Fixed Tritium front/Cylinder & Slide notched rear
Weight Unloaded: 24.5 oz.
Caliber: .38 Spl. +P/.357 Mag.
Capacity: 7
Features: Scandium N-frame; large exposed hammer; matte black finish
MSRP: $979

S&W MODEL 386 NIGHT GUARD

S&W MODEL 329PD

S&W MODEL 629 PERFORMANCE CENTER

S&W MODEL 640

Springfield Armory

(www.springfield-armory.com)

SPRINGFIELD ARMORY
G.I. 45 FULL-SIZE
(PARKERIZED)

SPRINGFIELD ARMORY
G.I. 45 FULL-SIZE
(OD GREEN)

SPRINGFIELD ARMORY
G.I. FULL-SIZE HI-CAP

SPRINGFIELD ARMORY
G.I. 45 MICRO COMPACT

SPRINGFIELD ARMORY
MIL SPEC (STAINLESS)

SPRINGFIELD ARMORY
MIL SPEC (PARKERIZED)

G.I. 45

Action: Autoloader, SA
Overall Length: 6.5 in. (Micro Compact), 7.5 in. (Champion), 8.5 in. (Full Size)
Overall Height: 5 in. (Micro Compact), 5.5 in. (Champion, Full Size)
Overall Width: 1.5 in.
Barrel: 3 in. (Micro Compact), 4 in. (Champion), 5 in. (Full Size)
Grips: Checkered hardwood
Sights: Fixed front/dovetail rear
Weight Unloaded: 33 oz. (Micro Compact), 37 oz. (Champion), 39 oz. (Full Size)
Caliber: .45 ACP
Capacity: 6 + 1 (Micro Compact), 7 + 1 (Champion, Full Size)
Features: Colt 1911 design; steel frame; thumb, grip safeties; lanyard loop
Micro Compact *(parkerized finish)*: $708
Champion *(parkerized finish)*: $656
Champion Lightweight *(parkerized finish, aluminum frame; weight: 30 oz.)*: $656
Full-size *(parkerized finish)*: $656
Full-size *(stainless finish)*: $708
Full-size *(OD green Armory Kote finish)*: $656
Full-size Hi-Cap *(parkerized finish, capacity), 14 + 1; weight: 40 oz.)*: $717

MIL SPEC

Action: Autoloader, SA
Overall Length: 8.5 in.
Overall Height: 5.5 in.
Overall Width: 1.5 in.
Barrel: 5 in.
Grips: Checkered hardwood
Sights: Fixed front/dovetail rear, 3-dot
Weight Unloaded: 39 oz.
Caliber: .45 ACP
Capacity: 7 + 1
Features: Colt 1911 design; steel frame; thumb, grip safeties; lanyard loop; lowered/flared ejection port; beveled magazine well
Parkerized finish: $768
Stainless finish: $842

HANDGUNS

Springfield Armory

(www.springfield-armory.com)

SPRINGFIELD ARMORY LOADED (OD GREENBLACK)

SPRINGFIELD ARMORY LOADED (BLACK STAINLESS)

SPRINGFIELD ARMORY LOADED

LOADED

Action: Autoloader, SA
Overall Length: 6.5 in. (Micro Compact, Ultra Compact), 7 in. (Champion), 8.5 in. (Full Size)
Overall Height: 5 in. (Micro Compact, Ultra Compact), 5.5 in. (Champion, Full Size)
Overall Width: 1.5 in.
Barrel: 3 in. (Micro Compact), 3.5 in. (Ultra Compact), 4 in. (Champion), 5 in. (Full Size)
Grips: Checkered cocobolo
Sights: Dovetail front/adj. rear
Weight Unloaded: 26 oz. (Micro Compact), 37 oz. (Champion), 40 oz. (Full Size)
Caliber: 9mm, .45 ACP
Capacity: 6 + 1 (Micro Compact, Ultra Compact), 7 + 1 (Champion, Full Size), 9 + 1 (9mm)
Features: Colt 1911 design; steel frame; ambidextrous extended thumb, beavertail grip safeties; lowered/flared ejection port; beveled magazine well; loaded-chamber indicator
Micro Compact Lightweight bi-tone *(aluminum frame; Picatinny rail)*: $1349
Ultra Compact stainless *(dovetail front/rear sights, Tritium)*: $1051
Champion Lightweight *(OD Green/ Black, aluminum frame; 30 oz., dovetail front/rear sights, Tritium; checkered rubber grips)*: $1011
Champion stainless *(dovetail front/ rear sights, Tritium)*: $1051
Full-size black stainless *(magazine funnel; textured composite grips)*: $1244
Full-size black stainless Combat *(textured composite grips; dovetail front/rear sights, Tritium)*: $999
Full-size bi-tone *(aluminum frame; 33 oz., dovetail front/rear sights, Tritium)*: $1033
Full-size parkerized *(dovetail front/ rear sights, Tritium)*: $981
Full-size stainless: $1081
Full-size stainless *(9mm)*: $1079

OPERATOR

Action: Autoloader, SA
Overall Length: 7.5 in. (Champion), 8.5 in. (Full Size)
Overall Height: 5.5 in. (Champion, Full Size)
Overall Width: 1.5 in.
Barrel: 4 in. (Champion), 5 in. (Full Size)
Grips: Checkered cocobolo
Sights: Dovetail front/rear, Tritium 3-dot
Weight: 31 oz. (Champion), 34 oz. (Full Size)
Caliber: .45 ACP
Capacity: 7 + 1
Features: Colt 1911 design; ambidextrous extended thumb, beavertail grip safeties; lowered/flared ejection port; beveled magazine well; loaded-chamber indicator; Picatinny rail; black Armory Kote finish
Champion Lightweight *(aluminum frame)*: $1076
Full-size Lightweight *(aluminum frame)*: $1305
Full-size MC *(steel frame, 42 oz., OD Green frame/black slide, Pachmayr wraparound grips)*: $1387

EMP

Action: Autoloader, SA
Overall Length: 6.5 in.
Overall Height: 5 in.
Overall Width: 1.5 in.
Barrel: 3 in.
Grips: Checkered cocobolo
Sights: Dovetail front/rear, Tritium 3-dot
Weight Unloaded: 26 oz. (9mm), 33 oz. (.40 S&W)
Caliber: 9mm, .40 S&W
Capacity: 9 + 1 (9mm), 8 + 1 (.40 S&W)
Features: Colt 1911 design; aluminum frame; ambidextrous extended thumb, beavertail grip safeties; lowered/flared ejection port; beveled magazine well; loaded-chamber indicator; magazine base pad; bi-tone finish
MSRP: $1345

HANDGUNS

SPRINGFIELD ARMORY OPERATOR

SPRINGFIELD ARMORY EMP

Springfield Armory

(www.springfield-armory.com)

SPRINGFIELD ARMORY TRP

SPRINGFIELD ARMORY XD-45 SERVICE

SPRINGFIELD ARMORY XD-45 TACTICAL (DARK EARTH)

TRP

Action: Autoloader, SA
Overall Length: 8.5 in.
Overall Height: 5.7 in.
Overall Width: 1.5 in.
Barrel: 5 in.
Grips: Textured G10 composite
Sights: Dovetail front/rear, Tritium 3-dot
Weight Unloaded: 42 oz.
Caliber: .45 ACP
Capacity: 7 + 1
Features: Colt 1911 design; FBI contract spec; ambidextrous extended thumb, beavertail grip safeties; lowered/flared ejection port; magazine funnel; loaded-chamber indicator
Black Armory Kote finish: $1777
Stainless: $1777

XD-45

Action: Autoloader, SA; striker-fired
Overall Length: 6.5 in. (Compact), 7.3 in. (Service), 8.3 in. (Tactical)
Overall Height: 4.9 in. (Compact), 5.6 in. (Service, Tactical)
Overall Width: 1.3 in.
Barrel: 4 in. (Compact), 5 in. (Service, Tactical)
Grips: Textured polymer
Sights: Dovetail front/rear, 3-dot
Weight Unloaded: 29 oz. (Compact), 30 oz. (Service, Tactical)
Caliber: .45 ACP
Capacity: 10 + 1 (Compact), 13 + 1 (Service, Tactical)
Features: Polymer frame; grip/trigger safeties; ambidextrous magazine release; loaded-chamber/striker-status indicators; textured front/rear grip straps; combat trigger guard; Picatinny rail
Compact *(bi-tone, OD or dark earth frame, 4 in. barrel)*: $666
Compact *(matte black, bi-tone, OD, or dark earth finish, 5-in. barrel)*: $646
Service *(bi-tone matte black frame/ matte stainless slide)*: $649
Service *(matte black, OD, or dark earth frame)*: $578
Service *(dark earth or OD frame/matte stainless slide)*: $649
Tactical *(bi-tone matte black frame/ matte stainless slide)*: $679
Tactical *(matte black, dark earth, or OD frame /matte black slide)*: $629

XD SUBCOMPACT

Action: Autoloader, SA; striker-fired
Overall Length: 6.5 in.
Overall Height: 4.8 in. (compact magazine), 5.5 in. (w/ grip extension)
Overall Width: 1.3 in.
Barrel: 3 in.
Grips: Textured polymer
Sights: Dovetail front/rear, 3-dot
Weight Unloaded: 26 oz. (compact magazine), 27 oz. (w/ grip extension)
Caliber: 9mm, .40 S&W
Capacity: 13 + 1 (9mm, compact magazine), 16 + 1 (9mm, grip extension), 9 + 1 (.40 S&W, compact magazine), 12 + 1 (.40 S&W, grip extension)
Features: Polymer frame; grip/trigger safeties; ambidextrous magazine release; loaded-chamber/striker-status indicators; textured front/rear grip straps; combat trigger guard; Picatinny rail; magazine/grip extension
Bi-tone matte black frame/ matte stainless slide *(9mm, .40 S&W)*: $616
Matte black or OD frame *(9mm, .40 S&W)*: $549
V-10 Ported: price TK

HANDGUNS

SPRINGFIELD ARMORY XD SERVICE (.45 GAP)

SPRINGFIELD ARMORY XD-9 SUBCOMPACT

SPRINGFIELD ARMORY XD-9 SERVICE V-10 (PORTED)

SPRINGFIELD ARMORY XD-45 TACTICAL WITH THUMB SAFETY

Springfield Armory

(www.springfield-armory.com)

SPRINGFIELD ARMORY
XD-9 SERVICE (BI-TONE)

XD SERVICE

Action: Autoloader, SA; striker-fired
Overall Length: 7.3 in.
Overall Height: 5.5 in.
Overall Width: 1.3 in.
Barrel: 4 in.
Grips: Textured polymer
Sights: Dovetail front/rear, 3-dot
Weight Unloaded: 28 oz. (9mm), 29 oz. (.40 S&W, .357 Sig.)
Caliber: 9mm, .40 S&W, .357 Sig.
Capacity: 16 + 1 (9mm), 12 + 1 (.40 S&W, .357 Sig.)
Features: Polymer frame; grip, trigger safeties; ambidextrous magazine release; loaded-chamber, striker-status indicators; textured front/rear grip straps; combat trigger guard; Picatinny rail
Matte black, dark earth, or OD frame: $549
Bi-tone matte black frame/ matte stainless slide: $616
Matte black or OD frame *(ported barrel)*: $584

XD TACTICAL

Action: Autoloader, SA; striker-fired
Overall Length: 8.3 in.
Overall Height: 5.5 in.
Overall Width: 1.3 in.
Barrel: 5 in.
Grips: Textured polymer
Sights: Dovetail front/rear, 3-dot
Weight Unloaded: 30 oz. (9mm), 32 oz. (.40 S&W, .357 Sig.)
Caliber: 9mm, .40 S&W, .357 Sig.
Capacity: 16 + 1 (9mm), 12 + 1 (.40 S&W, .357 Sig.)
Features: Polymer frame; grip, trigger safeties; ambidextrous magazine release; loaded-chamber/striker-status indicators; textured front/rear grip straps; combat trigger guard; Picatinny rail
Matte black, dark earth, or OD frame: $599

SPRINGFIELD ARMORY XD-40
TACTICAL (OD GREEN)

SPRINGFIELD ARMORY
XD-9 TACTICAL

Springfield Armory

(www.springfield-armory.com)

XD(M) and XD(M)45

Action: Autoloader, SA; striker-fired
Overall Length: 8 in.
Overall Height: 5.6 in. (9mm, .40 S&W), 5.8 in. (.45 ACP)
Overall Width: 1.3 in.
Barrel: 4.5 in.
Grips: Textured polymer; modular
Sights: Dovetail front/rear, 3-dot
Weight Unloaded: 32 oz. (9mm, .40 S&W), 31 oz. (.45 ACP)
Caliber: 9mm, .40 S&W, .45 ACP
Capacity: 19 + 1 (9mm), 16 + 1 (.40 S&W), 13 + 1 (.45 ACP)
Features: Polymer frame; grip, trigger safeties; ambidextrous magazine release; loaded-chamber/striker-status indicators; textured front/rear grip straps; combat trigger guard; Picatinny rail; three backstrap sizes
XD(M) 45 *(bi-tone)*: $771
XD(M) 45 *(bi-tone, Tritium sights)*: $886
XD(M) 45 *(matte black)*: $709
XD(M) 45 *(matte black, Tritium sights)*: $824
XD(M) *(matte black or OD green frame/ matte black slide)*: $697
XD(M) *(matte black or OD green frame/ matte black slide, Trijicon sights)*: $815
XD(M) *(bi-tone, matte black, or OD green frame /matte stainless slide)*: $763

SPRINGFIELD ARMORY XD(M)45

SPRINGFIELD ARMORY XD(M) (BI-TONE)

SPRINGFIELD ARMORY XD(M) 3.8

XD(M) 3.8 COMPACT and XD(M) 3.8

Action: Autoloader, SA; striker-fired
Overall Length: 7 in.
Overall Height: 4.6 in. (Compact), 5.6 in.
Overall Width: 1.3 in.
Barrel: 3.8 in.
Grips: Textured polymer; modular
Sights: Dovetail front/rear, 3-dot
Weight Unloaded: 27.5 oz. (9mm), 28 oz. (.40 S&W)
Caliber: 9mm, .40 S&W
Capacity: 13 + 1 (Compact 9mm), 19 + 1 (9mm), 11 + 1 (Compact .40 S&W), 16 + 1 (.40 S&W)
Features: Polymer frame; grip, trigger safeties; ambidextrous magazine release; loaded-chamber/striker-status indicators; textured front/rear grip straps; combat trigger guard; Picatinny rail; three backstrap sizes
Compact bi-tone: $769
Compact matte black: $705
Bi-tone: $763
Matte black: $697
Matte black *(Tritium sights)*: $815
OD: $697
OD frame/matte stainless slide: $763

SPRINGFIELD ARMORY XD(M) 3.8 COMPACT

SPRINGFIELD ARMORY XD(M) 3.8 COMPACT WITH MAGAZINE EXTENSION

STI

(www.stiguns.com)

STI TOTAL ECLIPSE

TOTAL ECLIPSE

Action: Autoloader, SA
Overall Length: 7 in.
Overall Height: 5 in.
Overall Width: 1.4 in.
Barrel: 3 in.
Grips: Checkered polymer
Sights: Fixed front/dovetail rear, Tritium 2-dot
Weight Unloaded: 23.1 oz.
Caliber: 9mm, .40 S&W, .45 ACP
Capacity: 13 + 1 (9 mm), 11 + 1 (.40 S&W), 9 + 1 (.45 ACP)
Features: Polymer frame; extended thumb, beavertail grip safeties; lowered/flared ejection port; beveled magazine well; combat trigger guard; textured front/rear grip straps; KG coat matte black finish
MSRP: $1825

STI TACTICAL 4.15

TACTICAL 4.15 and 5.0

Action: Autoloader, SA
Overall Length: 7.8 in. (model 4.15), 8.5 in. (model 5.0)
Overall Height: 5.6 in.
Overall Width: 1.3 in.
Barrel: 4.2 in. (model 4.15), 5 in. (model 5.0)
Grips: Checkered polymer
Sights: Fixed front/dovetail rear, Tritium 2-dot

STI TACTICAL 5.0

Weight Unloaded: 33.5 oz. (model 4.15), 35.1 oz. (model 5.0)
Caliber: 9mm, .40 S&W, .45 ACP
Capacity: 17 + 1 (9 mm), 14 + 1 (.40 S&W), 12 + 1 (.45 ACP)
Features: Polymer frame; ambidextrous extended thumb, beavertail grip safeties; lowered/flared ejection port; magazine funnel; combat trigger guard; textured front/rear grip straps; Picatinny rail; matte blue finish
MSRP: $1999

STI VIP ALUMINUM

VIP

Action: Autoloader, SA
Overall Length: 7.5 in.
Overall Height: 5 in.
Overall Width: 1.4 in.
Barrel: 3.9 in.
Grips: Checkered polymer
Sights: Fixed front/dovetail rear
Weight Unloaded: 33.5 oz.
Caliber: 9mm, .40 S&W, .45 ACP
Capacity: 13 + 1 (9 mm), 11 + 1 (.40 S&W), 9 + 1 (.45 ACP)
Features: Polymer frame; extended thumb, beavertail grip safeties; lowered/flared ejection port; beveled magazine well; combat trigger guard; textured front/rear grip straps; Picatinny rail; matte blue finish
MSRP: $1646

STI DUTY ONE

DUTY ONE

Action: Autoloader, SA
Overall Length: 8.5 in.
Overall Height: 5.3 in.
Overall Width: 1.5 in.
Barrel: 5 in.
Grips: Checkered micarta
Sights: Dovetail front/Heinie rear
Weight Unloaded: 37.2 oz.
Caliber: 9mm, .40 S&W, .45 ACP
Capacity: 9 + 1 (9mm), 8 + 1 (.40 S&W, .45 ACP)
Features: Colt 1911 design; steel frame; extended thumb, beavertail grip safeties; lowered/flared ejection port; beveled magazine well; checkered front/rear grip straps; Picatinny rail; matte blue finish
MSRP: $1299

STI SENTINEL PREMIER

SENTINEL PREMIER

Action: Autoloader, SA
Overall Length: 8.5 in.
Overall Height: 5.5 in.
Overall Width: 1.3 in.
Barrel: 5 in.
Grips: Checkered micarta
Sights: Dovetail front/adj. rear, Tritium
Weight Unloaded: 36.7 oz.
Caliber: .45 ACP
Capacity: 8 + 1
Features: Colt 1911 design; steel frame; ambidextrous extended thumb,

STI

(www.stiguns.com)

beavertail grip safeties; lowered/flared ejection port; magazine well; combat trigger guard; checkered front/rear grip straps; blue finish
MSRP: $1943

STI GUARDIAN

GUARDIAN

Action: Autoloader, SA
Overall Length: 7.5 in.
Overall Height: 5.3 in.
Overall Width: 1.5 in.
Barrel: 3.9 in.
Grips: Checkered micarta
Sights: Dovetail front/adj. rear, 3-dot
Weight Unloaded: 32.4 oz.
Caliber: 9mm, .45 ACP
Capacity: 9 + 1 (9mm), 8 + 1 (.45 ACP)
Features: Colt 1911 design; steel frame; extended thumb, beavertail grip safeties; lowered/flared ejection port; beveled magazine well; textured front/rear grip straps; blue frame/stainless slide
MSRP: $1110

STI OFF DUTY

OFF DUTY

Action: Autoloader, SA
Overall Length: 7 in.
Overall Height: 5 in.
Overall Width: 1.4 in.
Barrel: 3 in.
Grips: Checkered cocobolo
Sights: Dovetail front/adj. rear, 3-dot
Weight Unloaded: 31.3 oz.
Caliber: 9mm, .45 ACP
Capacity: 9 + 1 (9mm), 8 + 1 (.45 ACP)
Features: Colt 1911 design; steel frame; extended thumb, beavertail grip safeties; lowered/flared ejection port; beveled magazine well; checkered front/rear grip straps; Picatinny rail; blue frame/stainless slide
MSRP: $1231

STI ELEKTRA

ELEKTRA

Action: Autoloader, SA
Overall Length: 7 in.
Overall Height: 5 in.
Overall Width: 1.4 in.
Barrel: 3 in.
Grips: Pearlescent polymer
Sights: Fixed front/dovetail rear, Tritium
Weight Unloaded: 22.8 oz.
Caliber: 9mm, .45 ACP
Capacity: 9 + 1 (9mm), 8 + 1 (.45 ACP)
Features: Colt 1911 design; aluminum frame; extended thumb, beavertail grip safeties; lowered/flared ejection port; beveled magazine well; textured front/rear grip straps; KG coat finish
MSRP: $1370

LAWMAN

Action: Autoloader, SA
Overall Length: 8.5 in.
Overall Height: 5.3 in.
Overall Width: 1.4 in.
Barrel: 5 in.
Grips: Polymer
Sights: Dovetail front/adj. rear
Weight Unloaded: 37 oz.
Caliber: .45 ACP
Capacity: 8 + 1
Features: Colt 1911 design; steel frame; extended thumb, beavertail grip

STI LAWMAN

safeties; lowered/flared ejection port; beveled magazine well; checkered front/rear grip straps; blue or two-tone finishes
MSRP: $1420

STI SENTRY

SENTRY

Action: Autoloader, SA
Overall Length: 8.5 in.
Overall Height: 5.3 in.
Overall Width: 1.4 in.
Barrel: 5 in.
Grips: Checkered cocobola
Sights: Dovetail front/adj. rear
Weight Unloaded: 35.3 oz.
Caliber: 9mm, .40 S&W, .45 ACP
Capacity: 9 + 1 (9mm), 8 + 1 (.40 S&W, .45 ACP)
Features: Colt 1911 design; steel frame; ambidextrous extended thumb, beavertail grip safeties; lowered/flared ejection port; magazine well; checkered front/rear grip straps; blue finish
MSRP: $1598

TROJAN 5.0

Action: Autoloader, SA
Overall Length: 8.5 in.
Overall Height: 5.3 in.
Overall Width: 1.3 in.
Barrel: 5 in.
Grips: Checkered cocobola

HANDGUNS

STI

(www.stiguns.com)

STI TROJAN 5.0

Sights: Dovetail front/adj. rear
Weight Unloaded: 36 oz.
Caliber: 9mm, .40 S&W, .45 ACP
Capacity: 9 + 1 (9mm), 8 + 1 (.40 S&W, .45 ACP)
Features: Colt 1911 design; steel frame; ambidextrous extended thumb, beavertail grip safeties; lowered/flared ejection port; beveled magazine well; textured front/rear grip straps; blue finish
MSRP: $1598

STI ESCORT

ESCORT

Action: Autoloader, SA
Overall Length: 7 in.
Overall Height: 5.3 in.
Overall Width: 1.3 in.
Barrel: 3 in.
Grips: Checkered cocobola
Sights: Fixed front/dovetail rear, 3-dot
Weight Unloaded: 22.8 oz.
Caliber: 9mm, .45 ACP
Capacity: 9 + 1 (9mm), 8 + 1 (.45 ACP)
Features: Colt 1911 design; aluminum frame; extended thumb, beavertail grip safeties; lowered/flared ejection port; beveled magazine well; textured front/ rear grip straps; KG coat frame/blue slide finish
MSRP: $1155

STI LS

LS

Action: Autoloader, SA
Overall Length: 7 in.
Overall Height: 4.4 in.
Overall Width: 1.1 in.
Barrel: 3.4 in.
Grips: Checkered cocobola
Sights: Fixed front/Heinie dovetail rear
Weight Unloaded: 28 oz.
Caliber: 9mm
Capacity: 9 + 1
Features: Colt 1911 design; steel frame; extended thumb, beavertail grip safeties; lowered/flared ejection port; beveled magazine well; textured front/ rear grip straps; matte blue finish
MSRP: $1155

STI RANGER II

RANGER II

Action: Autoloader, SA
Overall Length: 7.8 in.
Overall Height: 5.3 in.
Overall Width: 1.3 in.
Barrel: 4.2 in.
Grips: Checkered cocobola
Sights: Dovetail front/rear
Weight Unloaded: 33 oz.
Caliber: 9mm, .40 S&W, .45 ACP
Capacity: 9 + 1 (9mm), 8 + 1 (.40 S&W, .45 ACP)
Features: Colt 1911 design; steel frame; ambidextrous extended thumb, beavertail grip safeties; lowered/flared ejection port; beveled magazine well; textured front/rear grip straps; blue finish
MSRP: $1110

STI SHADOW

SHADOW

Action: Autoloader, SA
Overall Length: 7 in.
Overall Height: 5.3 in.
Overall Width: 1.3 in.
Barrel: 3 in.
Grips: Checkered micarta
Sights: Fixed front/dovetail rear, Tritium
Weight Unloaded: 22.8 oz.
Caliber: 9mm, .40 S&W, .45 ACP
Capacity: 9 + 1 (9mm), 8 + 1 (.40 S&W, .45 ACP)
Features: Colt 1911 design; aluminum frame; ambidextrous extended thumb, beavertail grip safeties; lowered/flared ejection port; beveled magazine well; textured front/rear grip straps; KG coat finish
MSRP: $1370

STI GP5

GP5

Action: Autoloader, SA/DA
Overall Length: 7.5 in.
Overall Height: 5.3 in.
Overall Width: 1.3 in.
Barrel: 3.3 in.
Grips: Textured polymer
Sights: Fixed front/dovetail rear, 3-dot
Weight Unloaded: 23.8 oz.

HANDGUNS

STI

(www.stiguns.com)

Caliber: 9mm
Capacity: 17 + 1
Features: Beavertail polymer frame; ambidextrous extended thumb safety; textured front/rear grip straps; Picatinny rail; combat trigger guard; blue finish
MSRP: $663

STI GP6

GP6

Action: Autoloader, SA/DA
Overall Length: 7.9 in.
Overall Height: 5.3 in.
Overall Width: 1.3 in.
Barrel: 4.3 in.
Grips: Textured polymer
Sights: Fixed front/dovetail rear, 3-dot
Weight Unloaded: 26.1 oz.
Caliber: 9mm
Capacity: 17 + 1
Features: Beavertail polymer frame; ambidextrous extended thumb safety; textured front/rear grip straps; Picatinny rail; combat trigger guard; blue finish
MSRP: $663
GP6-C (fiber optic front/adj. rear): . . .
. . . . **$827**

STI GP6-C

Steyr Arms

(www.steyr-mannlicher.com)

STEYR ARMS M-A1

STEYR ARMS M-A1

Action: Autoloader, reset action system (DOA)
Overall Length: 7.2 in.
Overall Height: 5.1 in.
Overall Width: 1.2 in.
Barrel: 4 in.
Grips: Textured polymer
Sights: Fixed triangular/ trapezoid
Weight Unloaded: 27.2 oz.
Caliber: 9mm, .40 S&W
Capacity: 17 + 1 (9mm), 12 + 1 (.40 S&W)
Features: Polymer frame; trigger, internal striker, internal gun-lock safeties; polygonal rifling; black matte Mannox finish; Picatinny rail
MSRP: $649

Stoeger Industries

(www.stoegerindustries.com)

STOEGER COUGER 9MM (ANODIZED SILVER)

STOEGER COUGAR .45

STOEGER COUGAR

Action: Autoloader, single/DA
Overall Length: 7 in.
Overall Height: 5.6 in.
Overall Width: 1.4 in.
Barrel: 3.6 in.
Grips: Checkered polymer
Sights: Dovetail front and rear, white 3-dot
Weight Unloaded: 32.6 oz. (9mm), 32.4 oz. (.40 S&W), 32 oz. (.45 ACP)
Caliber: 9mm, .40 S&W, .45 ACP
Capacity: 15 + 1 (9mm), 11 + 1 (.40 S&W), 8 + 1 (.45 ACP)
Features: Beretta rotating barrel design; aluminum alloy frame/steel slide, barrel; ambidextrous thumb, firing pin block, and decocking safeties; Picatinny rail (.45 ACP), external hammer; loaded-chamber indicator; combat trigger guard; serrated front/back grip strap

Bruniton matte black *(9mm, .40 S&W)*: $469
Bruniton matte black *(.45 ACP)*: $499
Bruniton black slide/anodized silver frame *(9mm, .40 S&W)*: $499
Bruniton silver slide/anodized silver frame *(9mm, .40 S&W)*: $499

Sturm, Ruger & Co.

(www.ruger.com)

STURM, RUGER & CO. LCP

STURM, RUGER & CO. SR9

LCP

Action: Autoloader, DA
Overall Length: 5.2 in.
Overall Height: 3.6 in.
Overall Width: .8 in.
Barrel: 2.8 in.
Grips: Textured polymer
Sights: Fixed front/rear
Weight Unloaded: 9.4 oz.
Caliber: .380
Capacity: 6 + 1
Features: Loaded-chamber indicator; textured front/rear grip straps; black finish

MSRP: $364
Crimson Trace laser sight grip: $548

SR9

Action: Autoloader, striker-fired
Overall Length: 7.5 in.
Overall Height: 5.5 in.
Overall Width: 1.3 in.
Barrel: 4.1 in.
Grips: Textured polymer; modular
Sights: Adj. 3-dot
Weight Unloaded: 26.5 oz.
Caliber: 9mm
Capacity: 17 + 1
Features: Polymer frame; loaded-chamber/cocked indicators; reversible backstrap; textured front/rear grip straps; ambidextrous safety/magazine release; Picatinny rail; magazine base pad
Nitrodox Pro black: $565
Two-tone *(matte black frame/matte stainless slide)*: $525
OD green *(matte green frame/matte black slide)*: $565

HANDGUNS

Sturm, Ruger & Co.

(www.ruger.com)

STURM, RUGER & CO. SR9C

STURM, RUGER & CO. SR40

SR9C

Action: Autoloader, striker-fired
Overall Length: 6.9 in.
Overall Height: 4.6 in.
Overall Width: 1.3 in.
Barrel: 3.5 in.
Grips: Textured polymer; modular
Sights: Adj. 3-dot
Weight Unloaded: 23.4 oz.
Caliber: 9mm
Capacity: 10 + 1
Features: Polymer frame; loaded chamber/cocked indicators; textured front/rear grip straps; reversible backstrap; ambidextrous safety, magazine releases; Picatinny rail; magazine base pad
Nitrodox Pro black: $525
Two-tone *(matte black frame/matte stainless slide)*: $525

SR40

Action: Autoloader, striker-fired
Overall Length: 7.5 in.
Overall Height: 5.5 in.
Overall Width: 1.3 in.
Barrel: 4.1 in.
Grips: Textured polymer; modular
Sights: Adj. 3-dot
Weight Unloaded: 27.3 oz.
Caliber: .40 S&W
Capacity: 15 + 1
Features: Polymer frame; loaded-chamber/cocked indicators; reversible backstrap; textured front/rear grip straps; ambidextrous safety, magazine releases; Picatinny rail; magazine base pad; matte black frame/matte stainless slide finish
MSRP: $525

P345

Action: Autoloader, SA/DA
Overall Length: 7.5 in.
Overall Height: 5.8 in.
Overall Width: 1.2 in.
Barrel: 4.2 in.
Grips: Textured polymer
Sights: Adj. 3-dot
Weight Unloaded: 29 oz.
Caliber: .45 ACP
Capacity: 8 + 1
Features: Polymer frame; loaded-chamber indicator; textured front/rear grip straps; ambidextrous safety; magazine base pad; external hammer, extractor
Blue: $577
Two-tone *(matte black frame/matte stainless slide)*: $617

P95

Action: Autoloader, SA/DA
Overall Length: 7.3 in.
Overall Height: 5.8 in.
Overall Width: 1.2 in.
Barrel: 3.9 in.
Grips: Textured polymer
Sights: Fixed front/dovetail rear, 3-dot
Weight Unloaded: 27 oz.
Caliber: 9mm
Capacity: 15 + 1
Features: Polymer frame; loaded-chamber indicator; ambidextrous safety; magazine base pad; external hammer, extractor; full dust cover
Blue: $393
Two-tone *(matte black frame/matte stainless slide)*: $424

STURM, RUGER & CO. P345

STURM, RUGER & CO. P95

Sturm, Ruger & Co.

(www.ruger.com)

STURM, RUGER & CO. LCR

STURM, RUGER & CO. GP100

STURM, RUGER & CO. REDHAWK

STURM, RUGER & CO. SP101

LCR

Action: Revolver, DAO
Overall Length: 6.5 in.
Overall Height: 4.5 in.
Overall Width: 1.3 in.
Barrel: 1.9 in.
Grips: Rubber
Sights: Fixed front/rear
Weight Unloaded: 13.5 oz. (.38 Spl.), 17.10 oz (.357 Mag.)
Caliber: .38 Spl.; .357 Mag.
Capacity: 5
Features: Matte black aluminum frame; stainless fluted cylinder
Hogue Tamer *(textured rubber grip)*: $525
Hogue Tamer *(textured rubber grip, .357 Mag.)*: $575
Hogue Boot *(smooth rubber grip)*: $575
Crimson Trace laser sight grip: $792

SP101

Action: Revolver, SA/DA
Overall Length: 8 in. (3.1 in. barrel), 7 in. (2.3 in. barrel)
Overall Height: 4.8 in.
Overall Width: 1.4 in.
Barrel: 3.1 in., 2.3 in.
Grips: Rubber
Sights: Fixed front/groove rear, adj. rear (.327 Fed. Mag.)
Weight Unloaded: 25 oz. (2.3 in. barrel), 26 oz. (3.1 in. barrel), 28 oz. (.327 Fed. Mag.)
Caliber: .327 Fed. Mag.; .38 Spl.; .357 Mag.
Capacity: 5 (.38 Spl.; .357 Mag.), 6 (.327 Fed. Mag.)
Features: Matte stainless finish; bobbed hammer (.357 Mag./2.3 in. barrel)
MSRP: $607
Crimson Trace laser sight grip (.357 Mag./2.3 in. barrel): **$864**

GP100

Action: Revolver, SA/DA
Overall Length: 8.5 in. (3 in. barrel), 9.5 in. (4.2 in. barrel)
Overall Height: 6.3 in.
Overall Width: 1.6 in.
Barrel: 3 in., 4.2 in.
Grips: Hogue rubber Monogrip
Sights: Dovetail front/adj. rear, fixed front/rear (.357 Mag./3 in. barrel)
Weight Unloaded: 36 oz. (3 in. barrel), 40 oz.
Caliber: .327 Fed. Mag.; .357 Mag.
Capacity: 6 (.357 Mag.), 7 (.327 Fed. Mag.)
Features: Full underlug barrel
Blue: $634
Blue *(3 in. barrel)*: $679
Stainless *(.327 Fed. Mag.)*: $701

REDHAWK

Action: Revolver, SA/DA
Overall Length: 9.6 in.
Overall Height: 6.2 in.
Overall Width: 1.8 in.
Barrel: 4 in.
Grips: Hogue rubber finger groove Bantam
Sights: Fixed front/adj. rear
Weight Unloaded: 46.8 oz.
Caliber: .44 Mag., .45 LC
Capacity: 6
Features: Two cylinder lockup points, shrouded ejector rod; matte stainless finish
MSRP: $949

Taurus

(www.taurususa.com)

TAURUS 24/7 G2 COMPACT

TAURUS 24/7 G2

TAURUS 740 SLIM

TAURUS 709 SLIM

24/7 G2

Action: Autoloader, hybrid striker-fired
Overall Length: 6.6 in. (Compact), 7.3 in. (Standard)
Overall Height: 5 in.
Overall Width: 1.2 in.
Barrel: 3.5 in. (Compact), 4.2 in. (Standard)
Grips: Textured polymer, modular
Sights: Dovetail front/adj. rear
Weight Unloaded: 27 oz. (Compact), 28 oz. (Standard)
Caliber: 9mm, .40 S&W, .45 ACP
Capacity: 17 + 1 (9mm), 15 + 1 (.40 S&W), 12 + 1 (.45 ACP)
Features: Ambidextrous magazine release, thumb safety; polymer frame; external extractor; loaded-chamber indicator; Picatinny accessory rail; three backstraps configurations; cocked indicator; strike-two trigger allows second pull of trigger without resetting; black finish
MSRP: $475

22PLY and 25 PLY

Action: Autoloader, DAO
Overall Length: 4.8 in.
Barrel: 2.3 in.
Grips: Textured polymer
Sights: Fixed front/rear
Weight Unloaded: 10.8 oz.
Caliber: .22 LR; .25 ACP
Capacity: 8 + 1 (.22 LR), 9 + 1 (.25 ACP)
Features: Magazine disconnect, thumb safeties; polymer frame; external magazine finger grip; tip-up barrel; matte blue finish
MSRP: $240

732 TCP and 738 TCP

Action: Autoloader, striker-fired
Overall Length: 5.2 in.
Overall Height: 3.7 in.
Overall Width: .9 in.
Barrel: 3.3 in.
Grips: Textured polyme
Sights: Fixed front/rear
Weight Unloaded: 10.2 oz.
Caliber: .32 ACP; .380
Capacity: 6 + 1
Features: Polymer frame; magazine base pad; loaded-chamber indicator; black finish
Blue: $336
Bi-tone: $352

709 SLIM and 740 SLIM

Action: Autoloader, SA/DA
Overall Length: 6.2 in.
Barrel: 3.2 in.
Grips: Textured polymer
Sights: Fixed front/adj. rear
Weight Unloaded: 19 oz.
Caliber: 9mm, .40 S&W
Capacity: 7 + 1 (9mm), 6 + 1 (.40 S&W)
Features: Polymer frame; magazine base pad; loaded-chamber indicator; trigger, manual safeties
Blue: $483
Bi-tone: $498

800 SERIES

Action: Autoloader, hybrid striker-fired
Overall Length: 8.3 in.
Barrel: 4.2 in.
Grips: Textured polymer, modular
Sights: Dovetail front/rear, Novak
Weight Unloaded: 30.2 oz. (9mm), 29.6 oz. (.40 S&W), 28.2 oz. (.45 ACP)
Caliber: 9mm, .40 S&W, .45 ACP
Capacity: 17 + 1 (9mm), 15 + 1 (.40 S&W), 12 + 1 (.45 ACP)
Features: Polymer frame; strike-two trigger allows second pull of trigger without resetting; ambidextrous magazine release/thumb safety; external extractor; loaded-chamber indicator; Picatinny accessory rail; three backstrap sizes; cocked indicator; blue or bi-tone finish
.45 ACP: $674
9mm, .40 S&W: $656

800 SERIES COMPACT

Action: Autoloader, hybrid striker-fired
Overall Length: 6.7 in.
Barrel: 3.5 in.
Grips: Textured polymer, modular
Sights: Dovetail front/rear, 3-dot
Weight Unloaded: 24.7 oz.
Caliber: 9mm, .40 S&W
Capacity: 17 + 1 (9mm), 15 + 1 (.40 S&W)
Features: Polymer frame; strike-two trigger allows second pull of trigger without resetting; ambidextrous magazine release, thumb safety; external extractor; loaded-chamber indicator; Picatinny accessory rail; three backstrap sizes; cocked indicator; bi-tone finish
MSRP: $555

Taurus

(www.taurususa.com)

TAURUS 800 SERIES

TAURUS MODEL 22 (NICKEL)

TAURUS 738 TCP

TAURUS 92

TAURUS 1911 SERIES

MODELS 22 and 25

Action: Autoloader, SA/DA
Overall Length: 5.3 in.
Overall Height: 4.3 in.
Overall Width: 1.1 in.
Barrel: 2.8 in.
Grips: Textured polymer
Sights: Fixed front/rear
Weight Unloaded: 10.8 oz.
Caliber: .22 LR; .25 ACP
Capacity: 8 + 1 (.22 LR), 9 + 1 (.25 ACP)
Features: Beretta design; steel frame; magazine disconnect, thumb safeties; spurless hammer; extended magazine base; tip-up barrel
Blue *(wood grip)*: $262
Two-tone *(wood grip)*: $262
Blue *(pink, black, white pearl grips)*: $273
Blue/gold accents *(pink, black, white pearl grips)*: $311
Nickel *(wood grip)*: $262
Nickel *(pink, black, white pearl grips)*: $273
Nickel/gold accents *(pink, black, white pearl grips)*: $311

MILLENNIUM PRO SERIES COMPACT

Action: Autoloader, SA/DA
Overall Length: 6.1 in.
Overall Height: 4.9 in.

Overall Width: 1.3 in.
Barrel: 3.3 in.
Grips: Textured polymer, modular
Sights: Dovetail front/rear, Heinie "Straight Eight"
Weight Unloaded: 16 oz. (9mm, titanium), 18.7 oz. (.380; 9mm, .40 S&W), 19.9 oz. (.32 ACP), 22.2 oz. (.45 ACP)
Caliber: .32 ACP; .380; 9mm, .40 S&W, .45 ACP
Capacity: 12 + 1 (.380; 9mm), 10 + 1 (.32 ACP; .40 S&W), 6 + 1 (.45 ACP)
Features: Polymer frame; ambidextrous magazine release, thumb safety; external extractor; loaded-chamber indicator; cocked indicator
Blue: $483
Bi-tone: $498

1911 SERIES

Action: Autoloader, SA
Overall Length: 8.5 in.
Overall Height: 5.5 in.
Overall Width: 1.4 in.
Barrel: 5 in.
Grips: Checkered polymer
Sights: Dovetail front/rear, Novak style
Weight Unloaded: 38 oz.
Caliber: 9mm, .45 ACP
Capacity: 9 + 1 (9mm), 8 + 1 (.45 ACP)
Features: Colt 1911 design; steel frame; ambidextrous extended thumb, beavertail grip safeties; lowered/flared ejection port; beveled magazine well; magazine base pad; checkered front grip strap
Blue: $789
Stainless: $891

MODELS 92 and 99

Action: Autoloader, SA/DA
Overall Length: 8.5 in.
Overall Height: 5.4 in.
Overall Width: 1.5 in.
Barrel: 5 in.
Grips: Checkered rubber
Sights: Fixed front/dovetail rear (model 92), fixed front/adj. rear (model 99)
Weight Unloaded: 34 oz.
Caliber: 9mm
Capacity: 17 + 1
Features: Beretta design; steel frame; ambidextrous thumb safety; loaded-chamber indicator; combat trigger guard; Picatinny rail; external hammer; blue or stainless finish
MSRP: $571

MODELS 100 and 101

Action: Autoloader, SA/DA
Overall Length: 8.5 in.
Overall Height: 5.4 in.
Overall Width: 1.5 in.
Barrel: 5 in.
Grips: Checkered rubber
Sights: Fixed front/dovetail rear (model 100), fixed front/adj. rear (model 101)
Weight Unloaded: 34 oz.
Caliber: .40 S&W
Capacity: 11 + 1
Features: Beretta design; steel frame; ambidextrous thumb safety; loaded-chamber indicator; combat trigger guard; Picatinny rail; external hammer; blue or stainless finish
MSRP: $589

Taurus

(www.taurususa.com)

TAURUS MILLENIUM PRO COMPACT

TAURUS MODEL 85

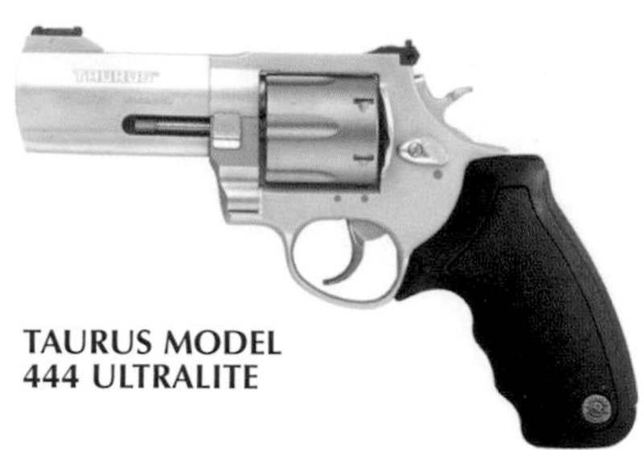
TAURUS MODEL 444 ULTRALITE

TAURUS MODEL 856

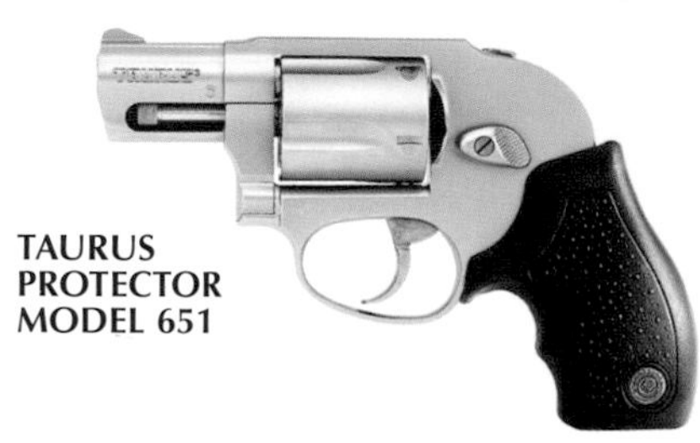
TAURUS PROTECTOR MODEL 651

MODEL 856

Action: Revolver, SA/DA
Overall Length: 6.5 in.
Barrel: 2 in.
Grips: Textured rubber
Sights: Fixed front/rear
Weight Unloaded: 22.2 oz.
Caliber: .38 Spl. +P
Capacity: 6
Features: Steel frame
Blue: $441
Matte stainless: $488

MODEL 85

Action: Revolver, SA/DA
Overall Length: 6.5 in. (2 in. barrel), 7.5 in. (3 in. barrel)
Barrel: 2 in., 3 in.
Grips: Textured rubber
Sights: Fixed front/rear
Weight Unloaded: 17 oz.
Caliber: .38 Spl. +P
Capacity: 6
Features: Ultra light frame
Blue: $400
Matte stainless *(ultralite frame)*: $461

MODEL 605, 731, and 905

Action: Revolver, SA/DA
Overall Length: 6.5 in.
Barrel: 2 in.
Grips: Textured rubber
Sights: Fixed front/rear
Weight Unloaded: 17 oz. (.32 Mag.), 21 oz. (9mm, .357 Mag.)
Caliber: .32 Mag.; 9mm, .357 Mag.
Capacity: 6 (.32 Mag.), 5 (9mm, .357 Mag.)
Features: Steel frame; transfer bar safety
605 *(.357 Mag.)*: $424
731 *(.32 Mag.)*: $514
905 *(9mm)*: $480

CIA MODELS 850 and 650

Action: Revolver, DAO
Overall Length: 6.5 in.
Barrel: 2 in.
Grips: Textured rubber
Sights: Fixed front/rear
Weight Unloaded: 23 oz. (.38 Spl.), 24.2 oz. (.357 Mag.)
Caliber: .38 Spl., .357 Mag.
Capacity: 5
Features: Steel frame; enclosed hammer
850 *(.38 Spl.)*: $520
650 *(.357 Mag.)*: $530

PROTECTOR MODELS 851 and 651

Action: Revolver, SA/DA
Overall Length: 6.5 in.
Barrel: 2 in.
Grips: Textured rubber
Sights: Fixed front/rear
Weight Unloaded: 16.8 oz. (.38 Spl.), 25 oz. (.357 Mag.)
Caliber: .38 Spl.; .357 Mag.
Capacity: 5
Features: Steel frame; shrouded hammer
851 *(.38 Spl.)*: $469
651 *(.357 Mag.)*: $480

MODELS 617 and 817

Action: Revolver, SA/DA
Overall Length: 6.6 in.
Barrel: 2 in.
Grips: Ribbed rubber
Sights: Fixed front/rear
Weight Unloaded: 21 oz. (.38 Spl. +P), 28.3 oz. (.357 Mag.)
Caliber: .38 Spl. +P; .357 Mag.
Capacity: 7
Features: Steel frame; exposed hammer
817 *(.38 Spl.)*: $459
671 *(.357 Mag.)*: $579

MODELS 65, 66, and 82

Action: Revolver, SA/DA
Overall Length: 9.3 in. (.38 Spl.), 10.5 in. (.357 Mag.)
Barrel: 4 in.
Grips: Textured rubber
Sights: Fixed front/rear, fixed front/adj. rear (Model 66)
Weight Unloaded: 36.5 oz. (.38 Spl.), 38 oz. (.357 Mag.)
Caliber: .38 Spl.; .357 Mag.
Capacity: 6 (.38 Spl.), 7 (.357 Mag.)
Features: Steel frame; exposed hammer
65 *(.357 Mag.)*: $541
66 *(.357 Mag.)*: $488
82 *(.38 Spl.)*: $424

MODEL 444 ULTRALITE

Action: Revolver, SA/DA
Overall Length: 9.8 in.
Barrel: 4 in.
Grips: Rubber with cushion inserts
Sights: Fixed fiber optic front/adj. rear
Weight Unloaded: 28.3 oz.
Caliber: .44 Mag.
Capacity: 6
Features: Titanium alloy frame; exposed hammer
Bi-tone: $748
Matte stainless: $795

HANDGUNS

Taurus

(www.taurususa.com)

TAURUS MODEL 905

TAURUS MODEL 82

TAURUS PUBLIC DEFENDER POLYMER

TAURUS PUBLIC DEFENDER

TAURUS RAGING JUDGE

TAURUS JUDGE 2.5-INCH CHAMBER

PUBLIC DEFENDER POLYMER

Action: Revolver, SA/DA
Overall Length: 9 in.
Barrel: 2.5 in.
Grips: Ribbed rubber
Sights: High visibility fixed front/adj. rear
Weight Unloaded: 27 oz.
Caliber: .45 LC/.410
Capacity: 5
Features: Polymer frame; bobbed hammer
Blue: $570
Bi-tone: $617

PUBLIC DEFENDER

Action: Revolver, SA/DA
Overall Length: 9 in.
Overall Height: 6.2 in.
Overall Width: 1.5 in.
Barrel: 2.5 in.
Grips: Ribbed rubber
Sights: Fiber optic dovetail front/fixed rear
Weight Unloaded: 20.7 oz. (Ultralite), 28.2 oz.
Caliber: .45 LC/.410
Capacity: 5
Features: Steel frame; bobbed hammer
Blue: $510
Matte stainless: $560

JUDGE 2.5 INCH CHAMBER

Action: Revolver, SA/DA
Overall Length: 9.5 in.
Overall Height: 6.2 in.
Overall Width: 1.5 in.
Barrel: 3 in.
Grips: Ribbed rubber
Sights: Fiber optic dovetail front/fixed rear
Weight Unloaded: 20.7 oz.
Caliber: .45 LC/.410 Gauge
Capacity: 5
Features: Steel frame; 2.5 in.
Blue: $570
Matte stainless: $592
Blue *(ported barrel)*: $630
Matte stainless *(ported barrel)*: $648
Ultra-Lite blue: $570
Ultra-Lite matte stainless: $592

JUDGE 3 INCH CHAMBER

Action: Revolver, SA/DA
Overall Length: 9.5 in.
Overall Height: 6.2 in.
Overall Width: 1.5 in.
Barrel: 3 in.
Grips: Ribbed rubber
Sights: Fiber optic dovetail front/fixed rear
Weight Unloaded: 36.8 oz.
Caliber: .45 LC/.410

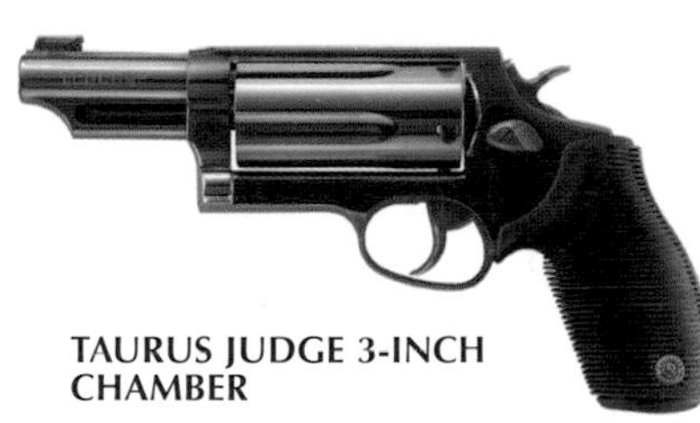
TAURUS JUDGE 3-INCH CHAMBER

Capacity: 5
Features: Steel frame; 3 in. chamber
Blue: $587
Matte stainless finish: $634

RAGING JUDGE MAGNUM

Action: Revolver, SA/DA
Overall Length: 10.2 in.
Barrel: 3 in.
Grips: Texture rubber w/ cushion insert
Sights: Fiber optic dovetail front/fixed rear
Weight Unloaded: 60.6 oz.
Caliber: .45 LC/.454 Casull/.410
Capacity: 6
Features: Steel frame; front/rear cylinder releases; 2.5 in. and 3 in. chambers
Blue Ultralite *(41.4 oz., .45 LC/.410 gauge)*: $936
Matte stainless: $936

Walther

(www.waltheramerica.com)

WALTHER PK380

WALTHER PPS

WALTHER PPK

WALTHER PPK/S (STAINLESS)

PK380

Action: Autoloader, SA/DA
Overall Length: 6.5 in.
Overall Height: 5.2 in.
Overall Width: 1.2 in.
Barrel: 3.2 in.
Grips: Polymer
Sights: Fixed blade front/drift adj. rear, 3-Dot
Weight Unloaded: 19.4 oz.
Caliber: .380
Capacity: 8 + 1
Features: Ambidextrous magazine release, safety; steel frame/slide; external hammer; Picatinny accessory rail
Black: $393
Two-tone: $458
***Black** (laser sight grip)*: $495

PPS

Action: Autoloader, striker-fired
Overall Length: 6.3 in.
Overall Height: 4.4 in.
Overall Width: 1.04 in.
Barrel: 3.2 in.
Grips: Polymer
Sights: Fixed front/adj. rear
Weight Unloaded: 19.4 oz. (9mm), 20.8 oz. (.40 S&W)
Caliber: 9mm, .40 S&W
Capacity: 6 +1 (9m
S&W)
Features: Ambidext
release; loaded-cha
indicators; small an
backstrap; trigger, internal striker, and Walther QuickSafe safeties; polymer receiver; extended magazines; black finish
MSRP: $735

PPK

Action: Autoloader, SA/DA
Overall Length: 6.1 in.
Overall Height: 3.8 in.
Overall Width: .98 in.
Barrel: 3.35 in.
Grips: Checkered polymer
Sights: Fixed blade front/adj. rear
Weight Unloaded: 20.8 oz.
Caliber: .32 ACP; .380
Capacity: 7 + 1 (.32 ACP), 6 +1 (.380)
Features: Steel frame/slide; manual, decocking, and firing pin safeties; extended beaver tail
Blued: $626
Stainless: $626

PPK/S

Action: Autoloader, single/DA
Overall Length: 6.1 in.
Overall Height: 4.3 in.
Overall Width: .98 in.
Barrel: 3.35 in.
Grips: Checkered polymer
Sights: Fixed blade front, drift adj. rear
Weight Unloaded: 22.4 oz.
Caliber: .32 ACP; .380
Capacity: 8 + 1 (.32 ACP), 7 + 1 (.380)
Features: Longer steel frame than PPK; manual, decocking, and firing pin safeties; extended beavertail
Blued: $626
Stainless: $626
Two-tone: $626
***.380** (laser sight grip grips)*: $862

P99

Action: Autoloader, striker-fired or DAO
Overall Length: 7.1 in. (9mm), 7.2 in. (.40 S&W)
Overall Height: 5.3 in.
Overall Width: 1.3 in.
Barrel: 4 in. (9mm), 4.17 in. (.40 S&W)
Grips: Polymer
Sights: 3-dot; adj.
Weight Unloaded: 21.3 oz. (9mm), 23.1 oz. (.40 S&W)
Caliber: 9mm, .40 S&W
Capacity: 15 + 1 (9mm), 12 + 1 (.40 S&W)
Features: Ambidextrous magazine release; cocking indicator; decocker safety; polymer receiver; black finish
***AS** (DAO)*: $825
***QA** (striker-fired)*: $825

Walther

(www.waltheramerica.com)

P99 COMPACT

Action: Autoloader, striker-fired or DAO
Overall Length: 6.6 in.
Overall Height: 4.3 in.
Overall Width: 1.3 in.
Barrel: 3.5 in.
Grips: Polymer
Sights: 3-dot, adj.
Weight Unloaded: 18.7 oz.
Caliber: 9mm, .40 S&W
Capacity: 10-round magazine (9mm), 8-round magazine (.40 S&W)
Features: Ambidextrous magazine release; cocking indicator; decocker safety; polymer receiver; black finish; flat-bottom and finger rest magazine butt plates
AS *(DAO)*: $825
QA *(striker-fired)*: $825

WALTHER P99 QA

WALTHER P99 COMPACT QA

Wilson Combat

(www.wilsoncombat.com)

WILSON COMBAT CQB

CQB

Action: Autoloader, SA
Overall Length: 7.6 in. (Compact), 8.7 in.
Overall Height: 5.1 in. (Compact), 5.6 in.
Overall Width: 1.3 in.
Barrel: 4 in. (Compact), 5 in.
Grips: Checkered diamondwood
Sights: Dovetail front/rear
Weight Unloaded: 33.8 oz. (Compact), 38.1 oz.
Caliber: .45 ACP
Capacity: 7 + 1 (Compact), 8 + 1
Features: Colt 1911 design; steel frame; ambidextrous extended thumb, beavertail grip safeties; lowered/flared ejection port; beveled magazine well; magazine base pad; checkered front grip strap; front/rear slide serrations; Armor-Tuff finish
MSRP: $2550
Elite *(G10 textured grips, serrated slide top, magazine well)*: $3050
Tactical LE *(Picatinny rail, G10 textured grips, serrated slide top, magazine well)*: $2775
Light-Rail Lightweight *(31.2 oz., aluminum frame, Picatinny rail, textured grips)*: $2800
Light-Rail Lightweight Professional *(28.5 oz., bob-tail aluminum frame, Picatinny rail, textured grips)*: $2850
Compact: $2575
Light-Rail Lightweight Compact *(27.3 oz., aluminum frame, Picatinny rail, textured grips)*: $2920

SUPERGRADE

Action: Autoloader, SA
Overall Length: 7.6 in. (Compact), 8.7 in.
Overall Height: 5.1 in. (Compact), 5.6 in.
Overall Width: 1.3 in.
Barrel: 4 in. (Compact), 5 in.
Grips: Checkered wood
Sights: Fixed front/adj. rear

WILSON COMBAT TACTICAL SUPERGRADE PROFESSIONAL

Weight Unloaded: 33.8 oz. (Compact), 39.1 oz.
Caliber: .45 ACP
Capacity: 7 + 1 (Compact), 8 + 1
Features: Colt 1911 design; steel frame; ambidextrous extended thumb, beavertail grip safeties; lowered/flared ejection port; magazine well; magazine base pad; checkered front grip strap; front/rear/top slide serrations
Classic *(two-tone finish)*: $4475
Tactical *(dovetail front/rear sights, Armor-Tuff matte black finish)*: $4350
Tactical Professional *(Speed-Chute magazine well, dovetail front/rear sights, Armor-Tuff matte black finish, G10 textured grips)*: $4350
Compact: $4350

Wilson Combat

(www.wilsoncombat.com)

ULTRALIGHT CARRY

Action: Autoloader, SA
Overall Length: 7.6 in. (Compact), 8.5 in.
Overall Height: 4.9 in. (Compact), 5.6 in.
Overall Width: 1.3 in.
Barrel: 4 in. (Compact), 5 in.
Grips: Textured G10
Sights: Dovetail front/rear, Tritium
Weight Unloaded: 26.5 oz. (Compact), 32.8 oz.
Caliber: .45 ACP
Capacity: 7 + 1 (Compact), 8 + 1
Features: Colt 1911 design; aluminum frame; ambidextrous extended thumb, beavertail grip safeties; lowered/flared ejection port; beveled magazine well; magazine base pad; checkered front grip strap; slide top serrations; Armor-Tuff matte black finish
MSRP: $3250
Compact: $3250

ULTRALIGHT CARRY SENTINEL

Action: Autoloader, SA
Overall Length: 7.2 in.
Overall Height: 4.8 in.
Overall Width: 1.3 in.
Barrel: 3.6 in.
Grips: Textured G10
Sights: Dovetail front/rear, Tritium
Weight Unloaded: 25.2 oz.
Caliber: 9mm
Capacity: 8 + 1
Features: Colt 1911 design; aluminum frame; ambidextrous extended thumb, beavertail grip safeties; lowered/flared ejection port; beveled magazine well; magazine base pad; checkered front grip strap; slide top serrations; Armor-Tuff matte black finish
MSRP: $3300

HANDGUNS

X-TAC

Action: Autoloader, SA
Overall Length: 8.7 in.
Overall Height: 5.6 in.
Overall Width: 1.3 in.
Barrel: 5 in.
Grips: Textured G10
Sights: Fiber optic dovetail front/ dovetail rear
Weight Unloaded: 38.1 oz.
Caliber: .45 ACP
Capacity: 8 + 1
Features: Colt 1911 design; steel frame; extended thumb, beavertail grip safeties; lowered/flared ejection port; beveled magazine well; magazine base pad; textured front grip strap; black parkerized finish
MSRP: $2395

PROFESSIONAL

Action: Autoloader, SA
Overall Length: 7.6 in.
Overall Height: 5.4 in.
Overall Width: 1.4 in.
Barrel: 4 in.
Grips: Checkered wood
Sights: Dovetail front/rear, Tritium
Weight Unloaded: 36.1 oz.
Caliber: .45 ACP
Capacity: 8 + 1
Features: Colt 1911 design; steel frame; extended thumb, beavertail grip safeties; lowered/flared ejection port; beveled magazine well; magazine base pad; checkered front grip strap; Armor-Tuff matte black finish
MSRP: $2600
Professional Lightweight (aluminum frame, 31 oz.): **$2750**

CLASSIC

Action: Autoloader, SA
Overall Length: 8.7 in.

WILSON COMBAT PROFESSIONAL LIGHTWEIGHT

WILSON COMBAT CLASSIC

WILSON COMBAT ULTRALIGHT COMPACT

WILSON COMBAT ULTRALIGHT CARRY SENTINEL

WILSON COMBAT X-TAC

Overall Height: 5.6 in.
Overall Width: 1.3 in.
Barrel: 5 in.
Grips: Checkered wood
Sights: Fixed front/adj. rear
Weight Unloaded: 39.1 oz.
Caliber: .45 ACP
Capacity: 8 + 1
Features: Colt 1911 design; steel frame; ambidextrous extended thumb, beavertail grip safeties; lowered/flared ejection port; beveled magazine well; magazine base pad; checkered front grip strap; Armor-Tuff matte black slide/matte gray frame finish
MSRP: $2700

PROTECTOR

Action: Autoloader, SA
Overall Length: 8.6 in.
Overall Height: 5.5 in.
Overall Width: 1.5 in.
Barrel: 5 in.
Grips: Checkered wood
Sights: Dovetail front/rear
Weight Unloaded: 37.1 oz.
Caliber: .45 ACP

Wilson Combat

(www.wilsoncombat.com)

WILSON COMBAT PROTECTOR

WILSON COMBAT TACTICAL ELITE

WILSON COMBAT ELITE PROFESSIONAL

WILSON COMBAT STEALTH

WILSON COMBAT SENTINAL

Capacity: 8 + 1
Features: Colt 1911 design; steel frame; extended thumb, beavertail grip safeties; lowered/flared ejection port; beveled magazine well; magazine base pad; checkered front grip strap; Armor-Tuff matte black slide/matte gray frame finish
MSRP: $2600

TACTICAL ELITE

Action: Autoloader, SA
Overall Length: 8.7 in.
Overall Height: 5.6 in.
Overall Width: 1.3 in.
Barrel: 5 in.
Grips: Checkered wood
Sights: Dovetail front/rear
Weight Unloaded: 39.5 oz.
Caliber: .45 ACP
Capacity: 8 + 1
Features: Colt 1911 design; steel frame; ambidextrous extended thumb, beavertail grip safeties; lowered/flared ejection port; beveled magazine well; magazine base pad; checkered front grip strap; Armor-Tuff matte black slide/matte gray frame finish
MSRP: $3250

ELITE PROFESSIONAL

Action: Autoloader, SA
Overall Length: 7.7 in.
Overall Height: 5.6 in.
Overall Width: 1.3 in.
Barrel: 4.1 in.
Grips: Checkered wood
Sights: Dovetail front/rear
Weight Unloaded: 36.2 oz.
Caliber: .45 ACP
Capacity: 8 + 1
Features: Colt 1911 design; steel frame; ambidextrous extended thumb, beavertail grip safeties; lowered/flared ejection port; beveled magazine well; magazine base pad; checkered front grip strap; Armor-Tuff matte black slide/matte gray frame finish
MSRP: $3250

STEALTH

Action: Autoloader, SA
Overall Length: 7.7 in.
Overall Height: 5.2 in.
Overall Width: 1.3 in.
Barrel: 4.1 in.

WILSON COMBAT BILL WILSON CARRY PISTOL

Grips: Checkered wood
Sights: Dovetail front/rear
Weight Unloaded: 35.3 oz.
Caliber: .45 ACP
Capacity: 7 + 1
Features: Colt 1911 design; steel frame; extended thumb, beavertail grip safeties; lowered/flared ejection port; beveled magazine well; magazine base pad; checkered front grip strap; Armor-Tuff matte black slide/matte gray frame finish
MSRP: $3150

SENTINEL

Action: Autoloader, SA
Overall Length: 7.2 in.
Overall Height: 4.8 in.
Overall Width: 1.3 in.
Barrel: 3.6 in.
Grips: Grooved wood
Sights: Dovetail front/rear
Weight Unloaded: 31.7 oz.
Caliber: 9mm
Capacity: 8 + 1
Features: Colt 1911 design; steel frame; extended thumb, beavertail grip safeties; lowered/flared ejection port; beveled magazine well; magazine base pad; checkered front grip strap; Armor-Tuff matte black slide/matte gray frame finish
MSRP: $2950
Ms. Sentinel (aluminum frame, 26.8 oz.): **$3300**

BILL WILSON CARRY PISTOL

Action: Autoloader, SA
Overall Length: 7.6 in.
Overall Height: 4.9 in.
Overall Width: 1.3 in.
Barrel: 4 in.

Wilson Combat

(www.wilsoncombat.com)

Grips: G10-textured polymer
Sights: Dovetail front/rear
Weight Unloaded: 35 oz.
Caliber: .45 ACP
Capacity: 7 + 1
Features: Colt 1911 design; round-butt steel frame; extended thumb, beavertail grip safeties; lowered/flared ejection port; beveled magazine well; magazine base pad; checkered front grip strap; Armor-Tuff matte black slide/matte gray frame finish
MSRP: $2850

SPEC-OPS 9

Action: Autoloader, SA
Overall Length: 7.9 in.
Overall Height: 5.3 in.
Overall Width: 1.3 in.
Barrel: 4.5 in.
Grips: Grooved polymer
Sights: Dovetail front/rear
Weight Unloaded: 31.7 oz.
Caliber: 9mm
Capacity: 16 + 1
Features: Polymer frame; extended thumb, beavertail grip safeties; lowered/flared ejection port; beveled magazine well; magazine base pad; checkered front grip strap; combat trigger guard; matte black finish
MSRP: $1995

CARRY COMP PROFESSIONAL

Action: Autoloader, SA
Overall Length: 8.1 in.
Overall Height: 5 in. (Compact), 5.4 in.
Overall Width: 1.4 in.
Barrel: 4.5 in.
Grips: Grooved wood
Sights: Dovetail front/rear, Tritium
Weight Unloaded: 35.2 oz. (Compact), 36.7 oz.
Caliber: .45 ACP
Capacity: 7 + 1 (Compact), 8 + 1
Features: Colt 1911 design; steel frame; extended thumb, beavertail grip safeties; lowered/flared ejection port; beveled magazine well; magazine base pad; checkered front grip strap; muzzle compensator; Armor-Tuff matte black finish
MSRP: $3350
Compact: $3350

WILSON COMBAT SPEC-OPS 9

WILSON COMBAT CARRY COMP PROFESSIONAL

9. Ammunition

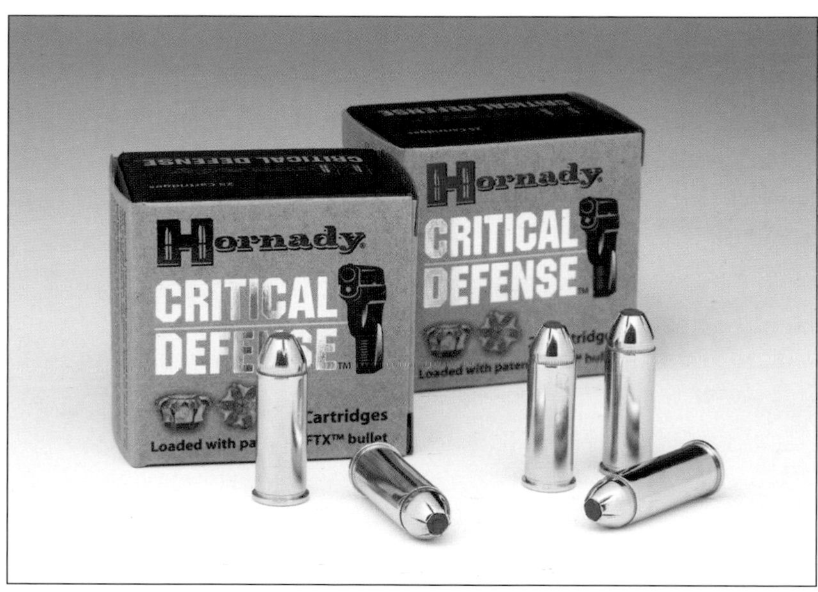

Image courtesy of Hornady.

LEGEND

BEB – Brass Enclosed Base
Bi-FMJ – Bimetal-Full Metal Jacket
BJHP – Brass Jacketed Hollow Point
CEHP – Controlled Expansion Hollow Point
CJPT LF – Copper Jacketed Polymer Tip Lead Free
EFMJ – Expanding Full Metal Jacket
EMJ – Encapsulated Metal Jacket
ETC – Encapsulated Truncated Cone
EXP JHP – Extra Power Jacketed Hollow Point
FMJ – Full Metal Jacket
FMJ-FN – Full Metal Jacket-Flat Nose
FMJ-FP – Full Metal Jacket-Flat Point
FMJ-SS – Full Metal Jacket-Subsonic
FMJ-TC – Full Metal Jacket-Truncated Cone
FN – Flat Nose
GDHP – Gold Dot Hollow Point
GDHP-SB – Gold Dot Hollow Point-Short Barrel
GR – Grain
HCFN – Hardcast Flat Nose
HP – Hollow Point
JHP – Jacketed Hollow Point
JSP – Jacketed Soft Point
JSP-LF – Jacketed Soft Point-Lead Free
LCN – Lead Conical Nose
LF – Lead Free
LRN – Lead Round Nose
LSW – Lead Semi Wadcutter
SFHP – StarFire Hollow Point
SJHP – Semi Jacketed Hollow Point
SW – Semi-Wadcutter
SWHC – Semi-Wadcutter Hardcast
SW HP – Semi-Wadcutter Hollow Point
TAC-XP HP LF – TAC-XP Hollow Point Lead Free
TSP – Truncated Soft point
TMJ – Total Metal Jacket
WFN GC – Wide Flat Nose Gas Check

Ammunition

Aguila (www.aguilaammo.com)

Aguila ammunition is new production, noncorrosive, and in Boxer-primed, reloadable brass cases loaded to SAAMI specifications.

Caliber	Manufacturer	Bullet Weight In Grains	Bullet Type	Case Type	Primer Type	Cartridges Per Box	MSRP
.25 ACP	Aguila	50	FMJ	Brass	Boxer	50	$18
.32 ACP	Aguila	71	FMJ	Brass	Boxer	50	$19
.380	Aguila	90	JHP	Brass	Boxer	50	$20
.380	Aguila	95	FMJ	Brass	Boxer	50	$18
9mm	Aguila	117	JHP	Brass	Boxer	50	$20
.38 Special	Aguila	158	SJHP	Brass	Boxer	50	$21

AGUILA 9MM 117-GR. JHP

Bear (www.dkgtrading.com)

Brown Bear pistol ammunition is new-production ammo manufactured with Berdan-primed, nonreloadable, lacquered steel cases that offer long shelf life and surefire ignition. It is loaded to military specifications.

Caliber	Bullet Weight in Grains	Bullet Type	Case Type	Primer Type	Cartridges Per Box	MSRP
9mm	115	FMJ	Nonreloadable Lacquer coated steel	Berdan	50	$12

Silver Bear pistol ammunition is new-production ammo manufactured with Berdan-primed, nonreloadable, nickel-plated steel cases.

Caliber	Bullet Weight in Grains	Bullet Type	Case Type	Primer Type	Cartridges Per Box	MSRP
9mm	115	FMJ	Nonreloadable Zinc plated Steel	Berdan	50	$12

BEAR BROWN BEAR 9MM 115-GR. FMJ

BEAR SILVER BEAR 9MM 115-GR. FMJ

Golden Bear shotgun ammunition is new-production ammo manufactured with nonreloadable, brass-coated steel cases.

Gauge	Length	Shot Size	Case Type	Cartridges Per Box	MSRP
.410	2.75 in.	5 #4 buck shot	Brass-plated steel hull	5	$4
.410	2.75 in.	97-grain slug	Brass-plated steel hull	5	$4

Black Hills Ammunition (www.black-hills.com)

All branches of the U.S. military and law-enforcement agencies nationwide, as well as firearms manufacturers, use Black Hills ammo during weapon development. It is new production, noncorrosive, and in Boxer-primed, reloadable brass cases with jacketed hollow point, full metal jacket, and Barnes TAC-XP 100 percent copper bullets.

Caliber	Bullet Weight in Grains	Bullet Type	Case Type	Primer Type	Cartridges Per Box	MSRP
32 H&R Magnum	85	JHP	Reloadable brass	Boxer	50	$35
.380	90	JHP	Reloadable brass	Boxer	50	$34
.380	100*	FMJ	Reloadable brass	Boxer	50	$30
9mm	115	EXP JHP	Reloadable brass	Boxer	50	$20
9mm	115	FMJ	Reloadable brass	Boxer	50	$28
9mm	124	JHP	Reloadable brass	Boxer	50	$31

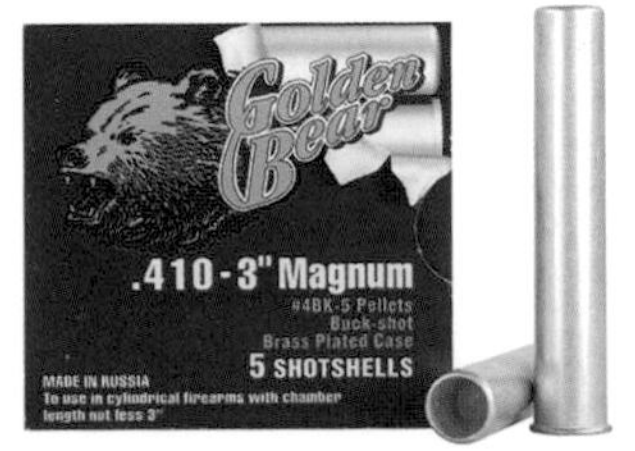

BEAR GOLDEN BEAR .410, 2.75 IN., 4-BUCK SHOT

AMMUNITION

Caliber	Bullet Weight in Grains	Bullet Type	Case Type	Primer Type	Cartridges Per Box	MSRP
9mm Luger +P	115	JHP	Reloadable brass	Boxer	50	$35
9mm Luger +P	124	JHP	Reloadable brass	Boxer	50	$35
.38 Special +P	125	JHP	Reloadable brass	Boxer	50	$34
.357 Magnum	125	JHP	Reloadable brass	Boxer	50	$37
.357 Magnum	158	JHP	Reloadable brass	Boxer	50	$37
.40 S&W	140	Barnes TAC-XP HP LF	Reloadable brass	Boxer	50	$53
.40 S&W	155	JHP	Reloadable brass	Boxer	50	$39
.40 S&W	180	JHP	Reloadable brass	Boxer	50	$39
.45 ACP	185	JHP	Reloadable brass	Boxer	50	$46
.45 ACP	230	FMJ	Reloadable brass	Boxer	50	$43
.45 ACP	230	JHP	Reloadable brass	Boxer	50	$47
.45 ACP +P	230	JHP	Reloadable brass	Boxer	50	$50

*This ammo, or any ball ammunition, is not for use with Seecamp LWS .380 handguns

Black Hills remanufactured ammunition is reloaded, once-fired brass suitable for training.

Caliber	Bullet Weight in Grains	Bullet Type	Case Type	Primer Type	Cartridges Per Box	MSRP
9mm	115	FMJ	Previously fired brass	Boxer	50	$20
9mm	124	FMJ	Previously fired brass	Boxer	50	$21
.40 S&W	180	JHP	Previously fired brass	Boxer	50	$28
.40 S&W	180	FMJ	Previously fired brass	Boxer	50	$25
.40 S&W	155	FMJ	Previously fired brass	Boxer	50	$27
.45 ACP	200	SW	Previously fired brass	Boxer	50	$28
.45 ACP	230	FMJ	Previously fired brass	Boxer	50	$28

Blazer (www.blazer-ammo.com)

Blazer ammo is new manufacture loaded to SAAMI standards in nonreloadable aluminum cases with Boxer primers and a variety of bullet types for training and defense.

Caliber	Bullet Weight in Grains	Bullet Type	Case Type	Primer Type	Cartridges Per Box	MSRP
.25 ACP	50	FMJ	Nonreloadable aluminum	Boxer	50	$19
.380	95	TMJ	Nonreloadable aluminum	Boxer	50	$18
9mm	115	FMJ	Nonreloadable aluminum	Boxer	50	$14
9mm	124	FMJ	Nonreloadable aluminum	Boxer	50	$13
9mm	147	TMJ	Nonreloadable aluminum	Boxer	50	$13
.38 Special	158	SJHP	Nonreloadable aluminum	Boxer	50	$21
.38 Special	158	LRN	Nonreloadable aluminum	Boxer	50	$17
.38 Special +P	125	JHP	Nonreloadable aluminum	Boxer	50	$18
.38 Special +P	158	TMJ	Nonreloadable aluminum	Boxer	50	$18
.357 Magnum	158	JHP	Nonreloadable aluminum	Boxer	50	$22
.40 S&W	155	TMJ	Nonreloadable aluminum	Boxer	50	$20
.40 S&W	165	TMJ	Nonreloadable aluminum	Boxer	50	$20
.40 S&W	180	FMJ	Nonreloadable aluminum	Boxer	50	$20
10mm	200	TMJ	Nonreloadable aluminum	Boxer	50	$26
.44 Special	200	Speer Gold Dot JHP	Nonreloadable aluminum	Boxer	50	$32
.45 Long Colt	200	JHP	Nonreloadable aluminum	Boxer	50	$37
.45 ACP	230	FMJ	Nonreloadable aluminum	Boxer	50	$26

BLAZER BRASS

Ammunition

BLAZER AMMO IS NOT RELOADABLE BUT IS ECONOMICAL FOR HIGH VOLUME PRACTICE AND TRAINING.

BLAZER CLEAN–FIRECASES (LEFT) COMPARED TO TYPICAL BLAZER AMMO (RIGHT)

Blazer Brass is new-production ammunition loaded to SAAMI standards in reloadable brass cases with Boxer primers and protected-base FMJ bullets.

Caliber	Bullet Weight in Grains	Bullet Type	Case Type	Primer Type	Cartridges Per Box	MSRP
.32 ACP	71	TMJ	Brass	Boxer	50	$23
.380	95	FMJ	Brass	Boxer	50	$19
9mm	115	FMJ	Brass	Boxer	50	$14
9mm	124	FMJ	Brass	Boxer	50	$14
.38 Special	125	FMJ	Brass	Boxer	50	$20
.40 S&W	165	FMJ	Brass	Boxer	50	$22
.40 S&W	180	FMJ	Brass	Boxer	50	$22
.45 ACP	230	FMJ	Brass	Boxer	50	$27

Blazer Clean-Fire Ammunition is new manufacture that uses CCI Clean-Fire primers and Speer TMJ bullets. It is designed for use in indoor ranges to eliminate airborne toxins.

Caliber	Bullet Weight in Grains	Bullet Type	Case Type	Primer Type	Cartridges Per Box	MSRP
9mm	124	TMJ	Nonreloadable aluminum	Boxer	50	$15
9mm	147	TMJ	Nonreloadable aluminum	Boxer	50	$19
.38 Special +P	158	TMJ	Nonreloadable aluminum	Boxer	50	$20
.40 S&W	180	TMJ	Nonreloadable aluminum	Boxer	50	$21
.45 ACP	230	TMJ	Nonreloadable aluminum	Boxer	50	$25

Buffalo Bore Ammunition (buffalobore.com)

Buffalo Bore produces powerful handgun ammunition loaded above normal factory ammunition specifications. It is new production, loaded in new brass, Boxer primed, and comes in a variety of bullets types including jacketed hollow point, full metal jacket, hardcast flat nose, and others for defense applications. Shooters should read the manufacturer's warnings and compatibility of this +P loaded ammunition before using it in their firearms.

Caliber	Bullet Weight in Grains	Bullet Type	Case Type	Primer Type	Cartridges Per Box	MSRP
.32 ACP +P	75	HCFN	Brass	Boxer	20	$22
.380 +P	100	FN	Brass	Boxer	20	$22
.380 +P	95	JHP	Brass	Boxer	20	$22
.380 +P	95	FMJ	Brass	Boxer	20	$22
.380 +P	90	JHP	Brass	Boxer	20	$22
.380	95	FMJ	Brass	Boxer	20	$22
.380	100	HCFN	Brass	Boxer	20	$22
.380	90	JHP	Brass	Boxer	20	$22
9mm +P+	147	JHP	Brass	Boxer	20	$24
9mm +P+	115	JHP	Brass	Boxer	20	$24
9mm +P+	124	JHP	Brass	Boxer	20	$24
9mm +P	115	JHP	Brass	Boxer	20	$24
9mm +P	124	JHP	Brass	Boxer	20	$24
.38 Special	158*	SWHP	Brass	Boxer	20	$25
.38 Special	125*	JHP	Brass	Boxer	20	$26

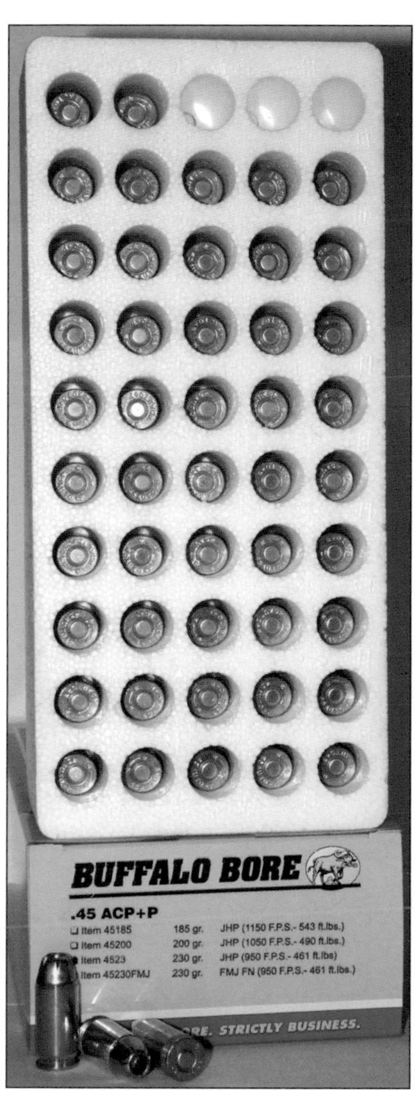

BUFFALO BORE .45 ACP +P 230-GR. JHP

Caliber	Bullet Weight in Grains	Bullet Type	Case Type	Primer Type	Cartridges Per Box	MSRP
.38 Special +P	158	SWHP	Brass	Boxer	20	$25
.38 Special +P	125	JHP	Brass	Boxer	20	$25
.357 Magnum	189	FN	Brass	Boxer	20	$26
.357 Magnum	158	SJHP	Brass	Boxer	20	$26
.357 Magnum	125**	JHP	Brass	Boxer	20	$26
.357 Magnum	158**	JHP	Brass	Boxer	20	$26
.357 Magnum	140**	JHP	Brass	Boxer	20	$26
.357 Sig	125	FMJ	Brass	Boxer	20	$26
.357 Sig	125	JHP	Brass	Boxer	20	$26
.40 S&W	180	JHP	Brass	Boxer	20	$25
.40 S&W	180	FMJ	Brass	Boxer	20	$25
.40 S&W +P	155	JHP	Brass	Boxer	20	$25
10mm	180	JHP	Brass	Boxer	20	$27

BUFFALO BORE 9MM +P+ PENETRATOR

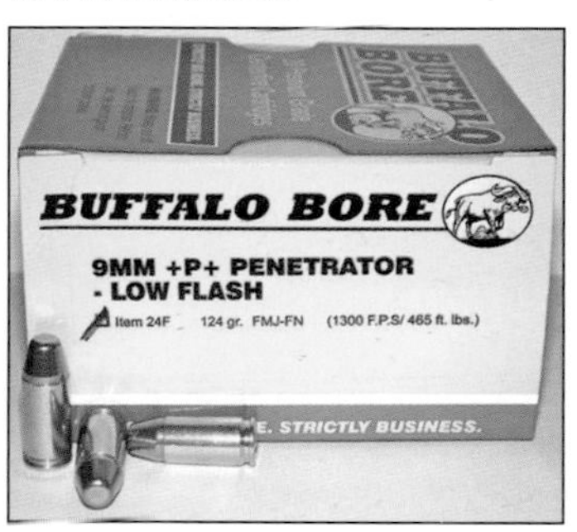

BUFFALO BORE .380 +P 90-GR. JHP

Caliber	Bullet Weight in Grains	Bullet Type	Case Type	Primer Type	Cartridges Per Box	MSRP
10mm	200	FMJ	Brass	Boxer	20	$27
10mm	220	HCFN	Brass	Boxer	20	$27
.44 Special	255***	Keith-Type Semi-Wadcutter Gas Check	Brass	Boxer	20	$36
.44 Special	180***	JHP	Brass	Boxer	20	$36
.45 Long Colt	200	JHP	Brass	Boxer	20	$34
.45 Long Colt	255	Keith-Type Semi-Wadcutter Gas Check	Brass	Boxer	20	$34
.45 Long Colt +P	260	JHP	Brass	Boxer	20	$34
.45 ACP +P	230	JHP	Brass	Boxer	20	$25
.45 ACP +P	255	HCFN	Brass	Boxer	20	$27
.45 ACP +P	185	JHP	Brass	Boxer	20	$27
.45 ACP +P	230	FMJ	Brass	Boxer	20	$25
.45 ACP +P	200	JHP	Brass	Boxer	20	$27

*This ammunition is safe for use in alloy frame and other non +P revolvers
**It is not recommended that this ammunition be fired from revolvers weighing less than 16 oz. due to the amount of recoil generated.
***Not intended for use in the Charter Arms Bulldog.

CorBon (www.corbon.com)

CorBon Self-Defense Ammunition is new production, noncorrosive, and loaded in Boxer-primed, reloadable brass cases. It uses flash-suppressed powder with scored bullet jackets that expand quickly with high weight retention and without overpenetration.

Caliber	Bullet Weight in Grains	Bullet Type	Case Type	Primer Type	Cartridges Per Box	MSRP
.25 NAA	35	JHP	Brass	Boxer	20	$22
.32 ACP	60	JHP	Brass	Boxer	20	$23
.32 NAA	60	JHP	Brass	Boxer	20	$23
.380	90	JHP	Brass	Boxer	20	$23
9mm +P	115	JHP	Brass	Boxer	20	$24
9mm +P	125	JHP	Brass	Boxer	20	$24

CORBON SELF-DEFENSE

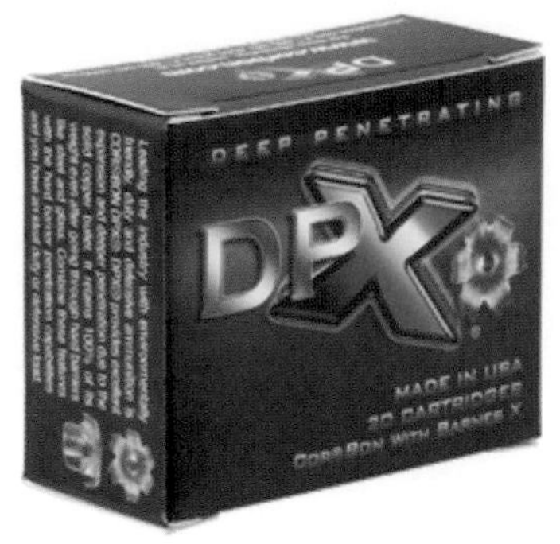

CORBON DPX

Caliber	Bullet Weight in Grains	Bullet Type	Case Type	Primer Type	Cartridges Per Box	MSRP
9mm +P	90	JHP	Brass	Boxer	20	$24
.38 Special +P	110	JHP	Brass	Boxer	20	$25
.38 Special +P	125	JHP	Brass	Boxer	20	$25
.357 Magnum	110	JHP	Brass	Boxer	20	$27
.357 Magnum	125	JHP	Brass	Boxer	20	$27
.357 Magnum	140	JHP	Brass	Boxer	20	$27
.357 Sig	115	JHP	Brass	Boxer	20	$30
.357 Sig	125	JHP	Brass	Boxer	20	$30
.40 S&W	135	JHP	Brass	Boxer	20	$29
.40 S&W	165	JHP	Brass	Boxer	20	$29
.40 S&W	150	JHP	Brass	Boxer	20	$29
10mm	165	JHP	Brass	Boxer	20	$30
10mm	135	JHP	Brass	Boxer	20	$30
10mm	150	JHP	Brass	Boxer	20	$30
.44 Special	165	JHP	Brass	Boxer	20	$34
.45 Long Colt +P	200	JHP	Brass	Boxer	20	$32
.45 GAP	200	JHP	Brass	Boxer	20	$29
.45 ACP +P	200	JHP	Brass	Boxer	20	$29
.45 ACP +P	165	JHP	Brass	Boxer	20	$29
.45 ACP +P	185	JHP	Brass	Boxer	20	$29
.45 ACP +P	230	JHP	Brass	Boxer	20	$29

CorBon DPX is new-manufacture ammunition that uses reloadable brass cases and Barnes XPB solid copper HP bullets for high velocity and hard barrier penetration on auto glass and steel while still maintaining safe soft-tissue penetration depths. DPX ammunition can achieve soft-tissue penetration of twelve to seventeen inches with reliable and consistent expansion. Recovered bullets have expanded 150 percent to 200 percent of the original size and retain 100 percent weight retention when recovered from ballistic gelatin.

Caliber	Bullet Weight in Grains	Bullet Type	Case Type	Primer Type	Cartridges Per Box	MSRP
.32 ACP	60	Barnes XPB HP LF	Brass	Boxer	20	$30
.380	80	Barnes XPB HP LF	Brass	Boxer	20	$29
9mm +P	115	Barnes XPB HP LF	Brass	Boxer	20	$33
9mm +P	95	Barnes XPB HP LF	Brass	Boxer	20	$34
.38 Special +P	110	Barnes XPB HP LF	Brass	Boxer	20	$33
.357 Magnum	125	Barnes XPB HP LF	Brass	Boxer	20	$38
.357 Sig	125	Barnes XPB HP LF	Brass	Boxer	20	$37
.40 S&W	140	Barnes XPB HP LF	Brass	Boxer	20	$39
10mm	155	Barnes XPB HP LF	Brass	Boxer	20	$39
.44 Special	200	Barnes XPB HP LF	Brass	Boxer	20	$52
.45 GAP	160	Barnes XPB HP LF	Brass	Boxer	20	$37
.45 Long Colt	225	Barnes XPB HP LF	Brass	Boxer	20	$51
.45 ACP	185	Barnes XPB HP LF	Brass	Boxer	20	$39
.45 ACP +P	160	Barnes XPB HP LF	Brass	Boxer	20	$35

CorBon Performance Match Ammunition is new manufacture loaded with match-grade components for accuracy and reliability.

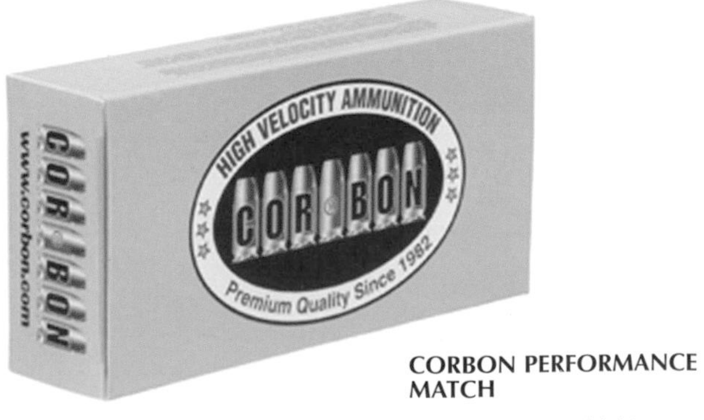

CORBON PERFORMANCE MATCH

Caliber	Bullet Weight in Grains	Bullet Type	Case Type	Primer Type	Cartridges Per Box	MSRP
.32 NAA	71	FMJ	Brass	Boxer	20	$25
9mm	147	FMJ	Brass	Boxer	20	$27
.38 Special	147	FMJ	Brass	Boxer	20	$12
.40 S&W	165	FMJ	Brass	Boxer	20	$37
.45 GAP	230	FMJ	Brass	Boxer	20	$34
.45 ACP	230	FMJ	Brass	Boxer	20	$33

Pow'RBall ammunition was designed to eliminate feeding problems in pistols that would not feed large cavity JHP bullets. The Pow'RBall projectile is a JHP bullet with a polymer ball crimped into the tip. The tip enhances feeding and delays the expansion of the projectile when it hits soft tissue. This controlled expansion provides deeper penetration, better weight retention, and more consistent expansion in soft tissue.

CORBON POW'RBALL .357 SIG 100-GR.

CORBOB GLASER BLUE SAFETY SLUG

Caliber	Bullet Weight In Grains	Bullet Type	Case Type	Primer Type	Cartridges Per Box	MSRP
.32 ACP	55	Pow'rBall	Brass	Boxer	20	$22
.380	70	Pow'rBall	Brass	Boxer	20	$23
9mm	100	Pow'rBall	Brass	Boxer	20	$23
.38 Special +P	100	Pow'rBall	Brass	Boxer	20	$26
.357 Magnum	100	Pow'rBall	Brass	Boxer	20	$25
.357 Sig	100	Pow'rBall	Brass	Boxer	20	$28
.40 S&W	135	Pow'rBall	Brass	Boxer	20	$27
10mm	135	Pow'rBall	Brass	Boxer	20	$28
.45 ACP +P	165	Pow'rBall	Brass	Boxer	20	$28

The Glaser Safety Slug was designed to address concerns of over penetration on soft tissue and ricochets on hard surfaces. Safety Slug ammo uses a copper jacket filled with a compressed load of lead shot capped with a round polymer ball that enhances feeding. Blue Safety Slugs use #12 shot, and Silver Safety Slugs use #6 shot.

Caliber	Bullet Weight In Grains	Bullet Type	Case Type	Primer Type	Cartridges Per Box	MSRP
.25 ACP	35	Blue Safety Slug	Brass	Boxer	6	$12
.32 ACP	55	Blue Safety Slug	Brass	Boxer	6	$12
.32 NAA	55	Blue Safety Slug	Brass	Boxer	6	$12
.380	70	Blue Safety Slug	Brass	Boxer	6	$12
.380	70	Silver Safety Slug	Brass	Boxer	6	$12
9mm +P	90	Blue Safety Slug	Brass	Boxer	6	$13
9mm +P	90	Silver Safety Slug	Brass	Boxer	6	$13
.38 Special +P	80	Blue Safety Slug	Brass	Boxer	6	$13
.38 Special	80	Blue Safety Slug	Brass	Boxer	6	$13
.38 Special	80	Silver Safety Slug	Brass	Boxer	6	$13
.357 Magnum	80	Blue Safety Slug	Brass	Boxer	6	$13
.357 Magnum	80	Silver Safety Slug	Brass	Boxer	6	$13
.357 Sig	80	Blue Safety Slug	Brass	Boxer	6	$13
.357 Sig	80	Silver Safety Slug	Brass	Boxer	6	$13
.40 S&W	115	Blue Safety Slug	Brass	Boxer	6	$14
.40 S&W	115	Silver Safety Slug	Brass	Boxer	6	$14
10mm	115	Blue Safety Slug	Brass	Boxer	6	$14
10mm	115	Silver Safety Slug	Brass	Boxer	6	$14
.44 Special	135	Blue Safety Slug	Brass	Boxer	6	$13
.44 Special	135	Silver Safety Slug	Brass	Boxer	6	$13
.45 Long Colt +P	145	Blue Safety Slug	Brass	Boxer	6	$14
.45 Long Colt +P	145	Silver Safety Slug	Brass	Boxer	6	$14
.45 ACP +P	145	Blue Safety Slug	Brass	Boxer	6	$14
.45 ACP +P	145	Silver Safety Slug	Brass	Boxer	6	$14

DoubleTap (www.doubletapammo.com)

DoubleTap ammunition is new manufacture using reloadable brass, is Boxer primed and loaded with a variety of bullet types for defensive applications.

Caliber	Bullet Weight in Grains	Bullet Type	Case Type	Primer Type	Cartridges Per Box	MSRP
.380	90	Bonded Defense JHP	Brass	Boxer	50	$37
.380	95	FMJ	Brass	Boxer	50	$37
.380	80	Barnes TAC-XP HP LF	Brass	Boxer	50	
9mm +P	124	Bonded Defense JHP	Brass	Boxer	50	$38
9mm +P	147	FMJ	Brass	Boxer	50	$36
9mm +P	147	Bonded Defense JHP	Brass	Boxer	50	$38
9mm +P	115	Barnes TAC-XP HP LF	Brass	Boxer	50	$63

Ammunition

DOUBLETAP 10MM 200–GR. WFN GC HARDCAST

Caliber	Bullet Weight in Grains	Bullet Type	Case Type	Primer Type	Cartridges Per Box	MSRP
9mm +P	115	Bonded Defense JHP	Brass	Boxer	50	$38
.38 Special +P	110	Barnes TAC-XP HP LF	Brass	Boxer	50	$63
.38 Special +P	125	Bonded Defense JHP	Brass	Boxer	50	$38
.38 Special +P	158	Lead SWHC	Brass	Boxer	50	$36
.357 Magnum	125	Bonded Defense JHP	Brass	Boxer	50	$41
.357 Magnum	158	JHP	Brass	Boxer	50	$41
.357 Magnum	200	Lead WFN GC	Brass	Boxer	50	$41
.357 Sig	115	Bonded Defense JHP	Brass	Boxer	50	$41
.357 Sig	125	Bonded Defense JHP	Brass	Boxer	50	$41
.357 Sig	125	FMJ	Brass	Boxer	50	$41
.357 Sig	147	Bonded Defense JHP	Brass	Boxer	50	$41
.357 Sig	147	FMJ	Brass	Boxer	50	$39
.40 S&W	135	JHP	Brass	Boxer	50	$41
.40 S&W	155	Bonded Defense JHP	Brass	Boxer	50	$41
.40 S&W	200	Lead WFN GC	Brass	Boxer	50	$41
.40 S&W	200	JHP	Brass	Boxer	50	$41
.40 S&W	165	Bonded Defense JHP	Brass	Boxer	50	$41
.40 S&W	180	Bonded Defense JHP	Brass	Boxer	50	$41
.40 S&W	200	FMJ	Brass	Boxer	50	$41
.40 S&W	140	Barnes TAC-XP HP LF	Brass	Boxer	50	$63
.40 S&W	180	CEHP	Brass	Boxer	50	$41
10mm	165	BJHP	Brass	Boxer	50	$40
10mm	180	CEHP	Brass	Boxer	50	$42
10mm	135	JHP	Brass	Boxer	50	$42
10mm	180	JHP	Brass	Boxer	50	$42
10mm	180	FMJ	Brass	Boxer	50	$42
10mm	200	FMJ	Brass	Boxer	50	$42
10mm	200	Lead WFN GC	Brass	Boxer	50	$42
10mm	155	Barnes XPB HP LF	Brass	Boxer	50	$39
10mm	200	JHP	Brass	Boxer	50	$42
10mm	230	Equalizer Jacketed Hollow Point*	Brass	Boxer	50	$46
10mm	155	Barnes XPB HP LF	Brass	Boxer	50	$64
10mm	230	Lead WFN GC	Brass	Boxer	50	$42
10mm	155	Bonded Defense JHP	Brass	Boxer	50	$42
10mm	165	Bonded Defense JHP	Brass	Boxer	50	$42
.44 Special	200	SWHC	Brass	Boxer	50	$44
.44 Special	240	Bonded Defense JHP	Brass	Boxer	50	$46
.45 GAP	230	Bonded Defense JHP	Brass	Boxer	50	$44
.45 GAP	185	Bonded Defense JHP	Brass	Boxer	50	$44
.45 GAP	200	Bonded Defense JHP	Brass	Boxer	50	$44
.45 GAP	230	FMJ	Brass	Boxer	50	$44
.45 Long Colt +P		Keith-Type SW	Brass	Boxer	50	$46
.45 Long Colt +P	225	Barnes TAC-XP HP LF	Brass	Boxer	20	$33
.45 ACP	230	Bonded Defense JHP	Brass	Boxer	50	$44
.45 ACP	185	Bonded Defense JHP	Brass	Boxer	50	$44
.45 ACP	200	Bonded Defense JHP	Brass	Boxer	50	$44
.45 ACP	230	FMJ	Brass	Boxer	50	$44
.45 ACP	160	Barnes TAC-XP HP LF	Brass	Boxer	50	$63

*The Equalizer bullet is a 135-grain jacketed hollow point loaded on top of a 95-grain lead ball. The lead ball hits higher than the jacketed hollow point–less than 1 in. high at 10 yds. and 2.5 in. high at 25 yds.

Extreme Shock (www.extremeshockusa.com)

The Enhanced Penetration Round (EPR) is new manufacture and engineered for greater penetration and greater terminal success through automobile glass, light sheet metal, and wood. It is also designed to penetrate thick skin and dense bone and then fragment once inside softer tissue. This round has a compressed tungsten core that will fragment on any surface that causes a lead bullet to ricochet. It is not an armor-piercing round.

EXTREME SHOCK'S EPR ROUNDS, LIKE THIS 115-GR. .38 SPECIAL, ARE MADE TO PENETRATE DEEPER AND PRODUCE CREATER TERMINAL IMPACT THAN TYPICAL .38 SPECIAL ROUNDS.

Caliber	Bullet Weight In Grains	Bullet Type	Case Type	Primer Type	Cartridges Per Box	MSRP	Pack of 6
.32 ACP	60	Frangible	Brass	Boxer	20	$19	$8
.380	70	Frangible	Brass	Boxer	20	$22	$8
9mm	115	Frangible	Brass	Boxer	20	$26	$8
.38 Special	115	Frangible	Brass	Boxer	20	$26	$8
.357 Magnum	115	Frangible	Brass	Boxer	20	$28	$9
.357 Sig	115	Frangible	Brass	Boxer	20	$28	$9
.40 S&W	150	Frangible	Brass	Boxer	20	$35	$11
10mm	150	Frangible	Brass	Boxer	20	$35	$11
.45 GAP	185	Frangible	Brass	Boxer	20	$35	$11
.45 Long Colt	185	Frangible	Brass	Boxer	20	$42	$12
.45 ACP	185	Frangible	Brass	Boxer	20	$37	$11

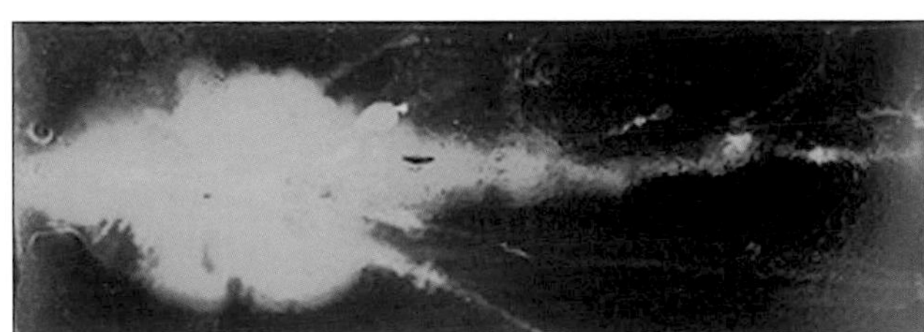

EXTREME SHOCK, .45 ACP FANG FACE IN BALLISTIC GEL.

EXTREME SHOCK'S 124-GR. 9MM AFR ROUND WAS DESIGNED TO MINIMIZE RICOCHET.

NyTrilium Handgun round (Fang Face and Personal Defense) is new-production ammo engineered for expansive fragmentation to expend energy in soft targets. The bullet is made of compressed Tungsten-NyTrilium designed to fragment.

Caliber	Bullet Weight In Grains	Bullet Type	Case Type	Primer Type	Cartridges Per Box	MSRP	Pack of 6
.380	90	Frangible	Brass	Boxer	20	$27	$9
9mm	124	Frangible	Brass	Boxer	20	$32	$11
.38 Special	124	Frangible	Brass	Boxer	20	$32	$11
.357 Magnum	124	Frangible	Brass	Boxer	20	$35	$11
.357 Sig	124	Frangible	Brass	Boxer	20	$36	$11
.40 S&W	165	Frangible	Brass	Boxer	20	$41	$13
.45 GAP	185	Frangible	Brass	Boxer	20	$41	$13
.45 ACP	185	Frangible	Brass	Boxer	20	$43	$13

The NyTrilium Air Freedom Round (AFR) is engineered to contain fired rounds inside of a structure and reduce ricochet and penetration. It will fragment when fired through standard sheetrock walls or on any surface that would cause a lead bullet to ricochet.

Caliber	Bullet Weight in Grains	Bullet Type	Case Type	Primer Type	Cartridges Per Box	MSRP	Pack of 6
.38 Special	70	Frangible	Brass	Boxer	20	$26.99	$9
.357 Magnum	70	Frangible	Brass	Boxer	20	$29.49	$10
.357 Sig	70	Frangible	Brass	Boxer	20	$30.49	$10
.40 S&W	100	Frangible	Brass	Boxer	20	$32.99	$11
10mm	100	Frangible	Brass	Boxer	20	$32.99	$11
.45 GAP	125	Frangible	Brass	Boxer	20	$36.49	$12
.45 ACP	125	Frangible	Brass	Boxer	20	$39.49	$12

The Copper Training/Tactical (CT-2) round projectile consists of a compressed copper powder blend encased in a copper jacket and topped with a green ballistic tip to aid in fragmentation and identification. It is new manufacture and is specifically engineered to fragment.

Caliber	Bullet Weight in Grains	Bullet Type	Case Type	Primer Type	Cartridges Per Box	MSRP	Pack of 6
.38 Special	90	CJPT LF	Brass	Boxer	20	$18	$5
.357 Magnum	90	CJPT LF	Brass	Boxer	20	$18	$5

EXTREME SHOCK CT-2 .45 ACP 150-GR.

EXTREME SHOCK FANG FACE .45 ACP 185-GR.

EXTREME SHOCK'S SW 137-GR. 9MM CARTRIDGE IS DESIGNED FOR USE IN SOUND-SUPPRESSED FIREARMS.

Caliber	Bullet Weight in Grains	Bullet Type	Case Type	Primer Type	Cartridges Per Box	MSRP	Pack of 6
.357 Sig	90	CJPT LF	Brass	Boxer	20	$18	$5
.40 S&W	100	CJPT LF	Brass	Boxer	20	$18	$5
.45 GAP	150	CJPT LF	Brass	Boxer	20	$18	$5
.45 ACP	150	CJPT LF	Brass	Boxer	20	$18	$5

The Silent Warrior (SW) round was designed to eliminate the loud and sharp sound produced by a bullet as it travels downrange. SW bullets have a tungsten core encased in a copper jacket and are designed for use in sound-suppressed firearms and to expend 100 percent of their kinetic energy into the target.

Caliber	Bullet Weight in Grains	Bullet Type	Case Type	Primer Type	Cartridges Per Box	MSRP	Pack of 6
9mm	137	Frangible	Brass	Boxer	20	$31	$10
.45 ACP	230		Brass	Boxer	20	$55	$16

FNH USA (www.fnhusa.com)

FNH ammunition is made specifically for the FNH five-seveN pistol.

Caliber	Bullet Weight in Grains	Bullet Type	Case Type	Primer Type	Cartridges Per Box	MSRP
5.7x28mm FN	27	JHP LF	Brass	Boxer	50	$22
5.7x28mm FN	40	Hornady V-Max	Brass	Boxer	50	$29

Federal (www.federalpremium.com)

American Eagle ammo is new production that uses reloadable brass, Boxer primers and bullet types suitable for training and practice.

Caliber	Bullet Weight in Grains	Bullet Type	Case Type	Primer Type	Cartridges Per Box	MSRP
.25 ACP	50	FMJ	Brass	Boxer	50	$19
.32 ACP	71	TMJ	Brass	Boxer	50	$23
.327 Federal Magnum	100	JSP	Brass	Boxer	50	$25
.380	95	FMJ	Brass	Boxer	50	$19
9mm	115	FMJ	Brass	Boxer	50	$14
9mm	124	FMJ	Brass	Boxer	50	$15
9mm	147	FMJ	Brass	Boxer	50	$15
9mm	124	TMJ	Brass	Boxer	50	$15
9mm	147	TMJ	Brass	Boxer	50	$15
.38 Special	130	FMJ	Brass	Boxer	50	$18
.38 Special	158	LRN	Brass	Boxer	50	$18
.357 Magnum	158	JSP	Brass	Boxer	50	$26
.357 Sig	125	FMJ	Brass	Boxer	50	$29
.40 S&W	155	FMJ	Brass	Boxer	50	$21
.40 S&W	165	FMJ	Brass	Boxer	50	$21
.40 S&W	180	FMJ	Brass	Boxer	50	$19
.40 S&W	180	TMJ	Brass	Boxer	50	$19
10mm	180	FMJ	Brass	Boxer	50	$29
.45 ACP	230	TMJ	Brass	Boxer	50	$24
.45 ACP	230	FMJ	Brass	Boxer	50	$25

FEDERAL AMERICAN EAGLE BRANDS, LIKE THIS 100-GR. .327 FEDERAL MAGNUM, OFFERS ECONOMY AND RELOADABLE BRASS.

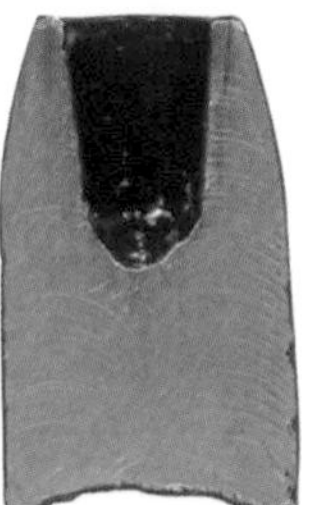

FEDERAL PREMIUM PERSONAL DEFENSE .38 SPECIAL, 125-GR. NYGLAD HP

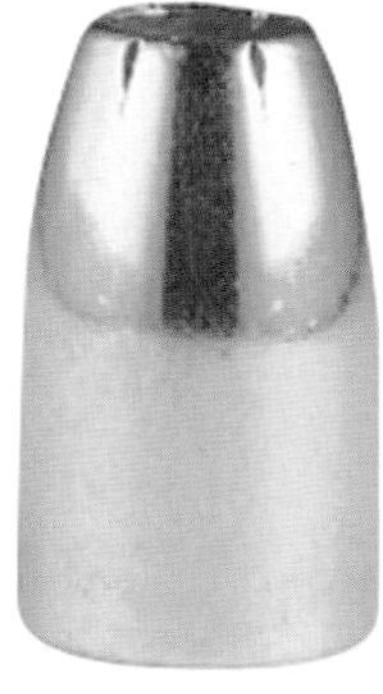

FEDERAL'S HYDRA SHOK BULLET, BEFORE AND AFTER

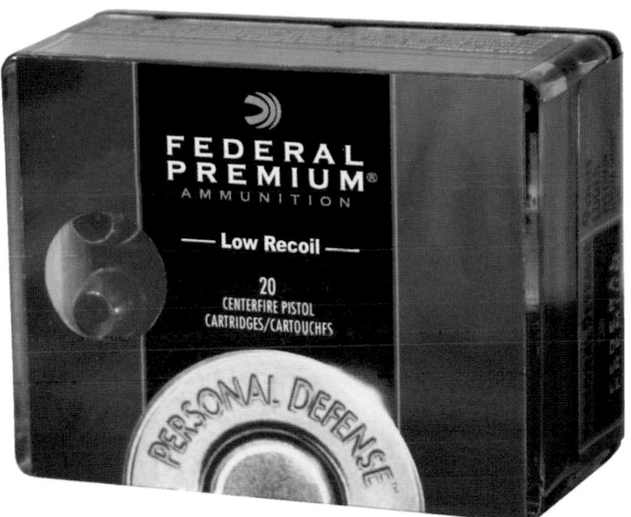

FEDERAL PREMIUM PERSONAL DEFENSE LOW RECOIL

Federal Premium Personal Defense ammunition is new manufacture using reloadable brass, noncorrosive Boxer primers and the center-post, hollow point design of the Hydra-Shok Hollow Point. The Hydra-Shok is designed to deliver controlled expansion while the notched jacket provides efficient energy transfer for maximum penetration. Many LE agencies and militaries use Hydra-Shok loads. The Nyclad bullet is nylon coated to help eliminate barrel fouling and reduce airborne lead. The .410 gauge loads are specifically designed to be employed in handguns for defensive purposes.

Caliber	Bullet Weight in Grains	Bullet Type	Case Type	Primer Type	Cartridges Per Box	MSRP
.32 ACP	65	Hydra-Shok JHP	Brass	Boxer	20	$20
.32 H&R Magnum	85	JHP	Brass	Boxer	20	$16
.327 Federal Magnum	100	JSP	Brass	Boxer	20	$25
9mm	115	JHP	Brass	Boxer	20	$17
9mm	124	Hydra-Shok JHP	Brass	Boxer	20	$20
9mm	147	Hydra-Shok JHP	Brass	Boxer	20	$20
.38 Special +P	129	Hydra-Shok JHP	Brass	Boxer	20	$20
.38 Special	125	Nyclad HP	Brass	Boxer	20	$20
.357 Magnum	125	JHP	Brass	Boxer	20	$18
.357 Magnum	158	JHP	Brass	Boxer	20	$18
.357 Magnum	158	Hydra-Shok JHP	Brass	Boxer	20	$23
.357 Sig	125	JHP	Brass	Boxer	20	$49
.40 S&W	180	Hydra-Shok JHP	Brass	Boxer	20	$22
.40 S&W	155	Hydra-Shok JHP	Brass	Boxer	20	$22
.40 S&W	165	Hydra-Shok JHP	Brass	Boxer	20	$22
.40 S&W	180	JHP	Brass	Boxer	20	$19
10mm	180	Hydra-Shok JHP	Brass	Boxer	20	$30
.45 ACP	230	Hydra-Shok JHP	Brass	Boxer	20	$23

Gauge	Length	Shot Size	Case Type	Cartridges Per Box	MSRP
.410	2.5 in.	.5 oz. #4	Plastic hull	20	$12
.410	2.5 in.	4 OOO buck	Plastic hull	20	$12

Premium Personal Defense Low Recoil ammunition is new manufacture using reloadable brass, noncorrosive Boxer primers and the center-post, hollow point design of the Hydra-Shok Hollow Point. The Expanding Full Metal Jacket (EFMJ) bullet provides higher energy, more reliable expansion (with lower risk of collateral damage), and reduced recoil.

Caliber	Bullet Weight in Grains	Bullet Type	Case Type	Primer Type	Cartridges Per Box	MSRP
.327 Federal Magnum	85	Hydra-Shok JHP	Brass	Boxer	20	$20
380	90	JHP	Brass	Boxer	20	$17
9mm	105	EFMJ	Brass	Boxer	20	$21
9mm	135	Hydra-Shok JHP	Brass	Boxer	20	$22
.38 Special	110	Hydra-Shok JHP	Brass	Boxer	20	$20
.357 Magnum	130	Hydra-Shok JHP	Brass	Boxer	20	$23
.40 S&W	135	Hydra-Shok JHP	Brass	Boxer	20	$24
.45 ACP	165	Hydra-Shok JHP	Brass	Boxer	20	$24

Power Shock ammunition features JHP bullets designed for reliable, quick, and positive expansion.

Caliber	Bullet Weight in Grains	Bullet Type	Case Type	Primer Type	Cartridges Per Box	MSRP
.32 H&R Magnum	85	JHP	Brass	Boxer	20	$16
9mm	115	JHP	Brass	Boxer	20	$17

Ammunition

FEDERAL POWER SHOCK .357 MAGNUM JHP

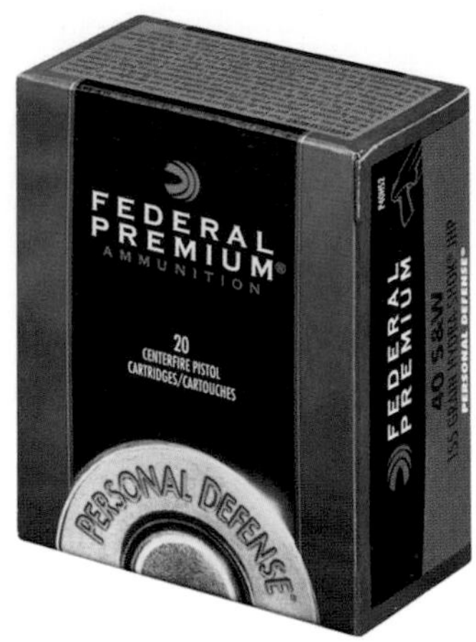

FEDERAL PREMIUM PERSONAL DEFENSE

Caliber	Bullet Weight in Grains	Bullet Type	Case Type	Primer Type	Cartridges Per Box	MSRP
.357 Magnum	125	JHP	Brass	Boxer	20	$18
.357 Magnum	158	JHP	Brass	Boxer	20	$19
.40 S&W	180	JHP	Brass	Boxer	20	$20
.45 ACP	185	JHP	Brass	Boxer	20	$21
.45 ACP	230	JHP	Brass	Boxer	20	$22

Fiocchi (www.fiocchiusa.com)

The Shooting Dynamics line of ammunition is designed for training. It is new manufactured with reloadable brass, Boxer primers, and a variety of bullet weights and velocities that provide the trajectory and recoil of Fiocchi's Extrema line of ammunition.

Caliber	Bullet Weight In Grains	Bullet Type	Case Type	Primer Type	Cartridges Per Box	MSRP
.25 ACP	50	FMJ	Brass	Boxer	50	$14
.32 ACP	60	JHP	Brass	Boxer	50	$17
.32 ACP	73	FMJ	Brass	Boxer	50	$15
.380	90	JHP	Brass	Boxer	50	$19
.380*	95	FMJ	Brass	Boxer	50	$19
9mm	115	FMJ	Brass	Boxer	50	$14
9mm	115	JHP	Brass	Boxer	50	$16
9mm	123	ETC	Brass	Boxer	50	$15
9mm	124	FMJ	Brass	Boxer	50	$14
9mm	147	FMJ	Brass	Boxer	50	$15
9mm	147	JHP	Brass	Boxer	50	$17
9mm	158	FMJ-SS	Brass	Boxer	50	$16
.38 Special +P	110	FMJ-FN	Brass	Boxer	50	$17
.38 Special	125	SJHP	Brass	Boxer	50	$20
.38 Special	130	FMJ	Brass	Boxer	50	$17
.38 Special	148	SJHP	Brass	Boxer	50	$20
.38 Special	158	FMJ	Brass	Boxer	50	$18
.38 Special	158	LRN	Brass	Boxer	50	$17
.357 Magnum	124	FMJ-TC	Brass	Boxer	50	$21
.357 Magnum	125	SJHP	Brass	Boxer	50	$20
.357 Magnum	142	FMJ-TC	Brass	Boxer	50	$18
.357 Magnum	148	SJHP	Brass	Boxer	50	$21
.40 S&W	165	JHP	Brass	Boxer	50	$20
.40 S&W	165	FMJ	Brass	Boxer	50	$19
.40 S&W	165	ETC	Brass	Boxer	50	$19
.40 S&W	170	FMJ-FN	Brass	Boxer	50	$18
.40 S&W	180	JHP	Brass	Boxer	50	$20
.40 S&W	180	FN	Brass	Boxer	50	$18
.44 Special	240	SW	Brass	Boxer	50	$30
.45 ACP	200	JHP	Brass	Boxer	50	$25
.45 ACP	230	FMJ	Brass	Boxer	50	$19
.45 ACP	230	TC	Brass	Boxer	50	$21
.45 ACP	230	JHP	Brass	Boxer	50	$26

*Not for use in Seecamp LWS .380

Fiocchi Extrema Pistol XTP line is manufactured to be reliable and accurate self-defense ammunition. The cartridges are loaded with the Hornady XTP bullet, which is known for controlled expansion and consistent penetration. This is new manufacture with nickel-plated cases to ensure positive feeding and extraction.

Caliber	Bullet Weight In Grains	Bullet Type	Case Type	Primer Type	Cartridges Per Box	MSRP
.25 ACP	35	XTP-JHP	Brass	Boxer	50	$23
.32 ACP	60	XTP-JHP	Brass	Boxer	50	$23
.380	90	XTP-JHP	Brass	Boxer	50	$26
9mm	115	XTP-JHP	Brass	Boxer	50	$25
9mm	124	XTP-JHP	Brass	Boxer	50	$24
9mm	147	XTP-JHP	Brass	Boxer	50	$25
.38 Special +P	110	XTP-JHP	Brass	Boxer	50	$29
.38 Special	125	XTP-JHP	Brass	Boxer	50	$29
.357 Magnum	158	XTP-JHP	Brass	Boxer	50	$31
.357 Sig	124	XTP-JHP	Brass	Boxer	50	$31
.40 S&W	155	XTP-JHP	Brass	Boxer	50	$27
.40 S&W	180	XTP-JHP	Brass	Boxer	50	$28
.45 ACP	200	XTP-JHP	Brass	Boxer	50	$31
.45 ACP	230	XTP-JHP	Brass	Boxer	50	$30

Fiocchi Frangible Nontoxic ammunition uses SinterFire frangible, lead-free bullets designed for training in indoor ranges or on steel plates. The copper and tin composite bullets crumble upon impact with hard surfaces.

Caliber	Bullet Weight In Grains	Bullet Type	Case Type	Primer Type	Cartridges Per Box	MSRP
9mm	92	Sinterfire-frangible	Brass	Boxer	50	$26
9mm	100	Sinterfire-frangible	Brass	Boxer	50	$25
.357 Sig	100	Sinterfire-frangible	Brass	Boxer	50	$55
.40 S&W	125	Sinterfire-frangible	Brass	Boxer	50	$26

Hornady (www.hornady.com)

Hornady TAP FPD ammo is new manufacture designed specifically for protection and defense. TAP FPD ammo is engineered to deliver reliable and consistent performance.

Caliber	Bullet Weight In Grains	Bullet Type	Case Type	Primer Type	Cartridges Per Box	MSRP
9mm	124	JHP	Nickel-plated brass	Boxer	25	$23
9mm	147	JHP	Nickel-plated brass	Boxer	25	$23
.40 S&W	155	JHP	Nickel-plated brass	Boxer	20	$18
.40 S&W	180	JHP	Nickel-plated brass	Boxer	20	$18
.45 ACP +P	200	JHP	Nickel-plated brass	Boxer	20	$19
.45 ACP +P	230	JHP	Nickel-plated brass	Boxer	20	$19

Hornady Critical Defense ammunition is new production loaded with the Flex Tip eXpanding (FTX) bullet that provides controlled expansion and large, deep wound cavities over a wide range of velocities.

Caliber	Bullet Weight In Grains	Bullet Type	Case Type	Primer Type	Cartridges Per Box	MSRP
.380	90	FTX	Brass	Boxer	25	$20
9mm	115	FTX	Brass	Boxer	25	$20

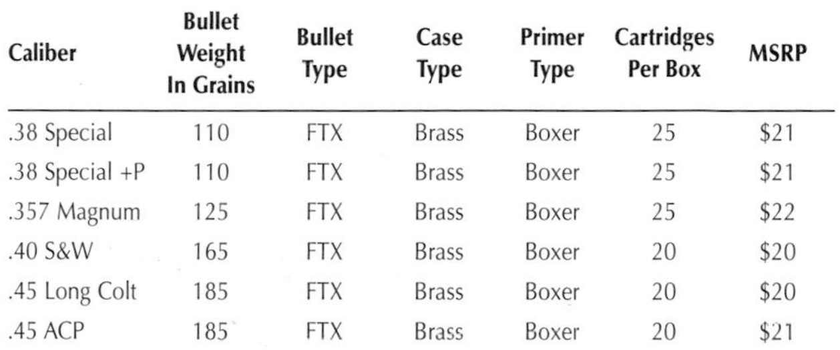

Caliber	Bullet Weight In Grains	Bullet Type	Case Type	Primer Type	Cartridges Per Box	MSRP
.38 Special	110	FTX	Brass	Boxer	25	$21
.38 Special +P	110	FTX	Brass	Boxer	25	$21
.357 Magnum	125	FTX	Brass	Boxer	25	$22
.40 S&W	165	FTX	Brass	Boxer	20	$20
.45 Long Colt	185	FTX	Brass	Boxer	20	$20
.45 ACP	185	FTX	Brass	Boxer	20	$21

HORNADY CRITICAL DEFENSE

HORNADY .380 CRITICAL DEFENSE 90-GR. BULLET (LEFT), CROSS SECTION (MIDDLE), AND EXPANDED (RIGHT)

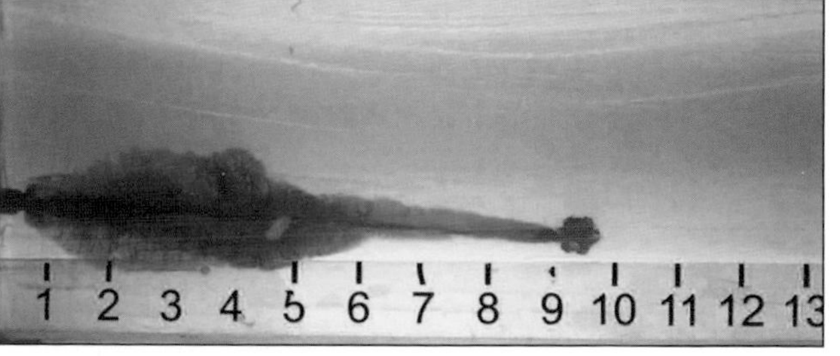

HORNADY .44 SPECIAL CUSTOM IN BALLISTIC GEL

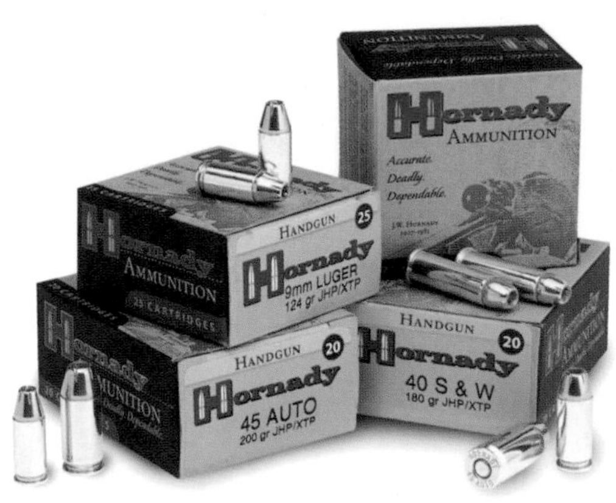

HORNADY CUSTOM AMMO

HORNADY .45 ACP +P 200-GR. TAP FPD

Hornady Custom pistol ammo is loaded with a variety of bullets including the Extreme Terminal Performance (XTP) bullet, a fully encapsulated FMJ, or the FTX bullet. All are designed to be accurate and deliver maximum knockdown power.

Caliber	Bullet Weight In Grains	Bullet Type	Case Type	Primer Type	Cartridges Per Box	MSRP
.25 ACP	35	XTP-JHP	Brass	Boxer	25	$17
.32 ACP	60	XTP-JHP	Brass	Boxer	25	$16
.380	90	XTP-JHP	Brass	Boxer	25	$18
9mm	115	XTP-JHP	Brass	Boxer	25	$17
9mm	124	XTP-JHP	Brass	Boxer	25	$17
9mm	147	XTP-JHP	Brass	Boxer	25	$18
.38 Special	125	XTP-JHP	Brass	Boxer	25	$19
.38 Special	158	XTP-JHP	Brass	Boxer	25	$18
.357 Magnum	125	XTP-JHP	Brass	Boxer	25	$20
.357 Magnum	140	XTP-JHP	Brass	Boxer	25	$20
.357 Magnum	158	XTP-JHP	Brass	Boxer	25	$22
.357 Sig	124	XTP-JHP	Brass	Boxer	20	$18
.357 Sig	147	XTP-JHP	Brass	Boxer	20	$18
.40 S&W	155	XTP-JHP	Brass	Boxer	20	$18
.40 S&W	180	XTP-JHP	Brass	Boxer	20	$18
10mm	155	XTP-JHP	Brass	Boxer	20	$17
10mm	180	XTP-JHP	Brass	Boxer	20	$20
10mm	200	XTP-JHP	Brass	Boxer	20	$17
.44 Special	165	FTX	Brass	Boxer	20	$19
.44 Special	180	XTP-JHP	Brass	Boxer	20	$17
.45 ACP	185	XTP-JHP	Brass	Boxer	20	$17
.45 ACP	200	XTP-JHP	Brass	Boxer	20	$19
.45 ACP +P	200	XTP-JHP	Brass	Boxer	20	$17
.45 ACP	230	FMJ	Brass	Boxer	20	$17
.45 ACP +P	230	XTP-JHP	Brass	Boxer	20	$18

Magtech (www.magtechammunition.com)

Magtech First Defense ammunition is new manufacture and is designed with a 100 percent solid copper bullet that is lead free and offers deep penetration and devastating expansion.

Caliber	Bullet Weight In Grains	Bullet Type	Case Type	Primer Type	Cartridges Per Box	MSRP
.380	77	Solid Copper HP	Brass	Boxer	20	$18
9mm	92.6	Solid Copper HP	Brass	Boxer	20	$22
.38 Special +P	95	Solid Copper HP	Brass	Boxer	20	$21
.357 Magnum	95	Solid Copper HP	Brass	Boxer	20	$25
.40 S&W	130	Solid Copper HP	Brass	Boxer	20	$25
.45 GAP	165	Solid Copper HP	Brass	Boxer	20	$25
.45 ACP +P	165	Solid Copper HP	Brass	Boxer	20	$26

Magtech's Guardian Gold ammunition line is new manufacture that offers stopping power, deep penetration, expansion, and accuracy.

Caliber	Bullet Weight In Grains	Bullet Type	Case Type	Primer Type	Cartridges Per Box	MSRP
.32 ACP	65	JHP	Brass	Boxer	20	$13
.380 +P	85	JHP	Brass	Boxer	20	$14
9mm +P	115	JHP	Brass	Boxer	20	$15
9mm	124	JHP	Brass	Boxer	20	$15
.38 Special +P	125	JHP	Brass	Boxer	20	$15
.357 Magnum	125	JHP	Brass	Boxer	20	$15
.40 S&W	155	JHP	Brass	Boxer	20	$19
.40 S&W	180	JHP	Brass	Boxer	20	$19
.44 Special	200	JHP	Brass	Boxer	20	$29
.45 GAP	185	JHP	Brass	Boxer	20	$19
.45 GAP	230	JHP	Brass	Boxer	20	$19
.45 ACP +P	185	JHP	Brass	Boxer	20	$19
.45 ACP +P	230	JHP	Brass	Boxer	20	$19

Ammunition

Magtech's CleanRange loads are new manufacture and designed to eliminate airborne lead and heavy metal exposure by using lead-free primers and fully encapsulated bullets.

Caliber	Bullet Weight In Grains	Bullet Type	Case Type	Primer Type	Cartridges Per Box	MSRP
.380	95	Encapsulated RN	Brass	Boxer	50	$20
9mm	115	Encapsulated RN	Brass	Boxer	50	$22
.38 Special	158	Encapsulated RN	Brass	Boxer	50	$23
.40 S&W	180	Encapsulated FN	Brass	Boxer	50	$25
.45 ACP	230	Encapsulated RN	Brass	Boxer	50	$31

MAGTECH CLEANRANGE

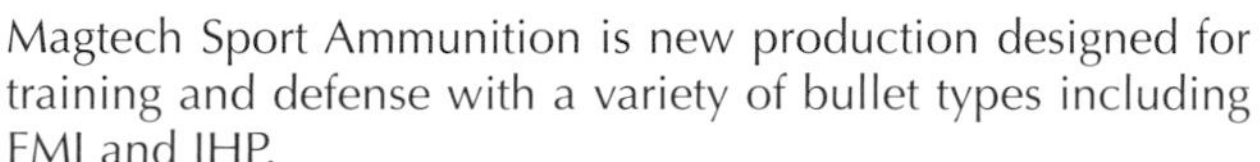
Magtech Sport Ammunition is new production designed for training and defense with a variety of bullet types including FMJ and JHP.

Caliber	Bullet Weight In Grains	Bullet Type	Case Type	Primer Type	Cartridges Per Box	MSRP
.25 ACP	50	FMJ	Brass	Boxer	50	$18
.32 ACP	71	FMJ	Brass	Boxer	50	$20
.32 ACP	71	JHP	Brass	Boxer	50	$24
.32 ACP	71	LRN	Brass	Boxer	50	$18
.380	95	FMJ	Brass	Boxer	50	$16
.380	95	JHP	Brass	Boxer	50	$23
.380	95	LRN	Brass	Boxer	50	$17
9mm	95	JSP	Brass	Boxer	50	$19
9mm	115	FMJ	Brass	Boxer	50	$12
9mm +P	115	JHP	Brass	Boxer	50	$25
9mm	124	FMJ	Brass	Boxer	50	$15
9mm	124	JSP	Brass	Boxer	50	$18
9mm	124	LRN	Brass	Boxer	50	$18
9mm Subsonic	147	JHP	Brass	Boxer	50	$22
9mm	147	FMJ	Brass	Boxer	50	$17
.38 Special	125	FMJ	Brass	Boxer	50	$18
.38 Special +P	125	SJHP	Brass	Boxer	50	$23
.38 Special +P	125	SJSP	Brass	Boxer	50	$23
.38 Special	130	FMJ	Brass	Boxer	50	$17
.38 Special	158	LRN	Brass	Boxer	50	$16
.38 Special	158	FMJ	Brass	Boxer	50	$18
.38 Special	158	SJHP	Brass	Boxer	50	$21
.38 Special	158	LSW	Brass	Boxer	50	$18
.38 Special	158	SJSP	Brass	Boxer	50	$21
.38 Special +P	158	SJHP	Brass	Boxer	50	$25
.38 Special +P	158	SJSP	Brass	Boxer	50	$23
.357 Magnum	125	FMJ	Brass	Boxer	50	$25
.357 Magnum	158	SJSP	Brass	Boxer	50	$23
.357 Magnum	158	FMJ	Brass	Boxer	50	$25
.357 Magnum	158	SJSP	Nickel-plated brass	Boxer	50	$23
.357 Magnum	158	LSW	Brass	Boxer	50	$25
.357 Magnum	158	SJHP	Brass	Boxer	50	$26

MAGTECH FIRST DEFENSE

MAGTECH GUARDIAN GOLD

Caliber	Bullet Weight In Grains	Bullet Type	Case Type	Primer Type	Cartridges Per Box	MSRP
.357 Sig	124	XTP-JHP	Brass	Boxer	50	$18
.357 Sig	147	XTP-JHP	Brass	Boxer	50	$18
.40 S&W	155	JHP	Brass	Boxer	50	$26
.40 S&W	160	LSW	Brass	Boxer	50	$28
.40 S&W	165	FMJ	Brass	Boxer	50	$19
.40 S&W	180	FMJ	Brass	Boxer	50	$18
.40 S&W	180	JHP	Brass	Boxer	50	$28
.40 S&W High Velocity	180	FMJ	Brass	Boxer	50	$19
.45 GAP	230	FMJ	Brass	Boxer	50	$27
.45 ACP	200	LSW	Brass	Boxer	50	$26
.45 ACP	230	FMJ	Brass	Boxer	50	$21
.45 ACP	230	FMJ-SW	Brass	Boxer	50	$35

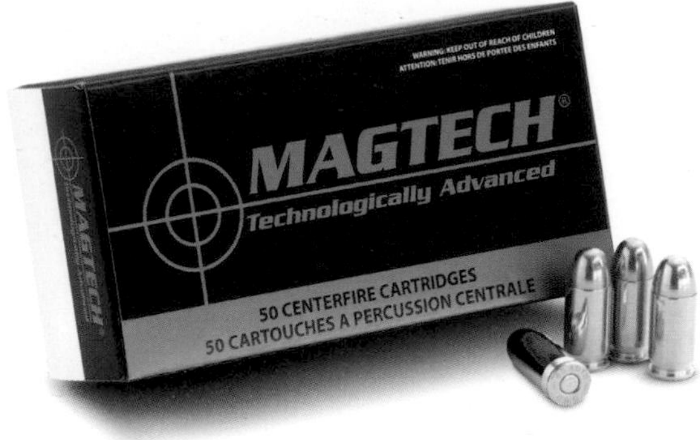

MAGTECH SPORT SHOOTING

PMC (www.pmcammo.com)

PMC's Gold line is new-production loaded with the Starfire bullet, which has a rib and flute design inside the hollow point cavity that offers maximum expansion to nearly twice the original size with average penetration of nine to fourteen inches. It comes in reloadable brass cases and is suitable for defense.

Caliber	Bullet Weight In Grains	Bullet Type	Case Type	Primer Type	Cartridges Per Box	MSRP
.380	95	SFHP	Brass	Boxer	20	$13
9mm	124	SFHP	Brass	Boxer	20	$15
.38 Special +P	125	SFHP	Brass	Boxer	20	$15
.357 Magnum	150	SFHP	Brass	Boxer	20	$16
.40 S&W	180	SFHP	Brass	Boxer	20	$18
.44 Magnum	240	SFHP	Brass	Boxer	20	$21
.45 ACP	230	SFHP	Brass	Boxer	20	$17

PMC GOLD LINE WITH STARFIRE BULLET

PMC Bronze line is new production manufactured with a variety of bullet types. It uses reloadable brass cases and is suitable for practice and training.

Caliber	Bullet Weight In Grains	Bullet Type	Case Type	Primer Type	Cartridges Per Box	MSRP
.25 ACP	50	FMJ	Brass	Boxer	50	$18
.32 ACP	60	JHP	Brass	Boxer	50	$19
.32 ACP	71	FMJ	Brass	Boxer	50	$20
.380	90	FMJ	Brass	Boxer	20	$16
9mm	115	FMJ	Brass	Boxer	20	$12
9mm	115	JHP	Brass	Boxer	20	$17
9mm	124	FMJ	Brass	Boxer	20	$13
.38 Special	132	FMJ	Brass	Boxer	20	$17
.38 Special +P	130	FMJ	Brass	Boxer	20	$15
.357 Magnum	125	JHP	Brass	Boxer	20	$18
.357 Magnum	158	JSP	Brass	Boxer	20	$21

PMC BRONZE LINE

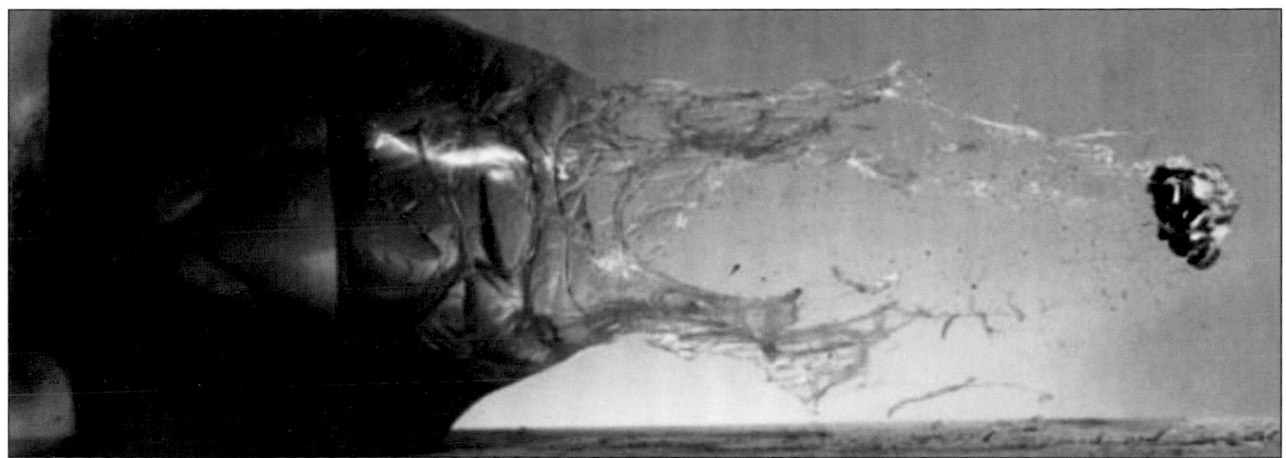

PMC STARFIRE IN BALLISTIC GEL

PMC SILVER LINE ERANGE AMMO

Caliber	Bullet Weight In Grains	Bullet Type	Case Type	Primer Type	Cartridges Per Box	MSRP
.40 S&W	165	FMJ	Brass	Boxer	20	$18
.40 S&W	165	JHP	Brass	Boxer	20	$18
.40 S&W	180	FMJ-FP	Brass	Boxer	20	$18
10mm	170	JHP	Brass	Boxer	20	$28
10mm	200	FMJ-TC	Brass	Boxer	20	$26
.44 Special	180	JHP	Brass	Boxer	20	$21
.44 Magnum	180	JHP	Brass	Boxer	20	$22
.44 Magnum	240	TSP	Brass	Boxer	20	$37
.45 ACP	180	JHP	Brass	Boxer	20	$19
.45 ACP	230	FMJ	Brass	Boxer	20	$21

PMC Silver Line eRange is new-production ammunition using a reduced hazard primer and Encapsulated Metal Jacket (EMJ) bullet. It is loaded in reloadable brass cases and suitable for practice and training.

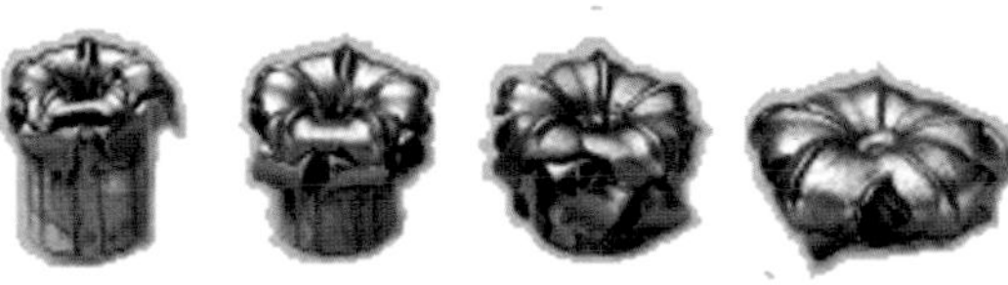

PMC STARFIRE BULLET IN VARIOUS STAGES OF EXPANSION

Caliber	Bullet Weight In Grains	Bullet Type	Case Type	Primer Type	Cartridges Per Box	MSRP
.380	90	EMJ	Brass	Boxer	50	$20
9mm	115	EMJ	Brass	Boxer	50	$17
9mm	124	EMJ	Brass	Boxer	50	$17
.38 Special	132	EMJ	Brass	Boxer	50	$20
.38 Special	158	EMJ	Brass	Boxer	50	$20
.357 Magnum	158	EMJ	Brass	Boxer	50	$30
.40 S&W	165	EMJ	Brass	Boxer	50	$23
.44 Magnum	240	EMJ	Brass	Boxer	50	$21
.45 ACP	230	EMJ	Brass	Boxer	50	$29

Prvi Partizan (www.prvipartizan.com)

PPU Pistol ammunition is new manufacture and designed for training and defensive.

Caliber	Bullet Weight In Grains	Bullet Type	Case Type	Primer Type	Cartridges Per Box	MSRP
.32 ACP	71	FMJ	Brass	Boxer	50	$17
.32 ACP	71	JHP	Brass	Boxer	50	$18
.380	94	FMJ	Brass	Boxer	50	$17
.380	94	JHP	Brass	Boxer	50	$19
.380	95	LRN	Brass	Boxer	50	$17

Ammunition

Caliber	Bullet Weight In Grains	Bullet Type	Case Type	Primer Type	Cartridges Per Box	MSRP
9mm	115	FMJ	Brass	Boxer	50	$15
9mm	124	FMJ	Brass	Boxer	50	$15
9mm	147	FMJ	Brass	Boxer	50	$18
9mm	147	JHP	Brass	Boxer	50	$19
.38 Special	158	LRN	Brass	Boxer	50	$18
.357 Magnum	158	SJHP	Brass	Boxer	50	$26
.357 Sig	124	FMJ	Brass	Boxer	50	$24
.40 S&W	180	FMJ	Brass	Boxer	50	$22
.40 S&W	180	JHP	Brass	Boxer	50	$27
.45 ACP	230	FMJ	Brass	Boxer	50	$27

REMINGTON EXPRESS

Remington (www.remington.com)

Remington's HD Ultimate Home Defense ammunition is new production loaded with Brass Jacket Hollow Point (BJHP) bullets that are designed to deliver massive expansion and deep penetration.

Caliber	Bullet Weight In Grains	Bullet Type	Case Type	Primer Type	Cartridges Per Box	MSRP
.380	102	BJHP	Brass	Boxer	25	$20
9mm	124	BJHP	Brass	Boxer	25	$22
.38 Special +P	125	BJHP	Brass	Boxer	25	$23
.40 S&W	165	BJHP	Brass	Boxer	25	$22
.45 ACP	230	BJHP	Brass	Boxer	25	$23

REMINGTON HD ULTIMATE HOME DEFENSE .40 S&W 165-GR. BJHP

Disintegrator CTF cartridges are all lead free and designed for training. The bullets are formed from powder using a compaction and sintering process that eliminates the need for a jacket to house the bullet core. They are made to breakup at distances as close as five feet.

Caliber	Bullet Weight In Grains	Bullet Type	Case Type	Primer Type	Cartridges Per Box	MSRP
9mm +P	100	Disintegrator CTF	Brass	Boxer	50	$45
.38 Special +P	101	Disintegrator CTF	Brass	Boxer	50	$41
.40 S&W	125	Disintegrator CTF	Brass	Boxer	50	$51
.45 ACP	155	Disintegrator CTF	Brass	Boxer	50	$50

Express ammunition is new manufacture with loads tailored to training and defense with a variety of bullet weights and types like Lead Round Nose (LRN), Semi-Jacketed Hollow Point (SJHP), Soft Point (SP), Semi-Wadcutter (SW), and Jacketed Hollow Point (JHP).

Caliber	Bullet Weight In Grains	Bullet Type	Case Type	Primer Type	Cartridges Per Box	MSRP
9mm	115	FMJ	Brass	Boxer	50	$34
9mm +P	115	JHP	Brass	Boxer	50	$40

REMINGTON GOLD SABER EXPANDED

Ammunition

Caliber	Bullet Weight In Grains	Bullet Type	Case Type	Primer Type	Cartridges Per Box	MSRP
9mm	124	FMJ	Brass	Boxer	50	$40
9mm	147	JHP	Brass	Boxer	50	$41
.38 Special	110	SJHP	Brass	Boxer	50	$38
.38 Special +P	110	LSW	Brass	Boxer	50	$39
.38 Special	158	LRN	Brass	Boxer	50	$28
.38 Special	158	LSW	Brass	Boxer	50	$30
.38 Special	158	JSP	Brass	Boxer	50	$41
.38 Special +P	158	LHP	Brass	Boxer	50	$33
.357 Magnum	110	SJHP	Brass	Boxer	50	$44
.357 Magnum	125	SJHP	Brass	Boxer	50	$44
.357 Magnum	158	SJHP	Brass	Boxer	50	$40
.357 Magnum	180	SJHP	Brass	Boxer	50	$43
.40 S&W	155	JHP	Brass	Boxer	50	$44
.45 Long Colt	225	LSW	Brass	Boxer	50	$43
.45 Long Colt	250	LRN	Brass	Boxer	50	$43
.45 ACP	185	JHP	Brass	Boxer	50	$45
.45 ACP	230	FMJ	Brass	Boxer	50	$45

Remington's Golden Saber High Performance Jacket (HPJ) ammunition is new manufacture designed for law enforcement and personal defense with match-type accuracy, deep penetration, maximum expansion, and nearly 100 percent weight retention. The bullet jacket is made of brass with a spiral nose-cut that allows expansion at lower velocities.

REMINGTON UMC

REMINGTON GOLDEN SABER

REMINGTON GOLD SABER HPJ BULLETS WITH SPIRAL NOSE-CUT

Caliber	Bullet Weight In Grains	Bullet Type	Case Type	Primer Type	Cartridges Per Box	MSRP
.380	102	BJHP	Nickel-plated brass	Boxer	25	$22
9mm	124	BJHP	Nickel-plated brass	Boxer	25	$26
9mm +P	124	BJHP	Nickel-plated brass	Boxer	25	$28
9mm	147	BJHP	Nickel-plated brass	Boxer	25	$26
.38 Special +P	125	BJHP	Nickel-plated brass	Boxer	25	$25
.357 Magnum	125	BJHP	Nickel-plated brass	Boxer	25	$27
.40 S&W	165	BJHP	Nickel-plated brass	Boxer	25	$30
.40 S&W	180	BJHP	Nickel-plated brass	Boxer	25	$30
.45 ACP	185	BJHP	Nickel-plated brass	Boxer	25	$30
.45 ACP +P	185	BJHP	Nickel-plated brass	Boxer	25	$34
.45 ACP	230	BJHP	Nickel-plated brass	Boxer	25	$30

UMC is new-manufacture ammunition intended for high volume practice and training. It is manufactured with either Full Metal Jacket (FMJ) or Jacketed Hollow Point (JHP) bullets.

Caliber	Bullet Weight In Grains	Bullet Type	Case Type	Primer Type	Cartridges Per Box	MSRP
.25 ACP	50	FMJ	Brass	Boxer	50	$17
.32 ACP	71	FMJ	Brass	Boxer	50	$19
.380	95	FMJ	Brass	Boxer	50	$19
.380	95	FNEB-lead free	Brass	Boxer	50	$19
9mm	115	JHP	Brass	Boxer	50	$18
9mm	115	FMJ	Brass	Boxer	50	$15
9mm	115	FNEB-lead free	Brass	Boxer	50	$16
9mm	124	FMJ	Brass	Boxer	50	$16
9mm	124	FNEB-lead free	Brass	Boxer	50	$16
9mm	147	FMJ	Brass	Boxer	50	$16
9mm	147	FNEB-lead free	Brass	Boxer	50	$16
.38 Special	125	FNEB-lead free	Brass	Boxer	50	$19
.38 Special +P	125	JHP	Brass	Boxer	50	$16
.38 Special	130	FMJ	Brass	Boxer	50	$19
.38 Special	158	LRN	Brass	Boxer	50	$17
.357 Magnum	125	JSP	Brass	Boxer	50	$23
.357 Sig	125	JHP	Brass	Boxer	50	$31
.357 Sig	125	FMJ	Brass	Boxer	50	$27
.40 S&W	165	FMJ	Brass	Boxer	50	$19
.40 S&W	180	JHP	Brass	Boxer	50	$23
.40 S&W	180	FNEB-lead free	Brass	Boxer	50	$21

Ammunition

Caliber	Bullet Weight In Grains	Bullet Type	Case Type	Primer Type	Cartridges Per Box	MSRP
10mm	180	FMJ	Brass	Boxer	50	$27
.45 GAP	230	FMJ	Brass	Boxer	50	$25
.45 ACP	185	FMJ	Brass	Boxer	50	$25
.45 ACP	230	FMJ	Brass	Boxer	50	$24
.45 ACP	230	JHP	Brass	Boxer	50	$30
.45 ACP	230	FNEB-lead free	Brass	Boxer	50	$27

SBR (sbrammunition.com)

SBR LaserMatch ammunition is designed for training. Cartridges are available in two trace ranges: Standard Range Visible Tracer (SRVT), which provides a visual ballistic signature to seventy-five yards and Extended Range Visible Tracer (ERVT), which provides a visual ballistic signature exceeding 150 yards. It is noncorrosive and will not harm firearm barrels. Tracer is visible at the muzzle and can be seen in full daylight.

Caliber	Bullet Weight In Grains	Bullet Type	Case Type	Primer Type	Cartridges Per Box	MSRP
9mm	124	FMJ-SRVT	Brass	Boxer	20	$16
9mm	124	FMJ-ERVT	Brass	Boxer	20	$17
9mm	147	FMJ-ERVT	Brass	Boxer	20	$17
9mm	147	FMJ-SRVT	Brass	Boxer	20	$17
.38 Special	158	FMJ-ERVT	Brass	Boxer	50	$37
.38 Special	158	FMJ-SRVT	Brass	Boxer	50	$36
.357 Sig	124	FMJ-ERVT	Brass	Boxer	50	$38
.357 Sig	124	FMJ-SRVT	Brass	Boxer	50	$37
.40 S&W	165	FMJ-ERVT	Brass	Boxer	20	$18
.40 S&W	165	FMJ-SRVT	Brass	Boxer	20	$18
.40 S&W	180	FMJ-ERVT	Brass	Boxer	50	$36
.40 S&W	180	FMJ-SRVT	Brass	Boxer	50	$35
.45 ACP	230	FMJ-ERVT	Brass	Boxer	20	$21
.45 ACP	230	FMJ-SRVT	Brass	Boxer	20	$20

SBR GreenMatch is lead-free ammunition loaded with lead-free primers and frangible SinterFire bullets, which are a blend of copper and tin powder composite materials. They have similar performance characteristics as a FMJ projectile.

Caliber	Bullet Weight In Grains	Bullet Type	Case Type	Primer Type	Cartridges Per Box	MSRP
9mm	90	Frangible	Brass	Boxer	50	$28
.40 S&W	125	Frangible	Brass	Boxer	50	$31
.45 ACP	155	Frangible	Brass	Boxer	50	$34

Sellier & Bellot (www.sellier-bellot.cz)

Sellier & Bellot ammunition is new manufacture and suitable for training and defense.

Caliber	Bullet Weight In Grains	Bullet Type	Case Type	Primer Type	Cartridges Per Box	MSRP
.25 ACP	50	FMJ	Brass	Boxer	50	$18
.32 ACP	73	FMJ	Brass	Boxer	50	$19
.380	92	FMJ	Brass	Boxer	50	$17
9mm	115	JHP	Brass	Boxer	50	$23
9mm	115	FMJ	Brass	Boxer	50	$12
9mm	124	FMJ	Brass	Boxer	50	$15
.38 Special	158	LRN	Brass	Boxer	50	$18
.38 Special	158	SJSP	Brass	Boxer	50	$22
.38 Special	158	FMJ	Brass	Boxer	50	$16
.357 Magnum	158	SP	Brass	Boxer	50	$23
.357 Magnum	158	FMJ	Brass	Boxer	50	$23
.357 Sig	140	FMJ	Brass	Boxer	50	$25
.40 S&W	180	FMJ	Brass	Boxer	50	$18
.40 S&W	180	FMJ-lead free	Brass	Boxer	50	$25
.45 ACP	230	FMJ	Brass	Boxer	50	$21

Gauge	Length	Shot Size	Case Type	Cartridges Per Box	MSRP
.410	3 in.	5 OO buck pellets	Plastic hull	25	$26

Sellier & Bellot NONTOX ammunition is new manufacture and suitable for training indoors.

SELLER & BELLOT NONTOX

SELLER & BELLOT 9MM 115-GR. FMJ

SPEER GOLD DOT

SPEER LAWMAN

Caliber	Bullet Weight In Grains	Bullet Type	Case Type	Primer Type	Cartridges Per Box	MSRP
.32 ACP	73	TFMJ	Brass	Boxer	50	$20
9mm	115	TFMJ	Brass	Boxer	50	$20
9mm	124	TFMJ	Brass	Boxer	50	$20
.38 Special	158	TFMJ	Brass	Boxer	50	$20
.357 Magnum	158	TFMJ	Brass	Boxer	50	$23
.357 Sig	140	TFMJ	Brass	Boxer	50	$25
.40 S&W	180	TFMJ	Brass	Boxer	50	$24
.45 ACP	230	TFMJ	Brass	Boxer	50	$24

Speer (www.speer-ammo.com)

Gold Dot ammunition offers performance, accuracy, and reliability with bonded-core bullets designed for optimum expansion and penetration. This is new-manufacture ammo suitable for personal protection loaded in nickel-plated, reloadable brass.

Caliber	Bullet Weight In Grains	Bullet Type	Case Type	Primer Type	Cartridges Per Box	MSRP
.25 ACP	35	GDHP	Nickel-plated brass	Boxer	20	$17
.32 ACP	60	GDHP	Nickel-plated brass	Boxer	20	$20
.327 Federal Magnum	100	GDHP	Nickel-plated brass	Boxer	20	$20
.327 Federal Magnum	115	GDHP	Nickel-plated brass	Boxer	20	$21
.380	90	GDHP	Nickel-plated brass	Boxer	20	$18
9mm	124	GDHP	Nickel-plated brass	Boxer	20	$20
9mm +P	124	GDHP	Nickel-plated brass	Boxer	20	$20
9mm	147	GDHP	Nickel-plated brass	Boxer	20	$20
9mm	115	GDHP	Nickel-plated brass	Boxer	20	$12
9mm	124	GDHP	Nickel-plated brass	Boxer	20	$15
.38 Special +P	125	GDHP	Nickel-plated brass	Boxer	20	$22
.357 Magnum	125	GDHP	Nickel-plated brass	Boxer	20	$23
.357 Magnum	158	GDHP	Nickel-plated brass	Boxer	20	$23
.357 Sig	125	GDHP	Nickel-plated brass	Boxer	20	$21
.40 S&W	155	GDHP	Nickel-plated brass	Boxer	20	$23
.40 S&W	165	GDHP	Nickel-plated brass	Boxer	20	$23
.40 S&W	180	GDHP	Nickel-plated brass	Boxer	20	$24
.44 Special	200	GDHP	Nickel-plated brass	Boxer	20	$29
.45 Long Colt	250	GDHP	Nickel-plated brass	Boxer	20	$29
.45 GAP	185	GDHP	Nickel-plated brass	Boxer	20	$25
.45 GAP	200	GDHP	Nickel-plated brass	Boxer	20	$23
.45 ACP	185	GDHP	Nickel-plated brass	Boxer	20	$25
.45 ACP +P	200	GDHP	Nickel-plated brass	Boxer	20	$24
.45 ACP	230	GDHP	Nickel-plated brass	Boxer	20	$24

Gold Dot Short Barrel ammunition is specifically designed for use in short barrel revolvers and pistols.

Caliber	Bullet Weight In Grains	Bullet Type	Case Type	Primer Type	Cartridges Per Box	MSRP
9mm +P	124	GDHP-SB	Nickel-plated brass	Boxer	20	$21
.38 Special +P	125	GDHP-SB	Nickel-plated brass	Boxer	20	$23
.357 Magnum	135	GDHP-SB	Nickel-plated brass	Boxer	20	$24
.40 S&W	180	GDHP-SB	Nickel-plated brass	Boxer	20	$25
.44 Magnum	200	GDHP-SB	Nickel-plated brass	Boxer	20	$24
.45 ACP	230	GDHP-SB	Nickel-plated brass	Boxer	20	$24

Speer's Lawman ammunition is specifically designed for training and duplicates Gold Dot loads. This is new manufacture in reloadable brass cases.

Caliber	Bullet Weight In Grains	Bullet Type	Case Type	Primer Type	Cartridges Per Box	MSRP
.32 ACP	71	TMJ	Brass	Boxer	50	$24
.380	95	TMJ	Brass	Boxer	50	$21
9mm	115	FMJ	Brass	Boxer	50	$16
9mm	124	TMJ	Brass	Boxer	50	$15
9mm	147	TMJ	Brass	Boxer	50	$16
.38 Special +P	158	TMJ	Brass	Boxer	50	$25

SPEER 9MM GOLD DOT EXPANDED

Caliber	Bullet Weight In Grains	Bullet Type	Case Type	Primer Type	Cartridges Per Box	MSRP
.357 Sig	125	TMJ	Brass	Boxer	50	$30
.40 S&W	155	TMJ	Brass	Boxer	50	$21
.40 S&W	165	TMJ	Brass	Boxer	50	$23
.40 S&W	180	TMJ	Brass	Boxer	50	$21
.45 GAP	185	TMJ	Brass	Boxer	50	$27
.45 GAP	200	TMJ	Brass	Boxer	50	$27
.45 ACP	185	TMJ	Brass	Boxer	50	$28
.45 ACP	200	TMJ	Brass	Boxer	50	$27
.45 ACP	230	FMJ	Brass	Boxer	50	$28

Lawman Cleanfire ammunition is loaded similar to Lawman ammo except for lead-free primers and a totally encased bullet. This ammo is designed for use in indoor range training.

Caliber	Bullet Weight In Grains	Bullet Type	Case Type	Primer Type	Cartridges Per Box	MSRP
.380	70	RHT	Brass	Boxer	50	$17
9mm	124	TMJ-RN	Brass	Boxer	50	$17
9mm	147	TMJ-FN	Brass	Boxer	50	$17
.38 Special +P	158	TMJ-FN	Brass	Boxer	50	$24
.357 Sig	125	TMJ-FN	Brass	Boxer	50	$29
.40 S&W	165	TMJ-FN	Brass	Boxer	50	$22
.40 S&W	180	TMJ-FN	Brass	Boxer	50	$22
.40 S&W	200	TMJ-FN	Brass	Boxer	50	$22
.45 GAP	200	TMJ-FN	Brass	Boxer	50	$29
.45 ACP	230	TMJ-RN	Brass	Boxer	50	$29

Ultramax (www.ultramaxammunition.com)

Ultramax uses previously fired brass cases. This is remanufactured ammunition that goes through a ten-step quality assurance process and is suitable for high volume training and practice.

Caliber	Bullet Weight In Grains	Bullet Type	Case Type	Primer Type	Cartridges Per Box	MSRP
.380	95	FMJ	Brass	Boxer	50	$14
.380	115	LRN	Brass	Boxer	50	$14
9mm	115	FMJ	Brass	Boxer	50	$14
9mm	115	JHP	Brass	Boxer	50	$18
9mm	125	LRN	Brass	Boxer	50	$12
9mm	125	FMJ	Brass	Boxer	50	$14
9mm	147	FMJ	Brass	Boxer	50	$19
.38 Special	125	LCN	Brass	Boxer	50	$15
.38 Special	125	JHP	Brass	Boxer	50	$20
.38 Special	130	FMJ	Brass	Boxer	50	$18
.38 Special	158	LSW	Brass	Boxer	50	$15
.38 Special	158	LRN	Brass	Boxer	50	$15
.357 Magnum	158	LSW	Brass	Boxer	50	$28
.357 Magnum	158	JHP	Brass	Boxer	50	$33
.357 Sig	125	FMJ	Brass	Boxer	50	$18
.40 S&W	165	FMJ	Brass	Boxer	50	$18
.40 S&W	180	LCN	Brass	Boxer	50	$15
.40 S&W	180	FMJ	Brass	Boxer	50	$18
.40 S&W	180	JHP	Brass	Boxer	50	$24
10mm	180	FMJ	Brass	Boxer	50	$25
.45 ACP	185	JHP	Brass	Boxer	50	$27
.45 ACP	200	LSW	Brass	Boxer	50	$25
.45 ACP	230	FMJ	Brass	Boxer	50	$23
.45 ACP	230	JHP	Brass	Boxer	50	$27

Winchester (www.winchester.com)

Super-X Silvertip ammunition offers power, precision, reliable functioning, and performance with a specially engineered jacketed bullet that delivers penetration and rapid energy release with virtually no weight loss or bullet fragmentation. It is new production in reloadable brass cases.

Caliber	Bullet Weight In Grains	Bullet Type	Case Type	Primer Type	Cartridges Per Box	MSRP
.32 ACP	60	Silvertip HP	Brass	Boxer	50	$44
.380	85	Silvertip HP	Brass	Boxer	50	$32
9mm	115	Silvertip HP	Brass	Boxer	50	$39
9mm	147	Silvertip HP	Brass	Boxer	50	$42
.38 Special	110	Silvertip HP	Brass	Boxer	50	$37
.38 Special +P	125	Silvertip HP	Brass	Boxer	50	$40
.38 Special	158	LRN	Brass	Boxer	50	$32
.38 Special	158	LSW	Brass	Boxer	50	$33
.38 Special +P	158	LHP-SW	Brass	Boxer	50	$35
.357 Magnum	125	JHP	Brass	Boxer	50	$48
.357 Magnum	145	Silvertip HP	Brass	Boxer	50	$48
.357 Magnum	158	JHP	Brass	Boxer	50	$48

WINCHESTER SUPER–X SILVERTIP 10MM

Caliber	Bullet Weight In Grains	Bullet Type	Case Type	Primer Type	Cartridges Per Box	MSRP
.40 S&W	155	Silvertip HP	Brass	Boxer	50	$44
10mm	175	Silvertip HP	Brass	Boxer	20	$20
.44 Special	200	Silvertip HP	Brass	Boxer	20	$24
.44 Special	246	LRN	Brass	Boxer	20	$43
.45 Long Colt	225	Silvertip HP	Brass	Boxer	20	$24
.45 Long Colt	225	LRN	Brass	Boxer	20	$20
.45 GAP	185	Silvertip HP	Brass	Boxer	50	$47
.45 ACP	185	Silvertip HP	Brass	Boxer	20	$19

Supreme Elite Bonded PDX1 ammo was chosen by the FBI as its primary service round and is engineered to maximize terminal ballistics, as defined by the demanding FBI test protocol. It is new manufacture loaded in nickel-plated, reloadable brass.

Caliber	Bullet Weight In Grains	Bullet Type	Case Type	Primer Type	Cartridges Per Box	MSRP
.380	95	Bonded PDX1 JHP	Nickel-plated brass	Boxer	20	$17
9mm +P	124	Bonded PDX1 JHP	Nickel-plated brass	Boxer	20	$19
9mm	147	Bonded PDX1 JHP	Nickel-plated brass	Boxer	20	$19
.38 Special +P	130	Bonded PDX1 JHP	Nickel-plated brass	Boxer	20	$21
.40 S&W	165	Bonded PDX1 JHP	Nickel-plated brass	Boxer	20	$22
.40 S&W	180	Bonded PDX1 JHP	Nickel-plated brass	Boxer	20	$22
.45 Long Colt	225	Bonded PDX1 JHP	Nickel-plated brass	Boxer	20	$27
.45 ACP	230	Bonded PDX1 JHP	Nickel-plated brass	Boxer	20	$23

WINCHESTER SUPREME ELITE BONDED PDX1

Gauge	Length	Shot Size	Case Type	Cartridges Per Box	MSRP
.410	2.5 in.	12 BB pellets and 3 defense disc projectiles	Plastic hull	10	$12

USA Ammunition is designed for high volume practice and training. It is new-production loaded in reloadable brass.

Caliber	Bullet Weight In Grains	Bullet Type	Case Type	Primer Type	Cartridges Per Box	MSRP
.25 ACP	50	FMJ	Brass	Boxer	50	$23
.32 ACP	71	FMJ	Brass	Boxer	50	$23
.380	95	FMJ	Brass	Boxer	50	$19
9mm	115	FMJ	Brass	Boxer	50	$14
9mm	115	JHP	Brass	Boxer	50	$22
9mm	147	FMJ	Brass	Boxer	50	$17
9mm	147	JHP	Brass	Boxer	50	$22
.38 Special	125	JFN	Brass	Boxer	50	$24
.38 Special +P	125	JHP	Brass	Boxer	50	$27
.38 Special	130	FMJ	Brass	Boxer	50	$19
.38 Special	150	LRN	Brass	Boxer	50	$22
.357 Magnum	110	JHP	Brass	Boxer	50	$30
.357 Sig	125	JHP	Brass	Boxer	50	$36
.357 Sig	125	FMJ	Brass	Boxer	50	$33
.40 S&W	165	FMJ	Brass	Boxer	50	$38
.40 S&W	180	FMJ	Brass	Boxer	50	$20
.40 S&W	180	JHP	Brass	Boxer	50	$29
.45 GAP	230	FMJ	Brass	Boxer	50	$31
.45 GAP	230	JHP	Brass	Boxer	50	$33
.45 ACP	185	FMJ	Brass	Boxer	50	$30
.45 ACP	230	FMJ	Brass	Boxer	50	$24
.45 ACP	230	JHP	Brass	Boxer	50	$35

Ammunition

Winclean ammunition offers lead- and heavy-metal-free primers and Brass Enclosed Base (BENB) bullets to eliminate airborne lead. Designed for practice and training, this is new production in reloadable brass cases.

Caliber	Bullet Weight In Grains	Bullet Type	Case Type	Primer Type	Cartridges Per Box	MSRP
.380	95	BEB	Brass	Boxer	50	$23
9mm	115	BEB	Brass	Boxer	50	$18
9mm	124	BEB	Brass	Boxer	50	$18
9mm	147	BEB	Brass	Boxer	50	$18
.38 Special	125	BEB	Brass	Boxer	50	$24
.357 Magnum	125	BEB	Brass	Boxer	50	$34
.357 Sig	125	BEB	Brass	Boxer	50	$34
.40 S&W	165	BEB	Brass	Boxer	50	$25
.40 S&W	180	BEB	Brass	Boxer	50	$25
.45 GAP	230	BEB	Brass	Boxer	50	$32
.45 ACP	185	BEB	Brass	Boxer	50	$33
.45 ACP	230	BEB	Brass	Boxer	50	$33

Super Clean NT ammunition is designed with jacketed soft-point tin core bullet that performs like lead. For use in practice and training where lead is not permitted.

Caliber	Bullet Weight In Grains	Bullet Type	Case Type	Primer Type	Cartridges Per Box	MSRP
9mm	105	JSP-LF	Brass	Boxer	50	$45
.40 S&W	140	JSP-LF	Brass	Boxer	50	$53

Wolf Performance Ammunition (wolfammo.com)

Wolf Gold Ammunition is new production using Hollow Point (HP) and Soft Point (SP) bullets in reloadable brass cases suitable for tactical and defensive situations.

WINCHESTER SUPER CLEAN NT

WINCHESTER USA

Caliber	Bullet Weight In Grains	Bullet Type	Case Type	Primer Type	Cartridges Per Box	MSRP
.32 ACP	71	JHP	Brass	Boxer	50	$18
.380	94	JHP	Brass	Boxer	50	$19
9mm	147	JHP	Brass	Boxer	50	$21
.357 Magnum	158	SJHP	Brass	Boxer	50	$24
.40 S&W	180	JHP	Brass	Boxer	50	$24
.45 ACP	185	JHP	Brass	Boxer	50	$27

Wolf Polyformance Ammunition is new production using Full Metal Jacket (FMJ) in nonreloadable steel cases coated in polymer for smooth feeding and extraction. It is suitable for practice and training.

Caliber	Bullet Weight In Grains	Bullet Type	Case Type	Primer Type	Cartridges Per Box	MSRP
.380	91	FMJ	Steel	Berdan	50	$16
9mm	115	FMJ	Steel	Berdan	50	$13
.40 S&W	180	FMJ	Steel	Berdan	50	$16
.45 ACP	230	FMJ	Steel	Berdan	50	$18

WPA Military Classic ammunition is new production in military calibers loaded in nonreloadable steel cases coated in polymer. It is suitable for high-volume practice and training.

Caliber	Bullet Weight In Grains	Bullet Type	Case Type	Primer Type	Cartridges Per Box	MSRP
.380	91	Bi-FMJ	Steel	Berdan	50	$16
9mm	115	Bi-FMJ	Steel	Berdan	50	$13
.40 S&W	180	Bi-FMJ	Steel	Berdan	50	$16
.45 ACP	230	Bi-FMJ	Steel	Berdan	50	$18

10. Ammunition Ballistics

Muzzle velocity is the time rate of change or speed of a projectile as it exits the muzzle of a firearm and is measured in feet per second (fps). A chronograph is used to measure fps. Muzzle energy is the kinetic energy of an object due to its motion. It is measured in foot pounds (ft. lbs.) at the muzzle of a firearm.

Ballistic data is taken from manufacturers' charts and is subject to change. Check the manufacturers' test barrel length since the data represented here may differ from your firearm's actual muzzle velocity and muzzle energy depending on your firearm's barrel length.

5.7x28mm

Manufacturer	Bullet Weight/Type	Muzzle Velocity	Muzzle Energy
FNH USA	40-grain Hornady V-Max	2034 fps	256 ft. lbs.

.25 ACP

Manufacturer	Bullet Weight/Type	Muzzle Velocity	Muzzle Energy
Federal—American Eagle	50-grain Full Metal Jacket	760 fps	64 ft. lbs.
Aguila	50-grain Full Metal Jacket	760 fps	64 ft. lbs.
Fiocchi—Extrema	35-grain Hornady XTP Jacketed Hollow Point	900 fps	63 ft. lbs.
Speer—Gold Dot	35-grain Jacketed Hollow Point	900 fps	63 ft. lbs.
CorBon—Blue Safety Slug	35-grain Safety Slug	1100 fps	94 ft lbs.
Hornady—Custom	35-grain XTP Jacketed Hollow Point	900 fps	63 ft. lbs.
Fiocchi—Shooting Dynamics	50-grain Full Metal Jacket	760 fps	65 ft. lbs.
Magtech—Sport	50-grain Full Metal Jacket	760 fps	64 ft. lbs.
Remington—UMC	50-grain Full Metal Jacket	760 fps	64 ft. lbs.
Sellier & Bellot	50-grain Full Metal Jacket	781 fps	68 ft. lbs.
Winchester—USA	50-grain Full Metal Jacket	760 fps	64 ft. lbs.
CCI—Blazer	50-grain Total Metal Jacket	755 fps	63 ft. lbs.
PMC—Bronze	50-grain Full Metal Jacket	750 fps	62 ft. lbs.

.25 NAA

Manufacturer	Bullet Weight/Type	Muzzle Velocity	Muzzle Energy
CorBon—Self-Defense	35-grain Jacketed Hollow Point	1300 fps	131 ft. lbs.

.32 ACP

Manufacturer	Bullet Weight/Type	Muzzle Velocity	Muzzle Energy
CorBon—Pow'Rball	55-grain	1100 fps	148 ft. lbs.
CorBon—Blue Safety Slug	55-grain Safety	1100 fps	148 ft. lbs.
Extreme Shock—EPR	60-grain Frangible	830 fps	92 ft. lbs.
CorBon—DPX	60-grain Barnes XPB Hollow Point Lead Free	1050 fps	147 ft. lbs.
Fiocchi—Extrema	60-grain Hornady XTP Jacketed Hollow Point	1000 fps	133 ft. lbs.
PMC—Bronze	60-grain Jacketed Hollow Point	980 fps	117 ft. lbs.
Fiocchi—Shooting Dynamics	60-grain Jacketed Hollow Point	1200 fps	205 ft. lbs.
Speer—Gold Dot	60-grain Jacketed Hollow Point	960 fps	123 ft. lbs.
Winchester—Super-X	60-grain Silvertip Hollow Point	970 fps	125 ft. lbs.
Hornady—Custom	60-grain XTP Jacketed Hollow Point	1000 fps	133 ft. lbs.
Federal—Premium Personal Defense	65-grain Hydra-Shok Jacketed Hollow Point	925 fps	123 ft. lbs.
Magtech—Guardian Gold	65-grain Jacketed Hollow Point	922 fps	123 ft. lbs.
Aguila	71-grain Full Metal Jacket	900 fps	126 ft. lbs.
PMC—Bronze	71-grain Full Metal Jacket	900 fps	126 ft. lbs.
Magtech—Sport	71-grain Full Metal Jacket	905 fps	129 ft. lbs.
Prvi Partizan	71-grain Full Metal Jacket	902 fps	129 ft. lbs.
Remington—UMC	71-grain Full Metal Jacket	905 fps	129 ft. lbs.
Winchester—USA	71-grain Full Metal Jacket	905 fps	129 ft. lbs.
Wolf—Gold	71-grain Full Metal Jacket	903 fps	Not published
Prvi Partizan	71-grain Jacketed Hollow Point	902 fps	129 ft. lbs.
Wolf—Gold	71-grain Jacketed Hollow Point	903 fps	Not published
CCI—Blazer	71-grain Total Metal Jacket	900 fps	128 ft. lbs.
Federal—American Eagle	71-grain Total Metal Jacket	900 fps	128 ft. lbs.
Speer—Lawman	71-grain Total Metal Jacket	950 fps	142 ft. lbs.
Fiocchi—Shooting Dynamics	73-grain Full Metal Jacket	980 fps	155 ft. lbs.
Sellier & Bellot	73-grain Full Metal Jacket	1043 fps	176 ft. lbs.
Buffalo Bore	75-grain Hardcast Flat Nose +P	1150 fps	220 ft. lbs.

.32 H&R Magnum

Manufacturer	Bullet Weight/Type	Muzzle Velocity	Muzzle Energy
Black Hills	85-grain Jacketed Hollow Point	1000 fps	200 ft. lbs.
Federal—Premium Personal Defense	85-grain Jacketed Hollow Point	1100 fps	228 ft. lbs.

.32 NAA

Manufacturer	Bullet Weight/Type	Muzzle Velocity	Muzzle Energy
CorBon—Blue Safety Slug	55-grain Safety	1250 fps	191 ft. lbs.
CorBon—Self-Defense	60-grain Jacketed Hollow Point	1200 fps	192 ft. lbs.
CorBon—Performance Match	71-grain Full Metal Jacket	1000 fps	158 ft. lbs.

Ammunition Ballistics

.327 Federal Magnum

Manufacturer	Bullet Weight/Type	Muzzle Velocity	Muzzle Energy
Speer—Gold Dot	100-grain Jacketed Hollow Point	1500 fps	500 ft. lbs.
Federal—American Eagle	100-grain Jacketed Soft Point	1500 fps	500 ft. lbs.
Speer—Gold Dot	115-grain Jacketed Hollow Point	1335 fps	455 ft. lbs.
Federal—Premium Personal Defense	85-grain Hydra-Shok Jacketed Hollow Point	1400 fps	370 ft. lbs.

.380

Manufacturer	Bullet Weight/Type	Muzzle Velocity	Muzzle Energy
CorBon—Pow'Rball	70-grain Jacket Hollow Point capped with polymer ball	1100 fps	188 ft. lbs.
Extreme Shock—EPR	70-grain Frangible	1080 fps	181 ft. lbs.
CorBon—Blue Safety Slug	70-grain Safety Slug	1200 fps	224 ft. lbs.
CorBon—Silver Safety Slug	70-grain Safety Slug	1200 fps	224 ft. lbs.
Magtech—First Defense	77-grain Solid Copper Hollow Point Lead Free	1099 fps	207 ft. lbs.
DoubleTap	80-grain Barnes TAC-XP Hollow Point Lead Free	1050 fps	196 ft. lbs.
CorBon—DPX	80-grain Barnes XPB Hollow Point Lead Free	1050 fps	196 ft. lbs.
Magtech—Guardian Gold	85-grain Jacketed Hollow Point +P	1082 fps	221 ft. lbs.
Winchester—Super-X	85-grain Silvertip Hollow Point	1000 fps	189 ft. lbs.
DoubleTap	90-grain Bonded Defense Jacketed Hollow Point	1100 fps	242 ft. lbs.
PMC—Silver	90-grain Encapsulated Metal Jacket	920 fps	169 ft. lbs.
Hornady—Critical Defense	90-grain Flex Tip eXpanding	1000 fps	200 ft. lbs.
Fiocchi—Extrema	90-grain Hornady XTP Jacketed Hollow Point	1000 fps	200 ft. lbs.
Black Hills	90-grain Jacketed Hollow Point	1000 fps	200 ft. lbs.
PMC—Bronze	90-grain Jacketed Hollow Point	920 fps	169 ft. lbs.
Buffalo Bore	90-grain Jacketed Hollow Point	1025 fps	210 ft. lbs.
Buffalo Bore	90-grain Jacketed Hollow Point	1025 fps	210 ft. lbs.
CorBon—Self-Defense	90-grain Jacketed Hollow Point	1050 fps	220 ft. lbs.
Federal—Premium Personal Defense Reduced Recoil	90-grain Jacketed Hollow Point	1000 fps	200 ft lbs.
Fiocchi—Shooting Dynamics	90-grain Jacketed Hollow Point	1000 fps	205 ft. lbs.
Speer—Gold Dot	90-grain Jacketed Hollow Point	900 fps	196 ft. lbs.
Aguila	90-grain Jacketed Hollow Point	945 fps	Not published
Buffalo Bore	90-grain Jacketed Hollow Point +P	1175 fps	276 ft. lbs.
Wolf—Polyformance	91-grain Full Metal Jacket	1010 fps	Not published
Sellier & Bellot	92-grain Full Metal Jacket	955 fps	186 ft. lbs.
Prvi Partizan	94-grain Full Metal Jacket	951 fps	188 ft. lbs.
Prvi Partizan	94-grain Jacketed Hollow Point	951 fps	188 ft. lbs.
Wolf—Gold	94-grain Jacketed Hollow Point	952 fps	Not published
Winchester—Supreme Elite	95-grain Bonded PDX1 Jacketed Hollow Point	1000 fps	211 ft. lbs.
Winchester—USA WinClean	95-grain Brass Enclosed Base	955 fps	192 ft. lbs.
Magtech—Clean Range	95-grain Encapsulated Round	951 fps	190 ft. lbs.
Remington—UMC	95-grain Flat Nose Enclosed Base Lead Free	955 fps	190 ft. lbs.
Buffalo Bore	95-grain Full Metal Jacket	975 fps	200 ft. lbs.
Buffalo Bore	95-grain Full Metal Jacket	975 fps	200 ft. lbs.
CCI—Blazer	95-grain Full Metal Jacket	945 fps	188 ft. lbs.
DoubleTap	95-grain Full Metal Jacket	1085 fps	248 ft. lbs.
Federal—American Eagle	95-grain Full Metal Jacket	960 fps	194 ft. lbs.
Fiocchi—Shooting Dynamics	95-grain Full Metal Jacket	1000 fps	215 ft. lbs.
Magtech—Sport	95-grain Full Metal Jacket	951 fps	190 ft. lbs.
Remington—UMC	95-grain Full Metal Jacket	955 fps	190 ft. lbs.
Ultramax	95-grain Full Metal Jacket	870 fps	Not published
Winchester—USA	95-grain Full Metal Jacket	955 fps	190 ft. lbs.
Buffalo Bore	95-grain Full Metal Jacket +P	1125 fps	267 ft. lbs.
Buffalo Bore	95-grain Full Metal Jacket +P	1125 fps	267 ft. lbs.
Magtech—Sport	95-grain Jacketed Hollow Point	951 fps	190 ft. lbs.
Aguila	95-grain Jacketed Hollow Point	945 fps	Not published
Buffalo Bore	95-grain Jacketed Hollow Point +P	1125 fps	267 ft. lbs.
Magtech—Sport	95-grain Lead Round Nose	951 fps	190 ft. lbs.
PMC—Gold	95-grain Semi-Jacketed Hollow Point	925 fps	180 ft. lbs.
Speer—Lawman	95-grain Total Metal Jacket	945 fps	188 ft. lbs.
Buffalo Bore	100-grain Flat Nose +P	1125 fps	280 ft. lbs.
Black Hills	100-grain Full Metal Jacket	950 fps	190 ft. lbs.
Buffalo Bore	100-grain Hardcast Flat Nose	975 fps	211 ft. lbs.
Buffalo Bore	100-grain Hardcast Flat Nose	975 fps	211 ft. lbs.
Remington—Golden Saber	102-grain Brass Jacketed Hollow Point	940 fps	200 ft. lbs.
Ultramax	115-grain Lead Round Nose	900 fps	Not published

Ammunition Ballistics

9mm

Manufacturer	Bullet Weight/Type	Muzzle Velocity	Muzzle Energy
CorBon—Blue Safety Slug	80-grain Safety Slug +P	1500 fps	399 ft lbs.
CorBon—Silver Safety Slug	80-grain Safety Slug +P	1650 fps	484 ft lbs.
Extreme Shock—AFR	85-grain Frangible	1531 fps	442 ft. lbs.
Extreme Shock—CT-2	90-grain Copper Jacketed Polymer Tip Lead Free	1449 fps	420 ft. lbs.
SBR—GreenMatch	90-grain Frangible	1300 fps	339 ft. lbs.
CorBon—Self-Defense	90-grain Jacketed Hollow Point +P	1500 fps	450 ft. lbs.
Magtech—First Defense	92.6-grain Solid Copper Hollow Point Lead Free	1330 fps	364 ft. lbs.
Fiocchi—Shooting Dynamics	92-grain Expansion Mono-Block	1300 fps	350 ft. lbs.
CorBon—DPX	95-grain Barnes XPB Hollow Point Lead Free	1250 fps	399 ft. lbs.
Magtech—Sport	95-grain Jacketed Soft Point	1345 fps	380 ft. lbs.
CorBon—Pow'Rball	100-grain +P	1450 fps	467 ft. lbs.
Federal—Guard Dog	105-grain Expanding Full Metal Jacket	1230 fps	353 ft. lbs.
Winchester—Super Clean NT	105-grain Jacketed Soft Point	1200 fps	336 ft. lbs.
DoubleTap	115-grain Barnes TAC-XP Hollow Point Lead Free +P	1320 fps	445 ft. lbs.
CorBon—DPX	115-grain Barnes XPB Hollow Point Lead Free +P	1250 fps	399 ft. lbs.
DoubleTap	115-grain Bonded Defense Jacketed +P Hollow Point	1415 fps	511 ft lbs.
Winchester—USA WinClean	115-grain Brass Enclosed Base	1190 fps	362 ft. lbs.
Magtech—Clean Range	115-grain Encapsulated	1135 fps	330 ft. lbs.
PMC—Silver	115-grain Encapsulated Metal Jacket	1150 fps	338 ft. lbs.
Black Hills	115-grain EXP Jacketed Hollow Point	1250 fps	400 ft. lbs.
Remington—UMC	115-grain Flat Nose Enclosed Base Lead Free	1145 fps	335 ft. lbs.
Hornady—Critical Defense	115-grain Flex Tip eXpanding	1140 fps	332 ft. lbs.
Extreme Shock—EPR	115-grain Frangible	1182 fps	385 ft lbs.
Bear (Brown line)	115-grain Full Metal Jacket	1180 fps	Not published
Bear (Golden line)	115-grain Full Metal Jacket	1215 fps	Not published
Bear (Silver line)	115-grain Full Metal Jacket	1180 fps	Not published
Black Hills	115-grain Full Metal Jacket	1150 fps	336 ft. lbs.
Black Hills (remanufactured)	115-grain Full Metal Jacket	1150 fps	Not published
PMC—Bronze	115-grain Full Metal Jacket	1150 fps	338 ft. lbs.

Manufacturer	Bullet Weight/Type	Muzzle Velocity	Muzzle Energy
CCI—Blazer	115-grain Full Metal Jacket	1145 fps	335 ft. lbs.
CCI—Blazer Brass	115-grain Full Metal Jacket	1125 fps	323 ft. lbs.
Federal—American Eagle	115-grain Full Metal Jacket	1160 fps	344 ft. lbs.
Fiocchi—Shooting Dynamics	115-grain Full Metal Jacket	1250 fps	400 ft. lbs.
Magtech—Sport	115-grain Full Metal Jacket	1135 fps	330 ft. lbs.
Prvi Partizan	115-grain Full Metal Jacket	1148 fps	335 ft. lbs.
Remington—Express	115-grain Full Metal Jacket	1135 fps	329 ft. lbs.
Remington—UMC	115-grain Full Metal Jacket	1145 fps	335 ft. lbs.
Sellier & Bellot	115-grain Full Metal Jacket	1280 fps	418 ft. lbs.
Speer—Lawman	115-grain Full Metal Jacket	1200 fps	368 ft. lbs.
Winchester—USA	115-grain Full Metal Jacket	1190 fps	362 ft. lbs.
Wolf—Military Classic	115-grain Full Metal Jacket	1150 fps	Not published
Wolf—Polyformance	115-grain Full Metal Jacket	1150 fps	Not published
Fiocchi—Extrema	115-grain Hornady XTP Jacketed Hollow Point	1160 fps	340 ft. lbs.
Fiocchi—Shooting Dynamics	115-grain Jacket Hollow Point	1250 fps	400 ft. lbs.
PMC— Bronze	115-grain Jacketed Hollow Point	1160 fps	344 ft. lbs.
Federal—Premium Personal Defense	115-grain Jacketed Hollow Point	1160 fps	344 ft. lbs.
Magtech—Sport	115-grain Jacketed Hollow Point	1155 fps	340 ft. lbs.
Sellier & Bellot	115-grain Jacketed Hollow Point	1237 fps	393 ft. lbs.
Ultramax	115-grain Jacketed Hollow Point	1150 fps	Not published
Winchester—USA	115-grain Jacketed Hollow Point	1225 fps	383 ft. lbs.
Black Hills	115-grain Jacketed Hollow Point +P	1300 fps	431 ft. lbs.
Buffalo Bore	115-grain Jacketed Hollow Point +P	1300fps	431 ft. lbs.
CorBon—Self-Defense	115-grain Jacketed Hollow Point +P	1350 fps	466 ft. lbs.
Magtech—Guardian Gold	115-grain Jacketed Hollow Point +P	1246 fps	397 ft. lbs.
Remington—Express	115-grain Jacketed Hollow Point +P	1250 fps	399 ft. lbs.
Buffalo Bore	115-grain Jacketed Hollow Point +P+	1400 fps	500 ft. lbs.
Magtech—Sport	115-grain Jacketed Hollow Point +P+	1328 fps	451 ft. lbs.
Winchester—Super-X	115-grain Silvertip Hollow Point	1225 fps	383 ft. lbs.
Hornady—Custom	115-grain XTP Jacketed Hollow Point	1155 fps	341 ft. lbs.

Ammunition Ballistics

Manufacturer	Bullet Weight/Type	Muzzle Velocity	Muzzle Energy
Aguila	117-grain Jacketed Hollow Point	1250 fps	Not published
Fiocchi—Shooting Dynamics	123-grain Encapsulated Truncated Cone	1140 fps	470 ft. lbs.
DoubleTap	124-grain Bonded Defense Jacketed +P Hollow Point	1310 fps	473 ft lbs.
Winchester—Supreme Elite	124-grain Bonded PDX1 Jacketed Hollow Point +P	1200 fps	396 ft. lbs.
Winchester—USA WinClean	124-grain Brass Enclosed Base	1130 fps	352 ft. lbs.
Remington—Golden Saber	124-grain Brass Jacketed Hollow Point	1125 fps	349 ft. lbs.
Remington—Golden Saber	124-grain Brass Jacketed Hollow Point +P	1180 fps	384 ft. lbs.
PMC—Silver	124-grain Encapsulated Metal Jacket	1110 fps	339 ft. lbs.
Remington—UMC	124-grain Flat Nose Enclosed Base Lead Free	1100 fps	339 ft. lbs.
Black Hills (remanu-factured)	124-grain Full Metal Jacket	1150 fps	Not published
PMC—Bronze	124-grain Full Metal Jacket	1110 fps	339 ft. lbs.
CCI—Blazer	124-grain Full Metal Jacket	1090 fps	327 ft. lbs.
CCI—Blazer Brass	124-grain Full Metal Jacket	1090 fps	327 ft. lbs.
Federal—American Eagle	124-grain Full Metal Jacket	1120 fps	345 ft. lbs.
Fiocchi—Shooting Dynamics	124-grain Full Metal Jacket	1250 fps	420 ft. lbs.
Magtech—Sport	124-grain Full Metal Jacket	1109 fps	339 ft. lbs.
Prvi Partizan	124-grain Full Metal Jacket	1099 fps	331 ft. lbs.
Remington—Express	124-grain Full Metal Jacket	1100 fps	339 ft. lbs.
Remington—UMC	124-grain Full Metal Jacket	1100 fps	339 ft. lbs.
Sellier & Bellot	124-grain Full Metal Jacket	1181 fps	420 ft. lbs.
Speer—Lawman	124-grain Full Metal Jacket	1090 fps	327 ft. lbs.
Winchester—USA	124-grain Full Metal Jacket	1140 fps	358 ft. lbs.
SBR	124-grain Full Metal Jacket ERVT	1080 fps	323 ft. lbs.
SBR	124-grain Full Metal Jacket SRVT	1080 fps	323 ft. lbs.
Fiocchi—Shooting Dynamics	124-grain Full Metal Jacket Truncated Cone	1250 fps	420 ft. lbs.
Fiocchi—Extrema	124-grain Hornady XTP Jacketed Hollow Point	1100 fps	333 ft. lbs.
Federal—Premium Personal Defense	124-grain Hydra-Shok Jacketed Hollow Point	1120 fps	345 ft. lbs.
Black Hills	124-grain Jacketed Hollow Point	1150 fps	363 ft. lbs.
Hornady—TAP Personal Defense	124-grain Jacketed Hollow Point	1100 fps	339 ft. lbs.
Magtech—Guardian Gold	124-grain Jacketed Hollow Point	1096 fps	331 ft. lbs.
Speer—Gold Dot	124-grain Jacketed Hollow Point	1150 fps	327 ft. lbs.
Black Hills	124-grain Jacketed Hollow Point +P	1250 fps	430 ft. lbs.
Buffalo Bore	124-grain Jacketed Hollow Point +P	1225 fps	413 ft. lbs.
Speer—Gold Dot	124-grain Jacketed Hollow Point +P	1220 fps	410 ft. lbs.
Speer—Gold Dot Short Barrel	124-grain Jacketed Hollow Point +P	1150 fps	364 ft. lbs.
Buffalo Bore	124-grain Jacketed Hollow Point +P+	1300 fps	461 ft. lbs.
Magtech—Sport	124-grain Jacketed Soft Point	1109 fps	339 ft. lbs.
Magtech—Sport	124-grain Lead Round Nose	1109 fps	339 ft. lbs.
PMC—Gold	124-grain Semi-Jacketed Hollow Point	1200 fps	327 ft. lbs.
CCI—Blazer Clean-Fire	124-grain Total Metal Jacket	1090 fps	327 ft. lbs.
Federal—American Eagle	124-grain Total Metal Jacket	1120 fps	345 ft. lbs.
Speer—Lawman Cleanfire	124-grain Total Metal Jacket	1090 fps	327 ft. lbs.
Hornady—Custom	124-grain XTP Jacketed Hollow Point	1110 fps	339 ft. lbs.
Ultramax	125-grain Full Metal Jacket	1100 fps	Not published
CorBon—Self-Defense	125-grain Jacketed Hollow Point +P	1250 fps	434 ft. lbs.
Ultramax	125-grain Lead Round Nose	1060 fps	Not published
Federal—Premium Personal Defense Reduced Recoil	135-grain Hydra-Shok Jacketed Hollow Point	1060 fps	337 ft. lbs.
Extreme Shock—SW	137-grain Frangible	950 fps	295 ft. lbs.
Ultramax	147-grain Full Metal Jacket	930 fps	Not published
Winchester—USA WinClean	147-grain Brass Enclosed Base	990 fps	320 ft. lbs.
DoubleTap	147-grain Bonded Defense Jacketed +P Hollow Point	1135 fps	421 ft. lbs.
Winchester—Supreme Elite	147-grain Bonded PDX1 Jacketed Hollow Point	1000 fps	326 ft. lbs.
Remington—Golden Saber	147-grain Brass Jacketed Hollow Point	990 fps	320 ft. lbs.
Remington—UMC	147-grain Flat Nose Enclosed Base Lead Free	990 fps	320 ft. lbs.
CorBon—Performance Match	147-grain Full Metal Jacket	900 fps	264 ft. lbs.
Federal—American Eagle	147-grain Full Metal Jacket	960 fps	301 ft. lbs.
Fiocchi—Shooting Dynamics	147-grain Full Metal Jacket	1050 fps	360 ft. lbs.
Prvi Partizan	147-grain Full Metal Jacket	984 fps	317 ft. lbs.

Ammunition Ballistics

Manufacturer	Bullet Weight/Type	Muzzle Velocity	Muzzle Energy
Remington—UMC	147-grain Full Metal Jacket	990 fps	320 ft. lbs.
Winchester—USA	147-grain Full Metal Jacket	990 fps	320 ft. lbs.
DoubleTap	147-grain Full Metal Jacket +P	1135 fps	421 ft. lbs.
SBR	147-grain Full Metal Jacket ERVT	900 fps	266 ft. lbs.
SBR	147-grain Full Metal Jacket SRVT	900 fps	266 ft. lbs.
Fiocchi—Extrema	147-grain Hornady XTP Jacketed Hollow Point	980 fps	310 ft. lbs.
Federal—Premium Personal Defense	147-grain Hydra-Shok Jacketed Hollow Point	1000 fps	326 ft. lbs.
Fiocchi—Shooting Dynamics	147-grain Jacket Hollow Point	975 fps	310 ft. lbs.
Hornady—TAP Personal Defense	147-grain Jacketed Hollow Point	975 fps	310 ft. lbs.
Prvi Partizan	147-grain Jacketed Hollow Point	984 fps	317 ft. lbs.
Remington—Express	147-grain Jacketed Hollow Point	990 fps	320 ft. lbs.
Speer—Gold Dot	147-grain Jacketed Hollow Point	985 fps	326 ft. lbs.
Winchester—USA	147-grain Jacketed Hollow Point	990 fps	320 ft. lbs.
Wolf—Gold	147-grain Jacketed Hollow Point	985 fps	Not published
Buffalo Bore	147-grain Jacketed Hollow Point +P+	1175 fps	451 ft. lbs.
Magtech—Sport	147-grain Jacketed Hollow Point Subsonic	990 fps	320 ft. lbs.
Winchester—Super-X	147-grain Silvertip Hollow Point	1010 fps	333 ft. lbs.
CCI—Blazer	147-grain Total Metal Jacket	985 fps	317 ft. lbs.
CCI—Blazer Clean-Fire	147-grain Total Metal Jacket	985 fps	317 ft. lbs.
Federal—American Eagle	147-grain Total Metal Jacket	960 fps	301 ft. lbs.
Speer—Lawman	147-grain Total Metal Jacket	985 fps	317 ft. lbs.
Hornady—Custom	147-grain XTP Jacketed Hollow Point	975 fps	310 ft. lbs.
Prvi Partizan	158-grain Full Metal Jacket	951 fps	317 ft. lbs.
Fiocchi—Shooting Dynamics	158-grain Full Metal Jacket Subsonic	940 fps	309 ft. lbs.

.38 Special

Manufacturer	Bullet Weight/Type	Muzzle Velocity	Muzzle Energy
Extreme Shock—AFR	70-grain Frangible	1586 fps	475 ft. lbs.
CorBon—Blue Safety Slug	80-grain Safety Slug	1200 fps	256 ft. lbs.
CorBon—Silver Safety Slug	80-grain Safety Slug	1300 fps	300 ft. lbs.
CorBon—Blue Safety Slug	80-grain Safety Slug +P	1250 fps	278 ft. lbs.
CorBon—Silver Safety Slug	80-grain Safety Slug +P	1400 fps	348 ft lbs.
Extreme Shock—CT-2	90-grain Copper Jacketed Polymer Tip Lead Free	1575 fps	496 ft. lbs.
Magtech—First Defense	95-grain Solid Copper Hollow Point Lead Free +P	1083 fps	247 ft. lbs.
CorBon—Pow'Rball	100-grain +P	1150 fps	294 ft. lbs.
DoubleTap	110-grain Barnes TAC-XP Hollow Point Lead Free +P	1250 fps	382 ft. lbs.
CorBon—DPX	110-grain Barnes XPB Hollow Point Lead Free +P	1200 fps	352 ft. lbs.
Hornady—Critical Defense	110-grain Flex Tip eXpanding	1010 fps	249 ft. lbs.
Hornady—Critical Defense	110-grain Flex Tip eXpanding +P	1090 fps	290 ft. lbs.
Fiocchi—Shooting Dynamics	110-grain Full Metal Jacket Flat Nose +P	1080 fps	175 ft. lbs.
Fiocchi—Extrema	110-grain Hornady XTP Jacketed Hollow Point +P	1000 fps	269 ft. lbs.
Federal—Premium Personal Defense Reduced Recoil	110-grain Hydra-Shok Jacketed Hollow Point	1000 fps	244 ft. lbs.
CorBon—Self-Defense	110-grain Jacketed Hollow Point +P	1050 fps	269 ft. lbs.
Remington—Express	110-grain Semi-Jacketed Hollow Point	950 fps	220 ft. lbs.
Remington—Express	110-grain Semi-Jacketed Hollow Point +P	995 fps	242 ft. lbs.
Winchester—Super-X	110-grain Silvertip Hollow Point	945 fps	218 ft. lbs.
Extreme Shock—EPR	115-grain Frangible	1185 fps	387 ft. lbs.
Remington—Golden Saber	125-grain Brass Jacketed Hollow Point +P	975 fps	264 ft. lbs.
Remington—Ultimate Home Defense	125-grain Brass Jacketed Hollow Point +P	975 fps	264 ft. lbs.
PMC—Silver	125-grain Encapsulated Metal Jacket +P	950 fps	250 ft. lbs.
CCI—Blazer Brass	125-grain Full Metal Jacket	945 fps	208 ft. lbs.
Magtech—Sport	125-grain Full Metal Jacket	938 fps	245 ft. lbs.
Fiocchi—Extrema	125-grain Hornady XTP Jacketed Hollow Point	900 fps	225 ft. lbs.
Winchester—USA	125-grain Jacketed Flat Nose	800 fps	185 ft. lbs.
Remington—UMC	125-grain Jacketed Flat Nose Enclosed Base Lead Free	800 fps	185 ft. lbs.
Buffalo Bore	125-grain Jacketed Hollow Point	921 fps	235 ft. lbs.
Ultramax	125-grain Jacketed Hollow Point	890 fps	Not published
Black Hills	125-grain Jacketed Hollow Point +P	1050 fps	306 ft. lbs.
Buffalo Bore	125-grain Jacketed Hollow Point +P	1050 fps	306 ft. lbs.

Ammunition Ballistics

Manufacturer	Bullet Weight/Type	Muzzle Velocity	Muzzle Energy
CCI—Blazer	125-grain Jacketed Hollow Point +P	940 fps	245 ft. lbs.
CorBon—Self-Defense	125-grain Jacketed Hollow Point +P	950 fps	251 ft. lbs.
Magtech—Guardian Gold	125-grain Jacketed Hollow Point +P	1017 fps	287 ft. lbs.
Remington—UMC	125-grain Jacketed Hollow Point +P	945 fps	248 ft. lbs.
Speer—Gold Dot	125-grain Jacketed Hollow Point +P	945 fps	248 ft. lbs.
Winchester—Super-X	125-grain Jacketed Hollow Point +P	945 fps	248 ft. lbs.
Winchester—USA	125-grain Jacketed Hollow Point +P	945 fps	248 ft. lbs.
Winchester—USA WinClean	125-grain Jacketed Soft Point	775 fps	167 ft. lbs.
Ultramax	125-grain Lead Conical Nose	850 fps	Not published
Federal—Premium Personal Defense	125-grain Nyclad Hollow Point	830 fps	191 ft. lbs.
Fiocchi—Shooting Dynamics	125-grain Semi-Jacketed Hollow Point	1000 fps	261 ft. lbs.
PMC—Gold	125-grain Semi-Jacketed Hollow Point +P	950 fps	251 ft. lbs.
Magtech—Sport	125-grain Semi-Jacketed Hollow Point +P	938 fps	245 ft. lbs.
Fiocchi—Shooting Dynamics	125-grain Semi-Jacketed Soft Point	950 fps	250 ft. lbs.
Magtech—Sport	125-grain Semi-Jacketed Soft Point +P	938 fps	245 ft. lbs.
Winchester—Super-X	125-grain Silvertip Hollow Point +P	945 fps	248 ft. lbs.
Hornady—Custom	125-grain XTP Jacketed Hollow Point	900 fps	225 ft. lbs.
Federal—Premium Personal Defense	129-grain Hydra-Shok Jacketed Hollow Point +P	950 fps	258 ft. lbs.
Winchester—Supreme Elite	130-grain Bonded PDX1 Jacketed Hollow Point +P	950 fps	260 ft. lbs.
Federal—American Eagle	130-grain Full Metal Jacket	890 fps	229 ft. lbs.
Fiocchi—Shooting Dynamics	130-grain Full Metal Jacket	950 fps	260 ft. lbs.
Magtech—Sport	130-grain Full Metal Jacket	800 fps	185 ft. lbs.
Remington—UMC	130-grain Full Metal Jacket	790 fps	173 ft. lbs.
Ultramax	130-grain Full Metal Jacket	850 fps	Not published
Winchester—USA	130-grain Full Metal Jacket	800 fps	185 ft. lbs.
PMC—Bronze	130-grain Full Metal Jacket +P	1090 fps	343 ft. lbs.
PMC—Silver	132-grain Encapsulated Metal Jacket	840 fps	207 ft. lbs.
PMC—Bronze	132-grain Full Metal Jacket	840 fps	207 ft. lbs.
Speer—Gold Dot Short Barrel	135-grain Jacketed Hollow Point +P	860 fps	222 ft. lbs.
CorBon—Performance Match	147-grain Full Metal Jacket	900 fps	264 ft. lbs.
Fiocchi—Shooting Dynamics	148-grain Semi-Jacketed Hollow Point	820 fps	225 ft. lbs.
Winchester—USA	150-grain Lead Round Nose	845 fps	238 ft. lbs.
Magtech—Clean Range	158-grain Encapsulated Flat Nose	755 fps	200 ft. lbs.
PMC—Silver	158-grain Encapsulated Metal Jacket	800 fps	225 ft. lbs.
Fiocchi—Shooting Dynamics	158-grain Full Metal Jacket	960 fps	320 ft. lbs.
Magtech—Sport	158-grain Full Metal Jacket	755 fps	200 ft. lbs.
Sellier & Bellot	158-grain Full Metal Jacket	889 fps	277 ft. lbs.
SBR	158-grain Full Metal Jacket ERVT	650 fps	Not published
SBR	158-grain Full Metal Jacket SRVT	650 fps	Not published
Remington—Express	158-grain Lead Hollow Point +P	945 fps	248 ft. lbs.
Winchester—Super-X	158-grain Lead Hollow Point Semi-Wadcutter +P	890 fps	278 ft. lbs.
CCI—Blazer	158-grain Lead Round Nose	750 fps	197 ft. lbs.
Federal—American Eagle	158-grain Lead Round Nose	760 fps	203 ft. lbs.
Fiocchi—Shooting Dynamics	158-grain Lead Round Nose	910 fps	295 ft. lbs.
Magtech—Sport	158-grain Lead Round Nose	755 fps	200 ft. lbs.
Prvi Partizan	158-grain Lead Round Nose	902 fps	283 ft. lbs.
Remington—Express	158-grain Lead Round Nose	755 fps	200 ft. lbs.
Remington—UMC	158-grain Lead Round Nose	755 fps	200 ft. lbs.
Sellier & Bellot	158-grain Lead Round Nose	997 fps	349 ft. lbs.
Ultramax	158-grain Lead Round Nose	800 fps	Not published
Winchester—Super-X	158-grain Lead Round Nose	755 fps	200 ft. lbs.
Remington—Express	158-grain Lead Semi Wadcutter	755 fps	200 ft. lbs.
Magtech—Sport	158-grain Lead Semi-Wadcutter	755 fps	200 ft. lbs.
Ultramax	158-grain Lead Semi-Wadcutter	800 fps	Not published
Winchester—Super-X	158-grain Lead Semi-Wadcutter	755 fps	200 ft. lbs.
DoubleTap	158-grain Lead Semi-Wadcutter Hardcast +P	1025 fps	369 ft. lbs.
Buffalo Bore	158-grain Lead Semi-Wadcutter Hollow Point	854 fps	256 ft. lbs.
Buffalo Bore	158-grain Lead Semi-Wadcutter Hollow Point Gas Check +P	1000 fps	351 ft. lbs.
Magtech—Sport	158-grain Semi-Jacketed Hollow Point	807 fps	230 ft. lbs.
Magtech—Sport	158-grain Semi-Jacketed Hollow Point +P	890 fps	278 ft. lbs.

Ammunition Ballistics

Manufacturer	Bullet Weight/Type	Muzzle Velocity	Muzzle Energy
Magtech—Sport	158-grain Semi-Jacketed Soft Point	744 fps	200 ft. lbs.
Sellier & Bellot	158-grain Semi-Jacketed Soft Point	899 fps	277 ft. lbs.
Magtech—Sport	158-grain Semi-Jacketed Soft Point +P	890 fps	278 ft. lbs.
Aguila	158-grain Semi-Jacketed Hollow Point	900 fps	Not published
CCI—Blazer	158-grain Total Metal Jacket +P	850 fps	253 ft. lbs.
CCI—Blazer Clean-Fire	158-grain Total Metal Jacket +P	850 fps	253 ft. lbs.
Speer—Lawman Cleanfire	158-grain Total Metal Jacket +P	900 fps	284 ft. lbs.
Hornady—Custom	158-grain XTP Jacketed Hollow Point	800 fps	225 ft. lbs.

.357 Magnum

Manufacturer	Bullet Weight/Type	Muzzle Velocity	Muzzle Energy
Extreme Shock—AFR	70-grain Frangible	1738 fps	570 ft. lbs.
CorBon—Blue Safety Slug	80-grain Safety Slug	1600 fps	455 ft. lbs.
CorBon—Silver Safety Slug	80-grain Safety Slug	1800 fps	575 ft. lbs.
Extreme Shock—CT-2	90-grain Copper Jacketed Polymer Tip Lead Free	1723 fps	593 ft. lbs.
Magtech—First Defense	95-grain Solid Copper Hollow Point Lead Free	1411 fps	420 ft. lbs.
CorBon—Pow'Rball	100-grain Jacket Hollow Point capped with polymer ball	1450 fps	467 ft. lbs.
CorBon—Self-Defense	110-grain Jacketed Hollow Point	1500 fps	549 ft. lbs.
Winchester—USA	110-grain Jacketed Hollow Point	1295 fps	410 ft. lbs.
Remington—Express	110-grain Semi-Jacketed Hollow Point	1295 fps	410 ft. lbs.
Extreme Shock—EPR	115-grain Frangible	1498 fps	618 ft lbs.
CorBon—DPX	125-grain Barnes XPB Hollow Point Lead Free	1300 fps	469 ft. lbs.
DoubleTap	125-grain Bonded Defense Jacketed Hollow Point	1600 fps	710 ft. lbs.
Remington—Golden Saber	125-grain Brass Jacketed Hollow Point	1220 fps	413 ft. lbs.
Hornady—Critical Defense	125-grain Flex Tip eXpanding	1500 fps	624 ft. lbs.
Magtech—Sport	125-grain Full Metal Jacket	1405 fps	548 ft. lbs.
Winchester—USA WinClean	125-grain Jacketed Flat Nose	1370 fps	521 ft. lbs.
Black Hills	125-grain Jacketed Hollow Point	1500 fps	625 ft. lbs.
PMC—Bronze	125-grain Jacketed Hollow Point	1450 fps	584 ft. lbs.
CorBon—Self-Defense	125-grain Jacketed Hollow Point	1450 fps	584 ft. lbs.
Federal—Premium Personal Defense	125-grain Jacketed Hollow Point	1450 fps	584 ft. lbs.

Manufacturer	Bullet Weight/Type	Muzzle Velocity	Muzzle Energy
Magtech—Guardian Gold	125-grain Jacketed Hollow Point	1378 fps	527 ft. lbs.
Winchester—Super-X	125-grain Jacketed Hollow Point	1450 fps	583 ft. lbs.
Buffalo Bore	125-grain Jacketed Hollow Point High Velocity	1700 fps	802 ft. lbs.
Remington—UMC	125-grain Jacketed Soft Point	1450 fps	583 ft. lbs.
Remington—Express	125-grain Semi-Jacketed Hollow Point	1450 fps	583 ft. lbs.
Fiocchi—Shooting Dynamics	125-grain Semi-Jacketed Soft Point	1450 fps	585 ft. lbs.
Hornady—Custom	125 grain XTP Jacketed Hollow Point	1500 fps	624 ft. lbs.
Buffalo Bore	125-grains Jacketed Hollow Point	1700 fps	802 ft. lbs.
Federal—Premium Personal Defense Reduced Recoil	130-grain Hydra-Shok Jacketed Hollow Point	1300 fps	490 ft. lbs.
Speer—Gold Dot Short Barrel	135-grain Jacketed Hollow Point	990 fps	294 ft. lbs.
CorBon—Self-Defense	140-grain Jacketed Hollow Point	1325 fps	546 ft. lbs.
Hornady—Custom	140-grain XTP Jacketed Hollow Point	1350 fps	566 ft lbs.
Fiocchi—Shooting Dynamics	142-grain Full Metal Jacket Truncated Cone	1420 fps	650 ft. lbs.
Winchester—Super-X	145-grain Silvertip Hollow Point	1290 fps	535 ft. lbs.
Fiocchi—Shooting Dynamics	148-grain Semi-Jacketed Hollow Point	1500 fps	720 ft. lbs.
PMC—Gold	150-grain Semi-Jacketed Hollow Point	1200 fps	480 ft. lbs.
PMC—Silver	158-grain Encapsulated Metal Jacket	1200 fps	505 ft. lbs.
Magtech—Sport	158-grain Full Metal Jacket	1235 fps	535 ft. lbs.
Sellier & Bellot	158-grain Full Metal Jacket	1263 fps	560 ft. lbs.
Fiocchi—Extrema	158-grain Hornady XTP Jacketed Hollow Point	1250 fps	545 ft. lbs.
Federal—Premium Personal Defense	158-grain Hydra-Shok Jacketed Hollow Point	1240 fps	539 ft. lbs.
Black Hills	158-grain Jacketed Hollow Point	1250 fps	548 ft. lbs.
Buffalo Bore	158-grain Jacketed Hollow Point	1475 fps	763 ft. lbs.
CCI—Blazer	158-grain Jacketed Hollow Point	1150 fps	464 ft. lbs.
DoubleTap	158-grain Jacketed Hollow Point	1400 fps	688 ft. lbs.
Federal—Premium Personal Defense	158-grain Jacketed Hollow Point	1240 fps	539 ft. lbs.
Speer—Gold Dot	158-grain Jacketed Hollow Point	1235 fps	535 ft. lbs.
Ultramax	158-grain Jacketed Hollow Point	1300 fps	Not Published
Winchester—Super-X	158-grain Jacketed Hollow Point	1235 fps	535 ft. lbs.

Ammunition Ballistics

Manufacturer	Bullet Weight/Type	Muzzle Velocity	Muzzle Energy
Winchester—USA WinClean	180-grain Brass-Enclosed Base	990 fps	392 ft. lbs.
Remington—Golden Saber	180-grain Brass Jacketed Hollow Point	1015 fps	412 ft. lbs.
DoubleTap	180-grain Controlled Expansion Hollow Point	1100 fps	484 ft. lbs.
Magtech—Clean Range	180-grain Encapsulated Flat Nose	990 fps	392 ft. lbs.
Magtech—Guardian Gold	180-grain Encapsulated Flat Nose	990 fps	392 ft. lbs.
Fiocchi—Shooting Dynamics	180-grain Flat Nose	1000 fps	400 ft. lbs.
Remington—UMC	180-grain Flat Nose Enclosed Base Lead Free	1015 fps	412 ft. lbs.
Black Hills (remanufactured)	180-grain Full Metal Jacket	1000 fps	Not published
Buffalo Bore	180-grain Full Metal Jacket	1100 fps	484 ft. lbs.
CCI—Blazer	180-grain Full Metal Jacket	985 fps	388 ft. lbs.
CCI—Blazer Brass	180-grain Full Metal Jacket	985 fps	388 ft. lbs.
Federal—American Eagle	180-grain Full Metal Jacket	990 fps	392 ft. lbs.
Magtech—Sport	180-grain Full Metal Jacket	990 fps	390 ft. lbs.
Prvi Partizan	180-grain Full Metal Jacket	935 fps	350 ft. lbs.
Sellier & Bellot	180-grain Full Metal Jacket	968 fps	375 ft. lbs.
Ultramax	180-grain Full Metal Jacket	930 fps	Not published
Winchester—USA	180-grain Full Metal Jacket	990 fps	390 ft. lbs.
Wolf—Polyformance	180-grain Full Metal Jacket	990 fps	Not published
SBR	180-grain Full Metal Jacket ERVT	900 fps	Not published
PMC—Bronze	180-grain Full Metal Jacket Flat Point	985 fps	388 ft. lbs.
Magtech—Sport	180-grain Full Metal Jacket High Velocity	1050 fps	441 ft. lbs.
Sellier & Bellot	180-grain Full Metal Jacket Lead Free	968 fps	375 ft. lbs.
SBR	180-grain Full Metal Jacket SRVT	900 fps	325 ft. lbs.
Fiocchi—Extrema	180-grain Hornady XTP Jacketed Hollow Point	950 fps	360 ft. lbs.
Federal—Premium Personal Defense	180-grain Hydra-Shok Jacketed Hollow Point	990 fps	392 ft. lbs.
Buffalo Bore	180-grain Jacketed Hollow Point	1100 fps	484 ft. lbs.
Federal—Premium Personal Defense	180-grain Jacketed Hollow Point	990 fps	392 ft. lbs.
Fiocchi—Shooting Dynamics	180-grain Jacketed Hollow Point	1000 fps	400 ft. lbs.
Hornady—TAP Personal Defense	180-grain Jacketed Hollow Point	950 fps	361 ft. lbs.
Magtech—Guardian Gold	180-grain Jacketed Hollow Point	990 fps	392 ft. lbs.
Magtech—Sport	180-grain Jacketed Hollow Point	990 fps	310 ft. lbs.
Remington—UMC	180-grain Jacketed Hollow Point	1015 fps	412 ft. lbs.
Speer—Gold Dot	180-grain Jacketed Hollow Point	985 fps	400 ft. lbs.
Speer—Gold Dot	180-grain Jacketed Hollow Point	950 fps	361 ft. lbs.
Ultramax	180-grain Jacketed Hollow Point	930 fps	Not published
Winchester—USA	180-grain Jacketed Hollow Point	1010 fps	408 ft. lbs.
Wolf—Gold	180-grain Jacketed Hollow Point	935fps	Not published
Black Hills	180-grain Jacketed Hollow Point	1000 fps	400 ft. lbs.
Black Hills (remanufactured)	180-grain Jacketed Hollow Point	1000 fps	Not published
Ultramax	180-grain Lead Conical Nose	930 fps	Not published
PMC—Gold	180-grain Semi-Jacketed Hollow Point	985 fps	388 ft. lbs.
CCI—Blazer Clean-Fire	180-grain Total Metal Jacket	985 fps	388 ft. lbs.
Federal—American Eagle	180-grain Total Metal Jacket	990 fps	392 ft. lbs.
Speer—Lawman	180-grain Total Metal Jacket	985 fps	388 ft. lbs.
Speer—Lawman Cleanfire	180-grain Total Metal Jacket	985 fps	388 ft. lbs.
Hornady—Custom	180-grain XTP Jacketed Hollow Point	950 fps	361 ft. lbs.
DoubleTap	200-grain Full Metal Jacket	1050 fps	490 ft. lbs.
DoubleTap	200-grain Jacketed Hollow Point	1050 fps	490 ft. lbs.
DoubleTap	200-grain Lead Wide Flat Nose Gas Check	1050 fps	490 ft. lbs.

10mm

Manufacturer	Bullet Weight/Type	Muzzle Velocity	Muzzle Energy
Extreme Shock—AFR	100-grain	1495 fps	496 ft. lbs.
CorBon—Silver Safety Slug	115-grain Safety Slug	1650 fps	695 ft lbs.
CorBon—Pow'Rball	135-grain Jacket Hollow Point capped with polymer ball	1400 fps	588 ft. lbs.
DoubleTap	135-grain Jacketed Hollow Point	1600 fps	767 ft. lbs.
CorBon—Self-Defense	135-grain Jacketed Hollow Point	1400 fps	588 ft. lbs.
Extreme Shock—EPR	150-grain Frangible	1209 fps	487 ft. lbs.
CorBon—Self-Defense	150-grain Jacketed Hollow Point	1325 fps	585 ft. lbs.
CorBon—DPX	155-grain Barnes XPB Hollow Point Lead Free	1200 fps	496 ft. lbs.
DoubleTap	155-grain Barnes XPB Lead Free	1400 fps	750 ft. lbs.
DoubleTap	155-grain Bonded Defense Jacketed Hollow Point	1475 fps	750 ft. lbs.

Manufacturer	Bullet Weight/Type	Muzzle Velocity	Muzzle Energy
Hornady—Custom	155-grain XTP Jacketed Hollow Point	1265 fps	551 ft. lbs.
DoubleTap	165-grain Bonded Defense Jacketed Hollow Point	1400 fps	718 ft. lbs.
DoubleTap	165-grain Brass Jacketed Hollow Point	1425 fps	744 ft. lbs.
CorBon—Self-Defense	165-grain Jacketed Hollow Point	1250 fps	573 ft. lbs.
PMC—Bronze	170-grain Jacketed Hollow Point	1200 fps	543 ft. lbs.
Winchester—Super-X	175-grain Silvertip Hollow Point	1290 fps	649 ft. lbs.
DoubleTap	180-grain Controlled Expansion Jacketed Hollow Point	1350 fps	728 ft. lbs.
Federal—American Eagle	180-grain Full Metal Jacket	1060 fps	449 ft. lbs.
Remington—UMC	180-grain Full Metal Jacket	1150 fps	529 ft. lbs.
Ultramax	180-grain Full Metal Jacket	1100 fps	Not published
Federal—Premium Personal Defense	180 grain Hydra-Shok Jacketed Hollow Point	1030 fps	424 ft. lbs.
Buffalo Bore	180 grain Jacketed Hollow Point	1350 fps	782 ft. lbs.
DoubleTap	180-grain Jacketed Hollow Point	1300 fps	676 ft. lbs.
DoubleTap	180-grain Match Full Metal Jacket	1250 fps	625 ft. lbs.
Hornady—Custom	180-grain XTP Jacketed Hollow Point	1180 fps	556 ft. lbs.
Buffalo Bore	200-grain Full Metal Jacket	1200 fps	639 ft. lbs.
DoubleTap	200-grain Full Metal Jacket	1275 fps	722 ft. lbs.
PMC—Bronze	200-grain Full Metal Jacket Truncated Cone	1050 fps	490 ft. lbs.
DoubleTap	200-grain Jacketed Hollow Point	1250 fps	694 ft. lbs.
DoubleTap	200-grain Lead Wide Flat Nose Gas Check	1300 fps	750 ft. lbs.
CCI—Blazer	200-grain Total Metal Jacket	1050 fps	490 ft. lbs.
Hornady—Custom	200-grain XTP Jacketed Hollow Point	1050 fps	490 ft. lbs.
Buffalo Bore	220-grain Hard Cast Flat Nose	1200 fps	703 ft. lbs.
DoubleTap	230-grain Equalizer Jacketed Hollow Point	1040 fps	553 ft. lbs.
DoubleTap	230-grain Lead Wide Flat Nose Gas Check	1125 fps	641ft. lbs.

.44 Special

Manufacturer	Bullet Weight/Type	Muzzle Velocity	Muzzle Energy
CorBon—Blue Safety Slug	135-grain Safety Slug	1300 fps	507 ft. lbs.
CorBon—Silver Safety Slug	135-grain Safety Slug	1300 fps	507 ft. lbs.
Hornady—Critical Defense	165-grain Flex Tip eXpanding	910 fps	279 ft. lbs.
CorBon—Self-Defense	165-grain Jacketed Hollow Point	1050 fps	404 ft. lbs.
PMC—Bronze	180-grain Jacketed Hollow Point	980 fps	383 ft. lbs.
Buffalo Bore	180-grain Jacketed Hollow Point	1150 fps	543 ft. lbs.
Hornady—Custom	180-grain XTP Jacketed Hollow Point	1000 fps	400 ft. lbs.
CorBon—DPX	200-grain Barnes XPB Hollow Point Lead Free	950 fps	401 ft. lbs.
DoubleTap	200-grain Bonded Defense Jacketed Hollow Point	1100 fps	538 ft. lbs.
Magtech—Guardian Gold	200-grain Jacketed Hollow Point	875 fps	340 ft. lbs.
Speer—Gold Dot	200-grain Jacketed Hollow Point	875 fps	340 ft. lbs.
Winchester—Super-X	200-grain Silvertip Hollow Point	900 fps	360 ft. lbs.
CCI—Blazer	200-grain Speer Gold Dot Jacketed Hollow Point	875 fps	340 ft. lbs.
Fiocchi—Shooting Dynamics	240-grain Semi-Wadcutter	760 fps	305 ft. lbs.
DoubleTap	240-grain Semi-Wadcutter Hardcast	950 fps	
Winchester—Super-X	246-grain Lead Round	755 fps	310 ft. lbs.
Buffalo Bore	255-grain Lead Keith-Type Semi-Wadcutter Gas Check	1000 fps	566 ft. lbs.

.44 Magnum

Manufacturer	Bullet Weight/Type	Muzzle Velocity	Muzzle Energy
PMC—Bronze	180-grain Jacketed Hollow Point	1400 fps	783 ft. lbs.
Extreme Shock—EPR	185-grain Frangible	1675 fps	1152 ft. lbs.
PMC—Silver	240-grain Encapsulated Metal Jacket	1300 fps	900 ft. lbs.
PMC—Bronze	240-grain Jacketed Hollow Point	1300 fps	900 ft. lbs.
PMC—Gold	240-grain Semi-Jacketed Hollow Point	1300 fps	900 ft. lbs.

.45 Long Colt

Manufacturer	Bullet Weight/Type	Muzzle Velocity	Muzzle Energy
CorBon—Blue Safety Slug	145-grain Safety Slug +P	1250 fps	503 ft. lbs.
CorBon—Silver Safety Slug	145-grain Safety Slug +P	1250 fps	503 ft. lbs.
DoubleTap	160-grain Barnes TAC-XP Hollow Point Lead Free	1125 fps	450 ft. lbs.
Hornady—Critical Defense	185-grain Flex Tip eXpanding	920 fps	348 ft. lbs.
Buffalo Bore	200-grain Jacketed Hollow Point	1100 fps	537 ft. lbs.

AimSHOT

(aimshot.com)

COMPACT RAIL LASER

Compatible Firearms: Most firearms with a rail
Activation: Slide switch and pressure pad switch
Master Switch: No
Beam Color/Intensity/Mode: Red/5mw, 632nm, class IIIa/constant
Sight Adjustments: Windage and elevation
Battery Size/Life: Three #LR44/5 hr.
Features: Aluminum construction
MSRP: $50

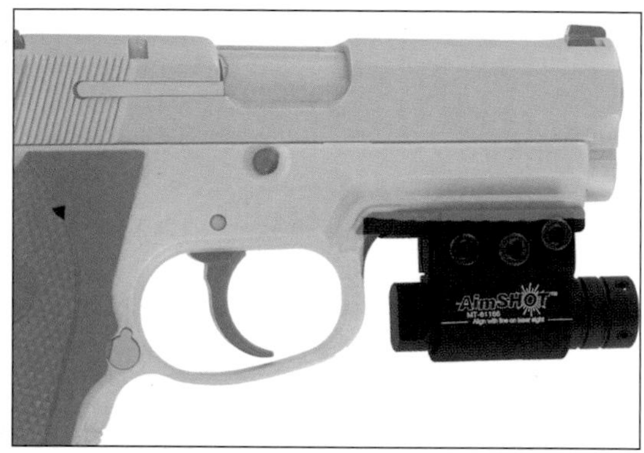

AIMSHOT 6132 RED LASER SIGHT

AIMSHOT 8268 GREEN LASER SIGHT

LASER AND LED FLASHLIGHT

Compatible Firearms: Most firearms with a rail
Activation: Slide switch and pressure pad switch
Master Switch: No
Beam Color/Intensity/Mode: Green/5mw, 532nm, class IIIa/constant
Sight Adjustments: Windage and elevation
Battery Size/Life: One #CR123/5 hr. (laser) and 6 hr. (flashlight)
Features: Aluminum construction; mounts to rail or trigger guard; matte black
MSRP: $158

AIMSHOT KT-6132-1

AIMSHOT LS8268 ON GLOCK

Crimson Trace

(crimsontrace.com)

CRIMSON TRACE
GLS630

CRIMSON TRACE
LG-085

CRIMSON TRACE
LG-302

LASER GUARD

Compatible Firearms: Glock, Kahr, Kel-Tec, Ruger, Smith & Wesson, Springfield, Taurus
Activation: Ambidextrous button under trigger guard, one hand operation
Master Switch: No
Beam Color/Intensity/Mode: Red/5mw, 633nm, class IIIa/constant
Sight Adjustments: Windage and elevation
Battery Size/Life: One 1/3N 3V lithium or two 357 silver oxide/4 hr.
Features: Polymer construction; matte black finish; water resistant; attaches to front of trigger guard and frame
MSRP: $209

PRO-CUSTOM LASER GRIP

Compatible Firearms: 1911, Smith & Wesson
Activation: Ambidextrous button under trigger guard, one hand operation/constant
Master Switch: Yes
Beam Color/Intensity/Mode: Red/5mw, 633nm, class IIIa/constant
Sight Adjustments: Windage and elevation
Battery Size/Life: Two #2032 lithium/4 hr.
Features: Water resistant; replaces original grips
Burlwood *(1911 models; double diamond checkered synthetic)*: $359
Carbon Fiber *(1911 models; hard textured polymer with carbon fiber pattern; matte black finish)*: $359
Chestnut *(J-frame models; chestnut finish with rubber overmold front and back strap)*: $329

LASER GRIP

Compatible Firearms: 1911, Beretta, Bersa, Browning, Charter Arms, CZ, Glock, Kahr, North American Arms, Ruger, Sig Sauer, Smith & Wesson, Springfield, Taurus, Walther
Activation: Ambidextrous button under trigger guard or dual side buttons, one hand operation
Master Switch: Yes
Beam Color/Intensity/Mode: Red/5mw, 633nm, class IIIa/constant
Sight Adjustments: Windage and elevation
Battery Size/Life: Two #2032 lithium/4 hr.
Features: Water resistant; checkered black finish; replaces original grips or fits over grip of polymer frame pistols
MSRP: . . . . $229 - $329
Mil-Spec Lasergrip (Beretta): **. . . $399**
Waterproof (Sig Sauer)**: $399**

CRIMSON TRACE
LG-407

CRIMSON TRACE
LG-431

LaserLyte

(laserlyte.com)

LASERLYTE LASER TRAINING SYSTEM

LASERLYTE REAR SIGHT ON A SPRINGFIELD EMP

REAR SIGHT LASER

Compatible Firearms: Glock, Springfield
Activation: Button behind rear sight
Master Switch: No
Beam Color/Intensity/Mode: Red/5mw, 650nm, class IIIa/constant and pulsating
Sight Adjustments: Windage and elevation
Battery Size/Life: Four #377/5 hr.
Features: Waterproof, replaces rear sight
MSRP: $199

SUB COMPACT RAIL LASER

Compatible Firearms: Any firearm with a minimum of .70 inches rail space
Activation: Ambidextrous button under trigger guard, one hand operation
Master Switch: No
Beam Color/Intensity/Mode: Red/5mw, 650nm, class IIIa/constant and pulsating
Sight Adjustments: Windage and elevation
Battery Size/Life: Four #377/5 hr.
Features: Waterproof; mounts to most weapon rails; auto-off
MSRP: $100

LASER TRAINING SYSTEM

Compatible Firearms: Firearms chambered in 9mm, .40 S&W, or .45ACP
Activation: Firearm's trigger/firing pin
Master Switch: No
Beam Color/Intensity/Mode: Red/5mw, 650nm, class IIIa/single pulse per trigger pull
Sight Adjustments: N/A
Battery Size/Life: Three #377/3,000 shots
Features: Installs in firearm's chamber for dry firing exercises
MSRP: $199

LaserMax

(lasermax.com)

LASERMAX FULL SIZE SABRE SERIES ON A GLOCK

INTERNAL GUIDE ROD LASERS

Compatible Firearms: 1911, Beretta, Glock, Sig Sauer, Smith & Wesson, Springfield, Taurus
Activation: Modified slide stop or take down
Master Switch: No
Beam Color/Intensity/Mode: Red/5mw, 635nm/pulsating
Sight Adjustments: Windage and elevation
Battery Size/Life: Three #393/1.5 hr.
Features: Water resistant; replaces factory guide rod
MSRP: $399

UNI-MAX LMS-UNI

Compatible Firearms: Most pistols with an accessory rail
Activation: Ambidextrous button on unit
Master Switch: Yes
Beam Color/Intensity/Mode: Red/5mw, 635nm/constant or pulsating
Sight Adjustments: Windage and elevation
Battery Size/Life: Two #357/3hr. (constant) or 6 hr. (pulsating)
Features: Water resistant; compact design; accessory rail; auto off; can be activated via optional cord
MSRP: $189

LaserMax

(lasermax.com)

UNI-MAX LMS-UNI-G

Compatible Firearms: Most pistols with an accessory rail
Activation: Ambidextrous button on unit
Master Switch: Yes
Beam Color/Intensity/Mode: Green/5mw, 532nm/pulsating
Sight Adjustments: Windage and elevation
Battery Size/Life: One 1/3N 3V lithium /1 hr.
Features: Water resistant; compact design; accessory rail; auto off; can be activated via optional cord
MSRP: $349

LASERMAX LMS-UNI-G

LASERMAX LMS-UNI ON A S&W M&P WITH LIGHT ACCESSORY

LASERMAX INTERNAL GUIDE ROD ON A SIG P226

SABRE SERIES LASERS

Compatible Firearms: Glock
Activation: Mode switch; grip pressure
Master Switch: Yes
Beam Color/Intensity/Mode: Red/5mw, 635nm/constant or pulsating
Sight Adjustments: Windage and elevation
Battery Size: Two #357
Features: Water resistant; attaches to grip; beavertail design
MSRP: $219

Leapers

(leapers.com)

UTG COMBAT TACTICAL W/E LASER

Compatible Firearms: Most pistols with an accessory rail
Activation: Ambidextrous push-button switch
Master Switch: No
Beam Color/Intensity/Mode: Red/3.1mw, 635nm/constant or pulsating
Sight Adjustments: Windage and elevation
Battery Size: Three #LR44
Features: Aluminum construction
MSRP: $30

Viridian

(viridiangreenlaser.com)

C5 and C5L

Compatible Firearms: Most pistols with an accessory rail
Activation: Ambidextrous button
Master Switch: No
Beam Color/Intensity/Mode: Green/5mw, 532nm/constant or multiple pulsating
Sight Adjustments: Windage and elevation
Battery Size/Life: One #CR12¾ hr. (constant), 7 hr. (pulsating)
Features: Zytel polymer construction; compact design
C5: $269
C5L (integrated 100 lumen tactical light): $329

GLOCK, RUGER SR9, SMITH & WESSON M&P, SPRINGFIELD XD/XDM, TAURUS PT 24/7, WALTHER P22, WALTHER PK380

Compatible Firearms: Designed for specific brand models
Activation: Ambidextrous button
Master Switch: No
Beam Color/Intensity/Mode: Green/5mw, 532nm/constant or multiple pulsating
Sight Adjustments: Windage and elevation
Battery Size/Life: One #CR12¾ hr. (constant), 7 hr. (pulsating)
Features: Zytel polymer construction; compact design; embossed with brand logo
Black: $279
OD (Glock, Ruger SR9, Walther P22): $284

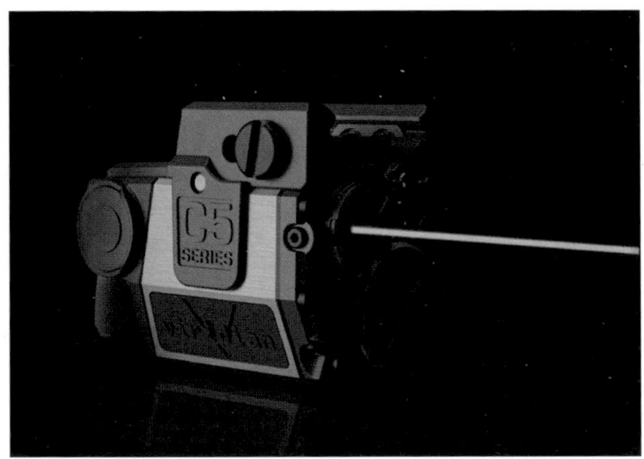

VIRIDIAN C5

VIRIDIAN C5L

TACTICAL LIGHTS

Blackhawk

(blackhawk.com)

BLACKHAWK NIGHT-OPS XIPHOS NT WEAPON MOUNTED LIGHT

NIGHT-OPS XIPHOS NT WEAPON MOUNTED LIGHT

Activation: Ambidextrous button
Compatible Firearms: Designed for specific brand models
Beam Output/Modes: 90 Lumens/ constant and strobe
Overall Length: 3.1 in.
Weight With Batteries: 2.5 oz.
Battery Size/Life: One 3-Volt CR123A/120 min.
Bulb Type: LED
Features: Anodized aluminum construction; cam-clamp mount; low battery indicator
MSRP: $200

Glock

(glock.com)

GLOCK GTL 10
AND GTL 11

GLOCK GTL 21
AND GTL 22

GTL 10 and GTL 11

Activation: Ambidextrous button
Compatible Firearms: All Glock models and most pistols with accessory rails
Beam Output/Modes: 60 Lumens/constant
Overall Length: 3.1 in.
Weight With Batteries: 1.8 oz.
Battery Size/Life: Two 3-Volt CR123A/1.1 hr.
Bulb Type: Xenon
Features: Polymer construction; focusable beam; waterproof
GTL 10: $100
GTL 11 (dimmable beam): $75

GTL 21 and GTL 22

Activation: Ambidextrous button
Compatible Firearms: All Glock models and most pistols with accessory rails
Light Beam Output/Modes: 60 Lumens/constant
Laser Beam Color/Intensity/Mode: Red/5mw, 630nm/constant or pulsating
Laser Adjustments: Windage and elevation
Overall Length: 3.2 in.
Weight With Batteries: 1.8 oz.
Battery Size/Life: Two 3-Volt CR123A/1.1 hr. (light), 2.1 hr. (laser), 1 hr. (light and laser)
Bulb Type: Xenon
Features: Polymer construction; focusable beam; waterproof
GTL 21: $230
GTL 22 (dimmable beam): $230

Insight

(insighttechgear.com)

INSIGHT WX150

INSIGHT M3

WX150

Activation: Ambidextrous button
Compatible Firearms: Most pistols with accessory rails
Light Beam Output/Modes: 150 Lumens/momentary on, constant, strobe
Overall Length: 3.2 in.
Weight With Batteries: 4 oz.
Battery Size/Life: Two 3-Volt CR123A/125 min.
Bulb Type: LED
Features: Aluminum construction; slide-lock mounting; waterproof; black finish
MSRP: $240

M3

Activation: Ambidextrous button
Compatible Firearms: Most pistols with accessory rails
Light Beam Output/Modes: 90 Lumens/momentary on, constant
Overall Length: 3.4 in.
Weight With Batteries: 3.3 oz.
Battery Size/Life: Two 3-Volt CR123A/1 hr.
Bulb Type: Xenon
Features: Side-lock clamp; black or tan finishes
MSRP: $120

M3X

Activation: Ambidextrous button
Compatible Firearms: Most pistols with accessory rails
Light Beam Output/Modes: 125 Lumens/momentary on, constant
Overall Length: 3.4 in.
Weight With Batteries: 3.9 oz.
Battery Size/Life: Two 3-Volt CR123A/60 min.
Bulb Type: Xenon
Features: Side-lock clamp; black or tan finishes
MSRP: $175

Insight

(insighttechgear.com)

M3X LED

Activation: Ambidextrous button
Compatible Firearms: Most pistols with accessory rails
Light Beam Output/Modes: 150 Lumens/momentary on, constant
Overall Length: 3.4 in.
Weight With Batteries: 3.9 oz.
Battery Size/Life: Two 3-Volt CR123A/120 min.
Bulb Type: LED
Features: Side-lock clamp; black finish
MSRP: $200

M6

Activation: Ambidextrous button
Compatible Firearms: Most pistols with accessory rails
Light Beam Output/Modes: 125 Lumens/momentary on, constant
Laser Beam Color/Intensity/Mode: Red/5mw, 640nm/constant
Laser Adjustments: Windage and elevation
Overall Length: 3.4 in.
Weight With Batteries: 3.7 oz.
Battery Size/Life: Two 3-Volt CR123A/1 hr.
Bulb Type: Xenon
Features: Integrated laser; side-lock clamp; black or tan finishes; 6-position selector for laser/light use
MSRP: $280

M6X

Activation: Ambidextrous button
Compatible Firearms: Most pistols with accessory rails
Light Beam Output/Modes: 125 Lumens/momentary on, constant
Laser Beam Color/Intensity/Mode: Red/5mw, 640nm/constant
Laser Adjustments: Windage and elevation
Overall Length: 3.4 in.
Weight With Batteries: 4.4 oz.
Battery Size/Life: Two 3-Volt CR123A/60 min.
Bulb Type: Xenon
Features: Integrated laser; rail-grabber mount fits most rails; black or tan finishes; 4-position selector for laser/light use
MSRP: $390

M6X LED

Activation: Ambidextrous button
Compatible Firearms: Most pistols with accessory rails
Light Beam Output/Modes: 150 Lumens/momentary on, constant
Laser Beam Color/Intensity/Mode: Red/5mw, 640nm/constant
Laser Adjustments: Windage and elevation
Overall Length: 3.4 in.
Weight With Batteries: 4.4 oz.
Battery Size/Life: Two 3-Volt CR123A/60 min.
Bulb Type: LED
Features: Integrated laser; rail-grabber mount fits most rails; black or tan finishes; 4-position selector for laser/light use
MSRP: $410

X2

Activation: Ambidextrous button
Compatible Firearms: Most pistols with accessory rails
Light Beam Output/Modes: 80 Lumens/momentary on, constant
Overall Length: 2.4 in.
Weight With Batteries: 1.7 oz.
Battery Size/Life: One 3-Volt CR123A/1 hr.
Bulb Type: LED
Features: Compact design; side-lock clamp; black finishes
MSRP: $190

X2L LED

Activation: Ambidextrous button
Compatible Firearms: Most pistols with accessory rails
Light Beam Output/Modes: 80 Lumens/momentary on, constant
Laser Beam Color/Intensity/Mode: Red/5mw, 640nm/constant
Laser Adjustments: Windage and elevation
Overall Length: 2.4 in.
Weight With Batteries: 1.9 oz.
Battery Size/Life: One 3-Volt CR123A/60 min.
Bulb Type: LED
Features: Integrated laser; black finish; 2-position selector for laser/light use
MSRP: $300

M2

Activation: Ambidextrous button
Compatible Firearms: Most pistols with accessory rails
Light Beam Output/Modes: 90 Lumens/momentary on, constant
Overall Length: 3.5 in.
Weight With Batteries: 4 oz.
Battery Size/Life: Two 3-Volt CR123A/1 hr.
Bulb Type: LED
Features: Designed for H&K USP; compact design; side-lock clamp; black finish
MSRP: $240

INSIGHT M2

INSIGHT M6

INSIGHT M3X LED

INSIGHT M6X LED

Leapers

(leapers.com)

LEAPERS UTG 23MM IRB XENON

LEAPERS COMBAT TACTICAL W/E RED LASER WITH WEAVER MOUNT

LEAPERS UTG XENON FLASHLIGHT AND W/E LASER

UTG 23MM IRB XENON

Activation: Ambidextrous toggle switch
Compatible Firearms: Most pistols with accessory rails
Beam Output/Modes: 126 Lumens/constant
Overall Length: 3.1 in.
Weight With Batteries: 5.1 oz.
Battery Size/Life: Two 3-Volt CR123A/70 min.
Bulb Type: LED
Features: Aluminum construction
MSRP: $34

COMBAT TACTICAL W/E RED LASER

Activation: Ambidextrous toggle switch
Compatible Firearms: Designed for most pistiols with an accessory rail
Activation: Push-button switch
Master Switch: No
Beam Color/Intensity/Mode: Red/5mw, 650nm, class IIIa/steady
Sight Adjustments: No
Battery Size/Life: Four #LR44/6000 hrs.
Features: Waterproof
MSRP: $29

UTG XENON FLASHLIGHT AND W/E LASER

Activation: Ambidextrous toggle switch
Compatible Firearms: Most pistols with accessory rails
Light Beam Output/Modes: 126 Lumens/constant
Laser Beam Color/Intensity/Mode: Red/3.1mw, 640nm/constant
Laser Adjustments: Windage and elevation
Overall Length: 3.6 in.
Weight With Batteries: 6.3 oz.
Battery Size/Life: Two 3-Volt CR123A/60 min. (flashlight), 80 min. (laser)
Bulb Type: Xenon
Features: Integrated laser; black finish
MSRP: $65

ACCESSORIES

Streamlight

(streamlight.com)

TLR-1 and TLR-1S

Activation: Ambidextrous toggle switch
Compatible Firearms: Most pistols with accessory rails
Beam Output/Modes: 135 Lumens/constant, momentary on
Overall Length: 3.3 in.
Weight With Batteries: 4.2 oz.
Battery Size/Life: Two 3-Volt CR123A/2.5 hr.
Bulb Type: LED
Features: Aluminum construction; waterproof; black finish
TLR-1: $100
TLR-1s (constant, momentary on beam modes; 160 Lumens): $200

STREAMLIGHT TLR-1

Streamlight

(streamlight.com)

TLR-2 and TLR-2S

Activation: Ambidextrous toggle switch
Compatible Firearms: Most pistols with accessory rails
Light Beam Output/Modes: 135 Lumens/momentary on and constant
Laser Beam Color/Intensity/Mode: Red/5mw, 650nm/constant
Laser Adjustments: Windage and elevation
Overall Length: 3.3 in.
Weight With Batteries: 4.7 oz.
Battery Size/Life: Two 3-Volt CR123A/2.5 hr. (beam), 45 hr. (laser)
Bulb Type: LED
Features: Aluminum construction; waterproof; black finish
TLR-2: $245
TLR-2s (strobe and constant mode; 160 Lumens): $260

TLR-3

Activation: Ambidextrous toggle switch
Compatible Firearms: Most pistols with accessory rails
Light Beam Output/Modes: 90 Lumens/constant
Overall Length: 7.2 in.

STREAMLIGHT TLR-2

STREAMLIGHT TLR-3

Weight With Batteries: 2.3 oz.
Battery Size/Life: One 3-Volt CR123A/1.5 hr.
Bulb Type: LED
Features: Polymer construction; waterproof; black finish
MSRP: $100

TLR-VIR

Activation: Ambidextrous toggle switch
Compatible Firearms: Most pistols with accessory rails
Light Beam Output/Modes: 160 Lumens/constant
Overall Length: 3.8 in.
Weight With Batteries: 6 oz.
Battery Size/Life: Two 3-Volt CR123A/1.5 hr. (beam), 20 hr. (IR)
Bulb Type: LED

STREAMLIGHT TLR-VIR

Features: Integrate IR (Infrared), aluminum construction; 3-position selector; waterproof; black finish
MSRP: $352

SureFire

(surefire.com)

X300

Activation: Ambidextrous toggle switch
Compatible Firearms: Most pistols with accessory rails
Light Beam Output/Modes: 170 Lumens/constant
Overall Length: 3.6 in.
Weight With Batteries: 3.8 oz.
Battery Size/Life: Two 3-Volt CR123A/2.4 hr.
Bulb Type: LED
Features: Aluminum construction; black finish
MSRP: $249

X400

Activation: Ambidextrous push/toggle switch
Compatible Firearms: Most pistols with accessory rails
Light Beam Output/Modes: 170 Lumens/constant
Laser Beam Color/Intensity/Mode: Red/5mw, 635nm/constant
Laser Adjustments: Windage and elevation
Overall Length: 3.6 in.
Weight With Batteries: 4.4 oz.
Battery Size/Life: Two 3-Volt CR123A/2.4 hr. (beam)
Bulb Type: LED
Features: Aluminum construction; weatherproof; black finish
MSRP: $460

SUREFIRE X400

SUREFIRE X300

Advanced Armament Corp.

(advanced-armament.com)

ADVANCED ARAMENT CORP. TI-RANT 9 END CAP

TI-RANT 9 and TI-RANT 9S

Caliber: 9mm
Overall Length: 5.1 in. (Ti-Rant 9S), 7.9 in.
Diameter: 1.4 in.
Weight: 7.6 oz. (Ti-Rant 9S), 8.6 oz.
Sound Reduction: 22 dB dry/27.2 dB wet (Ti-Rant 9S), 35-38 dB
Mounting Type: Threaded
Features: Titanium construction; recoil assist; black finish
MSRP: $850

TI-RANT 45 and TI-RANT 45S

Caliber: .45 ACP
Overall Length: 6.4 in. (Ti-Rant 45S), 8.7 in.

ADVANCED ARMAMENT CORP. ECO-9

Diameter: 1.4 in.
Weight: 9.2 oz. (Ti-Rant 45S), 11.5 oz.
Sound Reduction: 18 dB dry/28.5 dB wet (Ti-Rant 45S), 30-41 dB
Mounting Type: Threaded
Features: Titanium construction; recoil assist; black finish
MSRP: $850

ECO-9

Caliber: 9mm
Overall Length: 8.4 in.
Diameter: 1.3 in.
Weight: 10.5 oz.
Sound Reduction: 30 dB dry/38 dB wet
Mounting Type: Threaded
Features: Aluminum construction; recoil assist; black finish
MSRP: $450

ADVANCED ARMAMENT CORP. TI-RANT 45S

ADVANCED ARMAMENT CORP. EVOLUTION 40

EVOLUTION 9, 40 and 45

Caliber: 9mm, .40 S&W, .45ACP
Overall Length: 7.7 in. (9 Evolution), 7.8 in. (40 Evolution, 45 Evolution)
Diameter: 1.3 in.; 1.4 in. (40 Evolution, 45 Evolution)
Weight: 9.7 oz. (9 Evolution), 11.2 oz. (40 Evolution), 11.3 oz. (45 Evolution)
Sound Reduction: 34 dB dry/38 dB wet
Mounting Type: Threaded
Features: Aluminum construction; recoil assist; black finish
MSRP: $650

AWC Systems Technology

(awcsystech.com)

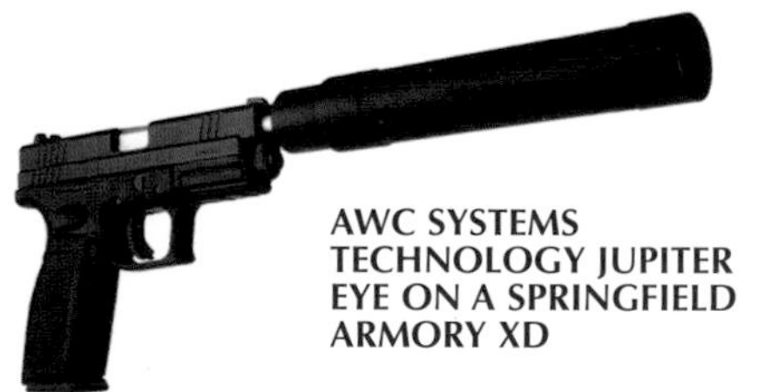

AWC SYSTEMS TECHNOLOGY JUPITER EYE ON A SPRINGFIELD ARMORY XD

JUPITER EYE

Caliber: 9mm, .40 S&W, 10mm
Overall Length: 7.8 in.
Diameter: 1.4 in.
Weight: 12 oz.
Sound Reduction: Not published
Mounting Type: Threaded
Features: Stainless construction; recoil assist; black finish
MSRP: $950

LIFE SUPPORT SYSTEM 5.7MM

Caliber: 5.7x28mm
Overall Length: 6 in.
Diameter: 1.3 in.
Weight: 7.2 oz.
Sound Reduction: Not published
Mounting Type: Threaded
Features: Titanium construction; recoil assist; black finish; design for FN Five-seveN
MSRP: $995

NEXUS III .45

Caliber: .45 ACP
Overall Length: 7.7 in.
Diameter: 1.4 in.
Weight: 13 oz.
Sound Reduction: not published
Mounting Type: Threaded
Features: Stainless/titanium construction; recoil assist; black finish
MSRP: $950

AWC SYSTEMS TECHNOLOGY ON A FN FIVE-SEVEN LIFE SUPPORT SYSTEM

AWC Systems Technology

(awcsystech.com)

TITANIUM ABRAXAS 9MM

Caliber: 9mm
Overall Length: 5.7 in.
Diameter: 1 in.
Weight: 3.3 oz.
Sound Reduction: not published
Mounting Type: Threaded
Features: Titanium construction; recoil assist; black finish
MSRP: $650

AWC SYSTEMS TECHNOLOGY TITANIUM ABRAXAS 9MM ON A BERETTA 90-TWO

GemTech

(gem-tech.com)

BLACKSIDE 40

Caliber: .40 S&W
Overall Length: 7.6 in.
Diameter: 1.4 in.
Weight: 10 oz.
Sound Reduction: 20 dB dry/30 dB wet
Mounting Type: Threaded
Features: Aluminum construction; recoil assist; black finish
MSRP: $740

BLACKSIDE 45

Caliber: .45 ACP
Overall Length: 7.6 in.
Diameter: 1.4 in.
Weight: 10 oz.
Sound Reduction: 20 dB dry/30 dB wet
Mounting Type: Threaded
Features: Aluminum construction; recoil assist; black finish
MSRP: $740

MULTIMOUNT

Caliber: 9mm
Overall Length: 7 in.
Diameter: 1.4 in.
Weight: 6.5 oz.
Sound Reduction: 20 dB dry/30 dB wet
Mounting Type: Threaded
Features: Aluminum construction; recoil assist; black finish
MSRP: $595

SFN-57

Caliber: 5.7x28mm
Overall Length: 5.8 in.
Diameter: 1.3 in.
Weight: 5.2 oz.
Sound Reduction: 20 dB dry/30 dB wet
Mounting Type: Threaded
Features: Aluminum construction; recoil assist; black finish; design for FN Five-seveN
MSRP: $575

TUNDRA

Caliber: 9mm
Overall Length: 7.2 in.
Diameter: 1.3 in.
Weight: 8.5 oz.
Sound Reduction: 20 dB dry/30 dB wet
Mounting Type: Threaded
Features: Aluminum construction; recoil assist; black finish; design for FN Five-seveN
MSRP: $750

GEMTECH TUNDRA

GEMTECH TUNDRA

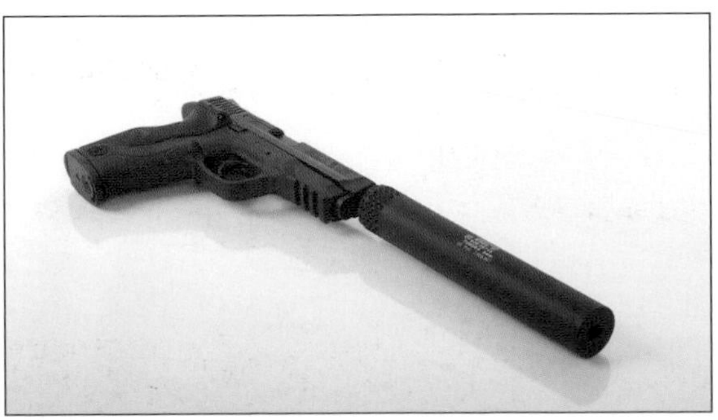

GEMTECH TUNDRA ON A S&W M&P

GEMTECH, S&W, AND LASERMAX COMBINATION

Knight's Armament

(knightarmco.com)

H&K USP-T

Caliber: .45 ACP
Overall Length: 7.5 in.
Diameter: 1.4 in.
Weight: 15.2 oz.
Sound Reduction: 28 dB dry/38 dB wet
Mounting Type: Threaded
Features: Designed for H&K USP; recoil assist; black finish
MSRP: . . . . not published

MK 23

Caliber: .45 ACP
Overall Length: 7.5 in.
Diameter: 1.4 in.
Weight: 15.2 oz.
Sound Reduction: 32 dB dry/38 dB wet
Mounting Type: Threaded
Features: Designed for H&K Mark 23; recoil assist; black finish
MSRP: . . . . not published

SRT Arms

(srtarms.com)

MATRIX M9

Caliber: 9mm
Overall Length: 7.7 in.
Diameter: 1.3 in.
Weight: 5.5 oz.
Sound Reduction: 33 dB dry/40 dB wet
Mounting Type: Threaded
Features: Aluminum construction; recoil assist; black finish
MSRP: $675

SRT ARMS
MATRIX M9

SWR Manufacturing

(swrmfg.com)

TRIDENT 9

Caliber: 9mm
Overall Length: 6.6 in.
Diameter: 1.4 in.
Weight: 7.5 oz.
Sound Reduction: Not published
Mounting Type: Threaded
Features: Aluminum construction; recoil assist; black finish
MSRP: $595

OCTANE-9 and OCTANE-9 HD

Caliber: 9mm
Overall Length: 7.4 in.
Diameter: 1.4 in.
Weight: 9.7 oz. (Octane-9), 12.5 oz. (Octane-9 HD)
Sound Reduction: Not published
Mounting Type: Threaded
Features: Recoil assist; black finish
Octane-9 (aluminum construction): $650
Octane-9 HD (stainless construction): $750

H.E.M.S.2 and H.E.M.S.C.T

Caliber: .45 ACP
Overall Length: 6.5 in. (H.E.M.S.C.T), 8.5 in.
Diameter: 1.4 in.
Weight: 10.8 oz.
Sound Reduction: Not published
Mounting Type: Threaded
Features: Aluminum/stainless construction; recoil assist; black finish
H.E.M.S.2: $745
H.E.M.S.C.T: $745

SWR MANUFACTURING
TRIDENT 9 DISASSEMBLED

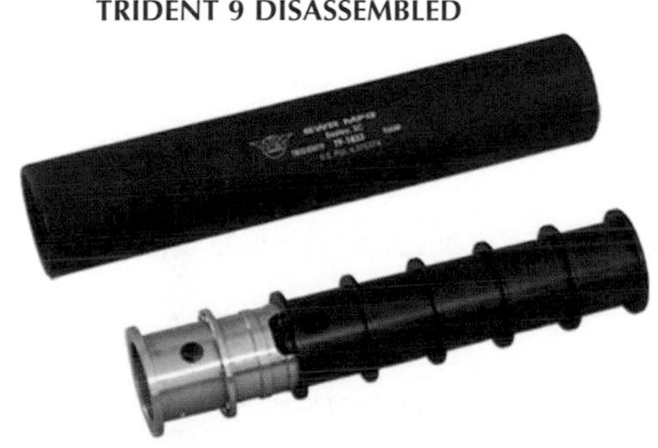

SWR MANUFACTURING
OCTANE-9

SWR MANUFACTURING
H.E.M.S.2

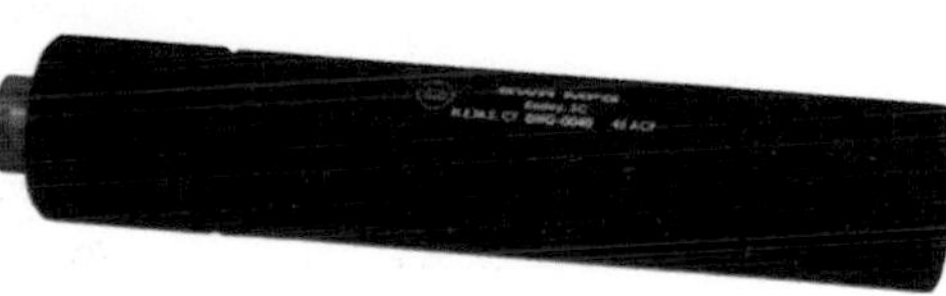

SWR MANUFACTURING
H.E.M.S.C.T

ACCESSORIES

SWR Manufacturing

(swrmfg.com)

GS-40

Caliber: .40 S&W
Overall Length: 8.3 in.
Diameter: 1.4 in.
Weight: 10.8 oz.
Sound Reduction: Not published
Mounting Type: Threaded
Features: Aluminum/stainless construction; recoil assist; black finish
MSRP: $745

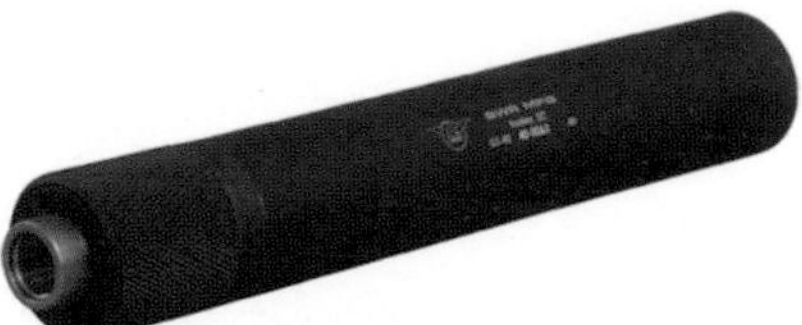

SWR MANUFACTURING GS-40

TROS

(trosusa.com)

DIPLOMAT-II

Caliber: 9mm, .45 ACP
Overall Length: 8.1 in. (9mm), 9 in. (.45 ACP)
Diameter: 1.3 in.
Weight: 9 oz.
Sound Reduction: Not published

TROS DIPLOMAT II ON A H&K USP TACTICAL 45

Mounting Type: Threaded
Features: Aluminum construction; recoil assist; black finish
MSRP: $595

Yankee Hill Machine (YHM)

(yhm.net)

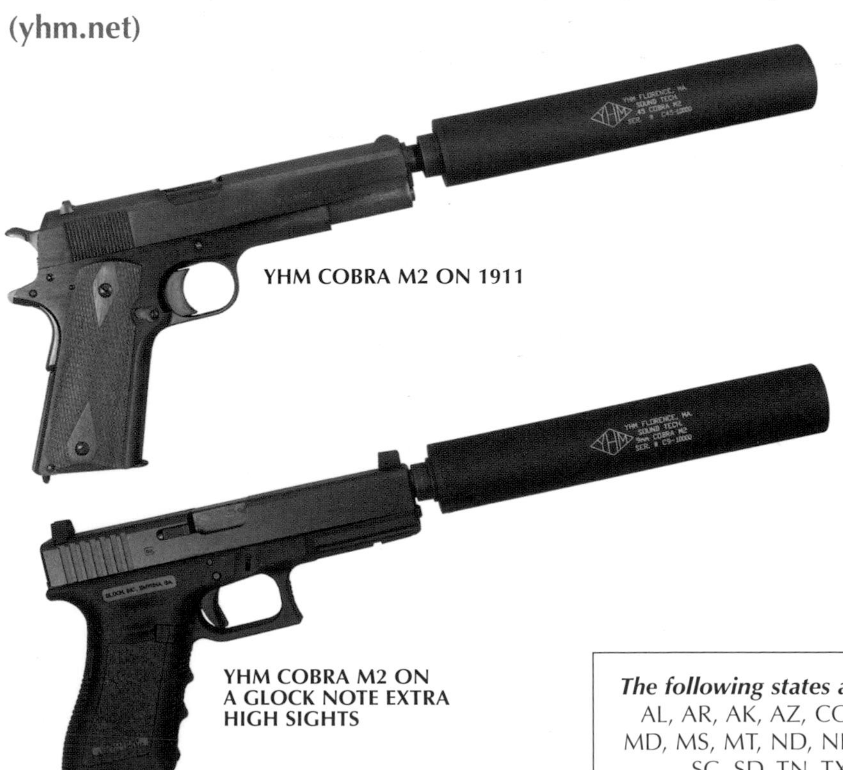

YHM COBRA M2 ON 1911

YHM COBRA M2 ON A GLOCK NOTE EXTRA HIGH SIGHTS

COBRA M2

Caliber: 9mm, .40 S&W, .45 ACP
Overall Length: 8 in.
Diameter: 1.4 in.
Weight: 11.5 oz.
Sound Reduction: 35 dB dry (9mm), 27 dB dry (.40 S&W), 22 dB dry (.45 ACP)
Mounting Type: Threaded
Features: Aluminum construction; recoil assist; black finish
MSRP: $627

The following states allow private ownership of suppressors: AL, AR, AK, AZ, CO, CT, FL, GA, ID, IN, KS, KY, LA, ME, MD, MS, MT, ND, NE, NV, NH, NM, NC, OH, OK, OR, PA, SC, SD, TN, TX, UT, VA, WA, WI, WV, and WY.

12. Holsters

Image courtesy of Safariland.

Bianchi

(www.bianchi-intl.com)

3S PISTOL POCKET

Use/Type: Concealment/inside waistband
Retention: Thumb break
Material/Finish: Leather/plain tan
Carry: Strong side or cross draw
Compatible Firearms: Compact and full-size pistols, small- and medium-frame revolvers
Features: Open muzzle; high ride; fits belts up to 1.8 in.
MSRP: $70

BIANCHI 3S PISTOL POCKET

5 BLACK WIDOW

Use/Type: Concealment/belt
Retention: Thumb snap
Material/Finish: Leather/plain tan or black
Carry: Strong side
Compatible Firearms: Compact and full-size pistols; small-, medium-, and large-frame revolvers
Features: Compact; open muzzle; high ride; fits belts up to 1.8 in.
MSRP: $50

5BH and BHL THUMBSNAP

Use/Type: Concealment/belt
Retention: Thumb break
Material/Finish: Leather/plain tan
Carry: Strong side
Compatible Firearms: Small- and medium-frame revolvers
Features: Closed muzzle; high ride; fits belts up from 1.8 in. to 2.3 in.
5BH: $55
5BHL (suede lined): **. $80**

6 and 6D WAISTBAND

Use/Type: Concealment/inside waistband
Retention: Thumb break (6D)
Material/Finish: Leather/rust suede
Carry: Strong side or cross draw
Compatible Firearms: Subcompact, compact, and full-size pistols; small-frame revolvers
Features: Open muzzle; high ride; fits belts up from 1.8 in. to 2.3 in.; spring-steel belt clip
6: $22
6D (thumb break): **. $27**

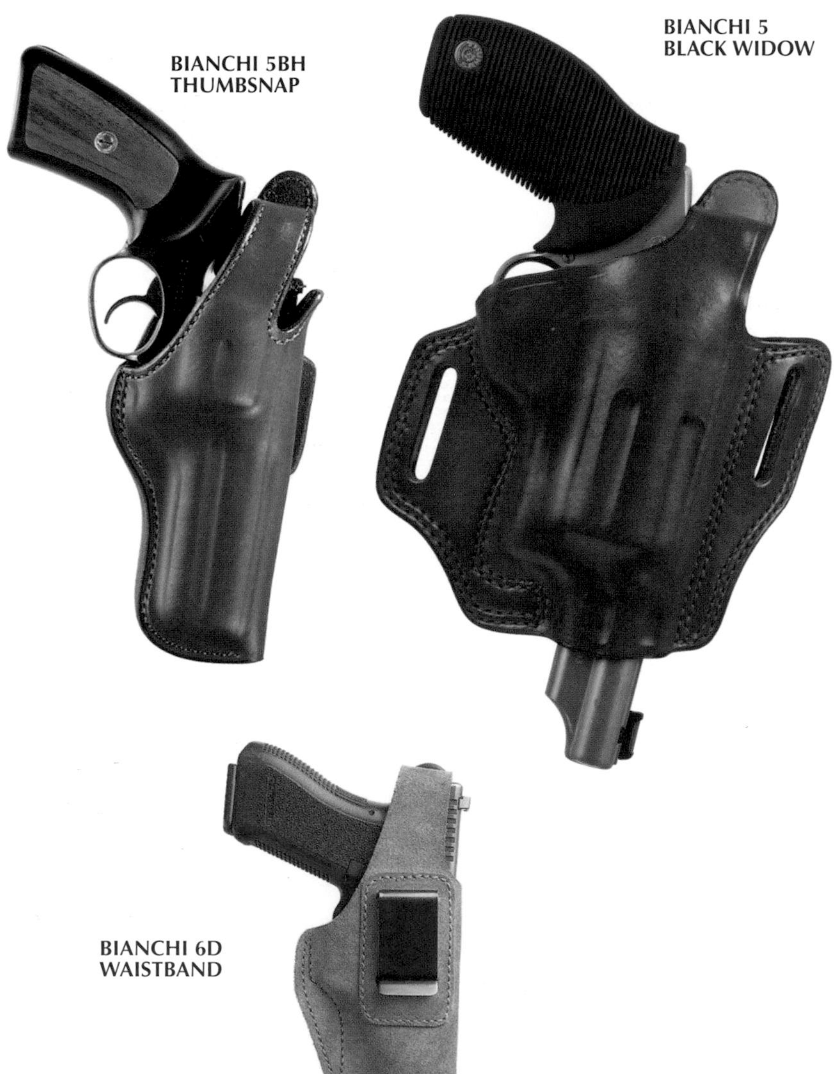

BIANCHI 5BH THUMBSNAP

BIANCHI 5 BLACK WIDOW

BIANCHI 6D WAISTBAND

Bianchi

(www.bianchi-intl.com)

BIANCHI
7 SHADOW

BIANCHI
19 THUMBSNAP

BIANCHI
55L LIGHTNIN'

7 SHADOW II

Use/Type: Concealment/belt, pancake-style
Material/Finish: Leather/plain tan or black
Carry: Strong side or cross draw
Compatible Firearms: Subcompact, compact- and full-size pistols; small- and medium-frame revolvers
Features: Open muzzle; high ride; fits belts up to 1.8 in.; three slots
MSRP: $55

19 and 19L THUMBSNAP

Use/Type: Concealment/belt
Retention: Thumb break
Material/Finish: Leather/plain tan
Carry: Strong side
Compatible Firearms: Full-size pistols
Features: Open muzzle; high ride; fits belts up to 1.8 in.
19: $55
19L (suede lined):**. $87**

55L LIGHT NIN'

Use/Type: Concealment/belt
Retention: Thumb break
Material/Finish: Leather/plain tan
Carry: Strong side
Compatible Firearms: Small-frame revolvers
Features: Designed for hammerless revolvers; closed muzzle; high ride; fits belts up from 1.8 in.
MSRP: $87

56 SERPENT

Use/Type: Concealment/belt
Retention: Thumb break
Material/Finish: Leather/plain tan or black
Carry: Strong side
Compatible Firearms: Compact and full-size pistols, small-frame revolvers
Features: Open muzzle; high ride; fits belts up to 1.5 in.
MSRP: $62

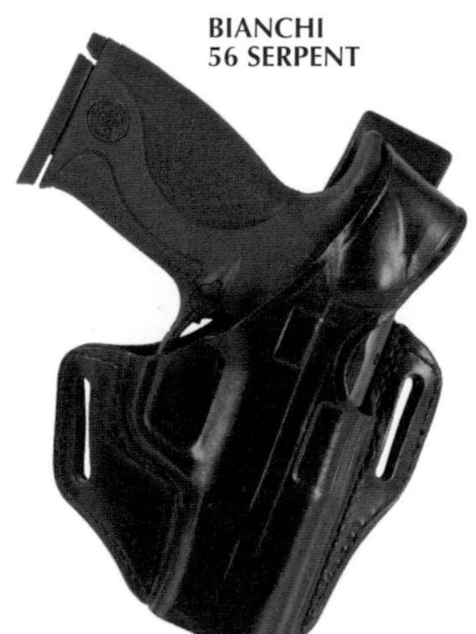

BIANCHI
56 SERPENT

57 REMEDY

Use/Type: Concealment/belt
Retention: None
Material/Finish: Leather/plain tan or black
Carry: Strong side
Compatible Firearms: Full-size pistols, small-frame revolvers
Features: Open muzzle; high ride; reinforced opening; fits belts up to 1.5 in.; two slots
MSRP: $56

BIANCHI
57 REMEDY

Bianchi

(www.bianchi-intl.com)

BIANCHI 58 P.I.

58 P.I.

Use/Type: Concealment/belt
Retention: None
Material/Finish: Leather/plain tan or black
Carry: Strong side
Compatible Firearms: Full-size pistols, small-frame revolvers
Features: Open muzzle; high ride; compact; fits belts up to1.5 in.; two slots
MSRP: $58

BIANCHI 77 PIRANHA

59 SPECIAL AGENT

Use/Type: Concealment/paddle design
Retention: Thumb break
Material/Finish: Leather/plain tan or black
Carry: Strong side or cross draw
Compatible Firearms: Subcompact, compact, and full-size pistols
Features: Open muzzle; adj. carry heights
MSRP: $85

75 VENOM

Use/Type: Concealment/belt slide
Retention: Thumb break
Material/Finish: Leather/plain tan or black
Carry: Strong side
Compatible Firearms: Subcompact, compact, and full-size pistols; small-frame revolvers
Features: Open muzzle; ultra high ride; fits belts up to 1.8 in.
MSRP: $62

77 PIRANHA

Use/Type: Concealment/belt, pancake-style
Retention: Thumb break
Material/Finish: Leather/plain tan or black
Carry: Strong side or cross draw
Compatible Firearms: Compact and full-size pistols, small-frame revolvers
Features: Fits belts up to 1.8 in.; three slots
MSRP: $62

82 CARRYLOK

Use/Type: Concealment/paddle design
Retention: Lever lock
Material/Finish: Leather/plain tan or black
Carry: Strong side
Compatible Firearms: Full-size pistols
Features: Open muzzle; fits belts up to 1.8 in.; two slots
MSRP: $76

BIANCHI 59 SPECIAL AGENT

BIANCHI 75 VENOM

BIANCHI 82 CARRYLOK

Bianchi

(www.bianchi-intl.com)

BIANCHI
83 PADDLELOK

83 PADDLELOK

Use/Type: Concealment/paddle design
Retention: Lever lock
Material/Finish: Leather/plain tan or black
Carry: Strong side
Compatible Firearms: Full-size pistols
Features: Open muzzle; high ride; fits belts up to 1.8 in.
MSRP: $88

BIANCHI
84 SNAPLOK

BIANCHI
100 PROFESSIONAL

84 SNAPLOK

Use/Type: Concealment/belt
Retention: Lever lock
Material/Finish: Leather/plain tan or black
Carry: Strong side
Compatible Firearms: Full-size pistols
Features: Open muzzle; fits belts up to 1.5 in.; adj. loops
MSRP: $96

100 PROFESSIONAL

Use/Type: Concealment/inside waistband
Retention: None
Material/Finish: Leather/plain tan
Carry: Strong side
Compatible Firearms: Subcompact, compact, and full-size pistols; small-frame revolvers
Features: Suede lined; fits belts up to 1.8 in.; spring-steel belt clip
MSRP: $57

101 FOLDAWAY

Use/Type: Concealment/belt slide
Retention: None
Material/Finish: Leather/plain tan or black
Carry: Strong side
Compatible Firearms: Compact and full-size pistols
Features: Minimalist design; fits belts up to 1.8 in.
MSRP: $13

BIANCHI
101 FOLDAWAY

Bianchi

(www.bianchi-intl.com)

BIANCHI
105 MINIMALIST

105 MINIMALIST

Use/Type: Concealment/belt slide
Retention: Hammer retainer tab
Material/Finish: Leather/plain tan or black
Carry: Strong side
Compatible Firearms: Subcompact, compact, and full-size pistols; small-frame revolvers
Features: Compact; open muzzle; suede lined; fits belts up to 1.8 in.
MSRP: $50

111 CYCLONE

Use/Type: Concealment/belt
Retention: Thumb break
Material/Finish: Leather/plain tan
Carry: Strong side
Compatible Firearms: Small- and medium-frame revolvers
Features: Open muzzle; suede lined; covered trigger guard; fits belts up to 1.8 in.
MSRP: $50

BIANCHI
111 CYCLONE

BIANCHI
120 COVERT OPTION

120 COVERT OPTION

Use/Type: Concealment/inside waistband
Retention: None
Material/Finish: Leather/russet
Carry: Strong side
Compatible Firearms: Subcompact, compact, and full-size pistols; small-frame revolvers
Features: Open muzzle; suede panel conforms to pistol; fit belts up to 1.8 in.
MSRP: $90

4584 EVADER

Use/Type: Concealment/belt
Retention: Lever lock
Material/Finish: Ballistic weave fabric/black
Carry: Strong side
Compatible Firearms: Compact and full-size pistols
Features: Open muzzle; low profile; fits belts up to 1.8 in.; adj. loops
MSRP: $32

BIANCHI
4584 EVADER

Bianchi

(www.bianchi-intl.com)

7000 ACCUMOLD SPORTING

Use/Type: Concealment/belt
Retention: Adj. strap with break
Material/Finish: Trilaminate/black
Carry: Strong side
Compatible Firearms: Compact and full-size pistols, small- and medium-frame revolvers
Features: Closed muzzle; high ride; polyknit lined; fits belts up to 1.8 in.
MSRP: $39

7001 ACCUMOLD THUMBSNAP

Use/Type: Concealment/belt
Retention: Thumb break
Material/Finish: Trilaminate/black
Carry: Strong side
Compatible Firearms: Compact and full-size pistols, small- and medium-frame revolvers
Features: Closed muzzle; high ride; polyknit lined; fits belts up to 1.8 in.
MSRP: $41

7500 ACCUMOLD PADDLE

Use/Type: Concealment/paddle design
Retention: Thumb break
Material/Finish: Trilaminate/black
Carry: Strong side
Compatible Firearms: Subcompact, compact, and full-size pistols; small- and medium-frame revolvers
Features: Closed muzzle; high ride; polyknit lined
MSRP: $59

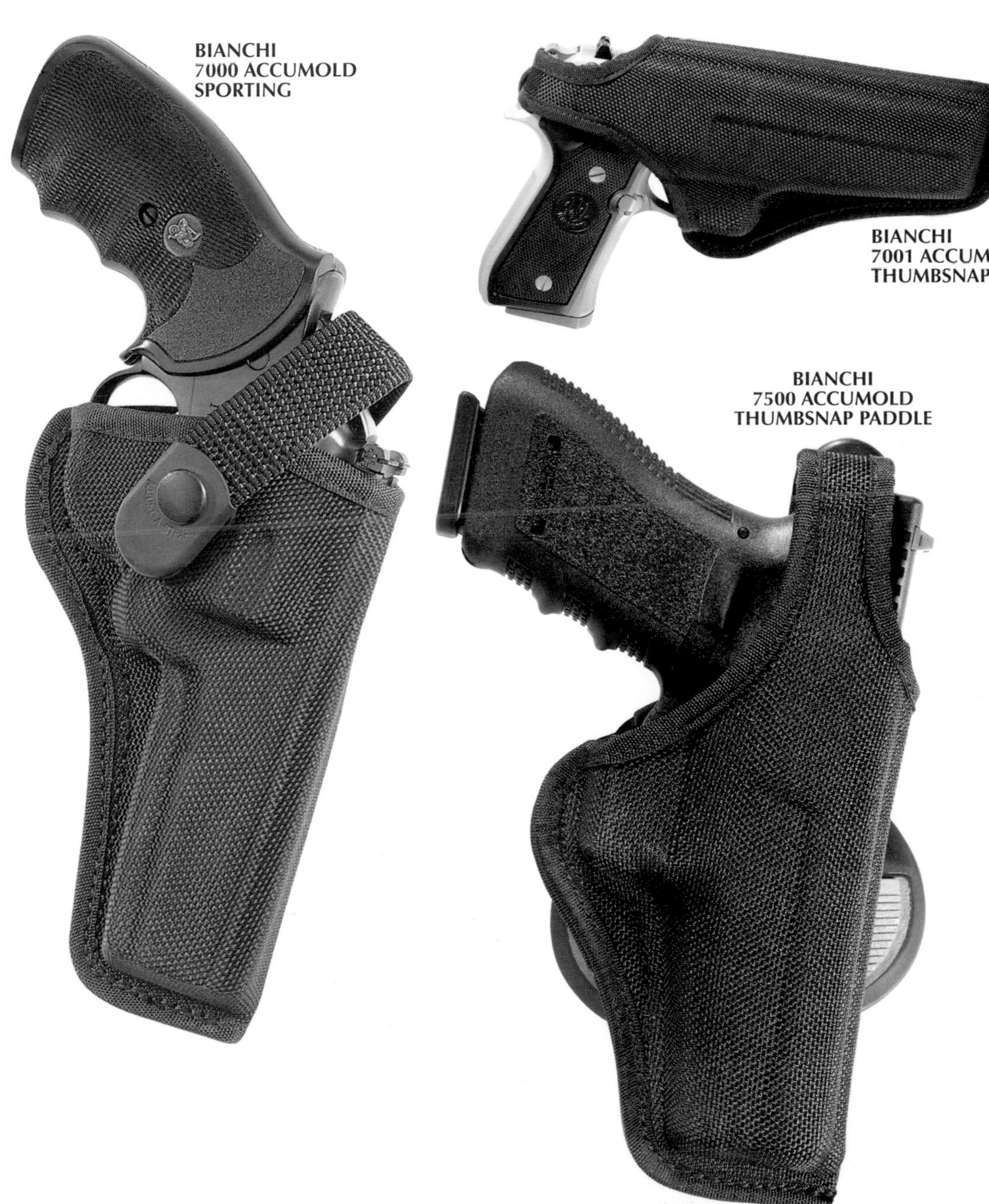

BIANCHI
7000 ACCUMOLD
SPORTING

BIANCHI
7001 ACCUMOLD
THUMBSNAP

BIANCHI
7500 ACCUMOLD
THUMBSNAP PADDLE

Bianchi

(www.bianchi-intl.com)

BIANCHI
7506 ACCUMOLD
BELT SLIDE

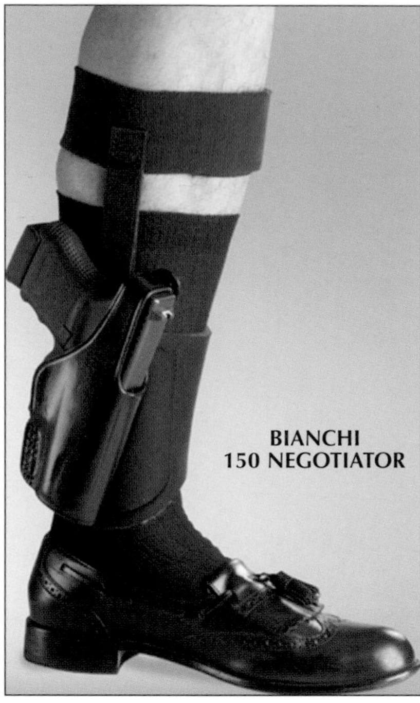

BIANCHI
150 NEGOTIATOR

BIANCHI X15 VERTICAL

7506 ACCUMOLD BELT SLIDE

Use/Type: Concealment/belt slide
Retention: Adj. strap with break
Material/Finish: Trilaminate/black
Carry: Strong side
Compatible Firearms: Subcompact, compact, and full-size pistols; small- and medium-frame revolvers
Features: Open muzzle; high ride; polyknit lined; fits belts up to 1.8 in.
MSRP: $41

4620 TUXEDO

Use/Type: Concealment/shoulder
Retention: Thumb break
Material/Finish: Trilaminate/black
Carry: Cross draw
Compatible Firearms: Compact and full-size pistols, small- and medium-frame revolvers
Features: Ambidextrous; x-harness; two tie-down straps; double magazine pouch or speedloader panel
MSRP: $123

X15 VERTICAL

Use/Type: Concealment/shoulder
Retention: Retainer strap, spring closure
Material/Finish: Leather/plain tan
Carry: Cross draw
Compatible Firearms: Compact and full-size pistols, small- and medium-frame revolvers
Features: Adj. harness; leather lined
MSRP: $159

X16 AGENT X

Use/Type: Concealment/shoulder
Retention: Thumb break
Material/Finish: Leather/plain tan
Carry: Cross draw
Compatible Firearms: Compact and full-size pistols, small- and medium-frame revolvers
Features: X-harness; two tie-down straps
MSRP: $156

150 and 150L NEGOTIATOR

Use/Type: Concealment/ankle
Retention: Thumb break
Material/Finish: Leather/plain black
Carry: Cross draw
Compatible Firearms: Compact pistols, small-frame revolvers
Features: Adj. elastic thigh strap; sheepskin lined
150: $83
150L (extended thigh strap): **. $83**

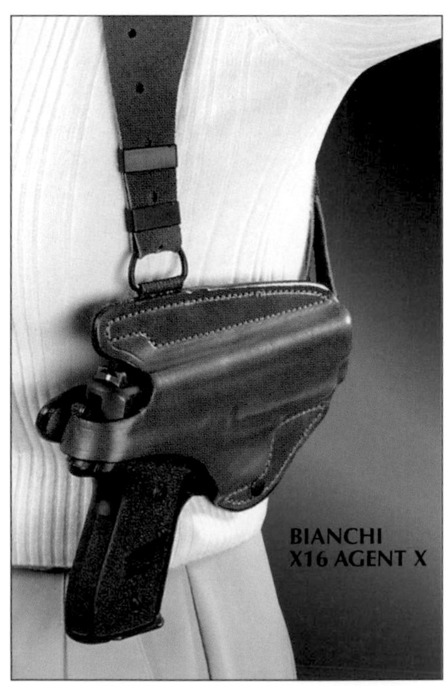

BIANCHI
X16 AGENT X

HOLSTERS

Bianchi

(www.bianchi-intl.com)

BIANCHI
4750 RANGER
TRIAD

BIANCHI
152 POCKET PIECE

4750 TRIAD

Use/Type: Concealment/ankle
Retention: Elastic strap with snap
Material/Finish: Nylon/black
Carry: Cross draw
Compatible Firearms: Compact pistols, small-frame revolvers
Features: Adj. elastic thigh strap; contoured fit
MSRP: $60

152 POCKET PIECE

Use/Type: Concealment/pocket
Retention: None
Material/Finish: Leather/rough side out tan
Carry: Strong side
Compatible Firearms: Compact pistols, small-frame revolvers
Features: Stabilizing two-pocket hooks
MSRP: $30

M12 UNIVERSAL MILITARY

Use/Type: Tactical/belt or shoulder
Retention: Elastic strap with snap
Material/Finish: Nylon/black
Carry: Ambidextrous
Compatible Firearms: Full-size pistols
Features: U.S. mil-spec for Beretta M9; removable flap
MSRP: $86

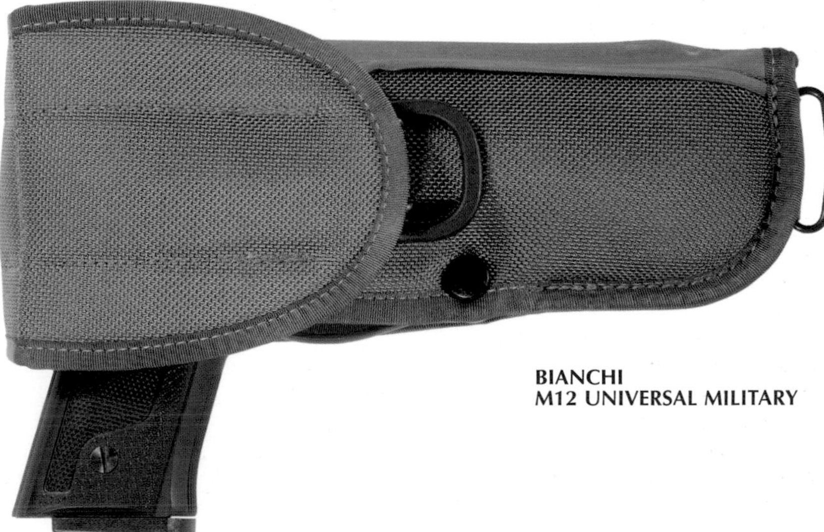

BIANCHI
M12 UNIVERSAL MILITARY

Bianchi

(www.bianchi-intl.com)

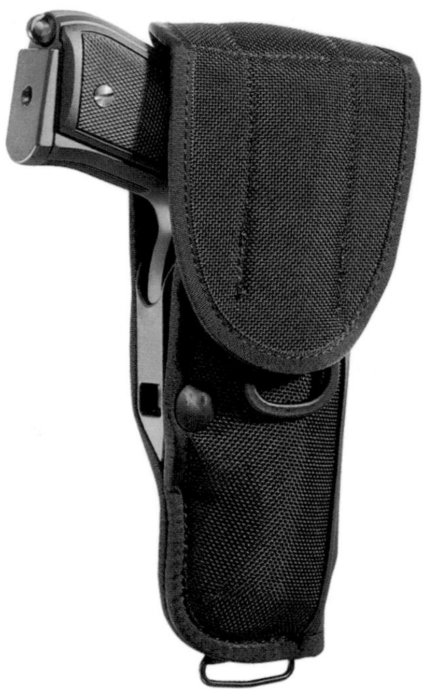

BIANCHI UM84I UNIVERSAL MILITARY

UM84I UNIVERSAL MILITARY

Use/Type: Tactical/belt or shoulder
Retention: Elastic strap with snap
Material/Finish: Nylon/OD green, black, woodland camo, desert camo, or digital camo
Carry: Ambidextrous
Compatible Firearms: Full-size pistols, medium- and large-frame revolvers
Features: Removable flap
MSRP: **$85**

T6505 TAC and T6500 TAC LT

Use/Type: Tactical/modular belt or thigh
Retention: Thumb break and retainer strap
Material/Finish: Trilaminate/black
Carry: Strong side
Compatible Firearms: Full-size pistols
Features: Compatible with any MOLLE system
Tac: **$90**
Tac LT (accommodates most pistols with mounted tactical lights): **$90**

BIANCHI T6505 TAC

HOLSTERS

Blackhawk

(www.blackhawk.com)

SERPA CQC

Use/Type: Concealment/hip, thigh, chest or shoulder
Retention: Retention screw and auto-lock release
Material/Finish: Carbon fiber/matte black, coyote tan, foliage green, carbon fiber, or matte gray
Carry: Strong side or cross draw
Compatible Firearms: Compact and full-size pistols, small- and large-frame revolvers
Features: Open muzzle; multiple platforms

Matte black, coyote tan, foliage green: **$50**
Carbon fiber: **$60**
Sporter (matte gray): **$34**
Light Bearing (accommodates most pistols with mounted tactical lights): **$50**

BLACKHAWK SERPA CQC CONCEALMENT

Blackhawk

(www.blackhawk.com)

SERPA LEVEL 2 TACTICAL

Use/Type: Tactical/thigh
Retention: Retention screw and auto-lock release
Material/Finish: Carbon fiber/matte black, coyote tan, foliage green, or olive drab
Carry: Strong side or cross draw
Compatible Firearms: Compact and full-size pistols
Features: Open muzzle; rubberized thigh straps; full-length holster body to protect rear sight
MSRP: **$133**

SERPA LEVEL 3 TACTICAL

Use/Type: Tactical/thigh
Retention: Retention screw, pivot guard and auto-lock release
Material/Finish: Carbon fiber/matte black

Carry: Strong side or cross draw
Compatible Firearms: Compact and full-size pistols
Features: Open muzzle; rubberized thigh straps; full-length holster body to protect rear sight
MSRP: **$156**
Light Bearing (accommodates most pistols with mounted tactical lights): **$156**

CQC CONCEALMENT

Use/Type: Concealment/belt and paddle platforms
Retention: Retention screw
Material/Finish: Carbon fiber/matte black, coyote tan, foliage green, carbon fiber, or matte gray
Carry: Strong side or cross draw
Compatible Firearms: Compact and full-size pistols
Features: Open muzzle

Matte black: **$33**
Carbon fiber: **$43**

3-SLOT PANCAKE

Use/Type: Concealment/belt, pancake-style
Retention: Thumb break
Material/Finish: Leather/plain brown or black
Carry: Strong side or cross draw
Compatible Firearms: Subcompact, compact, and full-size pistols
Features: Open muzzle; covered trigger guard
Leather: **$63**
Nylon (ambidextrous): **$28**

BLACKHAWK SERPA LEVEL 2 TACTICAL

BLACKHAWK 3-SLOT PANCAKE

CQC CONCEALMENT

BLACKHAWK SHERPA LEVEL 3 TACTICAL

Blackhawk

(www.blackhawk.com)

BLACKHAWK SPEEDCLASSIC

BLACKHAWK DETACHABLE SLIDE

BLACKHAWK INSIDE-THE-PANTS WITH CLIP

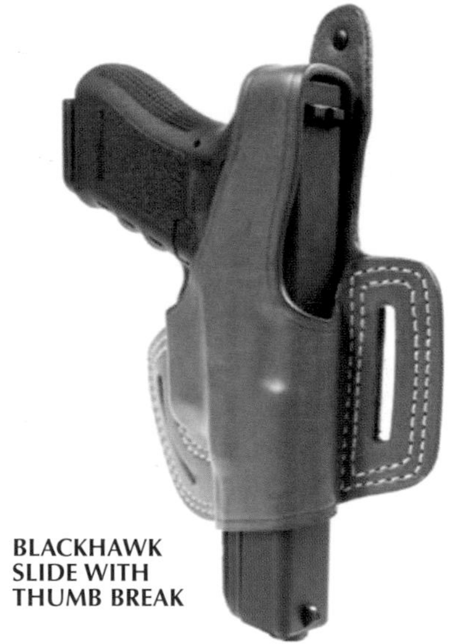

BLACKHAWK SLIDE WITH THUMB BREAK

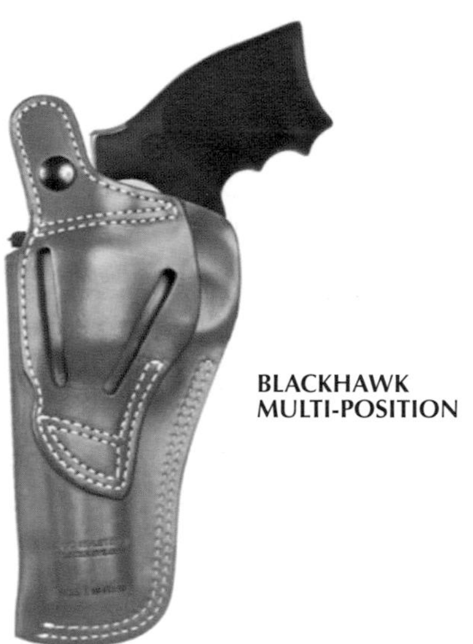

BLACKHAWK MULTI-POSITION

DETACHABLE SLIDE

Use/Type: Concealment/belt
Retention: Thumb break
Material/Finish: Leather/plain black
Carry: Strong side
Compatible Firearms: Subcompact, compact, and full-size pistols
Features: Open muzzle; covered trigger guard
MSRP: **$76**

INSIDE-THE-PANTS WITH CLIP

Use/Type: Concealment/inside waistband
Retention: None
Material/Finish: Leather/brown
Carry: Strong side
Compatible Firearms: Subcompact, compact, and full-size pistols; small-frame revolvers
Features: Open muzzle; covered trigger guard
Leather: **$59**
Nylon (black, retention strap): . . . **$19**
Nylon (black): **$13**

SLIDE WITH THUMB BREAK

Use/Type: Concealment/belt
Retention: Thumb break
Material/Finish: Leather/brown
Carry: Strong side
Compatible Firearms: Compact and full-size pistols
Features: Open muzzle; covered trigger guard
Leather: **$55**
Nylon (black): **$22**

MULTI-POSITION

Use/Type: Concealment/belt
Retention: Thumb break
Material/Finish: Leather/brown
Carry: Strong side or cross draw
Compatible Firearms: Full-size pistols; small-, medium-, and large-frame revolvers
Features: Open muzzle; covered trigger guard
MSRP: **$83**

TUCKABLE

Use/Type: Concealment/inside waistband
Retention: None
Material/Finish: Leather/rough side out
Carry: Strong side
Compatible Firearms: Subcompact and compact pistols, small-frame revolvers
Features: Allows user to tuck shirt
MSRP: **$37**

YAQUI SLIDE

Use/Type: Concealment/belt
Retention: Tension screw
Material/Finish: Leather/brown
Carry: Strong side
Compatible Firearms: Compact and full-size pistols
Features: Open muzzle; covered trigger guard
MSRP: **$53**

Blackhawk

(www.blackhawk.com)

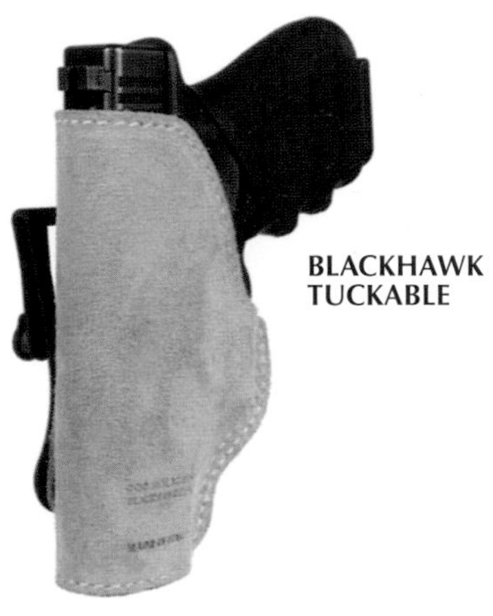

BLACKHAWK TUCKABLE

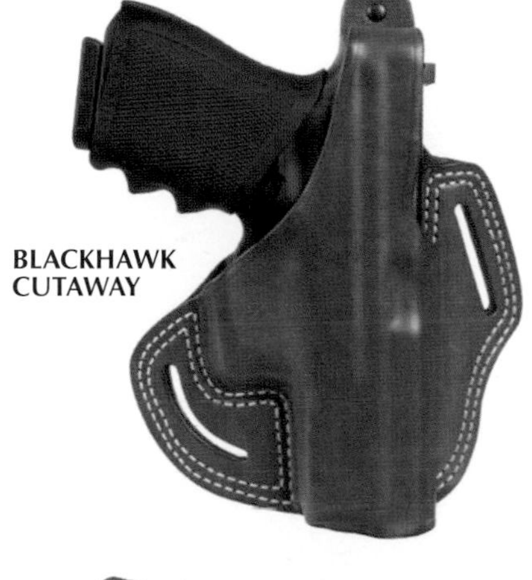

BLACKHAWK CUTAWAY

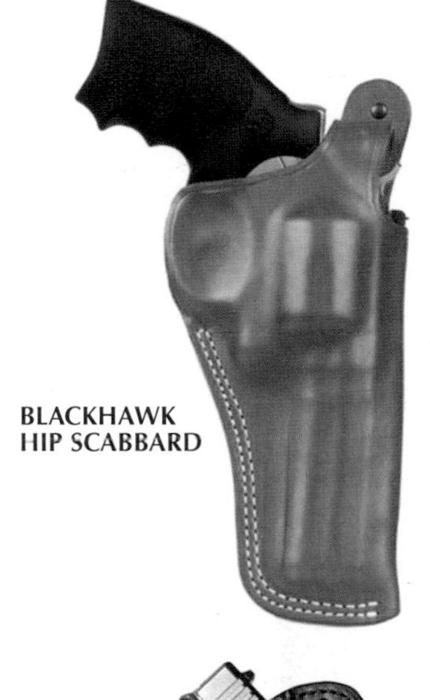

BLACKHAWK HIP SCABBARD

BLACKHAWK YAQUI SLIDE

BLACKHAWK COMPACT SLIDE WITH MAG POUCH

BLACKHAWK CHECK-SIX

HIP SCABBARD

Use/Type: Concealment/belt
Retention: Thumb break
Material/Finish: Leather/brown
Carry: Strong side or cross draw
Compatible Firearms: Medium- and large-frame revolvers
Features: Closed muzzle; covered trigger guard
Leather: **$63**
Nylon (black, thumb break): **$26**
Nylon (black, retaining strap, fits most medium-large pistols and small-large revolvers): **$18**

CUTAWAY

Use/Type: Concealment/belt
Retention: None
Material/Finish: Leather/brown
Carry: Strong side or cross draw
Compatible Firearms: Compact and full-size pistols
Features: Open muzzle; covered trigger guard
MSRP: **$67**

COMPACT SLIDE WITH MAG POUCH

Use/Type: Concealment/belt
Retention: Tension screw
Material/Finish: Leather/plain black
Carry: Strong side or cross draw
Compatible Firearms: Subcompact, compact, and full-size pistols
Features: Open muzzle; covered trigger guard; built-in magazine pouch
MSRP: **$67**

CHECK-SIX

Use/Type: Concealment/belt
Retention: Tension screw
Material/Finish: Leather/plain black
Carry: Strong side
Compatible Firearms: Subcompact, compact, and full-size pistols, small-frame revolvers
Features: Open muzzle; covered trigger guard; built-in magazine pouch
MSRP: **$67**

TUCKABLE

Use/Type: Concealment/inside waistband
Retention: Tension screw
Material/Finish: Leather/plain black
Carry: Strong side or cross draw
Compatible Firearms: Subcompact, compact, and full-size pistols; small-frame revolvers
Features: Molded sight track; adj. loops
MSRP: **$64**

COMPACT ASKINS

Use/Type: Concealment/belt
Retention: Tension screw
Material/Finish: Leather/plain black
Carry: Strong side
Compatible Firearms: Subcompact, compact, and full-size pistols, small- and medium-frame revolvers
Features: Molded sight track
MSRP: **$64**

Blackhawk

(www.blackhawk.com)

BLACKHAWK COMPACT ASKINS

BLACKHAWK ANGLE-ADJUSTABLE PADDLE

BLACKHAWK VERTICAL SHOULDER

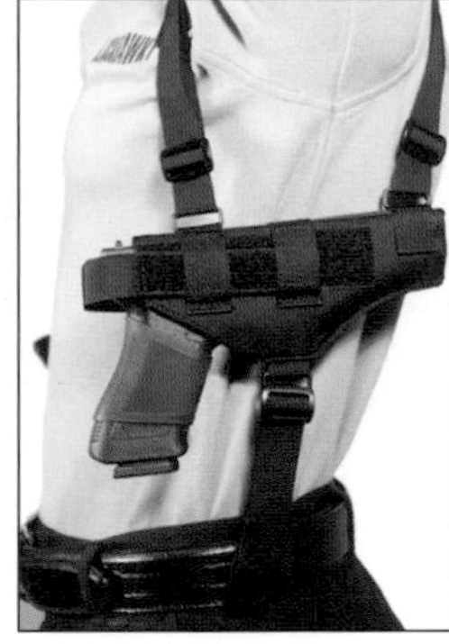

BLACKHAWK HORIZONTAL SHOULDER

BLACKHAWK UNIVERSAL SPEC OPS PISTOL HARNESS

BLACKHAWK NYLON LASER

BLACKHAWK AMBIDEXTROUS FLAT BELT

ANGLE-ADJUSTABLE PADDLE

Use/Type: Concealment/paddle
Retention: Thumb break
Material/Finish: Leather/black
Carry: Strong side
Compatible Firearms: Compact and full-size pistols, small-frame revolvers
Features: Open muzzle
Leather: $86
Nylon (retention strap): **$42**

VERTICAL SHOULDER

Use/Type: Concealment/shoulder
Retention: Adj. retainer strap
Material/Finish: Nylon/black
Carry: Cross draw
Compatible Firearms: Compact and full-size pistols, small- and medium-frame revolvers
Features: Adj. harness; off-set tie down
MSRP: $47

HORIZONTAL SHOULDER

Use/Type: Concealment/shoulder
Retention: Adj. retainer strap
Material/Finish: Nylon/black
Carry: Cross draw
Compatible Firearms: Compact and full-size pistols, small- and medium-frame revolvers
Features: Adj. harness; off-set tie down
Horizontal Shoulder: $57
Shoulder Holster-Concealed (adj. thumb break, insert stiffeners, ambidextrous, double magazine pouch): **$70**

UNIVERSAL SPEC OPS PISTOL HARNESS

Use/Type: Concealment/shoulder
Retention: Adj. thumb break
Material/Finish: Nylon/black
Carry: Cross draw
Compatible Firearms: Compact and full-size pistols
Features: Vertical, horizontal, or angled positions; adj. harness; built-in magazine pouch
MSRP: $70

NYLON LASER

Use/Type: Concealment/belt
Retention: Adj. thumb break
Material/Finish: Nylon/black
Carry: Strong side
Compatible Firearms: Compact and full-size pistols
Features: Accommodates pistols with under-barrel lasers
MSRP: $25

AMBIDEXTROUS FLAT BELT

Use/Type: Concealment/belt
Retention: Adj. thumb break
Material/Finish: Nylon/black
Carry: Ambidextrous
Compatible Firearms: Compact and full-size pistols; small-, medium-, and large-frame revolvers
MSRP: $21

BladeTech

(www.blade-tech.com)

BLADETECH HYBRID

BLADETECH UCH

BLADETECH SRB

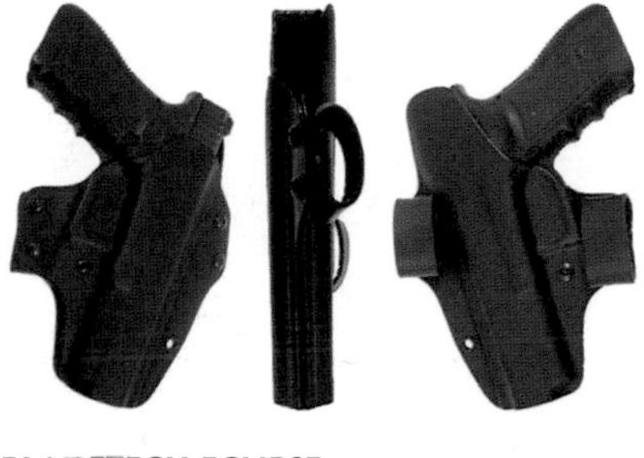
BLADETECH ECLIPSE

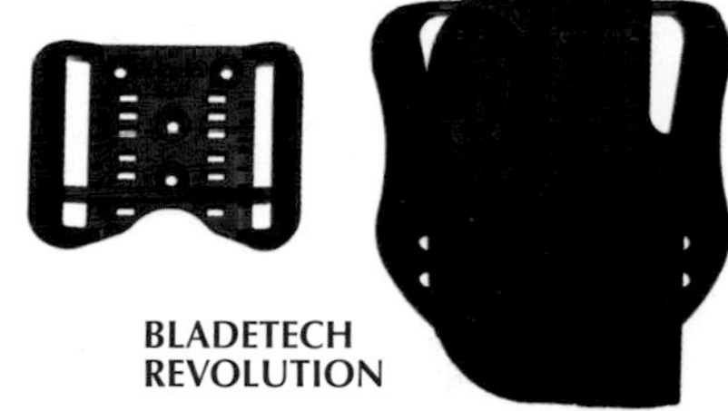
BLADETECH REVOLUTION

HYBRID

Use/Type: Concealment/hybrid belt
Retention: Tension screw
Material/Finish: Leather exterior, Kydex inner sleeve/brown or black
Carry: Strong side
Compatible Firearms: Compact and full-size pistols
Features: Open muzzle; covered trigger guard; converts from pancake-style to IWB
MSRP: **$90**

ULTIMATE CONCEALMENT HOLSTER (UCH)

Use/Type: Concealment/belt
Retention: Tension screw
Material/Finish: Kydex/black
Carry: Strong side
Compatible Firearms: Subcompact, compact, and full-size pistols; small- and medium-frame revolvers
Features: Open muzzle; covered trigger guard; adj. cant
MSRP: **$70**

IN THE WAISTBAND (IWB)

Use/Type: Concealment/belt
Retention: Tension screw
Material/Finish: Kydex/black
Carry: Strong side
Compatible Firearms: Subcompact, compact, and full-size pistols; small- and medium-frame revolvers
Features: Open muzzle; covered trigger guard; adj. cant; fits belts from 1.3 in. to 1.8 in.
IWB Universal Fits All Holster: . . **$65**
IWB Universal Fits All Holster (fits most large pistols): **$50**
IWB Razor (designed for specific size belt loops, fits most large pistols): **$70**
IWB Nano (constructed with thinner Kydex for light weight, fits most large pistols): **$60**
IWB Phantom (infection molded polymer, fits most large pistols): **$30**
IWB Weapon and Tactical Light (accommodates most pistols with mounted tactical lights, fits most large pistols and most tactical lights): **$80**

ECLIPSE

Use/Type: Concealment/belt or paddle
Retention: Tension screw
Material/Finish: Kydex/black
Carry: Strong side
Compatible Firearms: Compact and full-size pistols, small-frame revolvers
Features: Open muzzle; covered trigger guard
MSRP: **$30**

REVOLUTION

Use/Type: Concealment/belt, pancake-style
Retention: Tension screw
Material/Finish: Kydex/black
Carry: Strong side
Compatible Firearms: Compact and full-size pistols, small-frame revolvers
Features: Open muzzle; covered trigger guard
MSRP: **$70**

PADDLE

Use/Type: Concealment/paddle
Retention: Tension screw
Material/Finish: Kydex/black
Carry: Strong side
Compatible Firearms: Subcompact, compact, and full-size pistols; small-, medium-, and large-frame revolvers
Features: Open muzzle; covered trigger guard; adj. cant
MSRP: **$65**

STING RAY BELT (SRB)

Use/Type: Concealment/belt
Retention: Tension screw
Material/Finish: Kydex/black
Carry: Strong side
Compatible Firearms: Subcompact, compact, and full-size pistols; small-, medium-, and large-frame revolvers
Features: Open muzzle; covered trigger guard; interchangeable with paddle; Tek-Lok system; drop and offset loops; fits belts from 1.3 in. to 2.3 in.
MSRP: **$65**

WRS TACTICAL THIGH RIG

Use/Type: Concealment/thigh
Retention: Thumb break
Material/Finish: Kydex/black
Carry: Strong side
Compatible Firearms: Compact and full-size pistols, small-frame revolvers
Features: Open muzzle; covered trigger guard
WRS: **$135**
WRS Weapon and Tactical Light (accommodates most pistols with mounted tactical lights): **$140**

BladeTech

(www.blade-tech.com)

LEVEL II TACTICAL THIGH RIG

Use/Type: Concealment/thigh
Retention: Thumb break
Material/Finish: Polymer/black
Carry: Strong side
Compatible Firearms: Compact and full-size pistols, small-frame revolvers
Features: Open muzzle; covered trigger guard

Level II Tactical Thigh Rig: **$120**
Level II Tactical Thigh Rig Weapon and Tactical Light (accommodates most pistols with mounted tactical lights): . . . **$125**

Comp Tac

(www.comp-tac.com)

MINOTAUR MTAC

Use/Type: Concealment/inside waistband
Retention: Tension screw
Material/Finish: Kydex and leather/black
Carry: Strong side
Compatible Firearms: Subcompact, compact, and full-size pistols
Features: Open muzzle; adj. cant; allows shirt to be tucked; padded body panel; j-hooks

MTAC: **$80**
Spartan (unpadded body panel): **$64**

MINOTAUR GLADIATOR

Use/Type: Concealment/belt
Retention: Tension screw
Material/Finish: Kydex and leather/black
Carry: Strong side
Compatible Firearms: Subcompact, compact, and full-size pistols
Features: Open muzzle; adj. cant; two-snap belt loops

MSRP: **$80**

BELT and PADDLE

Use/Type: Concealment/belt or paddle
Retention: Tension screw
Material/Finish: Kydex/black
Carry: Strong side
Compatible Firearms: Subcompact, compact, and full-size pistols
Features: Open muzzle

Belt: **$68**
Paddle (vertical or forward cant, two stability tabs on paddle): **$58**

COMP TAC BELT HOLSTER

COMP TAC MINOTAUR MTAC

SETTABLE CANT

Use/Type: Concealment/belt or paddle
Retention: Tension screw
Material/Finish: Kydex/black
Carry: Strong side
Compatible Firearms: Subcompact, compact, and full-size pistols
Features: Open muzzle; modular system for belt or paddle

MSRP: **$70**

THE INFIDEL

Use/Type: Concealment/inside waistband
Retention: Tension screw
Material/Finish: Kydex/black
Carry: Strong side
Compatible Firearms: Subcompact, compact, and full-size pistols
Features: Open muzzle; covered trigger guard; modular system for snap belt loops, j-hooks or clips

MSRP: **$55**

COMP TAC MINOTAUR GLADIATOR

HOLSTERS

Comp Tac
(www.comp-tac.com)

COMP TAC SETTABLE CANT

COMP TAC INFIDEL

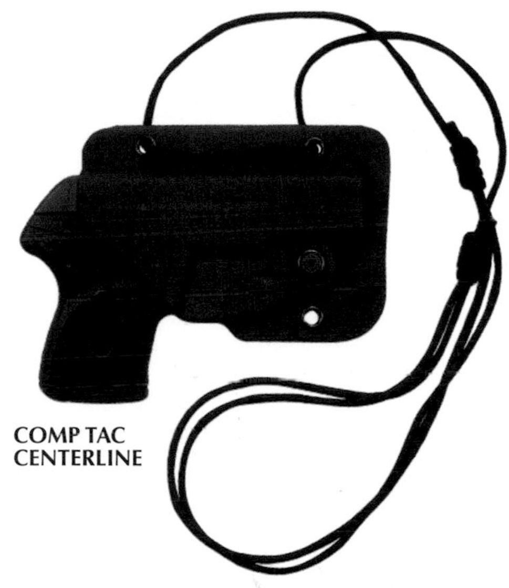

COMP TAC CENTERLINE

TWO–O'CLOCK
Use/Type: Concealment/inside waistband
Retention: Tension screw
Material/Finish: Kydex/black
Carry: Strong side
Compatible Firearms: Subcompact, compact, and full-size pistols; small-frame revolvers
Features: Open muzzle; covered trigger guard; clip
MSRP: $60

CENTERLINE
Use/Type: Concealment/lanyard
Retention: Tension screw
Material/Finish: Kydex/black
Carry: Around neck
Compatible Firearms: Subcompact pistols
Features: Closed bottom; covered trigger guard; designed to be worn around the neck
MSRP: $43

COMP TAC TWO-O'CLOCK

COMP TAC MINOTAUR MTAC SPARTAN

Cross Breed Holsters

(www.crossbreedholsters.com)

SUPER TUCK DELUXE

Use/Type: Concealment/inside waistband
Retention: Tension screw
Material/Finish: Kydex and leather/ black
Carry: Strong side
Compatible Firearms: Subcompact, compact, and full-size pistols; small-frame revolvers
Features: Open muzzle; adj. ride depth/cant; allows shirt to be tucked; leather body panel; metal v- or j-clips
MSRP: $70

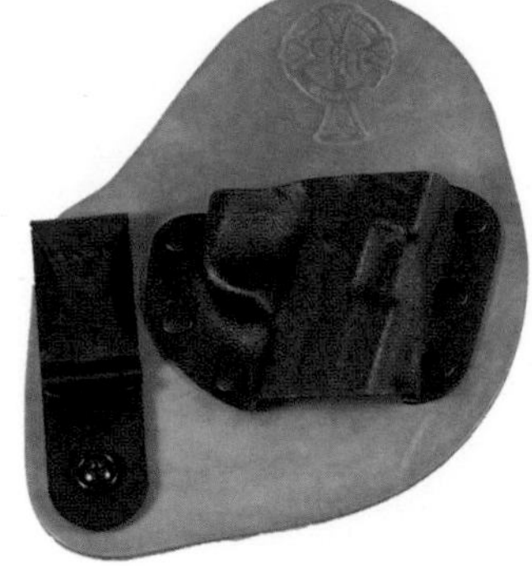

CROSS BREED MICROCLIP

MINITUCK

Use/Type: Concealment/inside waistband
Retention: Tension screw
Material/Finish: Kydex and leather/ black
Carry: Strong side
Compatible Firearms: Subcompact pistols
Features: Open muzzle; adj. ride depth/cant; allows shirt to be tucked; leather body panel; metal v- or j-clips
MSRP: $68

CROSS BREED MINITUCK

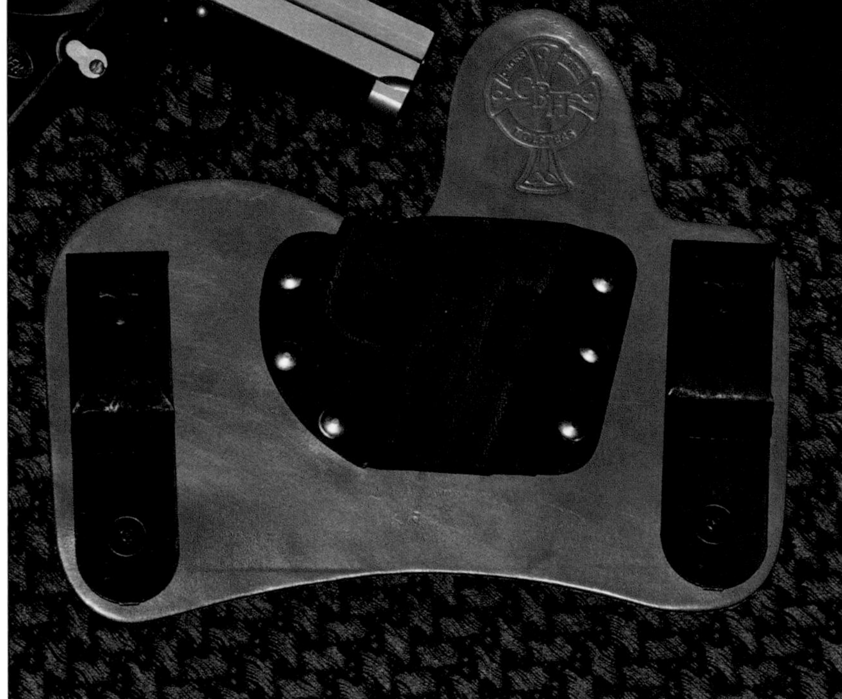

QWIKCLIP

Use/Type: Concealment/inside waistband
Retention: Tension screw
Material/Finish: Kydex and leather/ black
Carry: Strong side or cross draw
Compatible Firearms: Subcompact, compact, and full-size pistols; small-frame revolvers
Features: Open muzzle; adj. cant; allows shirt to be tucked; leather body panel; metal clip
MSRP: $67

MICROCLIP

Use/Type: Concealment/inside waistband
Retention: Tension screw
Material/Finish: Kydex and leather/ black
Carry: Strong side or cross draw
Compatible Firearms: Subcompact pistols
Features: Open muzzle; adj. cant; allows shirt to be tucked; leather body panel; metal clip
MSRP: $58

SNAPSLIDE

Use/Type: Concealment/ belt
Retention: Tension screw
Material/Finish: Kydex and leather/ black
Carry: Strong side
Compatible Firearms: Compact and full-size pistols
Features: Open muzzle; fits belts up to 1.5 in.
MSRP: $49

CROSS BREED MINISLIDE

Cross Breed Holsters

(www.crossbreedholsters.com)

MINISLIDE
Use/Type: Concealment/ belt
Retention: Tension screw
Material/Finish: Kydex and leather/ black
Carry: Strong side
Compatible Firearms: Subcompact pistols
Features: Open muzzle; fits belts up to 1.5 in.
MSRP: **$48**

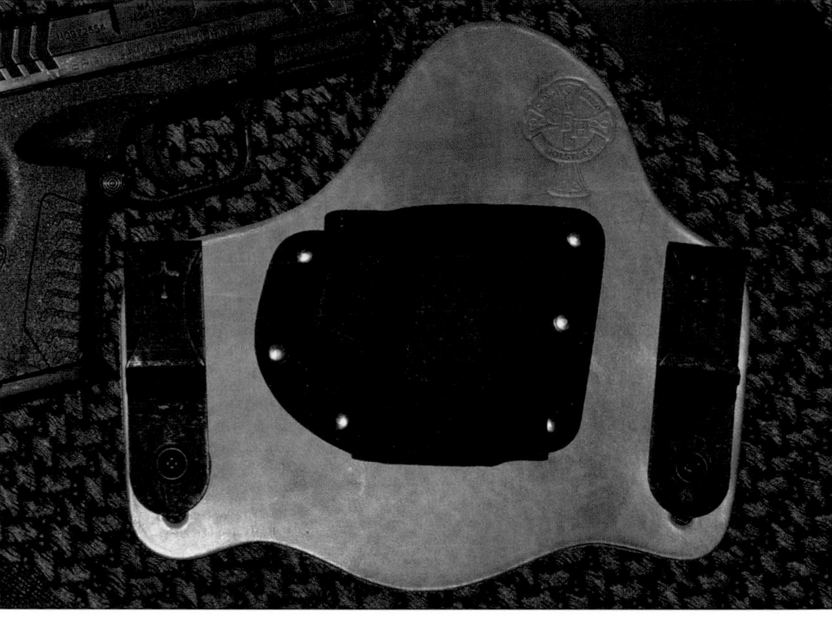

CROSS BREED SUPERTUCK

Don Hume

(www.donhume.com)

DON HUME 001 FRONT POCKET

001 FRONT POCKET
Use/Type: Concealment/pocket
Retention: None
Material/Finish: Leather/plain saddle brown
Carry: Ambidextrous
Compatible Firearms: Subcompact and, compact pistols, small-frame revolvers
Features: Open muzzle; covered trigger guard
MSRP: **$36**

002 HIP POCKET
Use/Type: Concealment/pocket
Retention: None
Material/Finish: Leather/plain saddle brown
Carry: Strong side
Compatible Firearms: Subcompact and compact pistols, small-frame revolvers
Features: Open muzzle; covered trigger guard; suede outside
MSRP: **$35**

DON HUME 002 HIP POCKET

Don Hume

(www.donhume.com)

AGENT

Use/Type: Concealment/belt, pancake-style
Retention: Thumb break
Material/Finish: Leather/plain saddle brown or black
Carry: Strong side or cross draw
Compatible Firearms: Compact and full-size pistols
Features: Open muzzle; high ride; fits belts up to 1.8 in.; three slots
Three Slot: $76
711 T.B. (two slot, strong side):. . . $72
Agent TAC (accommodates most pistols with mounted tactical lights): **$68**
Agent-SH TAC (accommodates most pistols with mounted tactical lights): **$140**

ANKLE SAFE

Use/Type: Concealment/ankle
Retention: Thumb break
Material/Finish: Leather/plain black
Carry: Cross draw
Compatible Firearms: Subcompact pistols, small-, medium-, and large-frame revolvers
Features: Adj. neoprene wrap; sheepskin padding
MSRP: $78

D.A.H.

Use/Type: Concealment/belt
Retention: None
Material/Finish: Leather/plain saddle brown or black
Carry: Small of the back or strong side
Compatible Firearms: Compact and full-size pistols
Features: Open muzzle; high ride; fits belts up to 1.8 in.; three slots
MSRP: $60

H710

Use/Type: Concealment/belt, inside waistband
Retention: None
Material/Finish: Leather/plain saddle brown or black
Carry: Strong side
Compatible Firearms: Compact and full-size pistols, small- and medium-frame revolvers
Features: Open muzzle; high ride; fits belts up to 1.8 in.
MSRP: $29

DON HUME
AGENT

DON HUME
H710

DON HUME
ANKLE SAFE

DON HUME
D.A.H.

H715

Use/Type: Concealment/belt
Retention: Thumb break
Material/Finish: Leather/plain saddle brown or black
Carry: Strong side
Compatible Firearms: Subcompact, compact, and full-size pistols; small- and medium-frame revolvers
Features: Open muzzle; fits belts up to 1.8 in.
M.O.S. (snap on belt loops): **$36**
Soft Pocket (natural, spring clip): **$19**
H715-M T.B. (spring clip): **$40**
H715-M W.C. (spring clip, reinforced opening, no retention): **$30**

Don Hume

(www.donhume.com)

H717

Use/Type: Concealment/belt
Retention: Thumb break
Material/Finish: Leather/plain black
Carry: Strong side
Compatible Firearms: Subcompact, compact, and full-size pistols; small- and medium-frame revolvers
Features: Open muzzle; fits belts up to 1.8 in.
MSRP: $50

H720

Use/Type: Concealment/paddle
Retention: Thumb break
Material/Finish: Leather/plain black
Carry: Strong side
Compatible Firearms: Subcompact, compact, and full-size pistols; small- and medium-frame revolvers
Features: Open muzzle; Kydex paddle
H720: $75
H720 O.T. (paddle and belt; reinforced opening, no retention):. **$61**

H721 DOUBLE NINE

Use/Type: Concealment/belt
Retention: Thumb break
Material/Finish: Leather/plain saddle brown or black
Carry: Strong side
Compatible Firearms: Subcompact, compact, and full-size pistols; small- and medium-frame revolvers
Features: Open muzzle; high ride; covered trigger guard; fits belts up to 1.8 in.
H721: $57
H721 O.T. (reinforced opening, no retention):. **$50**

DON HUME H717

DON HUME H715

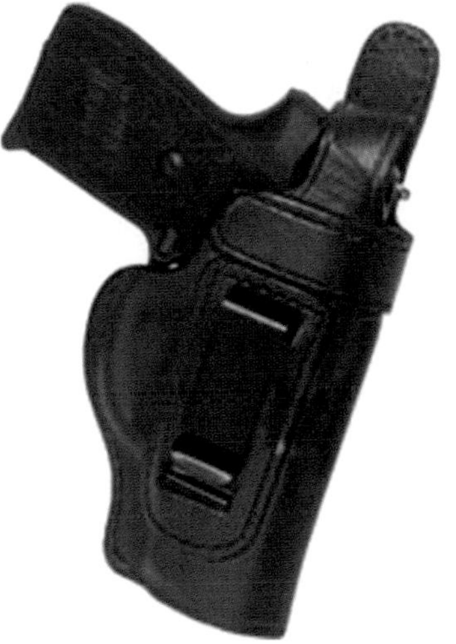

DON HUME H721 DOUBLE NINE

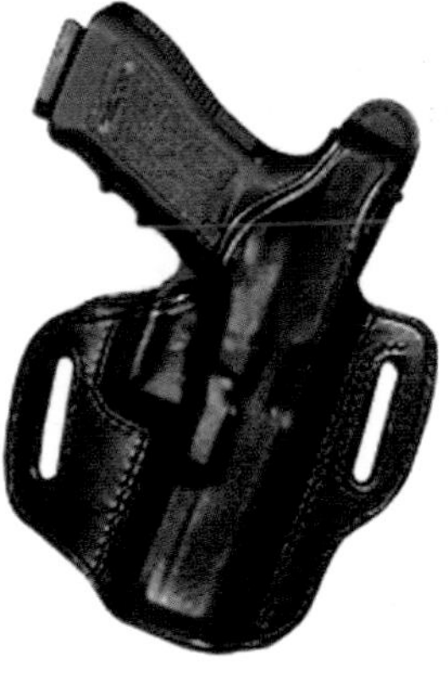

DON HUME H720

DeSantis

(www.desantisholster.com)

MINI SLIDE

Use/Type: Concealment/belt
Retention: Screw tension
Material/Finish: Leather/plain brown or black
Carry: Strong side
Compatible Firearms: Compact and full-size pistols, small- and medium-frame revolvers
Features: Open muzzle; covered trigger guard; fits belts up to 1.8 in.
Style 085 (thumb break): **$65**
Style 086: **$65**

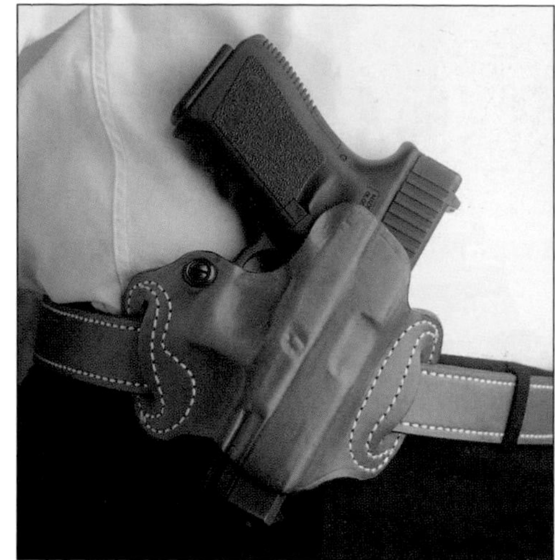

DESANTIS MINI SLIDE

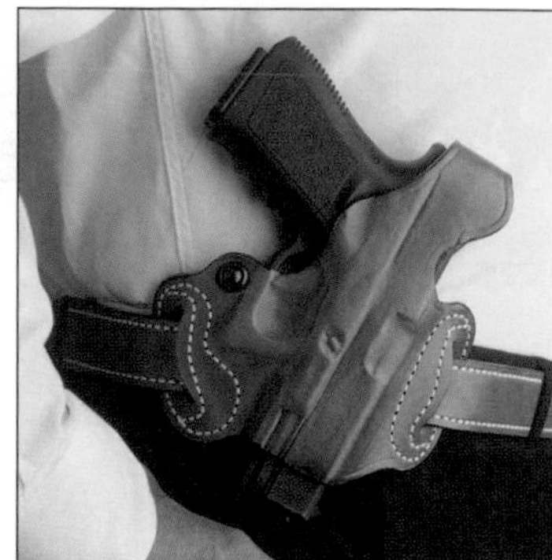

DESANTIS MINI SLIDE (STYLE 085)

SCABBARD

Use/Type: Concealment/belt
Retention: Screw tension
Material/Finish: Leather/plain brown or black
Carry: Strong side or cross draw
Compatible Firearms: Compact and full-size pistols, small- and medium-frame revolvers
Features: Open muzzle; covered trigger guard; fits belts up to 1.8 in.; three slots
Scabbard Style 001
(thumb break):................ **$85**
Speed Scabbard Style 002:..... $68
Mini Scabbard Style 019
(small pistols/revolvers):........ **$60**

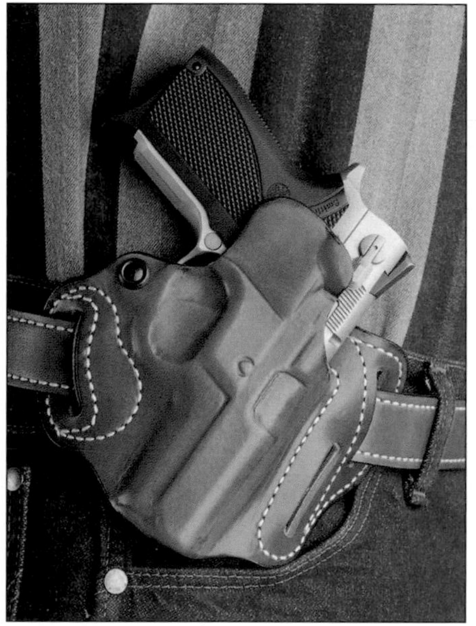

DESANTIS SCABBARD

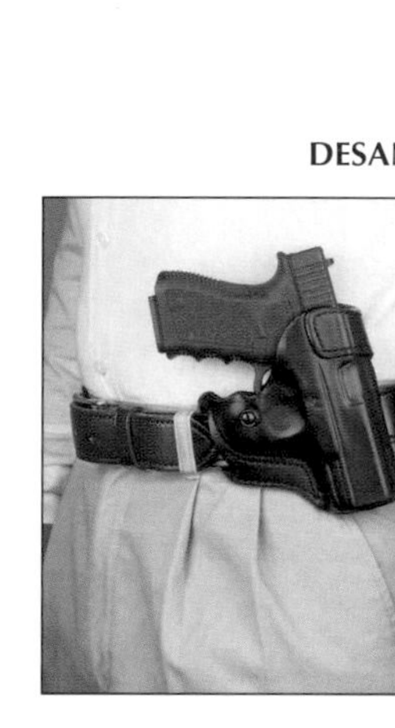

DESANTIS SKY COP

SKY COP

Use/Type: Concealment/belt
Retention: Screw tension
Material/Finish: Leather/plain black
Carry: Cross draw
Compatible Firearms: Full-size pistols, small-frame revolvers
Features: Open muzzle; covered trigger guard; fits belts up to 1.3 in.
Style 068: **$80**

SMALL-OF-BACK

Use/Type: Concealment/belt
Retention: Screw tension
Material/Finish: Leather/plain tan or black
Carry: Small of back
Compatible Firearms: Compact and full-size pistols, small- and medium-frame revolvers
Features: Open muzzle; covered trigger guard; fits belts up to 1.3 in.
Style 067: **$79**

DESANTIS SMALL-OF-BACK

HOLSTERS

DeSantis

(www.desantisholster.com)

DESANTIS I.C.E

I.C.E.

Use/Type: Concealment/belt
Retention: Thumb break
Material/Finish: Leather/plain black
Carry: Strong side
Compatible Firearms: Compact and full-size pistols, small- and medium-frame revolvers
Features: Open muzzle; covered trigger guard; lined; fits belts up to 1.3 in.
Style 011: $66

COCKED & LOCKED

Use/Type: Concealment/belt
Retention: Thumb break
Material/Finish: Leather/plain black
Carry: Strong side
Compatible Firearms: Full-size pistols
Features: Open muzzle; covered trigger guard; fits belts up to 1.3 in.
Style 1CL: $65

THE FACILITATOR

Use/Type: Concealment/belt
Retention: Screw tension
Material/Finish: Kydex/plain black
Carry: Strong side or cross draw
Compatible Firearms: Compact and full-size pistols
Features: Open muzzle; covered trigger guard; fits belts up to 1.3 in.
Style 042: $50

DESANTIS COCKED & LOCKED

F.F.D.O. WITH LOCK HOLE

Use/Type: Concealment/belt, pancake-style
Retention: Thumb break
Material/Finish: Leather/plain tan or black
Carry: Strong side or cross draw
Compatible Firearms: Compact and full-size pistols
Features: Open muzzle; high ride; padlock hole to secure weapon inside holster; fits belts up to 1.8 in.; three slots
Style 31L: $65

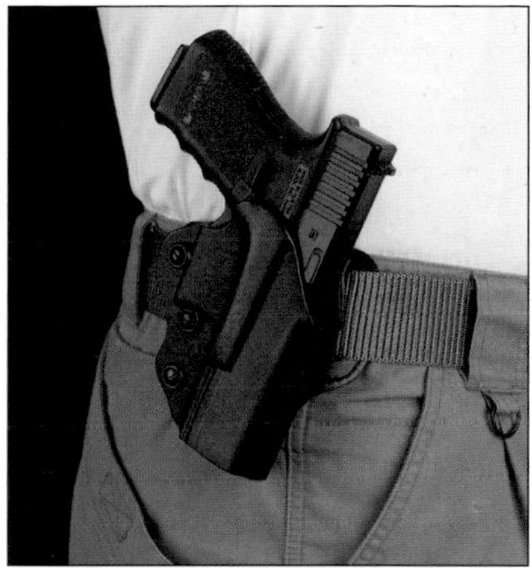

DESANTIS THE FACILITATOR

DESANTIS F.F.D.O.

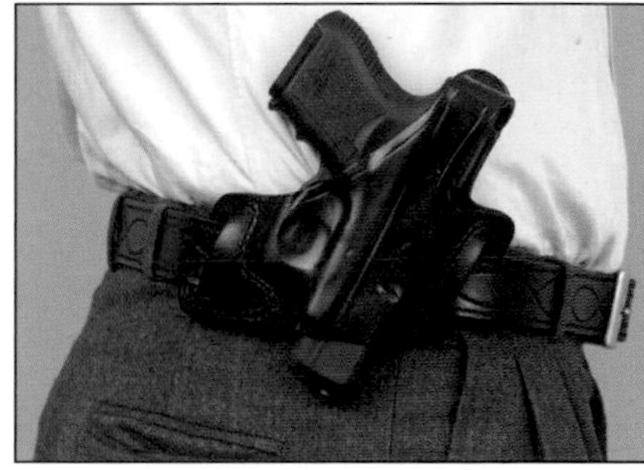

DESANTIS PARK ROW SLIDE

PARK ROW SLIDE

Use/Type: Concealment/belt slide
Retention: Thumb break
Material/Finish: Leather/plain black
Carry: Strong side
Compatible Firearms: Compact and full-size pistols
Features: Open muzzle; high ride; fits belts up to 1.8 in.
Style 034: $65

DeSantis

(www.desantisholster.com)

YAQUI

Use/Type: Concealment/belt slide
Retention: Screw tension
Material/Finish: Leather/plain tan or black
Carry: Strong side
Compatible Firearms: Compact and full-size pistols
Features: Open muzzle; high ride; fits belts up to 1.8 in.
Slide Style 023: $49
Paddle Style 029
(Kydex paddle): **$57**

DESANTIS YAQUI

DESANTIS QUICK SNAP

QUICK SNAP

Use/Type: Concealment/belt
Retention: Thumb break
Material/Finish: Leather/plain tan or black
Carry: Strong side
Compatible Firearms: Compact and full-size pistols
Features: Open muzzle; snap on belt loop; fits belts up to 1.8 in.
Style 027: $50

DESANTIS MAVERICK

DESANTIS SAFE-KEEPER

MAVERICK

Use/Type: Concealment/belt
Retention: Thumb break
Material/Finish: Leather/plain tan or black
Carry: Strong side
Compatible Firearms: Compact and full-size pistols
Features: Open muzzle; steel spring clip; fits belts up to 1.8 in.
Style 012: $50

QUIK-CHEK

Use/Type: Concealment/belt slide
Retention: Thumb release lever
Material/Finish: Leather/plain black
Carry: Strong side
Compatible Firearms: Compact and full-size pistols
Features: Open muzzle; high ride; polymer sight track; fits belts up to 1.5 in.
Style 043: $27

SAFE-KEEPER

Use/Type: Concealment/belt
Retention: Screw tension, thumb break
Material/Finish: Leather/plain tan or black
Carry: Strong side
Compatible Firearms: Compact and full-size pistols
Features: Open muzzle; high ride; padlock hole to secure weapon inside holster; snap on belt loops; fits belts up to 1.8 in.
Style 010: $58

F.A.M.S. WITH LOCK HOLE

Use/Type: Concealment/belt
Retention: Thumb break
Material/Finish: Leather/plain tan or black
Carry: Strong side or cross draw
Compatible Firearms: Compact and full-size pistols
Features: Open muzzle; high ride; padlock hole to secure weapon inside holster; fits belts up to 1.8 in.
Style 01L: $65

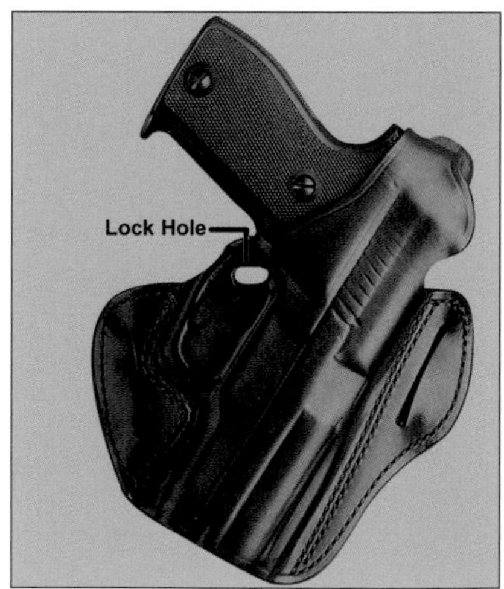

DESANTIS F.A.M.S. WITH LOCK HOLE

HOLSTERS

DeSantis

(www.desantisholster.com)

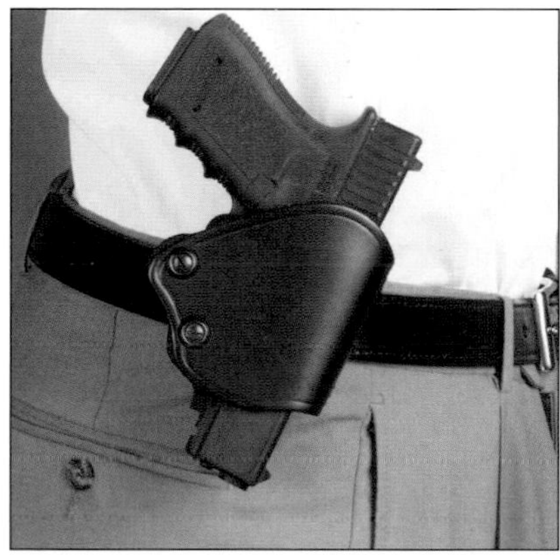

DESANTIS QUIK-CHEK

DESANTIS DS PADDLE

QUIK-CHEK

Use/Type: Concealment/belt slide, 1.5 in.
Retention: Thumb release lever, screw tension
Material/Finish: Leather/plain tan or black
Carry: Strong side
Compatible Firearms: Compact and full-size pistols
Features: Open muzzle; high ride; polymer sight track
Style 041: $83

DS PADDLE

Use/Type: Concealment/paddle design
Retention: Screw tension
Material/Finish: Kydex/black
Carry: Strong side
Compatible Firearms: Compact and full-size pistols
Features: Open muzzle; adj. cant
Style D49: $40

NYPAD

Use/Type: Concealment/paddle design
Retention: Screw tension
Material/Finish: Nylon/black
Carry: Strong side
Compatible Firearms: Compact and full-size pistols
Features: Open muzzle; adj. cant
Style N67: $51

DESANTIS NYPAD

DeSantis

(www.desantisholster.com)

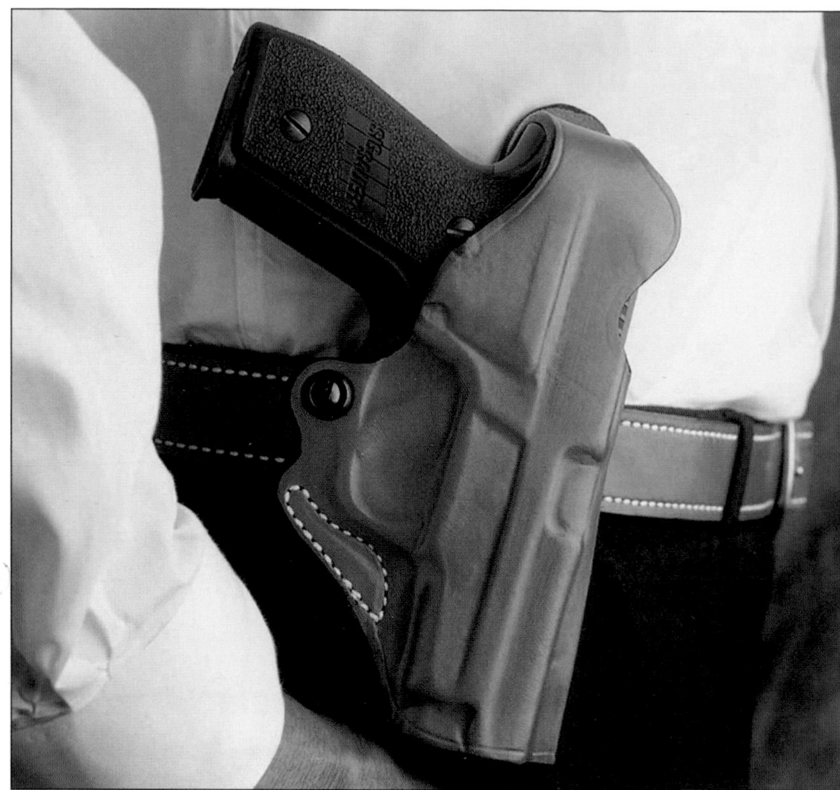

DESANTIS VIPER

VIPER

Use/Type: Concealment/paddle design
Retention: Screw tension
Material/Finish: Leather/plain tan or black
Carry: Strong side
Compatible Firearms: Compact and full-size pistols
Features: Open muzzle; adj. cant
Style 065: $86

PRO-FED

Use/Type: Concealment/paddle design
Retention: Screw tension
Material/Finish: Leather/plain tan or black
Carry: Strong side
Compatible Firearms: Compact and full-size pistols
Features: Open muzzle; adj. cant
Style 053: $85

TOP COP

Use/Type: Concealment/paddle design
Retention: Screw tension
Material/Finish: Leather/plain tan or black
Carry: Strong side
Compatible Firearms: Compact and full-size pistols
Features: Adj. cant
Style 037: $75

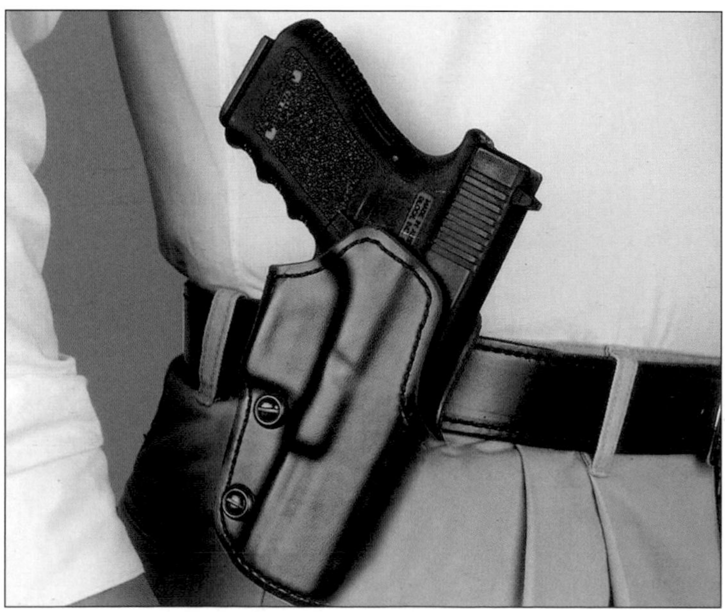

DEASNTIS PRO-FED

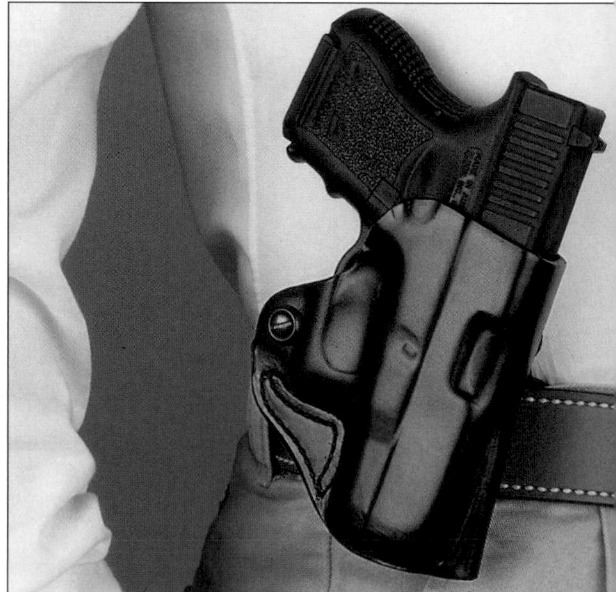

DESANTIS TOP COP

DeSantis

(www.desantisholster.com)

DUAL CARRY

Use/Type: Concealment/belt, inside waistband
Retention: Screw tension
Material/Finish: Leather/plain black
Carry: Strong side
Compatible Firearms: Subcompact pistols
Features: Loop and steel spring clip; fits belts up to 1.8 in.
Style 032: $32

COZY PARTNER

Use/Type: Concealment/belt, inside waistband
Retention: Screw tension
Material/Finish: Leather/plain black
Carry: Strong side
Compatible Firearms: Compact and full-size pistols
Features: Split belt loop; fits belts up to 1.8 in.
Style 028: $73

TUCK-THIS II

Use/Type: Concealment/belt, inside waistband
Retention: Screw tension
Material/Finish: Nylon/black
Carry: Strong side, small of back, cross draw
Compatible Firearms: Compact pistols, small-frame revolvers
Features: Allows shirt to be tucked; built-in magazine pouch; fits belts up to 1.8 in.
Style M24: $38

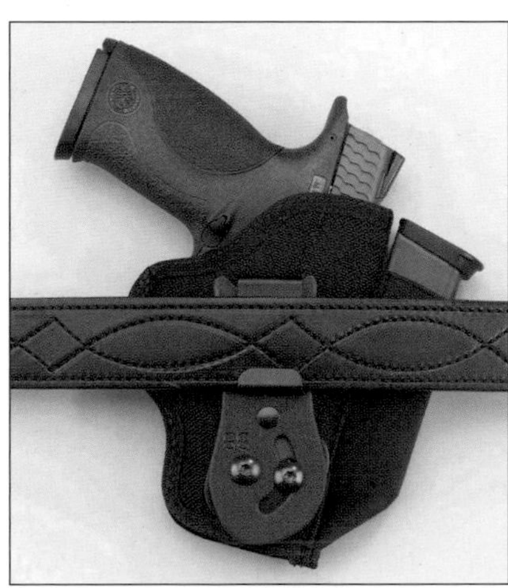

DESANTIS TUCK–THIS II

COMPANION

Use/Type: Concealment/belt, inside waistband
Retention: None
Material/Finish: Leather/plain black
Carry: Strong side
Compatible Firearms: Compact pistols, small-frame revolvers
Features: Belt loop or spring clip; fits belts up to 1.8 in.
Style 026: $65

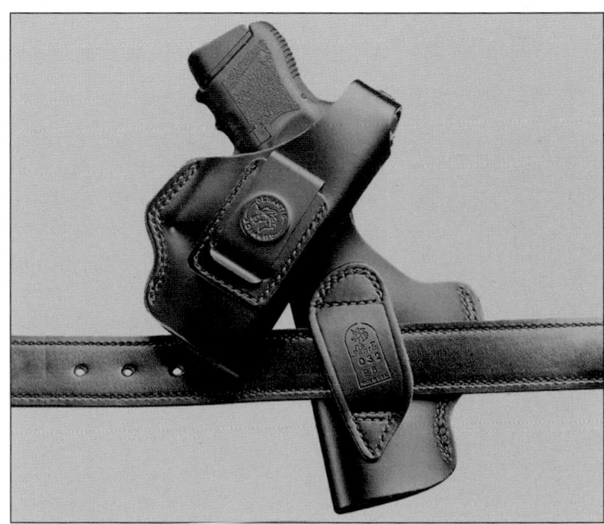

DESANTIS DUAL CARRY

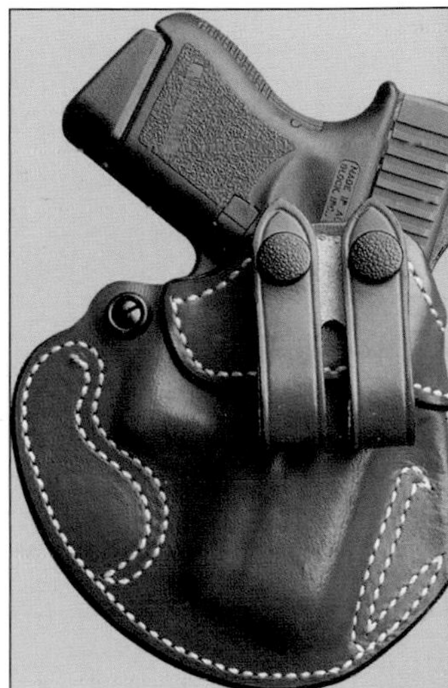

DESANTIS COZY PARTNER

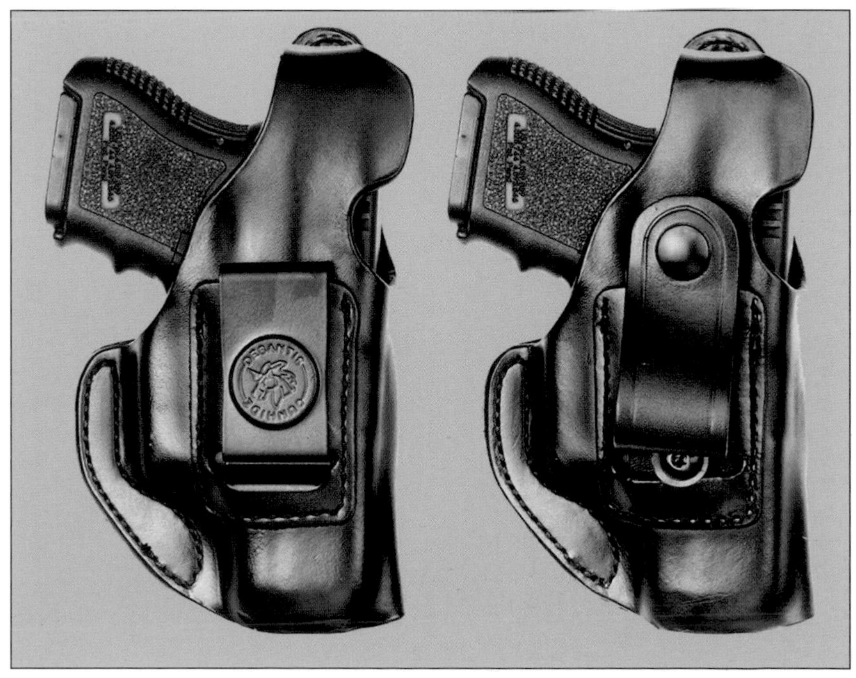

DESANTIS COMPANION WITH CLIP (LEFT) AND BELT LOOP (RIGHT)

HOLSTERS

DeSantis

(www.desantisholster.com)

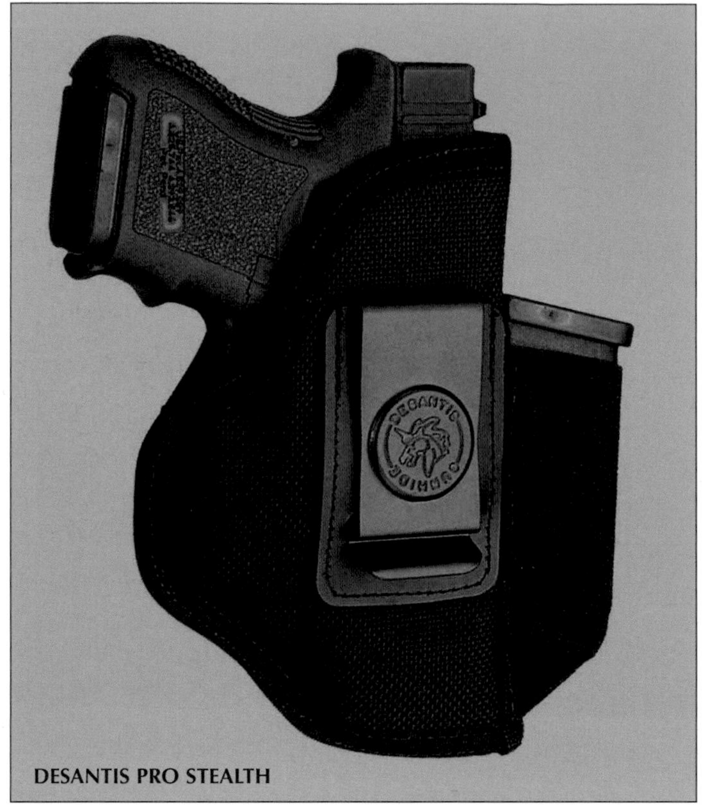

DESANTIS PRO STEALTH

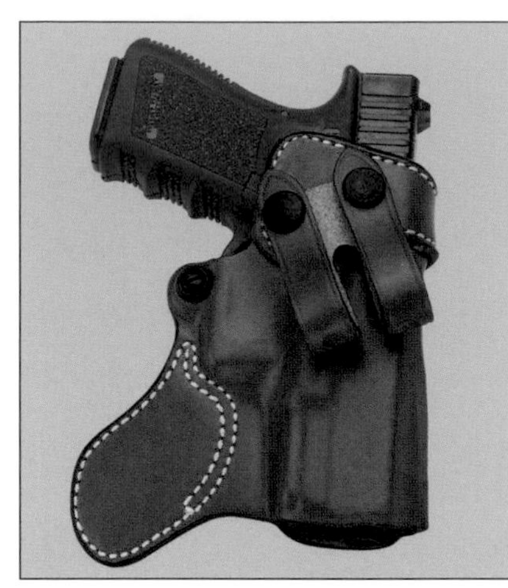

DESANTIS INNER PIECE

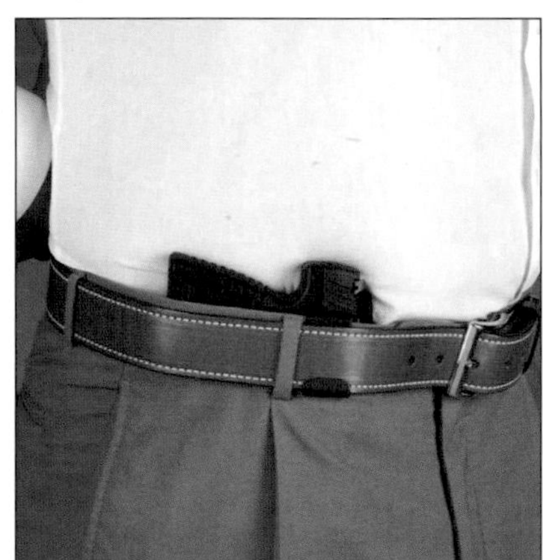

DESANTIS INVISIBLE AGENT WITH CLIP

DESANTIS INVISIBLE AGENT WITH LOOP

PRO STEALTH

Use/Type: Concealment/belt, inside waistband
Retention: None
Material/Finish: Nylon/black
Carry: Ambidextrous
Compatible Firearms: Compact pistols, small-frame revolvers
Features: Built-in magazine pouch; fits belts up to 1.8 in.
Style N87: $39

INNER PIECE

Use/Type: Concealment/belt, inside waistband
Retention: Screw tension
Material/Finish: Leather/plain tan or black
Carry: Strong side
Compatible Firearms: Compact and full-size pistols
Features: Split belt loop; reinforced opening; rear stabilizer wing; fits belts up to 1.8 in.
Style 057: $70
Style 098 (thumb break): **. $81**

THE INSIDER

Use/Type: Concealment/belt, inside waistband
Retention: None
Material/Finish: Leather/plain black
Carry: Strong side
Compatible Firearms: Compact pistols, small-frame revolvers
Features: Steel spring clip; fits belts up to 1.8 in.
Style 031: $26

INVISIBLE AGENT

Use/Type: Concealment/belt, inside waistband
Retention: None
Material/Finish: Leather/black
Carry: Strong side
Compatible Firearms: Compact pistols, small-frame revolvers
Features: Allows shirt to be tucked; belt loop or spring clip; fits belts up to 1.8 in.
Style 005: $28

DeSantis

(www.desantisholster.com)

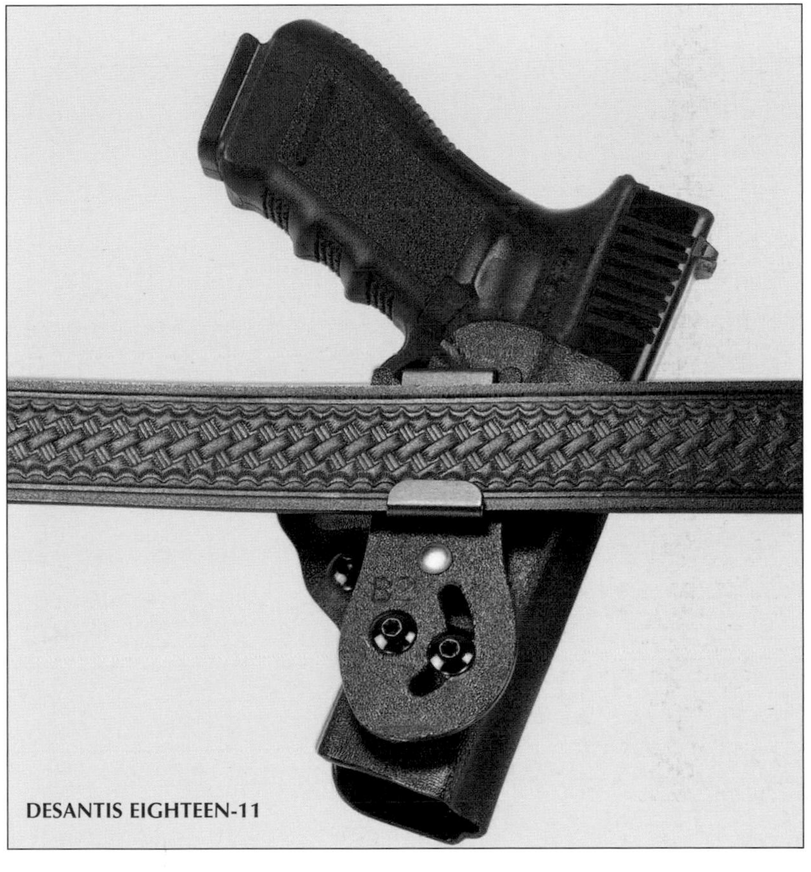
DESANTIS EIGHTEEN-11

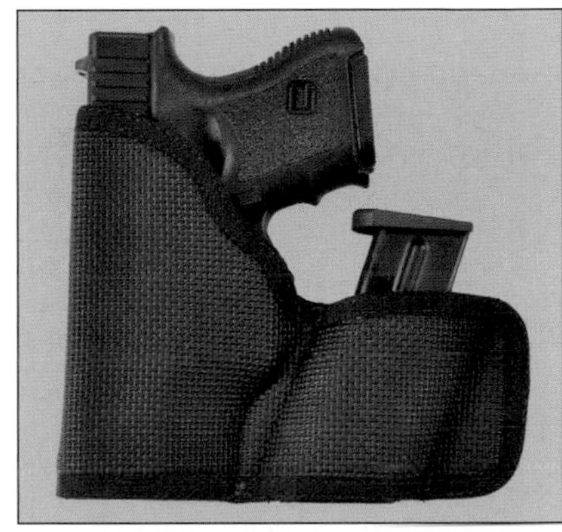
DESANTIS CARGO NEMESIS

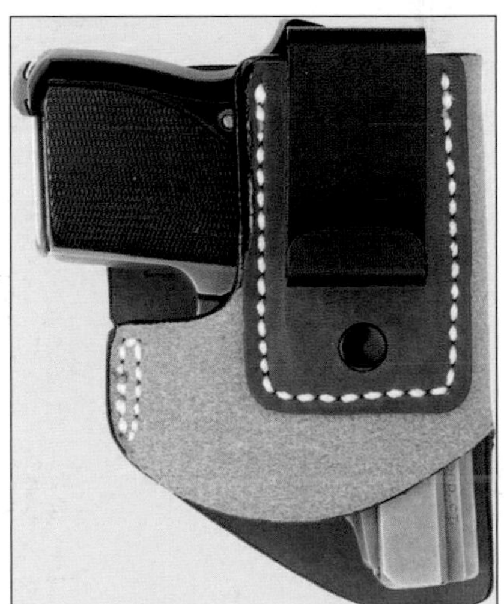
DESANTIS POP-UP

EIGHTEEN-11

Use/Type: Concealment/belt, inside waistband
Retention: Screw tension
Material/Finish: Kydex/black
Carry: Strong side, small of back, cross draw
Compatible Firearms: Compact and full-size pistols
Features: Adj. Roto-Tuck allows shirt to be tucked; fits belts up to 1.8 in.
Style D96: $40

THE NEMISIS and CARGO NEMISIS

Use/Type: Concealment/pocket
Retention: None
Material/Finish: Nylon/black
Carry: Ambidextrous
Compatible Firearms: Subcompact pistols, small-frame revolvers
Features: Sticky outside restricts movement in pocket
The Nemisis Style N38: $23
Cargo Nemisis Style M52 (built-in magazine pouch): **. $30**

POP-UP

Use/Type: Concealment/belt, inside waistband
Retention: None
Material/Finish: Leather/tan
Carry: Strong side
Compatible Firearms: Subcompact pistols, small-frame revolvers
Features: Low ride; fits belts up to 1.8 in.
Style 020: $45

SCORPION

Use/Type: Concealment/belt, inside waistband
Retention: None
Material/Finish: Kydex/black
Carry: Strong side
Compatible Firearms: Compact and full-size pistols, small and medium-frame revolvers
Features: Open muzzle, reinforced opening; fits belts up to 1.8 in.
Style 038: $63

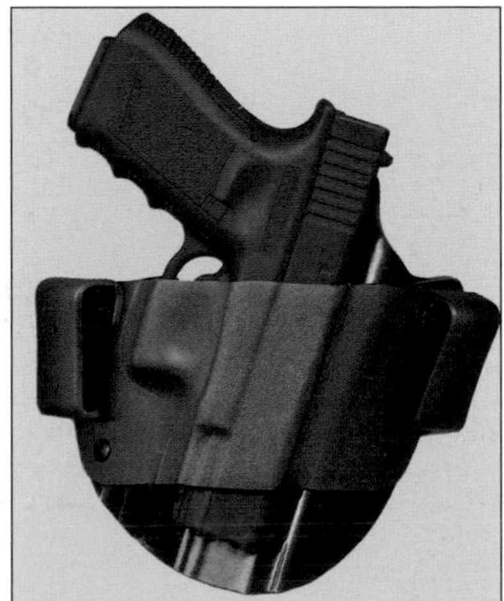
DESANTIS SCORPION

DeSantis

(www.desantisholster.com)

THE TRICKSTER and THE STING

Use/Type: Concealment/pocket
Retention: None
Material/Finish: Leather/black
Carry: Ambidextrous
Compatible Firearms: Subcompact pistols
Features: Design for back pant pocket
The Trickster Style 021: $27
The Sting Style 073 (built-in magazine pouch): **............ $33**

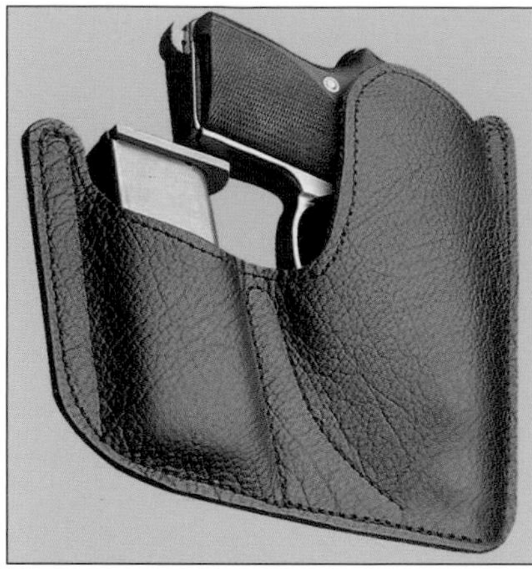

DESANTIS THE STING

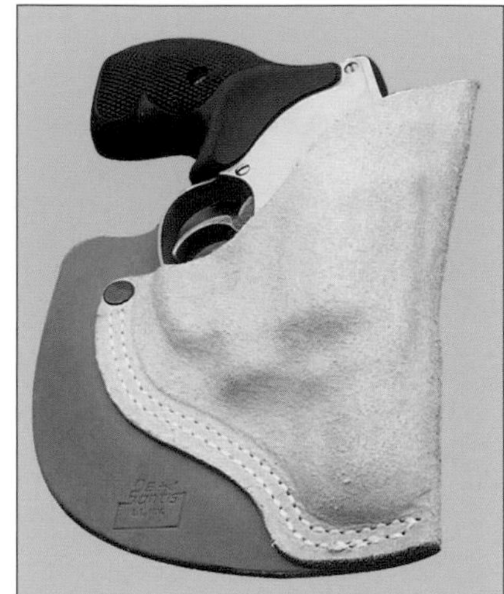

DESANTIS POCKET PAL

POCKET PAL

Use/Type: Concealment/pocket
Retention: None
Material/Finish: Leather/natural
Carry: Ambidextrous
Compatible Firearms: Subcompact pistols, small-frame revolvers
Features: Rough leather outside
Style 030: $46

SUPER FLY

Use/Type: Concealment/pocket
Retention: None
Material/Finish: Rubberized fabric/black
Carry: Ambidextrous
Compatible Firearms: Subcompact pistols, small-frame revolvers
Features: Sticky outside restricts movement in pocket
Style M44: $38
Style M44 (with flap): **......... $38**

DESANTIS SUPER FLY

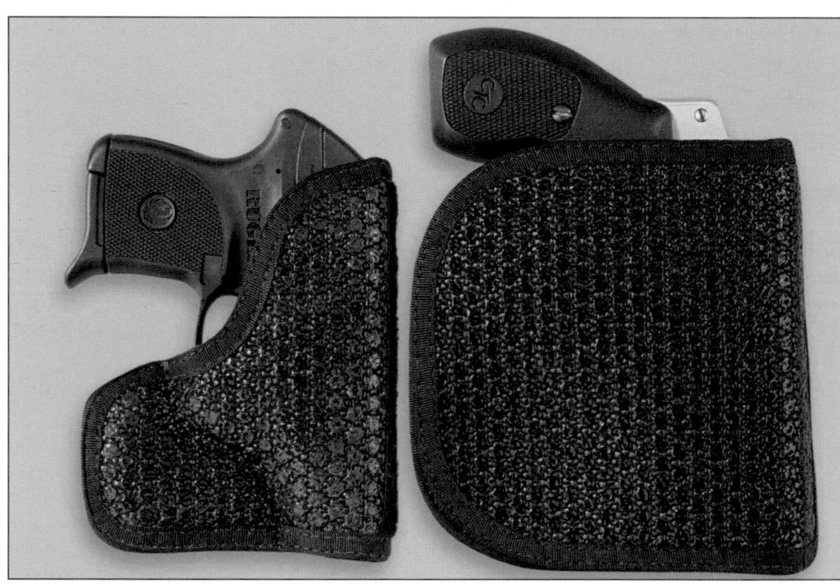

HOLSTERS

DESANTIS APACHE ANKLE RIG

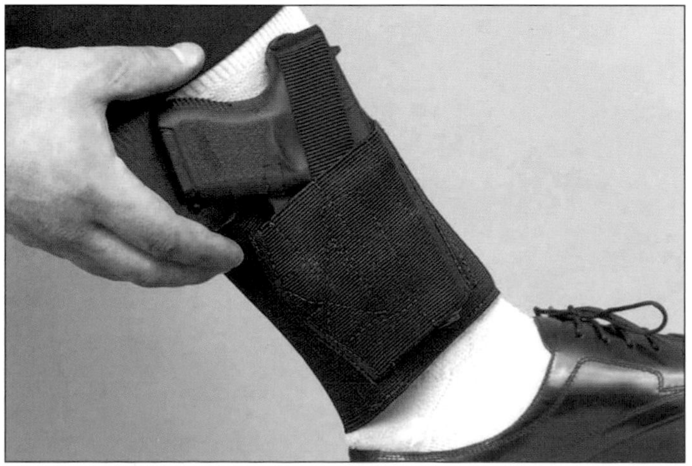

APACHE ANKLE RIG

Use/Type: Concealment/ankle
Retention: Thumb break
Material/Finish: Elastic fabric/black
Carry: Cross draw
Compatible Firearms: Subcompact and compact pistols, small-frame revolvers
Features: Sheepskin lined
Style 062: $51

DeSantis

(www.desantisholster.com)

LEATHER ANKLE

Use/Type: Concealment/ankle
Retention: Thumb break
Material/Finish: Leather/plain black
Carry: Cross draw
Compatible Firearms: Subcompact and compact pistols, small-frame revolvers
Features: Sheepskin lined
Style 044: $75

DIE HARD ANKLE RIG

Use/Type: Concealment/ankle
Retention: Thumb break
Material/Finish: Leather/plain black
Carry: Cross draw
Compatible Firearms: Subcompact and compact pistols, small-frame revolvers
Features: Synthetic or sheepskin lined
Style 014: $73

C.E.O. SHOULDER RIG

Use/Type: Concealment/shoulder
Retention: Thumb break, screw tension
Material/Finish: Leather/plain tan or black
Carry: Cross draw
Compatible Firearms: Compact and full-size pistols
Features: Ambidextrous; half-harness; one tie-down strap; suede lined
Style 11Z: $135

NEW YORK UNDERCOVER

Use/Type: Concealment/shoulder
Retention: Thumb break, screw tension
Material/Finish: Leather/plain tan or black
Carry: Cross draw
Compatible Firearms: Compact and full-size pistols
Features: Ambidextrous; x-harness; one tie-down strap; suede lined; double magazine pouch
Style 11D: $166

BODYGUARD

Use/Type: Concealment/shoulder
Retention: None
Material/Finish: Nylon/black
Carry: Cross draw
Compatible Firearms: Compact and full-size pistols, small- and medium-frame revolvers
Features: Designed to carry two weapons; ambidextrous; two tie-down straps; double magazine pouch
Style N90: $83

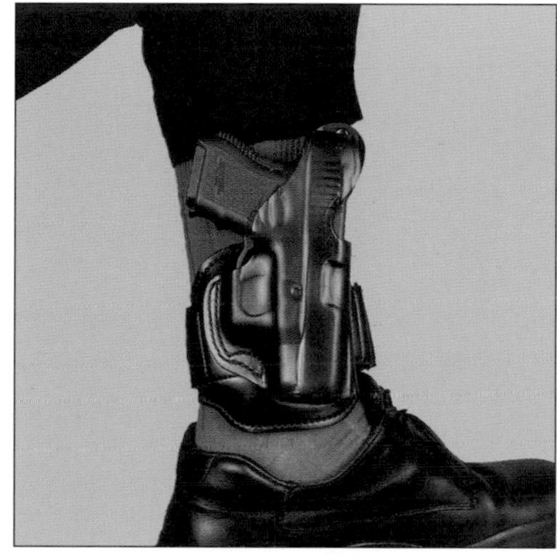

DESANTIS LEATHER ANKLE HOLSTER

DESANTIS DIE HARD ANKLE RIG

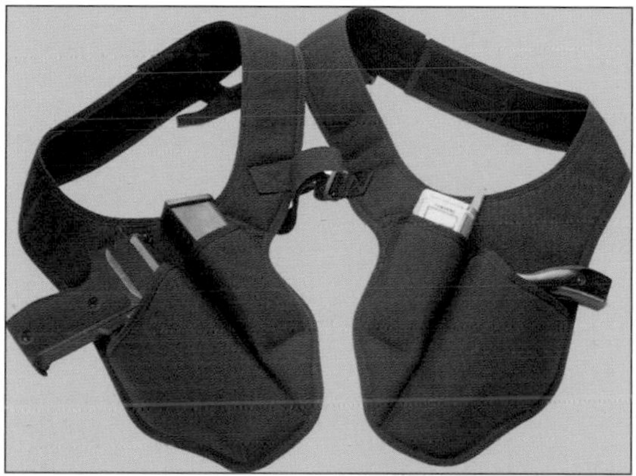

DESANTIS BODYGUARD

DESANTIS NEW YORK UNDERCOVER

DESANTIS C.E.O. SHOULDER RIG

DeSantis

(www.desantisholster.com)

DESANTIS THE PATRIOT

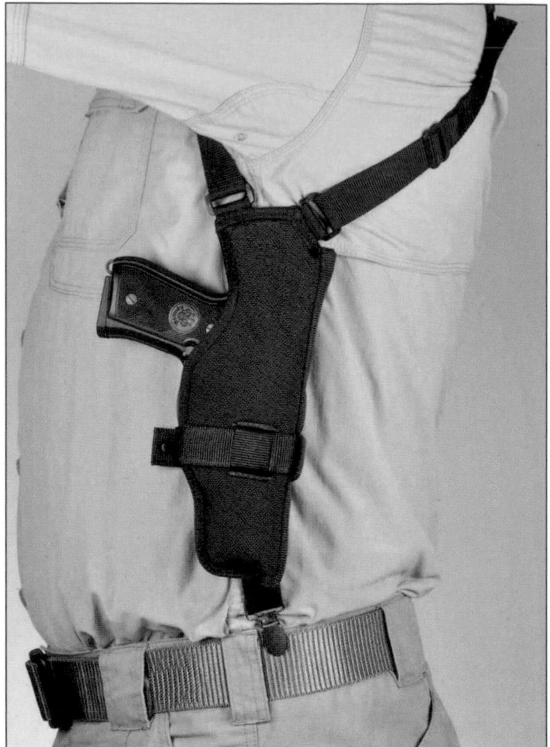

DESANTIS DRAGONFLY RIG

THE PATRIOT

Use/Type: Concealment/shoulder
Retention: Thumb break
Material/Finish: Nylon/black
Carry: Cross draw
Compatible Firearms: Compact and full-size pistols, small- and medium-frame revolvers
Features: Ambidextrous; two tie-down straps
Style N84: $84

DRAGONFLY RIG

Use/Type: Concealment/shoulder
Retention: Retaining strap
Material/Finish: Nylon/black
Carry: Cross draw
Compatible Firearms: Compact and full-size pistols, small- and medium-frame revolvers
Features: Ambidextrous; two tie-down straps; triple horizontal magazine pouch
Style 084: $90

HOLSTERS

Fobus

(www.fobusholster.com)

FOBUS STANDARD (PADDLE)

STANDARD

Use/Type: Concealment/belt or paddle
Retention: Passive retention around trigger guard
Material/Finish: Polymer/black
Carry: Strong side
Compatible Firearms: Compact and full-size pistols, small- and medium-frame revolvers
Features: Open muzzle; covered trigger guard; fits belts up to 1.8 in.; rubberized paddle
Belt or Paddle: $29

COMPACT

Use/Type: Concealment/belt or paddle
Retention: Passive retention around trigger guard
Material/Finish: Polymer/black
Carry: Strong side
Compatible Firearms: Compact and full-size pistols, small- and medium-frame revolvers
Features: Yaqui style; open muzzle; covered trigger guard; fits belts up to 1.8 in.; rubberized paddle
Belt or Paddle: $29

Fobus

(www.fobusholster.com)

FOBUS COMPACT

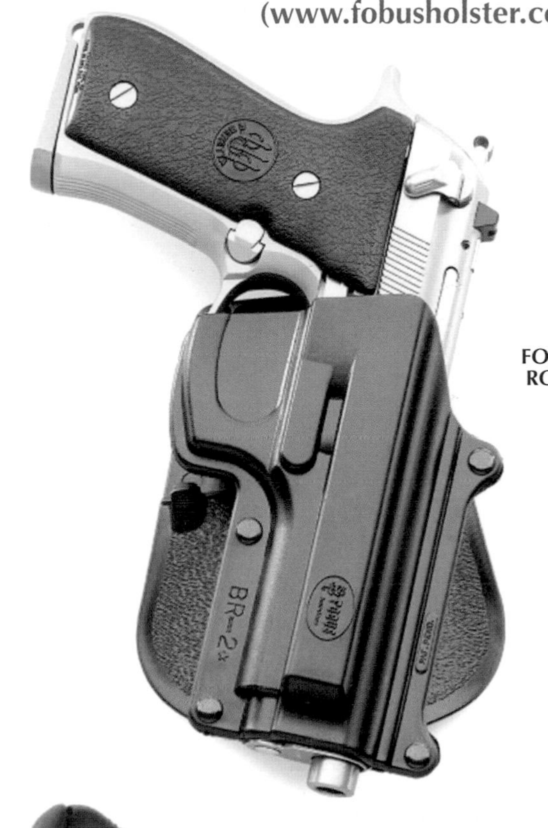

FOBUS ROTO

ROTO

Use/Type: Concealment/belt or paddle
Retention: Passive retention around trigger guard
Material/Finish: Polymer/black
Carry: Strong side, small of back, or cross draw
Compatible Firearms: Compact and full-size pistols, small- and medium-frame revolvers
Features: Open muzzle; covered trigger guard; 360-degree adj. cant; converts to either belt or paddle; fits belts up to 1.8 in.; rubberized paddle
Belt or Paddle: $34

FOBUS EVOLUTION

EVOLUTION SERIES

Use/Type: Concealment/belt or paddle
Retention: Screw tension
Material/Finish: Polymer/black
Carry: Strong side
Compatible Firearms: Compact and full-size pistols, small- and medium-frame revolvers
Features: Open muzzle; covered trigger guard; fits belts up to 1.8 in.; rubberized paddle
Belt or Paddle: $33
Roto Belt or Paddle (360-degree adj. cant, converts to either belt or paddle): **$37**

Fobus

(www.fobusholster.com)

FOBUS THUMB LEVER

FOBUS VARIO

THUMB LEVER

Use/Type: Concealment/belt or paddle
Retention: Thumb release lever lock
Material/Finish: Polymer/black
Carry: Strong side, small of back, or cross draw
Compatible Firearms: Compact and full-size pistols, small- and medium-frame revolvers
Features: Open muzzle; covered trigger guard; 360-degree adj. cant; converts to either belt or paddle; fits belts up to 1.8 in.; rubberized paddle
MSRP: $30

VARIO

Use/Type: Concealment/belt
Retention: Passive retention around trigger guard
Material/Finish: Polymer/black
Carry: Strong side
Compatible Firearms: Compact and full-size pistols, small- and medium-frame revolvers
Features: Open muzzle; covered trigger guard; fits belts from 1 in. to 2.3 in.; adj. loops
Belt or Paddle: $34

THUMB BREAK

Use/Type: Concealment/belt or paddle
Retention: Thumb break
Material/Finish: Polymer/black
Carry: Strong side
Compatible Firearms: Compact and full-size pistols, small- and medium-frame revolvers
Features: Open muzzle; covered trigger guard; 360-degree adj. cant; converts to either belt or paddle; fits belts up to 1.8 in.; rubberized paddle
Thumb Break: $33
Thumb Break Roto Belt or Paddle (360-degree adj. cant, converts to either belt or paddle): **. $37**

ANKLE

Use/Type: Concealment/ankle
Retention: Screw tension
Material/Finish: Polymer/black
Carry: Ambidextrous
Compatible Firearms: Subcompact and compact pistols, small-frame revolvers
Features: Adj. velcro strap; suede lined
MSRP: $46

FOBUS THUMB BREAK

FOBUS ANKLE

Fobus

(www.fobusholster.com)

INSIDE WAISTBAND IWB

Use/Type: Concealment/belt, inside waistband
Retention: Passive retention around trigger guard
Material/Finish: Polymer/black
Carry: Strong side
Compatible Firearms: Compact and full-size pistols
Features: Open muzzle; covered trigger guard; retention hooks
MSRP: $29

FOBUS IWB

TACTICAL

Use/Type: Concealment/belt or paddle
Retention: Muzzle stud, retaining strap
Material/Finish: Polymer/black
Carry: Strong side
Compatible Firearms: Compact and full-size pistols
Features: Open muzzle; covered trigger guard; accommodates most pistols with mounted tactical accessories; fits belts up to 1.8 in.; rubberized paddle
Tactical: $53
Tactical Roto Belt or Paddle
(360-degree adj. cant, converts to either belt or paddle): **$58**

FOBUS TACTICAL

Galco

(www.usgalco.com)

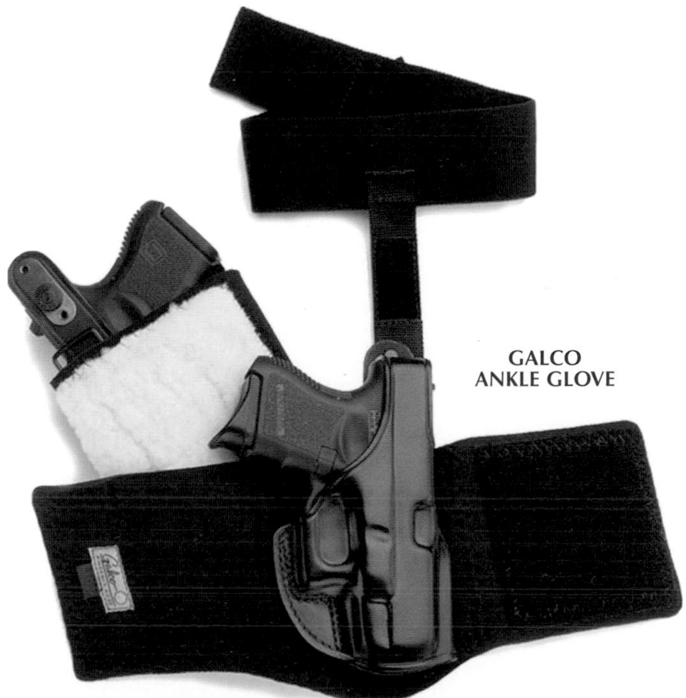

GALCO ANKLE GLOVE

ANKLE GLOVE

Use/Type: Concealment/ankle
Retention: Thumb break or retention screw
Material/Finish: Leather/plain black
Carry: Cross draw
Compatible Firearms: Subcompact and compact pistols, small-frame revolvers
Features: Neoprene ankle band
MSRP: $90

Galco

(www.usgalco.com)

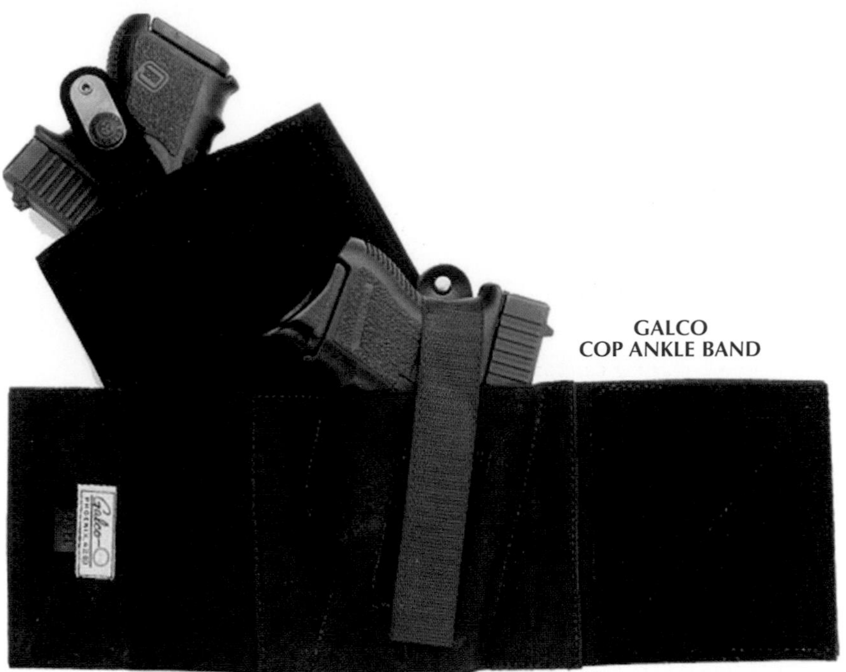

GALCO COP ANKLE BAND

COP ANKLE BAND

Use/Type: Concealment/ankle
Retention: Thumb break
Material/Finish: Nylon/black
Carry: Cross draw
Compatible Firearms: Subcompact and compact pistols, small-frame revolvers
Features: Neoprene ankle band
MSRP: $72

ANKLE LITE

Use/Type: Concealment/ankle
Retention: Thumb break
Material/Finish: Leather/plain black or khaki
Carry: Cross draw
Compatible Firearms: Subcompact and compact pistols, small-frame revolvers
Features: Elastic ankle band
MSRP: $53

GALCO ANKLE LITE

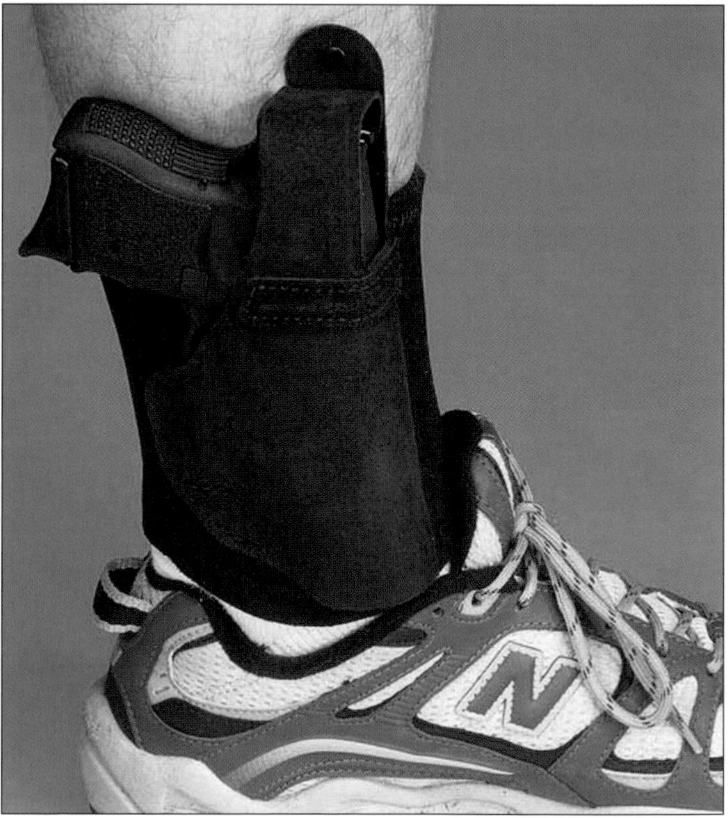

GALCO AVENGER

HOLSTERS

AVENGER

Use/Type: Concealment/belt
Retention: Screw tension
Material/Finish: Leather/plain black or tan
Carry: Strong side
Compatible Firearms: Full-size pistols
Features: Reinforced opening; sight rail; fits belts up to 1.8 in.
MSRP: $92

Galco

(www.usgalco.com)

COMBAT MASTER

Use/Type: Concealment/belt
Retention: None
Material/Finish: Leather/plain black or tan
Carry: Strong side
Compatible Firearms: Compact and full-size pistols, small- and medium-frame revolvers
Features: Reinforced opening; butt-forward cant; fits belts up to 1.8 in.
MSRP: $80

CONCEALABLE BELT

Use/Type: Concealment/belt
Retention: None
Material/Finish: Leather/plain black or brown
Carry: Strong side
Compatible Firearms: Compact and full-size pistols, small- and medium-frame revolvers
Features: Reinforced opening; butt-forward cant; fits belts up to 1.2 in.
Leather: $100
Exotic material (alligator, shark, stingray, ostrich, or english pigskin): . . . . **$174–$475**

COP 3 SLOT

Use/Type: Concealment/belt, pancake-style
Retention: Thumb break
Material/Finish: Leather/plain black
Carry: Strong side or cross draw
Compatible Firearms: Compact and full-size pistols, small- and medium-frame revolvers
Features: Open muzzle; high ride; fits belts up to 1.8 in.; three slots
MSRP: $70

COP SLIDE

Use/Type: Concealment/belt
Retention: Thumb break and tension screw
Material/Finish: Leather/plain black
Carry: Strong side or cross draw
Compatible Firearms: Compact and full-size pistols, small- and medium-frame revolvers
Features: Open muzzle; high ride; covered trigger guard; fits belts up to 1.8 in.
MSRP: $70

GALCO COMBAT MASTER

GALCO COP 3 SLOT

GALCO COP SLIDE

FLETCH and FX

Use/Type: Concealment/belt
Retention: Thumb break
Material/Finish: Leather/plain black or tan
Carry: Strong side
Compatible Firearms: Compact and full-size pistols, small- and medium-frame revolvers
Features: High ride; open muzzle; fits belts up to 1.8 in.
Fletch: $90
FX (suede lined): **$110**

GALCO FLETCH

Galco

(www.usgalco.com)

GALCO GLADIUS

GALCO M3X MATRIX

GLADIUS

Use/Type: Concealment/belt
Retention: Thumb break
Material/Finish: Leather/plain black
Carry: Strong side
Compatible Firearms: Compact and full-size pistols
Features: Open muzzle; snap belt loops; fits belts up to 1.5 in.
MSRP: $98

HALO

Use/Type: Concealment/belt
Retention: Thumb break
Material/Finish: Leather/plain black
Carry: Strong side or cross draw
Compatible Firearms: Compact and full-size pistols
Features: Open muzzle; high ride; accommodates most pistols with mounted tactical lights; fits belts up to 1.8 in.
MSRP: $90

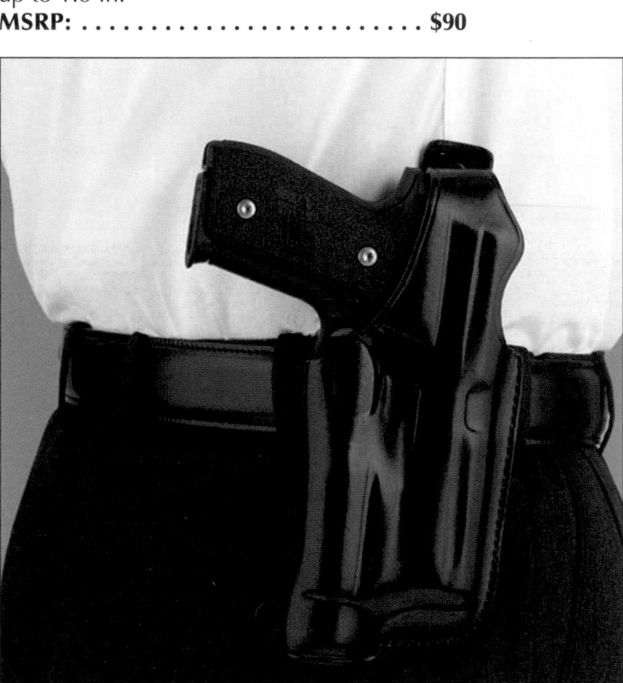

GALCO HALO

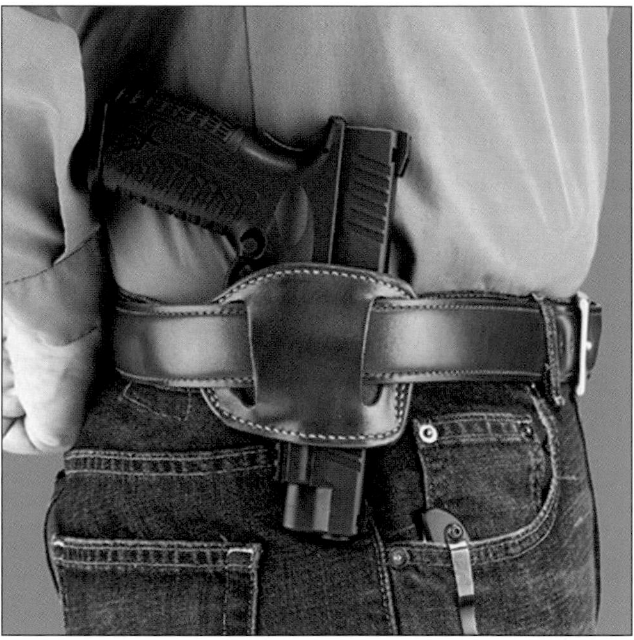

GALCO JAK SLIDE

JAK SLIDE

Use/Type: Concealment/belt
Retention: None
Material/Finish: Leather/plain black or tan
Carry: Strong side
Compatible Firearms: Compact and full-size pistols
Features: Open muzzle; high ride; covered trigger guard; fits belts up to 1.8 in.
MSRP: $65

M3X MATRIX

Use/Type: Concealment/belt
Retention: Twin retention screws
Material/Finish: Polymer/black
Carry: Strong side
Compatible Firearms: Compact and full-size pistols
Features: Open muzzle; covered trigger guard; fits belts up to 1.8 in.
MSRP: $30

Galco

(www.usgalco.com)

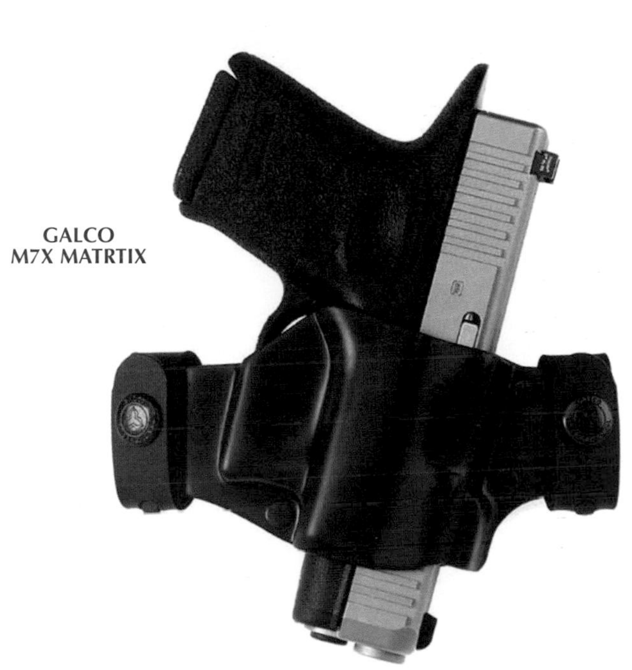

GALCO M7X MATRTIX

GALCO ROYAL DELUXE

M7X MATRIX

Use/Type: Concealment/belt
Retention: Retention screw
Material/Finish: Polymer/black
Carry: Strong side
Compatible Firearms: Compact and full-size pistols
Features: Open muzzle; covered trigger guard; snap belt loops; fits belts up to 1.8 in.
MSRP: $30

QUICK SLIDE

Use/Type: Concealment/belt
Retention: None
Material/Finish: Leather/plain black or brown
Carry: Strong side
Compatible Firearms: Compact and full-size pistols
Features: Open muzzle; high ride; covered trigger guard; fits belts up to 1.5 in.
MSRP: $100

ROYAL DELUXE

Use/Type: Concealment/belt 1.5 in.
Retention: None
Material/Finish: Leather/plain black or brown
Carry: Strong side
Compatible Firearms: Compact and full-size pistols
Features: Open muzzle; high ride; lined; premium hide; hand burnished; limited production
MSRP: $179

SILHOUETTE HIGH RIDE

Use/Type: Concealment/belt
Retention: Thumb break
Material/Finish: Leather/plain black or tan
Carry: Strong side
Compatible Firearms: Compact and full-size pistols, small- and medium-frame revolvers
Features: High ride; open muzzle; fits belts up to 1.8 in.
MSRP: $77

GALCO SILHOUETTE HIGH RIDE

Galco

(www.usgalco.com)

SMALL OF BACK (SOB)

Use/Type: Concealment/belt
Retention: Tension screw
Material/Finish: Leather/plain black or tan
Carry: Small of back
Compatible Firearms: Compact and full-size pistols, small- and medium-frame revolvers
Features: Reinforced opening; covered trigger guard; fits belts up to 1.8 in.
MSRP: $105

SIDE SNAP SCABBARD (SSS)

Use/Type: Concealment/belt
Retention: Tension screw
Material/Finish: Leather/plain black
Carry: Strong side
Compatible Firearms: Compact and full-size pistols, small- and medium-frame revolvers
Features: Open muzzle; covered trigger guard; snap belt loops; fits belts up to 1.5 in.
MSRP: $30

STINGER

Use/Type: Concealment/belt
Retention: None
Material/Finish: Leather/plain black
Carry: Strong side
Compatible Firearms: Subcompact, compact, and full-size pistols; small- and medium-frame revolvers
Features: Open muzzle; covered trigger guard; fits belts up to 1.5 in.
MSRP: $57

GALCO SOB

GALCO SSS

GALCO STINGER

GALCO TAC SLIDE

HOLSTERS

Galco

(www.usgalco.com)

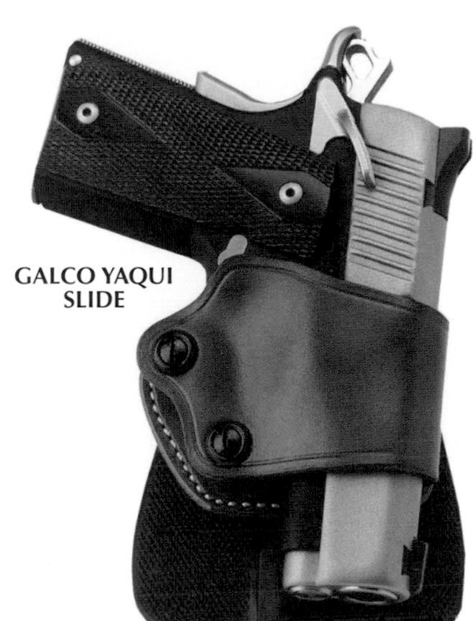

GALCO YAQUI SLIDE

TAC SLIDE

Use/Type: Concealment/belt
Retention: None
Material/Finish: Kydex and leather/black
Carry: Strong side
Compatible Firearms: Subcompact, compact, and full-size pistols; small- and medium-frame revolvers
Features: Open muzzle; high ride; covered trigger guard; fits belts up to 1.8 in.
MSRP: $40

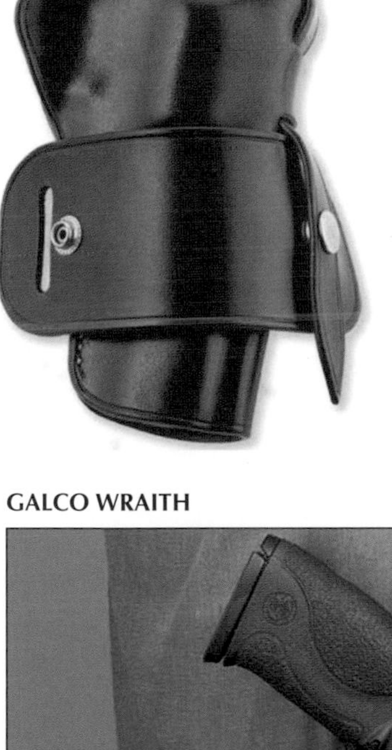

GALCO WHEELGUNNER

WHEELGUNNER

Use/Type: Concealment/belt
Retention: Hammer thong
Material/Finish: Leather/tan
Carry: Strong side or cross draw
Compatible Firearms: Medium- and large-frame revolvers
Features: Open muzzle; high ride; covered trigger guard; fits belts up to 1.8 in.
MSRP: $55

WRAITH

Use/Type: Concealment/belt
Retention: Thumb break
Material/Finish: Leather/plain black
Carry: Strong side
Compatible Firearms: Compact and full-size pistols, small- and medium-frame revolvers
Features: Covered trigger guard; fits belts up to 1.8 in.
MSRP: $30

GALCO WRAITH

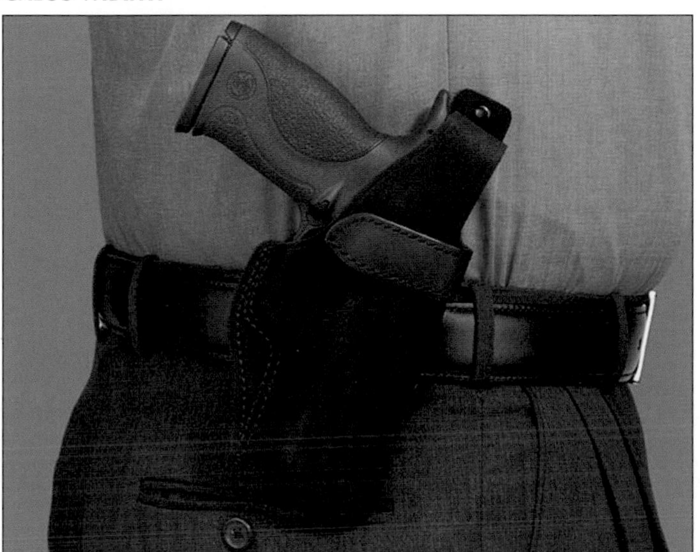

X PROJECT

Use/Type: Concealment/belt and shoulder
Retention: Strap
Material/Finish: Thermoplastic/plain black
Carry: Strong side with belt or cross draw with shoulder
Compatible Firearms: Compact and full-size pistols
Features: Covered trigger guard; converts from belt to shoulder holster; fits belts up to 1.5 in.
MSRP: $70

YAQUI SLIDE

Use/Type: Concealment/belt
Retention: Two tension screws
Material/Finish: Leather/black or tan
Carry: Strong side
Compatible Firearms: Subcompact, compact, and full-size pistols; small- and medium-frame revolvers
Features: Open muzzle; high ride; covered trigger guard; fits belts up to 1.8 in.
Belt: $65
Paddle: $77

FRONT POCKET

Use/Type: Concealment/pocket
Retention: None
Material/Finish: Leather/rough side out tan
Carry: Ambidextrous
Compatible Firearms: Subcompact pistols, small-frame revolvers
Features: Smooth leather inside
MSRP: $60

GALCO FRONT POCKET

Galco

(www.usgalco.com)

KINGTUK IWB

Use/Type: Concealment/belt, inside waistband
Retention: Thumb break
Material/Finish: Kydex and leather/ black
Carry: Strong side
Compatible Firearms: Compact and full-size pistols, small- and medium-frame revolvers
Features: Open muzzle; high ride; removable metal belt clips; allows shirt to be tucked; fits belts up to 1.8 in.
MSRP: $60

GALCO KINGTUK IWB

GALCO MOB

MIDDLE OF BACK (MOB)

Use/Type: Concealment/belt, inside waistband
Retention: Thumb break
Material/Finish: Leather/plain black
Carry: Middle of back
Compatible Firearms: Compact and full-size pistols, small- and medium-frame revolvers
Features: Reinforced opening; covered trigger guard; designed for palm-out draw; fits belts up to 1.8 in.
MSRP: $86

N3 IWB

Use/Type: Concealment/belt, inside waistband
Retention: None
Material/Finish: Leather/plain black
Carry: Strong side
Compatible Firearms: Compact and full-size pistols, small- and medium-frame revolvers

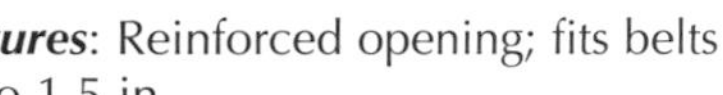

Features: Reinforced opening; fits belts up to 1.5 in.
MSRP: $77

GALCO N3 IWB

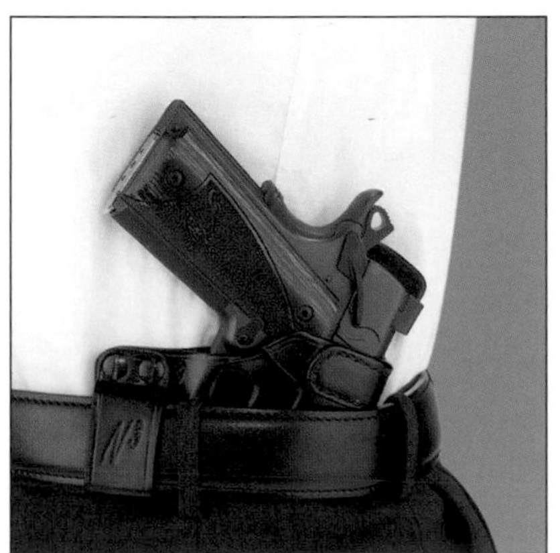

POCKET PROTECTOR

Use/Type: Concealment/pocket
Retention: None
Material/Finish: Leather/rough side out tan
Carry: Ambidextrous
Compatible Firearms: Subcompact pistols, small-frame revolvers
Features: Designed to catch on pocket during draw
MSRP: $25

PUSH UP

Use/Type: Concealment/belt, inside waistband
Retention: None
Material/Finish: Leather/natural
Carry: Strong side, inside waist band
Compatible Firearms: Subcompact pistols
Features: Low ride; fits belts up to 1.5 in.
MSRP: $50

GALCO PUSH UP

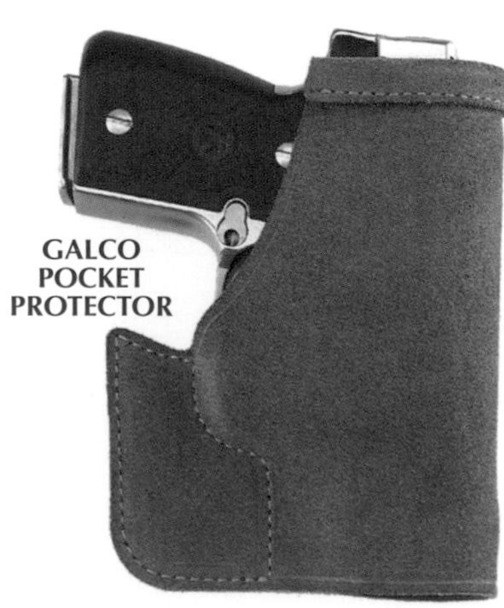

GALCO POCKET PROTECTOR

Galco

(www.usgalco.com)

ROYAL GUARD

Use/Type: Concealment/belt, inside waistband
Retention: None
Material/Finish: Leather/rough side out, tan or black
Carry: Strong side
Compatible Firearms: Compact and full-size pistols, small- and medium-frame revolvers
Features: Two belt loop snaps; fits belts up to 1.8 in.
MSRP: $129

GALCO ROYAL GUARD

SC2

Use/Type: Concealment/belt, inside waistband
Retention: Thumb break
Material/Finish: Leather/plain, black
Carry: Strong side
Compatible Firearms: Compact and full-size pistols, small- and medium-frame revolvers
Features: Two belt loop snaps; fits belts up to 1.8 in.
MSRP: $75

GALCO SC2

SCOUT

Use/Type: Concealment/belt, inside waistband
Retention: None
Material/Finish: Leather/plain, natural
Carry: Strong side or cross draw
Compatible Firearms: Subcompact, compact, and full-size pistols; small- and medium-frame revolvers
Features: Reinforced opening; fits belts up to 1.5 in.; hook
MSRP: $73

GALCO SCOUT

SKYOPS

Use/Type: Concealment/belt, inside waistband
Retention: None
Material/Finish: Leather/plain, natural
Carry: Strong side or cross draw
Compatible Firearms: Compact and full-size pistols
Features: Discrete belt hook; deep concealment; allows shirt to be tucked; fits belts up to 1.5 in.; hook
MSRP: $78

STOW-N-GO AND WALKABOUT

Use/Type: Concealment/belt, inside waistband
Retention: None
Material/Finish: Leather/natural
Carry: Strong side or cross draw
Compatible Firearms: Subcompact and compact pistols, small-frame revolvers
Features: No cant; fits belts up to 1.8 in.; clip
Stow-N-Go: $30
WalkAbout (built in magazine pouch): **$40**

SUMMER COMFORT

Use/Type: Concealment/belt, inside waistband
Retention: None
Material/Finish: Leather/plain, black
Carry: Strong side
Compatible Firearms: Compact and full-size pistols, small- and medium-frame revolvers
Features: Two belt loop snaps; lightweight; fits belts up to 1.8 in.
MSRP: $72

GALCO SUMMER COMFORT

GALCO SKYOPS

Galco

(www.usgalco.com)

TRITON IWB

Use/Type: Concealment/belt, inside waistband
Retention: Thumb break
Material/Finish: Kydex and leather/ black
Carry: Strong side
Compatible Firearms: Compact and full-size pistols, small- and medium-frame revolvers
Features: Open muzzle; high ride; fits belts up to 1.8 in.; clip
MSRP: $50

TUCK-N-GO

Use/Type: Concealment/belt, inside waistband
Retention: None
Material/Finish: Leather/natural
Carry: Strong side
Compatible Firearms: Subcompact and compact pistols, small-frame revolvers
Features: Reinforced top; allows shirt to be tucked; fits belts up to 1.5 in.; clip
MSRP: $30

ULTRA DEEP COVER (UDC)

Use/Type: Concealment/belt, inside waistband
Retention: None
Material/Finish: Leather/natural
Carry: Strong side
Compatible Firearms: Subcompact and compact pistols, small-frame revolvers

GALCO TRITON IWB

Features: Reinforced opening; allows shirt to be tucked; smooth leather interior; fits belts up to 1.3 in.; hook
MSRP: $79

USA ULTIMATE SECOND AMENDMENT

Use/Type: Concealment/belt, inside waistband
Retention: None
Material/Finish: Leather/natural
Carry: Strong side
Compatible Firearms: Subcompact and compact pistols, small-frame revolvers
Features: Allows shirt to be tucked; smooth leather interior; fits belts up to 1.3 in.; hook
MSRP: $70

GALCO TUCK-N-GO

V-HAWK

Use/Type: Concealment/belt, inside waistband
Retention: None
Material/Finish: Leather/plain, black
Carry: Strong side
Compatible Firearms: Compact and full-size pistols, small-frame revolvers
Features: Reinforced opening; two belt loop snaps or clip; fits belts up to 1.8 in.
MSRP: $112

WAISTBAND

Use/Type: Concealment/belt, inside waistband
Retention: Thumb break
Material/Finish: Leather/natural
Carry: Strong side or cross draw
Compatible Firearms: Subcompact and compact pistols, small-frame revolvers
Features: Smooth leather interior; no cant; fits belts up to 1.8 in.; clip
MSRP: $31

GALCO UDC

GALCO V-HAWK

GALCO WAISTBAND

Galco

(www.usgalco.com)

M5X MATRIX

Use/Type: Concealment/paddle
Retention: Two tension screws
Material/Finish: Injection molded polymer/black
Carry: Strong side
Compatible Firearms: Subcompact, compact, and full-size pistols
Features: Open muzzle
MSRP: $30

GALCO M5X MATRIX

CCP CONCEAL

CCP CONCEAL CARRY PADDLE

Use/Type: Concealment/paddle
Retention: None
Material/Finish: Leather/black or brown
Carry: Strong side or cross draw
Compatible Firearms: Compact and full-size pistols
Features: Open muzzle; adj. cant
MSRP: $117

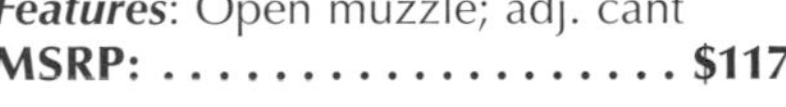

GALCO M4X MATRIX

GALCO FED PADDLE

FED PADDLE

Use/Type: Concealment/paddle
Retention: Thumb break
Material/Finish: Leather/black or tan
Carry: Strong side or cross draw
Compatible Firearms: Compact and full-size pistols
Features: Open muzzle; adj. cant; silicone suede lined
MSRP: $115

M4X MATRIX

Use/Type: Concealment/paddle
Retention: Thumb lever
Material/Finish: Injection molded polymer/black
Carry: Strong side
Compatible Firearms: Compact and full-size pistols
Features: Open muzzle
MSRP: $34

PADDLE LITE

Use/Type: Concealment/paddle
Retention: Thumb break
Material/Finish: Leather/black
Carry: Strong side or cross draw
Compatible Firearms: Subcompact, compact, and full-size pistols; small-frame revolvers
Features: Open muzzle
MSRP: $35

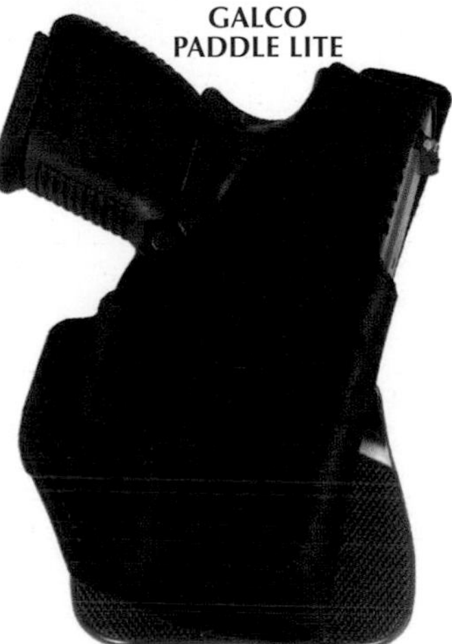

GALCO PADDLE LITE

Galco

(www.usgalco.com)

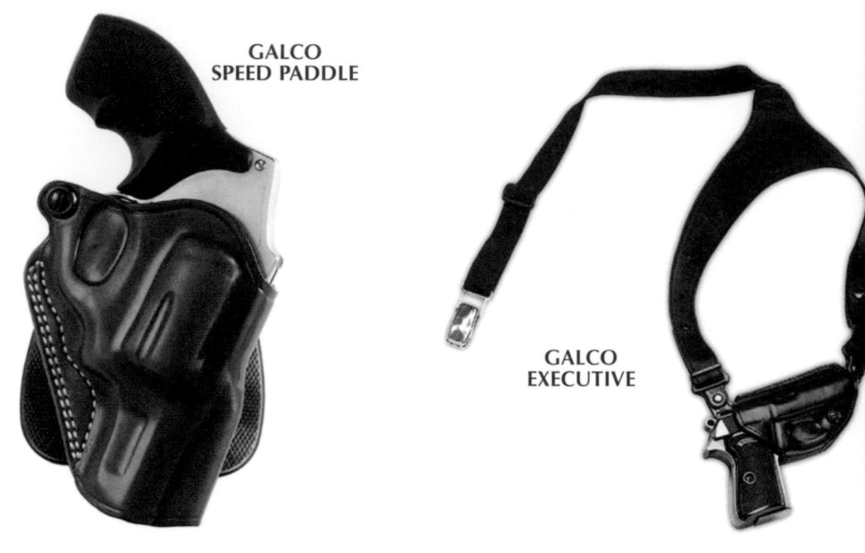

PLE PROFESSIONAL LAW ENFORCEMENT

Use/Type: Concealment/paddle
Retention: Thumb break
Material/Finish: Leather/black or tan
Carry: Strong side
Compatible Firearms: Subcompact, compact, and full-size pistols; small-frame revolvers
Features: Open muzzle
MSRP: $93

SPEED PADDLE

Use/Type: Concealment/paddle
Retention: Tension screw
Material/Finish: Leather/black or tan
Carry: Strong side
Compatible Firearms: Subcompact, compact, and full-size pistols; small-frame revolvers
Features: Open muzzle
MSRP: $75

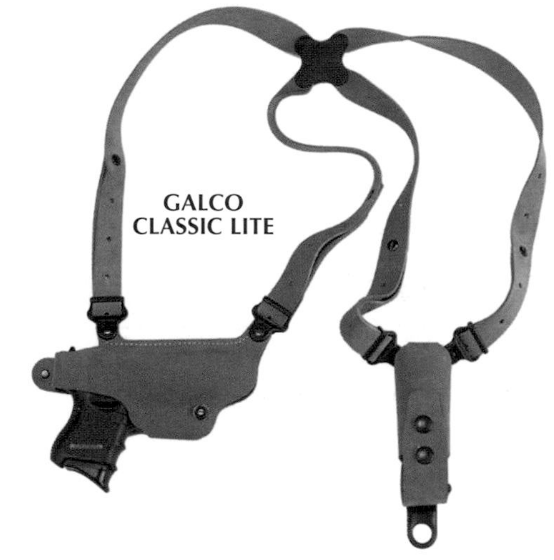

CLASSIC LITE

Use/Type: Concealment/shoulder
Retention: Thumb break
Material/Finish: Leather/natural
Carry: Cross draw
Compatible Firearms: Compact and full-size pistols, small-and medium-frame revolvers
Features: X-harness; two tie-down straps; single magazine pouch; horizontal carry
MSRP: $87

EXECUTIVE

Use/Type: Concealment/shoulder
Retention: Thumb break
Material/Finish: Leather/plain, black
Carry: Cross draw
Compatible Firearms: Subcompact and compact pistols, small-frame revolvers
Features: One tie-down strap; horizontal carry
MSRP: $200

JACKASS RIG

Use/Type: Concealment/shoulder
Retention: Thumb break
Material/Finish: Leather/plain, brown
Carry: Cross draw
Compatible Firearms: Compact and full-size pistols
Features: X-harness; two tie-down straps; two magazine pouches; adj. cant; modular system; horizontal carry
MSRP: $160

Galco

(www.usgalco.com)

MIAMI CLASSIC II

Use/Type: Concealment/shoulder
Retention: Thumb break
Material/Finish: Leather/plain, brown
Carry: Cross draw
Compatible Firearms: Compact and full-size pistols
Features: X-harness; two tie-down straps; two horizontal magazine pouches; modular system; horizontal carry
MSRP: $180

GALCO
MIAMI CLASSIC

MIAMI CLASSIC

Use/Type: Concealment/shoulder
Retention: Thumb break
Material/Finish: Leather/plain, brown
Carry: Cross draw
Compatible Firearms: Compact and full-size pistols
Features: X-harness; two tie-down straps; two vertical magazine pouches; modular system; horizontal carry
MSRP: $180

VHS

Use/Type: Concealment/shoulder
Retention: Strap
Material/Finish: Leather/plain, brown
Carry: Cross draw
Compatible Firearms: Compact and full-size pistols; small-, medium-, and large-frame revolvers
Features: X-harness; two tie-down straps; two vertical magazine pouches; modular system; vertical carry
MSRP: $190

GALCO
MIAMI CLASSIC II

Galco

(www.usgalco.com)

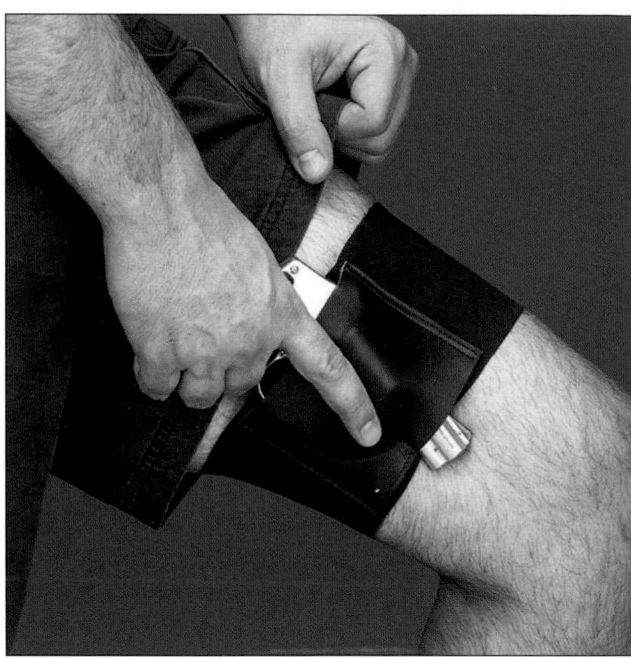

GALCO THIGH BAND

THIGH BAND

Use/Type: Concealment/thigh
Retention: None
Material/Finish: Leather/plain, black
Carry: Cross draw
Compatible Firearms: Compact and full-size pistols; small-, medium-, and large-frame revolvers
Features: Elastic band
MSRP: $57

UNDERWRAPS

Use/Type: Concealment/belly band
Retention: None
Material/Finish: Leather/plain, tan
Carry: Cross draw, strong side, or small of back
Compatible Firearms: Subcompact, compact, and full-size pistols; small-, medium-, and large-frame revolvers
Features: Elastic band; two handgun pockets; accessory pockets
MSRP: $53

GALCO UNDERWRAPS

HOLSTERS

Gould & Goodrich

(www.gouldusa.com)

B716 BOOTLOCK ANKLE

Use/Type: Concealment/ankle
Retention: Thumb break
Material/Finish: Leather/plain black
Carry: Cross draw
Compatible Firearms: Subcompact pistols, small-frame revolvers
Features: Designed to be worn over secured boot
MSRP: $113

GOULD & GOODRICH
B716 BOOTLOCK ANKLE

Gould & Goodrich

(www.gouldusa.com)

GOULD & GOODRICH B809 BELT SLIDE

GOULD & GOODRICH B816 ANKLE

B816 ANKLE PLUS GARTER

Use/Type: Concealment/ankle
Retention: Thumb break
Material/Finish: Leather/plain black
Carry: Cross draw
Compatible Firearms: Compact pistols, small-frame revolvers
Features: Adj. elastic thigh strap with garter; sheepskin liner
MSRP: $88

B809 BELT SLIDE

Use/Type: Concealment/belt
Retention: Thumb break
Material/Finish: Leather/black
Carry: Strong side
Compatible Firearms: Compact and full-size pistols
Features: Open muzzle; high ride; covered trigger guard; fits belts up to 1.8 in.
MSRP: $65

810 INSIDE PANTS

Use/Type: Concealment/inside waistband
Retention: Tension screw
Material/Finish: Leather/plain, brown
Carry: Strong side
Compatible Firearms: Compact and full-size pistols
Features: Two belt loop snaps; fits belts up to 1.8 in.
MSRP: $62

GOULD & GOODRICH 810 INSIDE PANTS

Gould & Goodrich

(www.gouldusa.com)

GOULD & GOODRICH 800 REIN-FORCED OPENING TWO SLOT

GOULD & GOODRICH 807 PADDLE

GOULD & GOODRICH 804 SHOULDER

800 REINFORCED OPENING TWO SLOT

Use/Type: Concealment/belt, pancake-style
Retention: None
Material/Finish: Leather/plain, brown or black
Carry: Strong side
Compatible Firearms: Compact and full-size pistols
Features: Open muzzle; fits belts up to 1.8 in.
MSRP: $65

807 PADDLE

Use/Type: Concealment/paddle
Retention: Thumb break
Material/Finish: Leather/plain black or brown
Carry: Strong side
Compatible Firearms: Compact and full-size pistols
Features: Open muzzle; flexible paddle wings
MSRP: $92

804 SHOULDER

Use/Type: Concealment/shoulder
Retention: Thumb break
Material/Finish: Leather/plain, brown or black
Carry: Cross draw
Compatible Firearms: Compact and full-size pistols
Features: Back swivel harness; two vertical magazine pouches; horizontal carry
MSRP: $164

GOULD & GOODRICH 806 SMALL-OF-BACK

806 SMALL-OF-BACK

Use/Type: Concealment/belt
Retention: Tension screw
Material/Finish: Leather/plain brown
Carry: Small of back
Compatible Firearms: Compact and full-size pistols, small- and medium-frame revolvers
Features: Reinforced opening; covered trigger guard; fits belts up to 1.5 in.
MSRP: $77

802 TWO-SLOT PANCAKE

Use/Type: Concealment/belt, pancake-style
Retention: None
Material/Finish: Leather/plain, black
Carry: Strong side
Compatible Firearms: Compact and full-size pistols
Features: Open muzzle; forward cant; fits belts up to 1.8 in.
MSRP: $67

GOULD & GOODRICH 802 TWO-SLOT PANCAKE

Gould & Goodrich

(www.gouldusa.com)

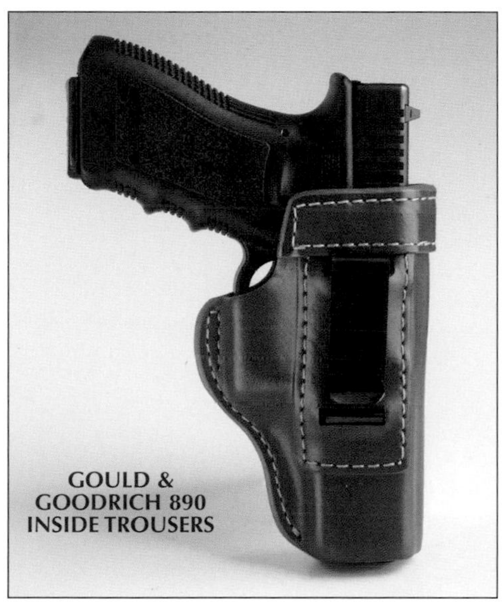

GOULD & GOODRICH 890 INSIDE TROUSERS

GOULD & GOODRICH 891 BELT SLIDE

803 THREE-SLOT PANCAKE

Use/Type: Concealment/belt, pancake-style
Retention: None
Material/Finish: Leather/plain, brown or black
Carry: Strong side
Compatible Firearms: Compact and full-size pistols
Features: Open muzzle; forward or vertical cant; fits belts up to 1.8 in.
MSRP: $67

801 YAQUI SLIDE

Use/Type: Concealment/belt
Retention: Two tension screws
Material/Finish: Leather/brown or black
Carry: Strong side
Compatible Firearms: Compact and full-size pistols
Features: Open muzzle; covered trigger guard; fits belts up to 2 in.
MSRP: $47

890 INSIDE TROUSERS

Use/Type: Concealment/belt
Retention: None
Material/Finish: Leather/brown or black
Carry: Strong side
Compatible Firearms: Subcompact, compact, and full-size pistols; small-frame revolvers
Features: Open muzzle; covered trigger guard; fits belts up to 1.8 in.
MSRP: $29

891 BELT SLIDE

Use/Type: Concealment/belt, inside waistband
Retention: None
Material/Finish: Leather/brown or black
Carry: Strong side
Compatible Firearms: Subcompact, compact, and full-size pistols; small-frame revolvers
Features: Open muzzle; covered trigger guard; fits belts up to 1.8 in.; metal clip
MSRP: $34

GOULD & GOODRICH 803 THREE-SLOT PANCAKE

Gould & Goodrich

(www.gouldusa.com)

T727 THE BODY GUARD

Use/Type: Concealment/belly band
Retention: None
Material/Finish: Leather/plain, tan
Carry: Cross draw, strong side, or small of back
Compatible Firearms: Subcompact, compact, and full-size pistols; small-, medium-, and large-frame revolvers
Features: Elastic band with hook and loop closure; one handgun pocket; two accessory pockets
MSRP: **$50**

701 POCKET

Use/Type: Concealment/pocket
Retention: None
Material/Finish: Leather/plain tan
Carry: Ambidextrous
Compatible Firearms: Subcompact pistols, small-frame revolvers
Features: Open muzzle; no-slip outer layer; suede lined
MSRP: **$17**

GOULD & GOODRICH 701 POCKET

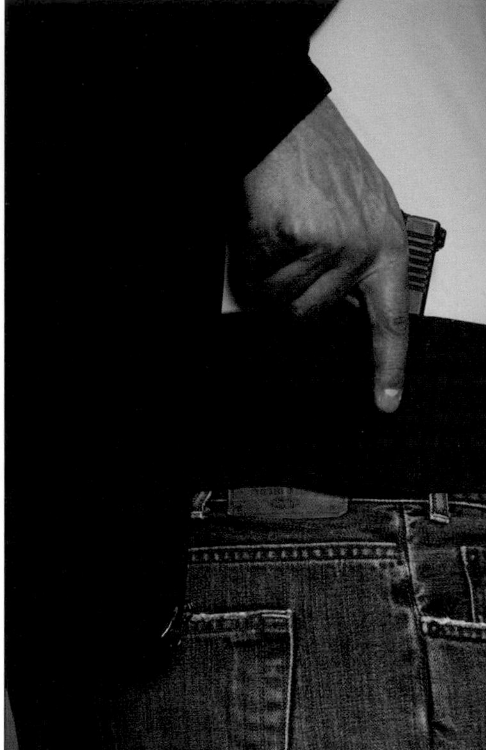

GOULD & GOODRICH
T727 THE BODY GUARD

HOLSTERS

Hunter

(www.huntercompany.com)

2800 THREE-SLOT PANCAKE

Use/Type: Concealment/belt, pancake-style
Retention: None
Material/Finish: Leather/plain, brown
Carry: Strong side
Compatible Firearms: Full-size pistols
Features: Open muzzle; forward or vertical cant; fits belts up to 1.8 in.
MSRP: **$80**

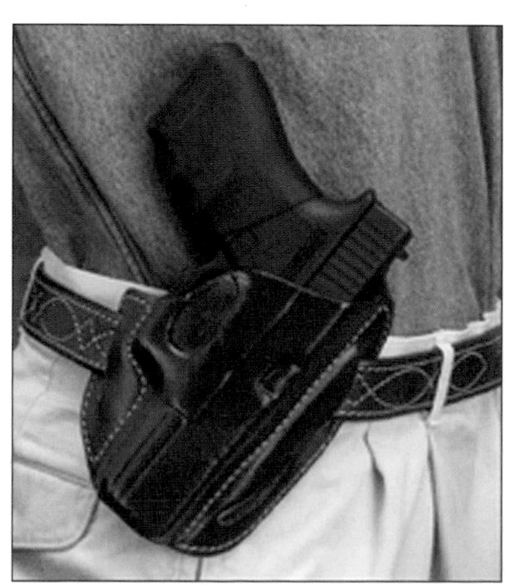

HUNTER 2800
THREE-SLOT
PANCAKE

Hunter

(www.huntercompany.com)

HUNTER 4800 PADDLE

HUNTER 4900 CROSSDRAW

HUNTER 5000

4800 PADDLE

Use/Type: Concealment/paddle
Retention: Thumb break
Material/Finish: Leather/plain, brown
Carry: Strong side
Compatible Firearms: Full-size pistols
Features: Open muzzle; Kydex paddle
MSRP: $100

4900 CROSSDRAW

Use/Type: Concealment/belt
Retention: Thumb break and tension screw
Material/Finish: Leather/plain, brown
Carry: Strong side
Compatible Firearms: Full-size pistols
Features: Open muzzle; fits belts up to 1.8 in.
MSRP: $95

5000

Use/Type: Concealment/belt
Retention: Thumb break
Material/Finish: Leather/plain, brown
Carry: Strong side
Compatible Firearms: Full-size pistols; small-, medium-, and large-revolvers
Features: Open muzzle; fits belts up to 1.8 in.
MSRP: $80

5200 REINFORCED OPENING

Use/Type: Concealment/belt
Retention: Tension screw
Material/Finish: Leather/plain, brown

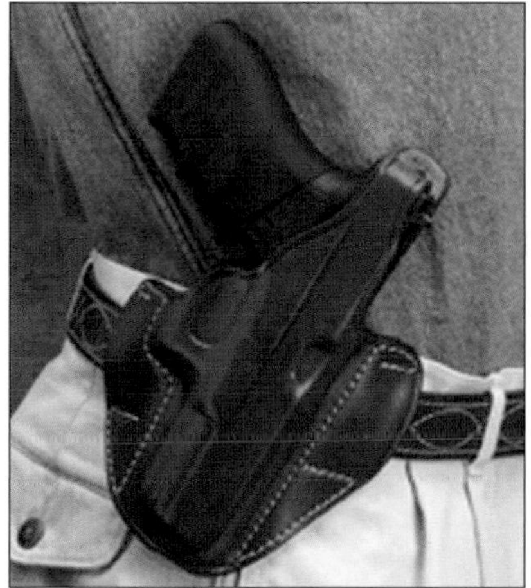

HUNTER 5300

Carry: Strong side
Compatible Firearms: Full-size pistols; small-, medium-, and large-revolvers
Features: Open muzzle; reinforced opening; fits belts up to 1.8 in.
MSRP: $70

5300

Use/Type: Concealment/belt, pancake-style
Retention: Thumb break
Material/Finish: Leather/plain, brown
Carry: Strong side
Compatible Firearms: Full-size pistols
Features: Open muzzle; forward or vertical cant; fits belts up to 1.8 in.
MSRP: $82

HUNTER 5200 REINFORCED OPENING

5100 SHOULDER

Use/Type: Concealment/shoulder
Retention: Thumb break
Material/Finish: Leather/plain, brown
Carry: Cross draw
Compatible Firearms: Compact and full-size pistols, small-frame revolvers
Features: Suede harness; two vertical magazine pouch; horizontal carry
MSRP: $167

Hunter

(www.huntercompany.com)

HUNTER 1300 INSIDE-THE-PANTS

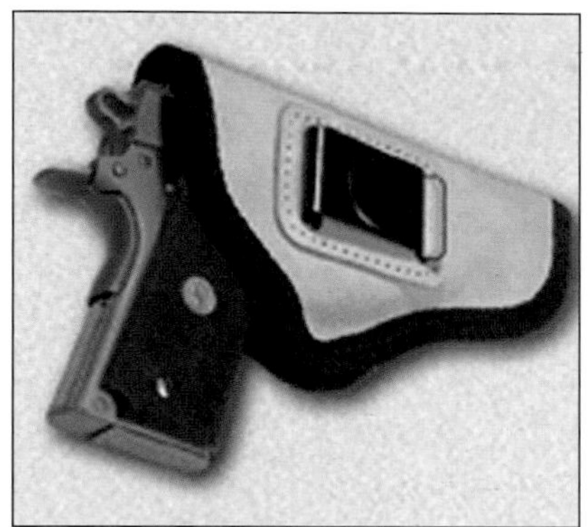

HUNTER 2500 POCKET

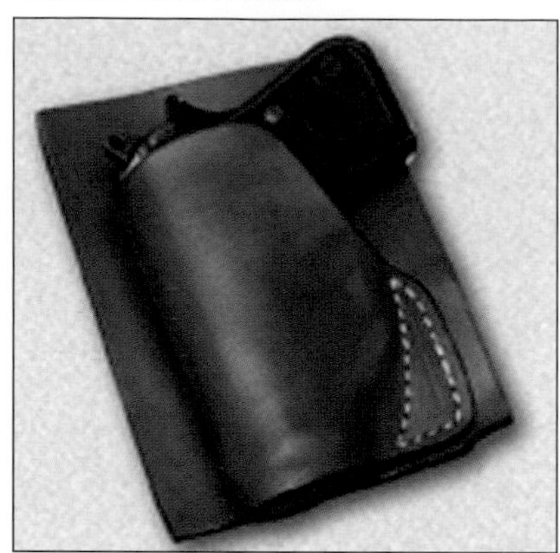

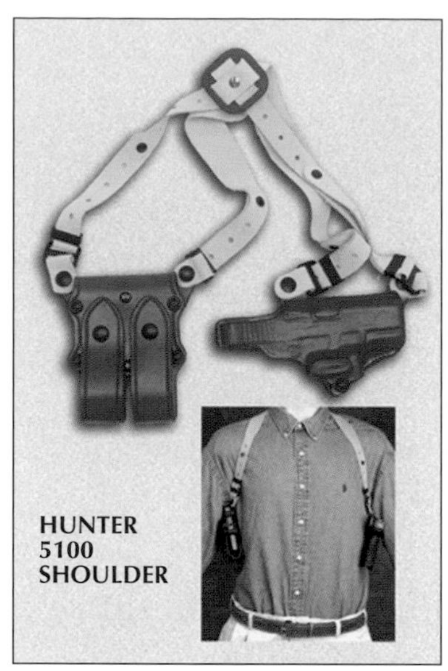

HUNTER 5100 SHOULDER

1300 INSIDE-THE-PANTS

Use/Type: Concealment/belt
Retention: None
Material/Finish: Leather/suede natural
Carry: Strong side
Compatible Firearms: Subcompact, compact, and full-size pistols; small-frame revolvers
Features: Open muzzle; covered trigger guard; fits belts up to 1.8 in.; metal clip
MSRP: $23

2500 POCKET

Use/Type: Concealment/pocket
Retention: None
Material/Finish: Leather/plain tan
Carry: Strong side
Compatible Firearms: Subcompact pistols, small-frame revolvers
Features: Open muzzle
MSRP: $31

Ross Leather

(www.rossleather.com)

M2, M4 and M4H FIELD

Use/Type: Concealment/belt, pancake-style
Retention: Thumb break
Material/Finish: Leather/plain or basketweave, tan or black
Carry: Strong side
Compatible Firearms: Compact and full-size pistols; small-, medium-, and large-frame revolvers
Features: Closed bottom for revolvers; open muzzle for pistols; forward cant; low ride; fits belts up to 1.8 in.
M2: $78
M4 (high ride):. **$84**
M4H (designed for hammerless revolvers, open muzzle, reinforced opening, high ride): **$84**

ROSS M2 FIELD

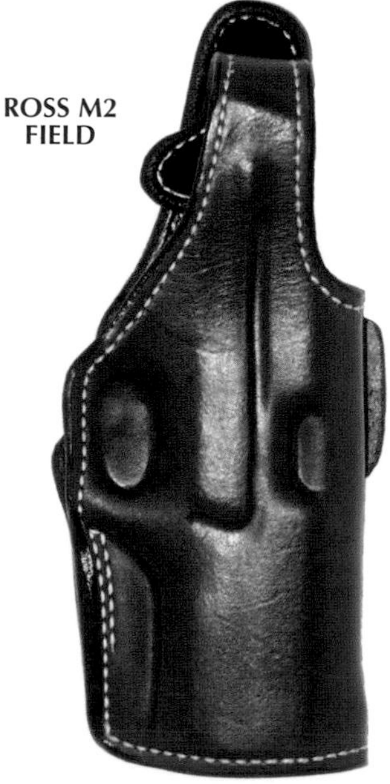

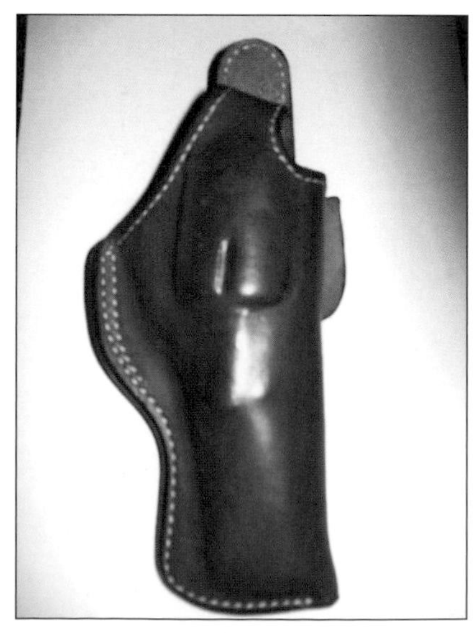

ROSS M4 FIELD

Ross Leather

(www.rossleather.com)

ROSS M4H FIELD

ROSS M3L SPEED SCABBARD

M3L SPEED SCABBARD

Use/Type: Concealment/belt
Retention: Two tension screws
Material/Finish: Leather/plain, tan or black
Carry: Strong side
Compatible Firearms: Compact and full-size pistols; small-, medium-, and large-frame revolvers
Features: Open muzzle; fits belts up to 1.8 in.
MSRP: **$85**
M4 (high ride):. **$84**
M4H (designed for hammerless revolvers, open muzzle, reinforced opening, high ride): **$84**

M5 FORWARD-CANT PANCAKE

Use/Type: Concealment/belt, pancake-style
Retention: Thumb break
Material/Finish: Leather/plain or basketweave, tan or black
Carry: Strong side
Compatible Firearms: Subcompact, compact, and full-size pistols; small-, medium-, and large-frame revolvers
Features: Closed bottom; forward or vertical cant; fits belts up to 1.8 in.
M5: **$82**
M5N (open muzzle): **$82**
M5WN (open muzzle, no thumb break): **$82**

M6 SMALL-OF-BACK

Use/Type: Concealment/belt
Retention: None
Material/Finish: Leather/plain or basketweave, tan or black
Carry: Small of back
Compatible Firearms: Compact and full-size pistols, small- and medium-frame revolvers
Features: Reinforced opening; covered trigger guard; fits belts up to 1.5 in.
MSRP: **$86**

M7 STINGRAY

Use/Type: Concealment/belt
Retention: None
Material/Finish: Leather/plain or basketweave, tan or black
Carry: Strong side
Compatible Firearms: Subcompact, compact, and full-size pistols; small-, medium-, and large-frame revolvers
Features: Open muzzle; forward cant; fits belts up to 1.8 in.
MSRP: **$75**

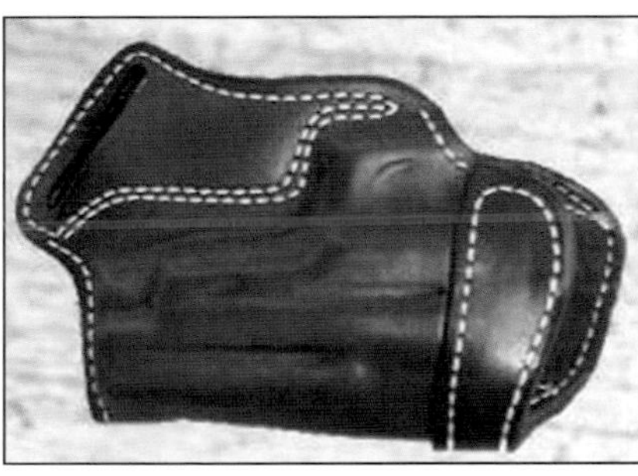

ROSS M6 SMALL-OF-BACK

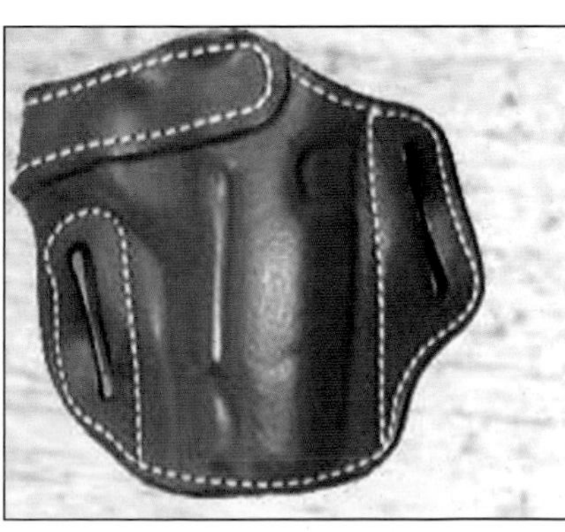

ROSS M7 STINGRAY

Ross Leather

(www.rossleather.com)

M8 and M9 BELT SLIDE

Use/Type: Concealment/belt
Retention: Thumb break
Material/Finish: Leather/plain or basketweave, tan or black
Carry: Strong side
Compatible Firearms: Subcompact, compact, and full-size pistols; small-, medium-, and large-frame revolvers
Features: Open muzzle; forward cant; fits belts up to 1.8 in.
M8: $77
M9 (no thumb break): **. $71**

ROSS M8 BELT SLIDE WITH THUMB BREAK

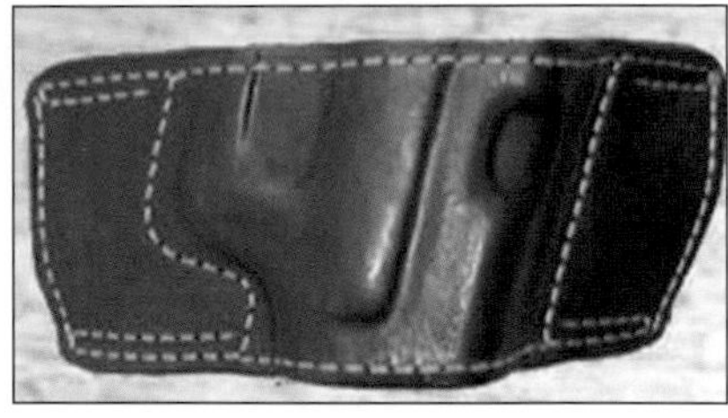

ROSS M9 BELT SLIDE

M10L and M10LC MINI BELT SLIDE

Use/Type: Concealment/belt
Retention: None
Material/Finish: Leather/plain, tan or black
Carry: Strong side
Compatible Firearms: Subcompact, compact, and full-size pistols; small-, medium-, and large-frame revolvers
Features: Open muzzle; fits belts up to 1.8 in.
M10L:. $68
M10LC (j-hook): **. $72**

ROSS M10LC BELT SLIDE WITH HOOK

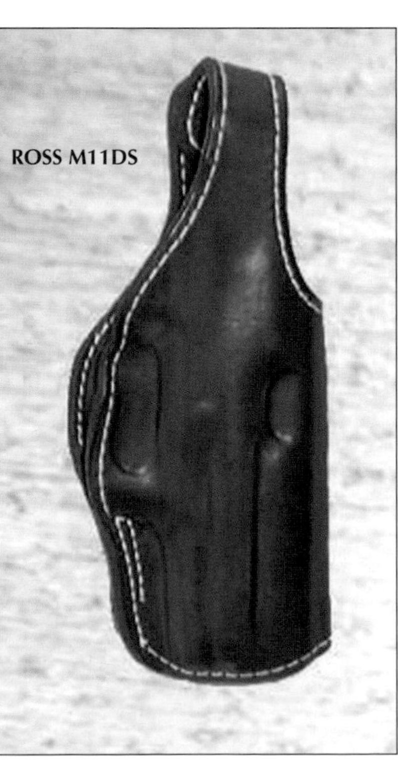

ROSS M11DS

M11DS TWO-POSITION FIELD

Use/Type: Concealment/belt
Retention: Thumb break
Material/Finish: Leather/plain or basketweave, tan or black
Carry: Strong side or cross draw
Compatible Firearms: Compact and full-size pistols; small-, medium-, and large-frame revolvers
Features: Closed bottom for revolvers; open muzzle for pistols; suede lined; fits belts up to 1.8 in.
MSRP: $101

M12 ASKINS AVENGER

Use/Type: Concealment/belt
Retention: None
Material/Finish: Leather/plain or basketweave, tan or black
Carry: Strong side
Compatible Firearms: Compact and full-size pistols; small-, medium-, and large-frame revolvers
Features: Open muzzle; fits belts up to 1.8 in.
MSRP: $75

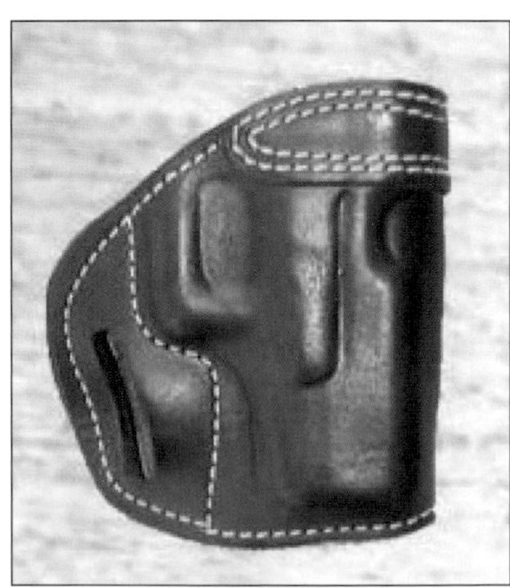

ROSS M12 ASKINS AVENGER

Ross Leather

(www.rossleather.com)

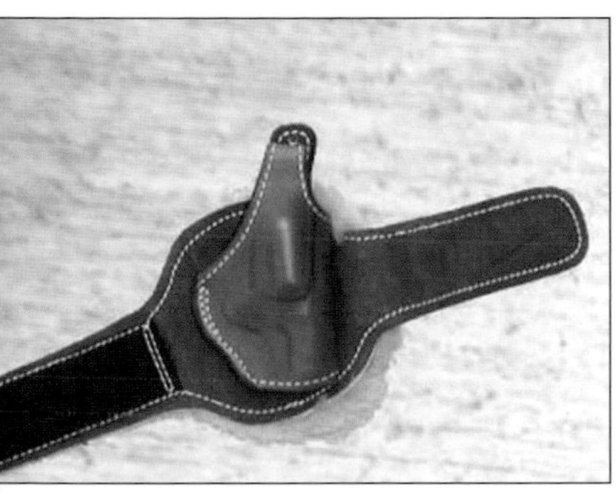

ROSS M13 ANKLE

ROSS M14A

M13 and M13H ANKLE

Use/Type: Concealment/ankle
Retention: Thumb break
Material/Finish: Leather/plain or basketweave, tan or black
Carry: Cross draw
Compatible Firearms: Compact pistols, small-frame revolvers
Features: Velcro strap; sheepskin liner; open muzzle
M13: **$93**
M13H (designed for hammerless revolvers): **$93**

M14 SUEDE J-HOOK

Use/Type: Concealment/belt
Retention: None
Material/Finish: Leather/suede, natural
Carry: Strong side
Compatible Firearms: Subcompact, compact, and full-size pistols; small-, medium-, and large-frame revolvers
Features: Open muzzle; fits belts up to 1.8 in.
M14: **$41**
M14A (plain tan finish): **$53**

M15 ROUGH-SIDE-OUT TUCK

Use/Type: Concealment/belt
Retention: None
Material/Finish: Leather/suede, natural
Carry: Strong side
Compatible Firearms: Subcompact, compact, and full-size pistols; small-, medium-, and large-frame revolvers
Features: Open muzzle; allows shirt to be tucked; metal j-hook
MSRP: **$67**

M16 SNAP-ON BELT LOOP

Use/Type: Concealment/belt
Retention: None
Material/Finish: Leather/plain, tan or black
Carry: Strong side
Compatible Firearms: Compact and full-size pistols; small-, medium-, and large-frame revolvers
Features: Open muzzle; body shield; suede lined; metal j-hook
MSRP: **$84**

ROSS M14

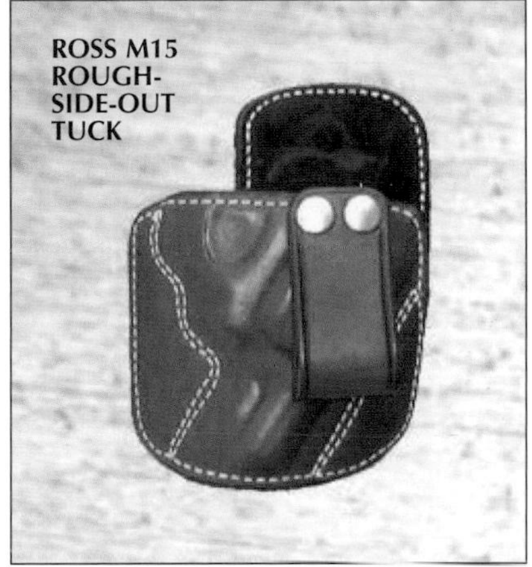

ROSS M15 ROUGH-SIDE-OUT TUCK

ROSS M16 SNAP-ON BELT LOOP

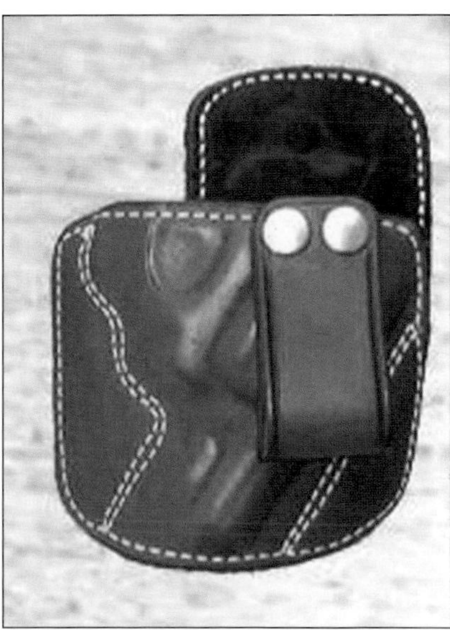

Ross Leather

(www.rossleather.com)

M17 ROUGH-SIDE-OUT BELT LOOP

Use/Type: Concealment/belt
Retention: None
Material/Finish: Leather/plain, tan
Carry: Strong side
Compatible Firearms: Compact and full-size pistols; small-, medium-, and large-frame revolvers
Features: Open muzzle; body shield; metal j-hook
MSRP: $84

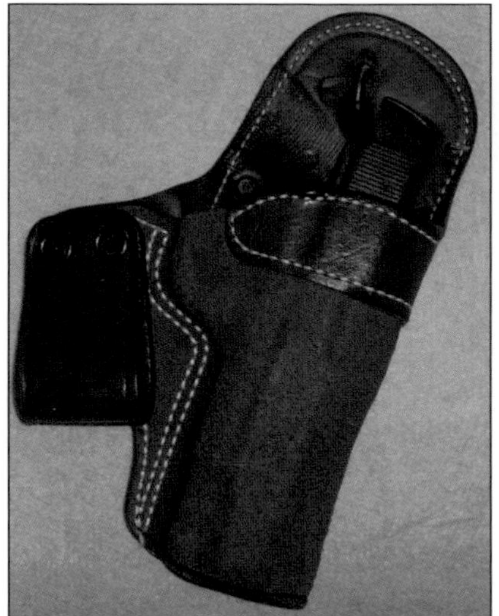

ROSS M17 ROUGH-SIDE-OUT BELT LOOP

ROSS M18TB SNAP-ON BELT LOOP WITH THUMB BREAK

M18 and M18TB SNAP-ON BELT LOOP

Use/Type: Concealment/belt
Retention: None
Material/Finish: Leather/plain, tan or black
Carry: Strong side
Compatible Firearms: Compact and full-size pistols; small-, medium-, and large-frame revolvers
Features: Open muzzle; suede lined; metal j-hook
M18: $82
M18TB (thumb break): **$90**

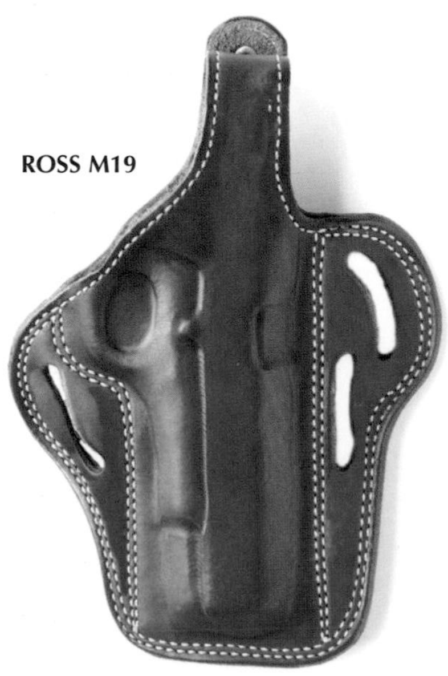

ROSS M19

M19 TWO-POSITION PANCAKE

Use/Type: Concealment/belt, pancake-style
Retention: Thumb break
Material/Finish: Leather/plain or basketweave, tan or black
Carry: Strong side or cross draw
Compatible Firearms: Subcompact, compact, and full-size pistols; small-, medium-, and large-frame revolvers
Features: Closed bottom; forward or vertical cant; fits belts up to 1.8 in.
M19: $79
M19N (open muzzle): **$79**
M19WN (open muzzle, no thumb break): **$79**

ROSS M18S SNAP-ON-BELT LOOP

M22LC CROSSDRAW

Use/Type: Concealment/belt
Retention: None
Material/Finish: Leather/plain or basketweave, tan or black
Carry: Cross draw
Compatible Firearms: Compact and full-size pistols; small-, medium-, and large-frame revolvers
Features: Open muzzle; low ride; fits belts up to 1.8 in.
MSRP: $96

ROSS M22LC CROSSDRAW

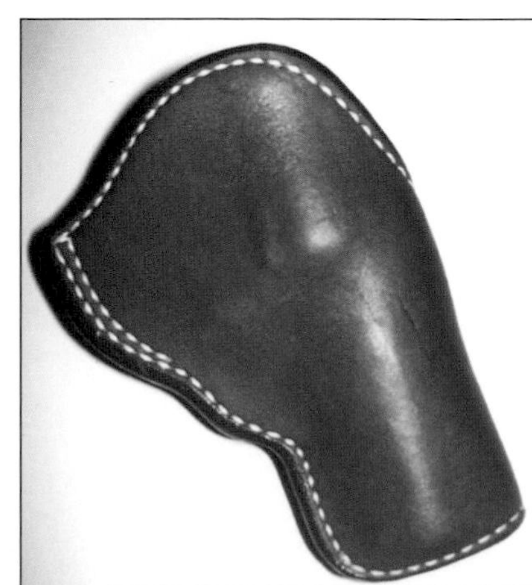

Ross Leather

(www.rossleather.com)

M23 CROSSDRAW DRIVING

Use/Type: Concealment/belt
Retention: Thumb break
Material/Finish: Leather/plain or basketweave, tan or black
Carry: Cross draw
Compatible Firearms: Compact and full-size pistols; small-, medium-, and large-frame revolvers
Features: Open muzzle; fits belts up to 1.8 in.
MSRP: $92

ROSS M23 CROSSDRAW DRIVING

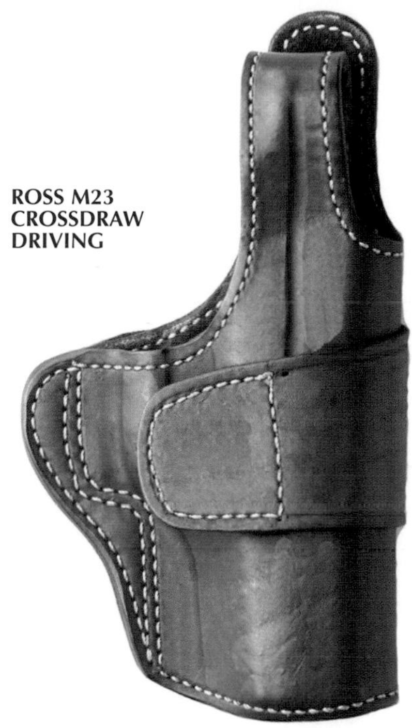

ROSS PD1 PADDLE

PD1 PADDLE

Use/Type: Concealment/paddle
Retention: None
Material/Finish: Leather/plain or basketweave, tan or black
Carry: Strong side
Compatible Firearms: Full-size pistols, Compact and full-size pistols; small-, medium-, and large-frame revolvers
Features: Open muzzle
MSRP: $94

POC1 POCKET

Use/Type: Concealment/pocket
Retention: None
Material/Finish: Leather/plain tan
Carry: Ambidextrous
Compatible Firearms: Subcompact pistols, small-frame revolvers
Features: Closed bottom
MSRP: $48

ROSS POC1 POCKET

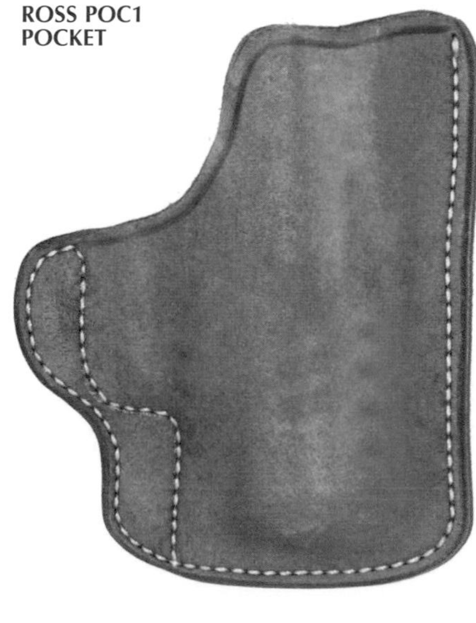

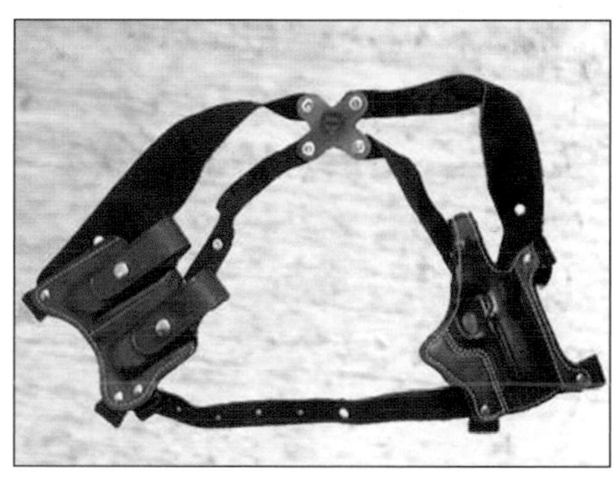

ROSS M42A HORIZONTAL SHOULDER

M42 and M42A HORIZONTAL SHOULDER

Use/Type: Concealment/shoulder
Retention: Thumb break
Material/Finish: Leather/plain, tan or black
Carry: Cross draw
Compatible Firearms: Compact and full-size pistols, small-fame revolvers
Features: Elastic and leather harness; horizontal carry
M42: $125
M42A (leather harness, two vertical magazine pouch): **. . $173**

M43 and M43A VERTICAL SHOULDER

Use/Type: Concealment/shoulder
Retention: Strap
Material/Finish: Leather/plain, tan or black
Carry: Cross draw
Compatible Firearms: Compact and full-size pistols, small-fame revolvers
Features: Elastic and leather harness; closed muzzle; vertical carry
M43: $125
M43D (leather harness, two vertical magazine pouch): **. . $173**

ROSS M43D

Safariland

(www.safariland.com)

SAFARILAND 18 IWB

SAFARILAND 0701 CONCELAMENT BELT

SAFARILAND 25 INSIDE-THE-POCKET

SAFARILAND 329 CONTOUR CONCEALMENT

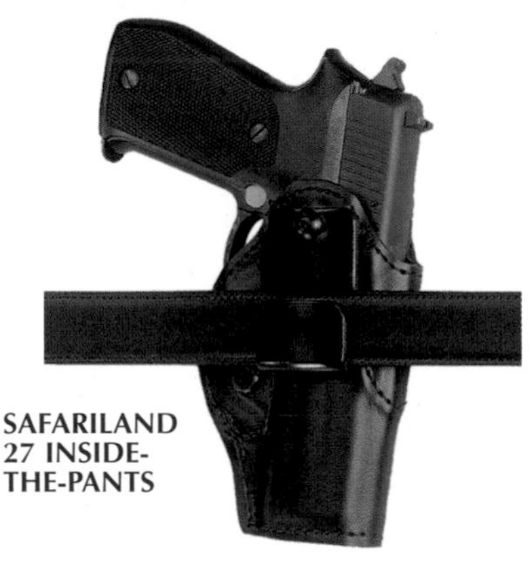
SAFARILAND 27 INSIDE-THE-PANTS

SAFARILAND 328 PANCAKE

0701 CONCEALMENT BELT

Use/Type: Concealment/belt
Retention: Strap and internal lock
Material/Finish: Laminate/STX Tactical black
Carry: Strong side
Compatible Firearms: Compact and full-size pistols
Features: Open muzzle; midride; forward cant
MSRP: $75

18 IWB

Use/Type: Concealment/belt
Retention: None
Material/Finish: Safarilaminate, synthetic suede/black
Carry: Strong side
Compatible Firearms: Subcompact pistols, small-frame revolvers
Features: Reinforced opening; double snap loops; adj. cant; fits belts up to 1.5 in.
MSRP: $78

25 INSIDE-THE-POCKET

Use/Type: Concealment/pocket
Retention: None
Material/Finish: Leather/plain black
Carry: Ambidextrous
Compatible Firearms: Small-frame revolvers
Features: Extra thin leather
MSRP: $37

27 INSIDE-THE-PANTS

Use/Type: Concealment/belt
Retention: None
Material/Finish: Leather/plain black
Carry: Strong side
Compatible Firearms: Subcompact pistols, small-frame revolvers
Features: Open muzzle; j-hook
MSRP: $46

328 PANCAKE

Use/Type: Concealment/belt, pancake-style, 1.8 in., three slots
Retention: Thumb break
Material/Finish: Leather/plain black
Carry: Strong side or cross draw
Compatible Firearms: Subcompact, compact, and full-size pistols; small- and medium-frame revolvers
Features: Open muzzle; high ride
MSRP: $64

329 CONTOUR CONCEALMENT

Use/Type: Concealment/belt
Retention: Thumb break, tension screw
Material/Finish: Safarilaminate/plain black
Carry: Strong side
Compatible Firearms: Compact and full-size pistols
Features: Designed for women; open muzzle; low-cut front; fits belts up to 1.3 in.
MSRP: $87

HOLSTERS

Safariland

(www.safariland.com)

SAFARILAND 4092 ANKLE

SAFARILAND 518 PADDLE

SAFARILAND 5181 OPEN-TOP PADDLE

SAFARILAND 5187 BELT

4092 ANKLE

Use/Type: Concealment/ankle
Retention: Thumb break
Material/Finish: Leather, nylon/plain black
Carry: Cross draw
Compatible Firearms: Small-frame revolvers
Features: Attaches to shoe
MSRP: $66

518 PADDLE

Use/Type: Concealment/paddle
Retention: Thumb break, tension screw
Material/Finish: Leather/plain or basketweave black
Carry: Strong side
Compatible Firearms: Subcompact, compact, and full-size pistols; small- and medium-frame revolvers
Features: Open muzzle
MSRP: $84

5181 OPEN-TOP PADDLE

Use/Type: Concealment/paddle
Retention: Tension screw
Material/Finish: Leather/plain or STX Tactical black
Carry: Strong side
Compatible Firearms: Subcompact, compact, and full-size pistols; small- and medium-frame revolvers
Features: Open muzzle
MSRP: . . . .$54–$62

5187 BELT

Use/Type: Concealment/belt
Retention: Tension screw
Material/Finish: Safarilaminate/plain black
Carry: Strong side
Compatible Firearms: Compact and full-size pistols
Features: Open muzzle; adj. belt loop
MSRP: $34

5188 CONCEALMENT PADDLE

Use/Type: Concealment/paddle
Retention: Tension screw
Material/Finish: Safarilaminate/STX plain black
Carry: Strong side
Compatible Firearms: Compact and full-size pistols
Features: Open muzzle; suede lining
MSRP: . . . .$39–$54

5189 OPEN-TOP, CLIP-ON

Use/Type: Concealment/belt
Retention: Tension screw
Material/Finish: Safarilaminate/STX plain black
Carry: Strong side
Compatible Firearms: Compact and full-size pistols
Features: Open muzzle; clip
MSRP: $34

527 PANCAKE

Use/Type: Concealment/belt, pancake-style
Retention: None
Material/Finish: Leather/plain black
Carry: Strong side
Compatible Firearms: Subcompact, compact, and full-size pistols; small- and medium-frame revolvers
Features: Open muzzle; high ride; forward cant; fits belts up to 1.8 in.; two slots
MSRP: $47

SAFARILAND 5188 CONCEALMENT PADDLE

SAFARILAND 5189 OPEN-TOP CLIP-ON

SAFARILAND 527 PANCAKE

Safariland

(www.safariland.com)

SAFARILAND 529 OPEN-TOP CONCCEALMENT BELT SLIDE

SAFARILAND 6287 SLS CONCEALMENT

SAFARILAND 567 CUSTOM FIT

SAFARILAND 6367 ALS BELT SLIDE

529 OPEN-TOP CONCEALMENT BELT SLIDE

Use/Type: Concealment/belt
Retention: None
Material/Finish: Safarilaminate/STX plain black
Carry: Strong side
Compatible Firearms: Compact and full-size pistols
Features: Open muzzle; two-snap belt loops; fits belts up to 1.8 in.
MSRP: $94

567 CUSTOM FIT

Use/Type: Concealment/belt
Retention: Two tension screws
Material/Finish: Safarilaminate/carbon fiber or STX plain black
Carry: Strong side
Compatible Firearms: Subcompact, compact, and full-size pistols; small- and medium-frame revolvers
Features: Open muzzle; suede lined
MSRP: $48

568 CUSTOM FIT PADDLE

Use/Type: Concealment/paddle
Retention: Two tension screws
Material/Finish: Safarilaminate/carbon fiber or STX plain black
Carry: Strong side or cross draw
Compatible Firearms: Subcompact, compact, and full-size pistols; small- and medium-frame revolvers
Features: Open muzzle; suede lined
MSRP: $53

569 CUSTOM FIT BELT CLIP

Use/Type: Concealment/belt
Retention: Two tension screws
Material/Finish: Safarilaminate/carbon fiber or STX plain black
Carry: Strong side
Compatible Firearms: Subcompact, compact, and full-size pistols; small- and medium-frame revolvers
Features: Open muzzle; suede lined; clip
MSRP: $48

6287 SLS CONCEALMENT

Use/Type: Concealment/belt
Retention: Tension screw
Material/Finish: Safarilaminate/plain black or STX Tactical
Carry: Strong side
Compatible Firearms: Subcompact, compact, and full-size pistols; small- and medium-frame revolvers
Features: Open muzzle; semi-high ride; forward cant
MSRP: . . . . $87–$120

6367 ALS BELT SLIDE

Use/Type: Concealment/belt
Retention: Thumb break, tension screw, thumb lever
Material/Finish: Safarilaminate /plain black or STX Tactical
Carry: Strong side
Compatible Firearms: Compact and full-size pistols
Features: Open muzzle; high ride; forward cant
MSRP: . . . . $103–$123

6377 ALS BELT

Use/Type: Concealment/belt
Retention: Thumb lever, tension screw
Material/Finish: Safarilaminate/carbon fiber or STX plain black
Carry: Strong side
Compatible Firearms: Subcompact, compact and full-size pistols; small- and medium-frame revolvers
Features: Open muzzle; semi-high ride; forward cant
MSRP: . . . . $48–$58

6377 ALS PADDLE

Use/Type: Concealment/paddle
Retention: Thumb lever, tension screw
Material/Finish: Safarilaminate/STX plain black
Carry: Strong side
Compatible Firearms: Compact and full-size pistols
Features: Open muzzle; semi-high ride; forward cant
MSRP: . . . . $54–$69

SAFARILAND 6377 ALS BELT

Safariland

(www.safariland.com)

SAFARILAND 6379 ALS CLIP-ON

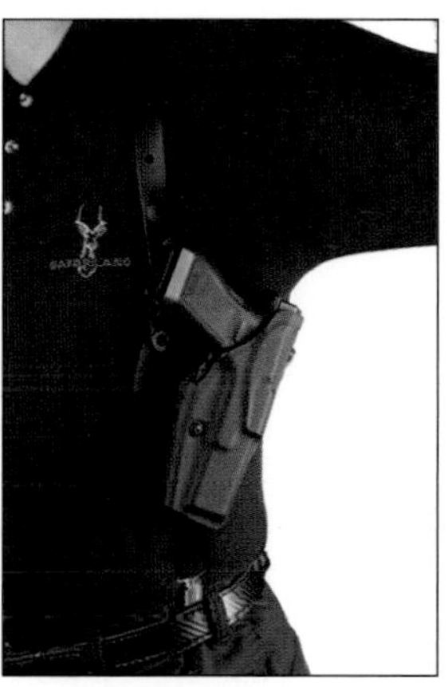

SAFARILAND 1051 ALS SHOULDER

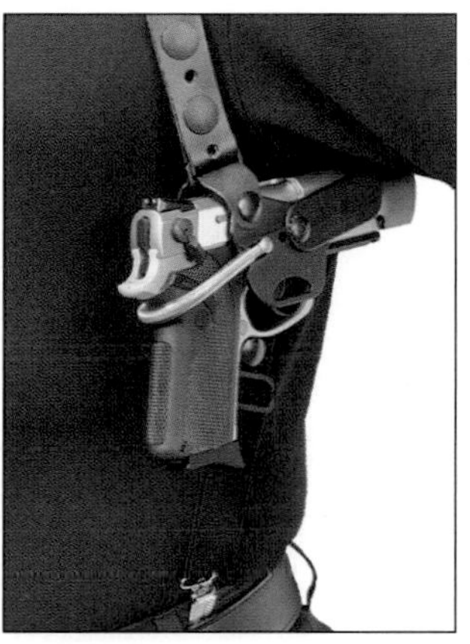

SAFARILAND 1090 "GUN QUICK" SHOULDER

SAFARIALND 3084 MILITARY TACTICAL

6379 ALS CLIP-ON

Use/Type: Concealment/belt
Retention: Thumb lever, tension screw
Material/Finish: Safarilaminate/carbon fiber or STX plain black
Carry: Strong side
Compatible Firearms: Compact and full-size pistols
Features: Open muzzle; low ride; adj. cant; clip
MSRP: . . . .$48–$58

474 PANCAKE CONCEALMENT

Use/Type: Concealment/belt, pancake-style
Retention: Thumb break
Material/Finish: Leather/plain black
Carry: Strong side
Compatible Firearms: Compact and full-size pistols
Features: Open muzzle; fits belts up to 1.8 in.; two slots
MSRP: $68

478 THUMBSNAP CONCEALMENT

Use/Type: Concealment/belt
Retention: Thumb break
Material/Finish: Leather/plain black
Carry: Strong side
Compatible Firearms: Compact and full-size pistols
Features: Open muzzle; two-snap belt loops; fits belts up to 1.8 in.
MSRP: . . . .$33–$37

1051 ALS SHOULDER

Use/Type: Concealment/shoulder
Retention: Thumb lever, tension screw
Material/Finish: Safarilaminate/plain black
Carry: Cross draw
Compatible Firearms: Compact and full-size pistols
Features: Horizontal or vertical carry; tie-down strap
MSRP: $161

1090 "GUN QUICK" SHOULDER

Use/Type: Concealment/shoulder
Retention: Spring
Material/Finish: Safarilaminate/plain black
Carry: Cross draw
Compatible Firearms: Compact and full-size pistols
Features: Tie-down strap; horizontal carry
MSRP: $125

3084 and 3085 MILITARY TACTICAL

Use/Type: Tactical/thigh
Retention: Rotating hood
Material/Finish: Safarilaminate/plain black or STX FDE brown
Carry: Ambidextrous
Compatible Firearms: Beretta M9 or 92F
Features: Double leg straps; accommodates light-mounted pistols
3084 (plain black): **. $190**
3085 (STX FDE brown): **. $200**

3280 MILITARY MIDRIDE

Use/Type: Tactical/belt
Retention: Rotating hood
Material/Finish: Safarilaminate/STX Tactical, FDE brown, OD, foliage green
Carry: Ambidextrous
Compatible Firearms: Beretta M9 or 92F
Features: Accommodates light-mounted pistols; compatible with MOLLE system
MSRP: $135

SAFARILAND 3280 MILITARY MIDRIDE

Safariland

(www.safariland.com)

SAFARILAND MILITARY 3285 TACTICAL

SAFARILAND 6004 SLS TACTICAL

SAFARILAND 6005 SLS TACTICAL WITH QUICK-RELEASE LEG HARNESS

SAFARILAND 6035 MILITARY TACTICAL

3285 MILITARY TACTICAL

Use/Type: Tactical/belt
Retention: Rotating hood
Material/Finish: Safarilaminate/STX Tactical black, FDE brown, OD, foliage green
Carry: Ambidextrous
Compatible Firearms: Full-size pistol
Features: Accommodates light-mounted pistols; compatible with MOLLE system; molded sight track
MSRP: **$135**

6004 and 6005 SLS TACTICAL

Use/Type: Tactical/thigh
Retention: Rotating hood
Material/Finish: Safarilaminate/STX Tactical black, FDE brown, foliage green
Carry: Strong side
Compatible Firearms: Full-size pistol
Features: Double leg straps; molded sight track
6004: **$170**
6005 (quick-release leg harness): **$180**

6034 and 6035 SLS MILITARY TACTICAL

Use/Type: Tactical/thigh
Retention: Rotating hood
Material/Finish: Safarilaminate/STX Tactical black, FDE brown, foliage green
Carry: Ambidextrous
Compatible Firearms: Beretta M9, 92F, or Sig P226
Features: Double leg straps; accommodates light-mounted pistols
6034: **$190**
6035 (quick release leg harness):. **$200**

6074 SPECIAL OPS TACTICAL

Use/Type: Tactical/thigh
Retention: Middle finger tab release
Material/Finish: Safarilaminate/STX Tactical Black
Carry: Strong side
Compatible Firearms: Compact and full-size pistols
Features: Double leg straps
MSRP: **$238**

6304 and 6305 ALS TACTICAL

Use/Type: Tactical/thigh
Retention: Thumb lever, rotating hood
Material/Finish: Safarilaminate/STX Tactical black, FDE brown, foliage green
Carry: Strong side
Compatible Firearms: Compact and full-size pistols
Features: Double leg straps
6304: **$195**
6305 (quick-release leg harness): **$205**

6354 and 6355 ALS TACTICAL THIGH

Use/Type: Tactical/thigh
Retention: Thumb lever
Material/Finish: Safarilaminate/STX Tactical black, FDE brown, foliage green
Carry: Strong side
Compatible Firearms: Compact and full-size pistols
Features: Double leg straps
6304: **$167**
6355 (quick-release leg harness): **$177**

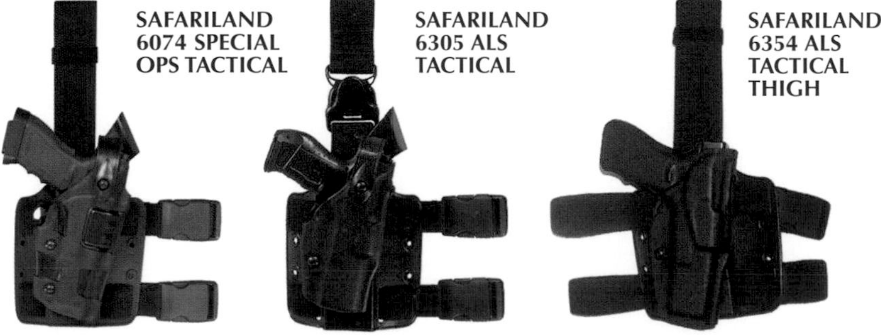

SAFARILAND 6074 SPECIAL OPS TACTICAL

SAFARILAND 6305 ALS TACTICAL

SAFARILAND 6354 ALS TACTICAL THIGH

13. Training Facilities

Image courtesy of Chuck Taylor's Small Arms Academy.

Training Facilities

Chuck Taylor's Small Arms Academy

(www.chucktayloramericansmallarmsacademy.com)

Location: Prescott, AZ

Training Offered: handgun, rifle, shotgun, submachine gun, and specialty courses available.

COURSE: 2-DAY DEFENSIVE HANDGUN

Duration: 2 days
Prerequisite: None, entry level
Estimated Round Count: 300
Tuition: $395
Details: Loading and unloading; weapon checking procedures; proper grip and stance; sight picture and alignment; trigger control; weapon presentations; speed and tactical reloading; malfunction clearing; stress management; target-engagement techniques from point-blank range to fifteen meters

Images Courtesy Chuck Taylor's Small Arms Academy.

CHUCK TAYLOR DEMONSTRATES PROPER ENTRY TECHNIQUES.

SHOOTING WHILE MOVING: ONE OF MANY SKILLS TAUGHT AT CHUCK TAYLOR'S SMALL ARMS ACADEMY.

ACCURACY DRILLS

STUDENTS ARE TAUGHT HOW TO MOVE AROUND CORNERS.

TAYLOR DEMONSTRATES PROPER MACHINE GUN GRIP AND STANCE.

COURSE: 4-DAY DEFENSIVE HANDGUN

Duration: 4 days
Prerequisite: None, entry level
Estimated Round Count: 900
Tuition: $595
Details: Loading and unloading; weapon checking procedures; proper grip and stance; sight picture and alignment; trigger control; weapon presentations; speed and tactical reloading; malfunction clearing; stress management; target-engagement techniques from point-blank range to fifteen meters; open and concealed carry; single and multiple target engagements; responses right and left; close range emergency responses; low-light shooting with and without a flashlight

Training Facilities

COURSE: 2-DAY ADVANCED TACTICAL SKILLS

Duration: 2 days
Prerequisite: 4-Day Advanced Defensive Handgun
Estimated Round Count: 600
Tuition: $395
Details: Close quarters confrontation defenses; enhanced marksmanship skills development; weapon retention and recovery techniques; force-on-force scenarios; vehicular defense and deployment; reduced-light operations

HIGH SPEED WEAPON PRESENTATIONS AND TARGET ENGAGEMENT

ENGAGING SMALL TARGETS

ENGAGING TARGETS WHILE SHOOTING AROUND COVER

IMPROVISED SHOOTING POSITIONS AND SHOOTING THROUGH ODDLY SHAPED OPENINGS

LOST WEAPON RECOVERY DRILLS

SHOOTING AROUND COVER DRILLS

SHOOTING FROM STOPPED VEHICLE

COURSE: 4-DAY ADVANCED DEFENSIVE HANDGUN

Duration: 4 days
Prerequisite: 2-Day Defensive Handgun
Estimated Round Count: 1000
Tuition: $595
Details: Loading and unloading; weapon checking procedures; proper grip and stance; sight picture and alignment; trigger control; weapon presentations; speed and tactical reloading; malfunction clearing; stress management; target-engagement techniques from point-blank range to fifteen meters; open and concealed carry; single and multiple target engagements; responses right and left; close range emergency responses; low-light shooting with and without a flashlight; vehicular defense and deployment; reduced-light operations

COURSE: HANDGUN COMBAT MASTER

Duration: 4 days
Prerequisite: 4-Day Defensive Handgun and 4-Day Advanced Defensive Handgun
Estimated Round Count: 1100
Tuition: $595
Details: Small classes; loading and unloading; weapon checking procedures; proper grip and stance; sight picture and alignment; trigger control; weapon presentations; speed and tactical reloading; malfunction clearing; stress management; target-engagement techniques from point-blank range to fifteen meters; open and concealed carry; single and multiple target engagements; responses right and left; close range emergency responses; low-light shooting with and without a flashlight; vehicular defense and deployment; reduced-light operations; hostage situations; small targets at close range; targets at odd angles; partially obscured targets; close-range emergency response drills

WEAK HAND SHOOTING

Image Courtesy Chuck Taylor's Small Arms Academy.

STUDENTS ARE TAUGHT HOW TO TRANSITION TO A HANDGUN FROM A SHOULDER WEAPON.

Front Sight Firearms Training Institute

(www.frontsight.com)

Location: Las Vegas, NV

Training Offered: handgun, rifle, shotgun, auto weapons, armorer, martial arts and specialty courses available

COURSE: 2-DAY DEFENSIVE HANDGUN

Duration: 2 days
Prerequisite: None, entry level
Estimated Round Count: 200
Tuition: $1000
Details: Loading and unloading; grip and stance; sight picture and alignment; trigger control; presentation from ready position and holster; speed and tactical reloading; malfunction clearing; target engagement; live-fire tactical simulator

COURSE: 4-DAY DEFENSIVE HANDGUN

Duration: 4 days
Prerequisite: None, entry level
Estimated Round Count: 600
Tuition: $2000
Details: Loading and unloading; grip and stance; sight picture and alignment; trigger control; presentation from ready position and holster; speed and tactical reloading; malfunction clearing; target engagement; live-fire tactical simulator; emphasis on concealed carry; shoot and no-shoot scenarios; target engagement from arms length to fifteen yards under time pressure

PROPER GRIP AND STANCE ARE STRESSED AT FRONT SIGHT FIREARMS TRAINING INSTITUTE.

Images Courtesy Front Sight Firearms Training Institute.

Training Facilities

HANDGUN COACHING AT FRONT SIGHT

COURSE: 5-DAY ARMED CITIZEN CORP

Duration: 5 days
Prerequisite: None, entry level
Estimated Round Count: 700
Tuition: $2500
Details: Elements of the 4-Day Defensive Handgun, Advanced Tactical Handgun, and 1-Day Concealed Carry Class including loading and unloading; grip and stance; sight picture and alignment; trigger control; presentation from ready position and holster; speed and tactical reloading; malfunction clearing; target engagement; live-fire tactical simulator; emphasis on concealed carry; shoot and no-shoot scenarios; target engagement from arms length to fifteen yards under time pressure

Training Facilities

HANDGUN FROM CONCEALMENT DRILL AT FRONT SIGHT

COURSE: 2-DAY HANDGUN SKILL BUILDER

Duration: 2 days
Prerequisite: 2-Day Defensive Handgun
Estimated Round Count: 200
Tuition: $1000
Details: Follow-up to 2-Day Defensive Handgun course; loading and unloading; grip and stance; sight picture and alignment; trigger control; presentation from ready position and holster; speed and tactical reloading; malfunction clearing; target engagement; live-fire tactical simulator

COURSE: 2-DAY ADVANCED TACTICAL HANDGUN

Duration: 2 days
Prerequisite: 4-Day Defensive Handgun
Estimated Round Count: 400
Tuition: $1000
Details: Follow-up to 4-Day Defensive Handgun course; close-contact shooting; moving and shooting; moving targets; cover and concealment; shooting from vehicles; precision-distance shooting; low light and night shooting

COURSE: 2-DAY HANDGUN COMBAT MASTER PREP

Duration: 2 days
Prerequisite: 4-Day Defensive Handgun
Estimated Round Count: 1000
Tuition: $1000
Details: Follow-up to 4-Day Defensive Handgun course; builds on speed shooting; accuracy and consistency

COURSE: 4-DAY HANDGUN COMBAT MASTER PREP

Duration: 4 days
Prerequisite: 4-Day Defensive Handgun
Estimated Round Count: 1000
Tuition: $2000
Details: Follow-up to 4-Day Defensive Handgun course; builds on speed shooting; accuracy and consistency

COURSE: 2-DAY DEFENSIVE HANDGUN (NIGHT)

Duration: 2 days
Prerequisite: 2-Day Defensive Handgun
Estimated Round Count: 400
Tuition: $1000
Details: Low-light techniques for loading and unloading; grip and stance; sight picture and alignment; trigger control; presentation from ready position and holster; speed and tactical reloading; malfunction clearing; target engagement

COURSE: 4-DAY DEFENSIVE HANDGUN (NIGHT)

Duration: 4 days
Prerequisite: None, entry level
Estimated Round Count: 700
Tuition: $2000
Details: Low-light techniques for loading and unloading; grip and stance; sight picture and alignment; trigger control; presentation from ready position and holster; speed and tactical reloading; malfunction clearing; target engagement; live-fire tactical simulator; emphasis on concealed carry

COURSE: 2-DAY HANDGUN SKILL BUILDER (NIGHT)

Duration: 2 days
Prerequisite: 2-Day Defensive Handgun or 4-Day Defensive Handgun
Estimated Round Count: 400
Tuition: $1000
Details: Low-light techniques for loading and unloading; grip and stance; sight picture and alignment; trigger control; presentation from ready position and holster; speed and tactical reloading; malfunction clearing; target engagement

HANDGUN HOME INVASION DRILL

INSTRUCTOR DEMONSTRATES HANDGUN LOADING TECHNIQUES.

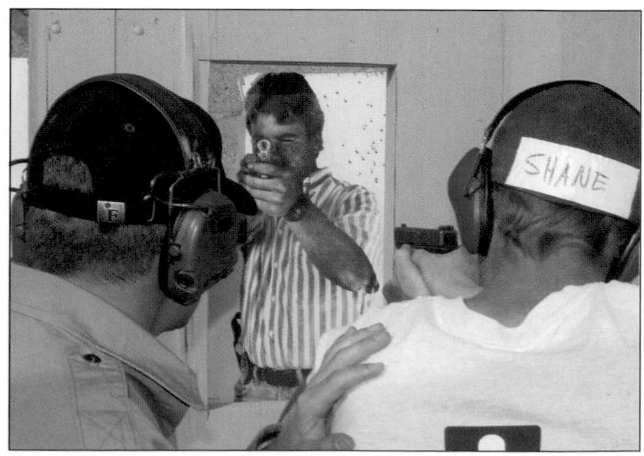

ENGAGING THREATS IN A HOME INVASION SCENARIO

HANDGUN NIGHT FIRE

COURSE: 2-DAY ADVANCED TACTICAL HANDGUN (NIGHT)
Duration: 2 days
Prerequisite: 2-Day Advanced Tactical Handgun
Estimated Round Count: 300
Tuition: $1000
Details: Low-light techniques for close-contact shooting; moving and shooting; moving targets; cover and concealment; shooting from vehicles; precision-distance shooting

Gunsite Academy

(www.gunsite.com)

Location: Paulden, AZ

Training Offered: pistol, carbine, rifle, shotguns, and specialty courses available

COURSE: 150 PISTOL
Duration: 3 days
Prerequisite: None, entry level
Estimated Round Count: 500
Tuition: $933
Details: Basic safety and weapons-handling procedures; basic range procedures; marksmanship skills

Training Facilities

COURSE: 250 PISTOL

Duration: 5 days
Prerequisite: 150 Pistol
Estimated Round Count: 1050
Tuition: $1428
Details: Introduction to Col. Jeff Cooper's "Modern Technique of the Pistol"; marksmanship; gun handling; combat mindset; elements of the Combat Triad

COURSE: 350 INTERMEDIATE PISTOL

Duration: 5 days
Prerequisite: 250 Pistol
Estimated Round Count: 1200
Tuition: $1648
Details: Builds on "Modern Technique of the Pistol"; advanced fighting skills; shooting on the move; moving target arrays; live-fire simulators; indoor and outdoor low-light encounters

AT GUNSITE STUDENTS RECEIVE INDIVIDUALIZED COACHING.

SIGHT ALIGNMENT IS A FUNDAMENTAL SKILL TAUGHT AT GUNSITE.

Images Courtesy of Gunsite Academy.

Training Facilities

STUDENTS AT READY POSITION

CLOSE CONTACT DRILL

Training Facilities

COURSE: 499 ADVANCED PISTOL

Duration: 5 days
Prerequisite: 350 Intermediate Pistol
Estimated Round Count: 1350
Tuition: $1793
Details: Advance skill sets on inhibited equipment manipulations; clear equipment malfunctions while physically impaired; improve presentation speed and accuracy; complex tactical problems; live-fire simulators; low-light work

COURSE: CLOSE QUARTERS PISTOL

Duration: 5 days
Prerequisite: 250 Pistol
Estimated Round Count: 1050
Tuition: $1648
Details: Designed specifically for concealed carry; close-encounter threats; car jacking; force-on-force scenarios; low-light night shooting

COURSE: CONCEALED CARRY PISTOL

Duration: 2 days
Prerequisite: None
Estimated Round Count: 600
Tuition: $571
Details: Training with concealed carry pistols; carry methods; presentation from a purse, pocket, fanny pack, or holster; practical uses and limitations of small pistols and revolvers

COURSE: DEFENSIVE REVOLVER

Duration: 3 days
Prerequisite: None
Estimated Round Count: 600
Tuition: $933
Details: Application of double-action revolver with the "Modern Technique of the Pistol"; marksmanship; manipulation; care and maintenance; tactical live-fire simulators; low-light conditions

COURSE: LADIES PISTOL 1

Duration: 2 days
Prerequisite: None
Estimated Round Count: 300
Tuition: $571
Details: Classes taught by women for women; introduction to the "Modern Technique of the Pistol"

COURSE: LADIES PISTOL 2

Duration: 3 days
Prerequisite: Ladies Pistol 1
Estimated Round Count: 300
Tuition: $933
Details: Classes taught by women for women; follow-up to Ladies Pistol 1

A GUNSITE INSTRUCTOR TIMES A STUDENT IN DRAW AND FIRE.

InSights Training Center

(www.insightstraining.com)

Locations: Seattle and Bellevue, WA; Harrisburg, PA; Rochester, NY; Winchester, VA; Atlanta, GA; Austin, Dallas, and Fort Worth, TX

Training Offered: handgun, combative, long arms, and tactics courses available

COURSE: BASIC HANDGUN SAFETY & RESPONSIBILITY

Duration: 6 hours.
Prerequisite: None
Estimated Round Count: Minimal
Tuition: $195, equipment provided
Details: Basic gun safety; marksmanship; familiarization with handgun types; handgun maintenance; justifiable self-defense

COURSE: WOMEN'S BASIC HANDGUN SAFETY & RESPONSIBILITY

Duration: 6 hours.
Prerequisite: None
Estimated Round Count: Minimal
Tuition: $185, equipment provided
Details: Basic gun safety; marksmanship; familiarization with handgun types; handgun maintenance; justifiable self-defense

COURSE: GENERAL DEFENSIVE HANDGUN

Duration: 2 days
Prerequisite: Basic weapons handling skills
Estimated Round Count: 600
Tuition: $350
Details: Basic gun safety; marksmanship; stance, grip and, sight alignment; trigger press; follow-through; rapid engagement of multiple targets; single or multiple opponent situations

COURSE: INTERMEDIATE DEFENSIVE HANDGUN

Duration: 3 days
Prerequisite: General Defensive Handgun
Estimated Round Count: 1500
Tuition: $600
Details: Drawing and shooting; tactical management; cover and concealment; one-handed shooting; injury drills; stress-fire techniques

COURSE: INTENSIVE HANDGUN SKILLS I

Duration: 3 days
Prerequisite: General Defensive Handgun
Estimated Round Count: 2000
Tuition: $600
Details: Long-range exercises; barricade drills; movement; shooting while moving; moving targets

COURSE: INTENSIVE HANDGUN SKILLS II

Duration: 3 days
Prerequisite: Intensive Handgun Skills I
Estimated Round Count: 2500
Tuition: $600
Details: Builds on Intensive Handgun Skills I with drills and shooting scenarios

COURSE: LOW-LIGHT HANDGUN SKILLS

Duration: 1 day
Prerequisite: Basic weapons handling skills
Estimated Round Count: 150
Tuition: $100
Details: Use of handgun safely, quickly, and reflexively in a low-light or limited-visibility situations

COURSE: CLOSE-QUARTERS CONFRONTATIONS

Duration: 3 days
Prerequisite: General Defensive Handgun
Estimated Round Count: 1000
Tuition: $600
Details: Stunning and disabling opponent; contact distance confrontation; lethal and nonlethal handgun-retention techniques; transitioning from lethal to nonlethal force; integrating unarmed skills; handgun; other self-defense

COURSE: BACK-UP GUN AND DEEP CONCEALMENT

Duration: 1 day
Prerequisite: General Defensive Handgun
Estimated Round Count: 800
Tuition: $200
Details: Class concentrates on how to get your gun out of concealment and into the fight; deep-concealment gun; drawing gun quickly while moving from cover, in low light, at close range, from alternate positions, and under duress

Training Facilities

I.C.E.

(www.icetraining.us)

Location: Virginia Beach, VA

Training Offered: firearms, driving, counterterrorism, and specialty courses available

COURSE: COMBAT FOCUS SHOOTING
Duration: 2 days
Prerequisite: None
Estimated Round Count: 1100–1500
Tuition: $500
Details: Combat accuracy; lateral motion; speed and precision shooting; reload; volume of fire; shooting in motion; one-hand and weak-hand shooting

COURSE: ADVANCED PISTOL HANDLING
Duration: 2 days
Prerequisite: Combat Focus Shooting
Estimated Round Count: 1100–1500
Tuition: $600
Details: Builds on Combat Focus Shooting; malfunction drills; one-hand and weak-hand reloads; unorthodox shooting positions

Magpul Dynamics

(www.magpuldynamics.com)

Location: Boulder; CO

Training Offered: weapon manipulation, tactical operations, medical, and airborne operations available

COURSE: DYNAMIC HANDGUN 1
Duration: 2 days or 3 days
Prerequisite: None, entry level
Estimated Round Count: 1500 (2 days), 2000 (3 days)
Tuition: $550 (2 days), $650 (3 days)
Details: Gear selection and placement; shooting stance; the draw; proper grip; axis and mechanics of recoil; grip; sight alignment and picture; trigger control; speed reloads; tactical reloads; malfunctions; strong- and weak-hand shooting; shooting on the move; situation-specific shooting positions

COURSE: DYNAMIC HANDGUN 2
Duration: 2 days or 3 days
Prerequisite: Dynamic Handgun 1 or equivalent
Estimated Round Count: 1500 (2 days), 2000 (3 days)
Tuition: $550 (2 days), $650 (3 days)
Details: Builds on Dynamic Handgun 1; terminal ballistics; rapid threat analysis and acquisition; shooting on the move; multiple target engagement; natural and improvised shooting positions; barricade shooting; shooting from vehicles; concealed shooting; low-light tactics

Shootrite Firearms Academy

(www.shootrite.org)

Location: Langston, AL

Training Offered: handgun, precision rifle, carbine, and specialty courses available

COURSE: DEFENSIVE HANDGUN
Duration: 14 hours.
Prerequisite: NRA First Steps or equivalent
Estimated Round Count: 600
Tuition: $400
Details: Gun safety and handling; combative marksmanship; threat response including shooter movement; combative mind-set; environmental awareness and avoidance

Training Facilities

Image Courtesy Shootrite Firearms Academy.

THREAT RESPONSE WITH REALISTIC TARGET AT SHOOTRITE.

Images Courtesy Shootrite Firearms Academy.

SHOOTRITE OFFERS SPECIALIZED REVOLVER TRAINING.

Training Facilities

COURSE: HANDGUN TACTICS

Duration: 24 hours.
Prerequisite: Defensive Handgun
Estimated Round Count: 1400
Tuition: $130
Details: Builds on Defensive Handgun; intensive drills that include movement; the use of cover; low-light operations; mental and physical skills required for combative engagements

COURSE: COMBATIVE HANDGUN

Duration: 24 hours.
Prerequisite: Defensive Handgun
Estimated Round Count: 1400
Tuition: $130
Details: Drills that apply skills to realistic conditions; low-light operations; reactive and moving targets; close quarters battle skills; ground fighting; retention techniques

MANEUVERING AND USING COVER AT THE "WALL"

Images Courtesy Shootrite Firearms Academy.

COURSE: REVOLVER

Duration: 14 hours.
Prerequisite: Defensive Handgun
Estimated Round Count: 600
Tuition: $130
Details: Intensive study of revolver use for self-defensive or combative situations

COURSE: CONCEAL CARRY

Duration: 14 hours.
Prerequisite: NRA First Steps or equivalent
Estimated Round Count: 600
Tuition: $130
Details: Gun safety and handling; combative marksmanship; threat response including shooter movement; combative mind-set; environmental awareness and avoidance; stresses conceal carry

DRAW AND FIRE FROM SITTING POSITION DRILL

Sig Sauer Academy

(www.sigsaueracademy.com)

Locations: Epping, NH; Orlando, FL; San Bernardino, CA ; Midland, VA

Training Offered: armorer, instructor development, learn to shoot, skill development, and specialty courses available

COURSE: HANDGUN ORIENTATION 101 and 101 FOR WOMEN

Duration: 1 day
Prerequisite: None, entry level
Estimated Round Count: Minimal
Tuition: $195, includes ammunition and loan of equipment
Details: Course 101: designed for new gun owners; and those who have never had formal training; provides the foundation and skills necessary to safely handle handguns; Course 101 for Women: specifically designed for female students

COURSE: BASIC PRACTICAL HANDGUN SKILLS 102 and 102 FOR WOMEN

Duration: 1 day
Prerequisite: Handgun Orientation 101
Estimated Round Count: 200
Tuition: $195, includes loan of equipment
Details: Efficient use of a handgun; working from the holster; performing reloads; clearing stoppages; manipulating trigger to maximize accuracy; Course 102 for Women: specifically design for female students

COURSE: INTERMEDIATE PRACTICAL HANDGUN SKILLS 103

Duration: 1 day
Prerequisite: Basic Practical Handgun Skills 102
Estimated Round Count: 300
Tuition: $195, includes loan of equipment
Details: Review and practice of safe and efficient use of a handgun; advanced concepts including movement; use of cover

Images Courtesy Sig Sauer Academy.

FIRING WHILE MOVING IS AN ADVANCED SKILL TAUGHT AT SIG ACADEMY.

Training Facilities

DRAW AND FIRE FROM SEATED POSITION

COURSE: BULLETS ON VEHICLES 1

Duration: 1 day
Prerequisite: Intermediate Practical Handgun Skills 103
Estimated Round Count: 200
Tuition: $195, includes loan of equipment
Details: Disabled vehicle procedures under fire; high speed driving and shooting drills; vehicle extractions under fire; live fire shooting scenarios from vehicles

COURSE: BULLETS ON VEHICLES 2

Duration: 1 day
Prerequisite: Bullets On Vehicles 1
Estimated Round Count: 200
Tuition: $195, includes loan of equipment
Details: Builds on Bullets On Vehicles 1; disabled vehicle procedures under fire; high speed driving and shooting drills; vehicle extractions under fire; live-fire shooting scenarios from vehicles

COURSE: HOME DEFENSE TACTICS

Duration: 1 day
Prerequisite: Basic weapons handling skills
Estimated Round Count: 150
Tuition: $195, includes loan of equipment
Details: Home movement tactics; handgun shooting for inside the home; prevailing in low-light drills; shooting from bed

COURSE: SPEED SHOOTING I

Duration: 1 day
Prerequisite: Intermediate Practical Handgun Skills 103
Estimated Round Count: 500
Tuition: $195, includes loan of equipment
Details: High speed target engagement exercises; static; multiple targets; shooting while moving; moving targets; target saturation

COURSE: SPEED SHOOTING II

Duration: 1 day
Prerequisite: Speed Shooting I
Estimated Round Count: 500
Tuition: $195, includes loan of equipment
Details: Builds on Speed Shooting I; high speed target engagement exercises; multiple targets; shooting while moving; static and moving targets; target saturation

COURSE: CONCEALED CARRY

Duration: 2 days
Prerequisite: Intermediate Practical Handgun Skills 103
Estimated Round Count: 300
Tuition: $495, includes loan of equipment
Details: Safety concerns and practices while carrying concealed; choosing a concealed-carry firearm; selecting concealed-carry equipment; presentation of firearm from a concealed-carry posture; close proximity shooting; techniques for violent encounters; one-handed operation; multiple shot techniques; alternative carry techniques

COURSE: ADVANCED CONCEALED CARRY

Duration: 2 days
Prerequisite: Concealed Carry
Estimated Round Count: 500
Tuition: $495, includes loan of equipment
Details: Builds on Concealed Carry course; shooting, movement, and communication; shooting outside of your comfort zone; cover utilization drills; low-light shooting drills with and without flashlights; shooting from and around vehicles; identification and engagement of moving opponents

COURSE: CONCEALED CARRY TECHNIQUES

Duration: 4 hours.
Prerequisite: Basic weapons handling skills
Estimated Round Count: 200
Tuition: $125, includes loan of equipment
Details: Selecting concealment gear; concealed-carry techniques; presentation and engagement from concealment

COURSE: DEFENSIVE PISTOL

Duration: 2 days
Prerequisite: Basic weapons handling skills
Estimated Round Count: 750
Tuition: $395, includes loan of equipment
Details: Pistol fundamentals; gear selection; developing combative mindset; basic diagnostic and evaluation exercises; draw techniques; methods of point and precision shooting; movement while shooting and shooting at moving targets; seated shooting and shooting around vehicles; multiple shot techniques; multiple targets of variable size and distance; reloading drills; single-hand techniques

COURSE: ADVANCED DEFENSIVE PISTOL

Duration: 2 days
Prerequisite: Defensive Pistol
Estimated Round Count: 600
Tuition: $395, includes loan of equipment
Details: Tactical live-fire movements; engagement of moving threats; close-quarter pistol operations; bilateral pistol manipulations; low-light pistol techniques; operating in and around vehicles; force-on-force dynamic training scenarios utilizing training munitions

COURSE: DEFENSIVE KNIFE AND PISTOL

Duration: 2 days
Prerequisite: Basic weapons handling skills
Estimated Round Count: 250
Tuition: $395, includes loan of equipment
Details: Use of force guidelines; knife types; carry methods; drawing techniques; defensive knife techniques; transitions to handgun; weapon retention and disarming techniques; hand-to-hand and close-quarters battle techniques

COURSE: LOW-LIGHT OPERATOR

Duration: 1 day
Prerequisite: Basic weapons handling skills
Estimated Round Count: 300
Tuition: $195, includes loan of equipment
Details: Low-light operation concepts and handgun flashlight techniques; moving in low-light environments; alternative uses of the flashlight; survival with and without alternative lighting source

PERSONALIZED INSTRUCTION AT SIG ACADEMY

Training Facilities

LAW ENFORCEMENT ROOM-CLEARING EXERCISE

COURSE: ADVANCED LOW-LIGHT WITH FOF

Duration: 1 day
Prerequisite: Low-Light Operator
Estimated Round Count: 200
Tuition: $195, includes loan of equipment
Details: Dynamic and methodic low-light movement and searching techniques; individual and team tactics in low light; operating pistol mounted systems in conjunction with hand-held lights

COURSE: LOW-LIGHT PISTOL TECHNIQUES

Duration: 4 hours.
Prerequisite: Basic weapons handling skills
Estimated Round Count: 200
Tuition: $95, includes loan of equipment
Details: Safe, efficient deployment of a light with a handgun; single-hand pistol techniques; low-light operation concepts; handgun-flashlight techniques

COURSE: CLOSE-QUARTER PISTOL OPERATOR

Duration: 1 day
Prerequisite: Basic weapons handling skills
Estimated Round Count: 300
Tuition: $195, includes loan of equipment
Details: Principles of close-quarters engagements; point versus precision shooting; bent-elbow shooting; strike and shoot techniques; dealing with multiple threats up close

COURSE: THE "Q" COURSE

Duration: 1 day
Prerequisite: Intermediate Practical Handgun Skills 103
Estimated Round Count: 300
Tuition: $150, includes loan of equipment
Details: Compilation of military special operations, federal law enforcement, and competition qualification courses;

COURSE: EXTREME CLOSE-QUARTERS BATTLE (CQB)

Duration: 2 days
Prerequisite: Basic weapons handling skills
Estimated Round Count: 400
Tuition: $395, includes loan of equipment
Details: Fundamentals of CQB and deadly threat-encounter matrix; point shooting; multiple adversaries; hand-to-hand tactics; ground fighting and shooting; zero-clearance and point-contact shooting

COURSE: CIVILIAN RESPONSE TO TERRORIST THREATS

Duration: 2 days
Prerequisite: Basic weapons handling skills
Estimated Round Count: 500
Tuition: $395, includes loan of equipment
Details: Fundamentals of CQB; hand-to-hand tactics; concealed-carry techniques; fundamental and advanced pistol techniques; how to spot an impending attack and survival mindset; terrorist weapons familiarization; edged-weapon tactics; counter ambush tactics; shooting from and around vehicles

Training Facilities

LOW-LIGHT DRILL AT SIG SAUER ACADEMY

SIG SAUER ACADEMY DIRECTOR, GEORGE HARRIS, EXPLAINING TECHNIQUES

COURSE: REFLEXIVE SHOOTING

Duration: 2 days
Prerequisite: Basic weapons handling skills
Estimated Round Count: 600–800
Tuition: $395, includes loan of equipment
Details: Point versus precision shooting concepts; working without sights; target focus versus gun focus; body indexing; movement; man-on-man dueling

COURSE: REFLEXIVE SHOOTING II

Duration: 2 days
Prerequisite: Reflexive Shooting
Estimated Round Count: 300
Tuition: $395, includes loan of equipment
Details: Reflexive shooting; dry and live-fire techniques; timed speed drills at varying distances with reactive targets; moving targets and shooter; offensive pursuit drills; dynamic dueling; seated and table shooting with movement to cover; low-light response with maneuver; support-hand shooting; distraction drills

COURSE: BACKUP-GUN OPERATOR

Duration: 1 day
Prerequisite: Basic weapons handling skills
Estimated Round Count: 150
Tuition: $195, includes loan of equipment
Details: Gear selection; concealed-carry techniques; presentation techniques; reloads

COURSE: PRACTICAL REVOLVER

Duration: 1 day
Prerequisite: Basic weapons handling skills
Estimated Round Count: 300
Tuition: $195, includes loan of equipment
Details: Efficient use of a revolver; working from the holster; performing reloads; reloading drills; multiple shot techniques; movement while shooting; single-hand techniques

The Combat Mindset: John "Jeff" Cooper started the American Pistol Institute (API) in Arizona in 1976, which later became the Gunsite Training Center. Cooper is known for the modern technique of handgun shooting and devised a color code for the combat mindset. The color progression indicates a person's mental state to act in any given situation:

- **White –** Person is unaware and unprepared.
- **Yellow –** Person is relaxed alert.
- **Orange –** Person observes a specific alert.
- **Red –** Person fights.

Training Facilities

Tactical Firearms Training Team

(www.tftt.com)

Location: Huntington Beach, CA

Training Offered: pistol, sniper, M4, shotgun, and specialty courses available

COURSE: TACTICAL PISTOL 1
Duration: 1 day
Prerequisite: None, entry level
Estimated Round Count: 300
Tuition: $165
Details: Fundamentals of incorporating speed; tactics and accuracy; use of cover; tactical reloading

COURSE: TACTICAL PISTOL 2
Duration: 1 day
Prerequisite: Tactical Pistol 1
Estimated Round Count: 300
Tuition: $165
Details: Advanced combat shooting; concealment presentation; speed loading; stoppage drills; casualty arms fire and reloads

COURSE: TACTICAL PISTOL 3
Duration: 2 days
Prerequisite: Tactical Pistol 2
Estimated Round Count: 300
Tuition: $350
Details: High level course; structure clearing drills; supine fire; weak-hand fire and reloads; obstacle and barrier shooting

COURSE: ADVANCED PISTOL OPERATOR
Duration: 4 day
Prerequisite: Tactical Pistol 3
Estimated Round Count: 1000
Tuition: $650
Details: High level course; target discretion drills; weak-hand fire and reloads; obstacle and barrier shooting; dynamic movement to cover; low-light fire; firing in pairs; fighting from vehicles

Thunder Ranch

(www.thunderranchinc.com)

Locations: Lakeview, OR; Mt. Home, TX

Training Offered: pistol, rifle, and specialty courses available; (class sizes limited to ten to twelve students)

COURSE: DEFENSIVE CONCEALED CARRY–CC
Duration: 3 days
Prerequisite: None, entry level
Estimated Round Count: 800
Tuition: $930
Details: Methods and techniques for carrying a handgun concealed in warm or cold weather

COURSE: DEFENSIVE HANDGUN–TH
Duration: 3 days
Prerequisite: None, entry level
Estimated Round Count: 800
Tuition: $930
Details: Basic safety skills: drawing, loading, malfunctions; advanced skills, i.e. distance firing; injury drills; ground fighting; shooting and moving

COURSE: DEFENSIVE HANDGUN 2–TH2
Duration: 3 days
Prerequisite: Defensive Handgun–TH
Estimated Round Count: 900
Tuition: $930
Details: Builds on Defensive Handgun–TH course with advanced timing and tactical problems

COURSE: DEFENSIVE REVOLVER–R
Duration: 3 days
Prerequisite: Defensive Handgun–TH
Estimated Round Count: 700
Tuition: $930
Details: Techniques and idiosyncrasies of the revolving handgun for personal defense

INDEX

HOLSTERS